Sexual Practices

To the memory of

Alfred C. Kinsey

Still the most spectacular light
in the history of
the study of human sexuality

Executive Editor: James Hughes
Art editor: Jane Owen
Picture Researcher: Diana Korchien
Editorial Assistant: Barbara Gish
Production: Barry Baker

The publishers wish to give special thanks to
Peter Webb and John Field,
Senior Lecturers at the Department of Art History,
Middlesex Polytechnic,
for their invaluable assistance and advice
in the provision of illustrations for, respectively,
the Thematic and the Geographic sections
of this book.

Edited and designed by
Mitchell Beazley International Limited
Mill House, 87–89 Shaftesbury Avenue, London, W1V 7AD
© Mitchell Beazley Publishers 1982
First published in the United Kingdom in 1982 by Mitchell Beazley Publishers
First United States publication 1983 by Franklin Watts, 387 Park Avenue South,
New York, New York 10016

Library of Congress Cataloging in Publication Data

Gregersen, Edgar.
   Sexual practices.

   Bibliography: p.
   Includes index.
   1. Sex customs—Cross cultural studies. I. Title.
HQ12.G73 1983   392'.6   83–6965
ISBN 0-531-09899-0

Composition in Palatino by Filmtype Services Limited, Scarborough, North Yorkshire
Printed in the United States of America

EDGAR GREGERSEN

Sexual Practices

The Story of
Human
Sexuality

With 320 illustrations
and 9 maps

FRANKLIN WATTS
NEW YORK 1983

A GROLIER COMPANY

AUTHOR'S
NOTE ON SPELLING AND
PRONUNCIATION

*T*he spelling of foreign words adopted here avoids unusual letters but still tries to show pronunciation accurately. For example, no special symbol is used for the *ng* sound as in *singer*, but where the *g* is "hard," as in *finger*, the spelling *ngg* has been used. Thus the well-known Indian erotic manual, elsewhere written *Ananga ranga* (*n* pronounced *ng*), is here written **Ananggā rangga**.

Long vowels are shown by doubling the relevant character, so that the *a* as in *father* is written *aa*. Thus we write **Kaama suutra**, elsewhere written as *Kāma sūtra*. This method is followed for Hebrew and Arabic, as well as ancient Greek, but vowel length is ignored for Latin, following Church Latin conventions.

To help the reader with the pronunciation of the names of the societies mentioned here, a stress mark (´) is written over the stressed vowel except where the next to the last vowel is stressed; thus:

Kágaba	Múria	Wógeo	Bororó	Samoyéd	Kachín
Yóruba	Wálbiri	Árapesh	Sirionó	Mossí	Apinayé

But no stress mark is written on:

Lepcha	Sarakatsani	Murngin	Malekula
Tikopia	Nambikwara	Ifugao	Miao

or in names that have a special English form (e.g., **Blackfoot**, **Burmese**), or in the common forms **Navaho**, **Eskimo**.

Chinese words are written in accordance with the official Pin-yin romanization, where *x* = a kind of *sh* sound, and *q* = a kind of *ch* sound. Indonesian words are written in accordance with the latest official spelling, thus **Toraja** (not the older *Toradja*).

The names of many societies have a number of variant spellings, e.g., **Navaho** *vs.* Navajo, **Chaga** *vs.* Chagga, **Maasai** *vs.* Masai, **Nambikwara** *vs.* Nambicuara, **Karajá** *vs.* Carajá. I have used the first spelling for each of these. In every case I have tried to use a form where the spelling corresponds most nearly to the conventions of World Orthography, in which, for example, a *k* sound is written with *k* (not *c* or *ch* or *qu*), an *h* sound with *h*, etc. In some instances, the variants reflect something other than spelling conventions, e.g., **Zande** *vs.* Azande, **Yãnomamö** *vs.* Yanoama, **Timbira** *vs.* Canella. I have used the name that is either most common or else is preferable for some other reason.

In the general spelling of English, American conventions are usually followed (e.g., *color, center, catalog, connection, canonize*), but spellings with *ae* and *oe* are generally kept because they are better than ones with *e*: *anaemic* (with a long *ee*) does not rime with *systemic* (with a short *e*) in my pronunciation. Hence, I write *paedophilia* but *pederastry* because for me the vowels are different.

Summary of special values for letters

Vowels
a as in f*a*ther, or (in Indian words) as *u* in b*u*t
e as in m*e*n, or v*ei*l
i as in sk*i*, or p*i*n
o as in g*o*, or *o*r
u as in r*u*le, or p*u*t

Consonants
c or č as in *c*ello, *ch*urch
š (or x in Chinese, Portuguese, Spanish, and names of American Indian groups) as sh in *sh*ip
x or kh as in *Kh*omeini (or ch in Ba*ch*, lo*ch*, *ch*utzpah)
ngg as in fi*ngg*er not si*ng*er

Other
´ stress (in Chinese and some other languages, high tone) as in **Bororó**
˜ nasalized vowel as in **Yãnomamö**

CONTENTS

Author's note on spelling and pronunciation 4

Part One   SEXUAL THEMES

One Sex: the anthropological perspective 7
Two The Western cultural background 15
Three History of the study of sex 31
Four Evolution of human sexuality 41
Five Sex techniques 55
Six Physical types 65
Seven Physical attractiveness 81
Eight Clothing and modesty 111
Nine Marriage and incest 129
Ten Prostitution 149
Eleven Current developments 167

Part Two   THE GEOGRAPHY OF SEXUAL PRACTICES

Twelve Africa 185
Thirteen The Middle East 201
Fourteen India and Southern Asia 215
Fifteen The Far East 233
Sixteen Oceania 247
Seventeen The Americas 261
Eighteen Europe and European outposts 275
Nineteen Cross-cultural survey 289

Bibliography 308
Author's acknowledgments 309
Illustration acknowledgments and sources 310
Index 313

Part One

SEXUAL THEMES

There is no reason why
sexual customs cannot be examined
as are other customs, to find out
when and where they
originated, how they spread,
and why they are maintained.

One ❦ SEX: THE ANTHROPOLOGICAL PERSPECTIVE

Sex began as a biological adaptation, but in all human cultures it has become a focal point for social and moral codes, as well as generating themes that permeate religion and art.

Sex began more than 2,000,000,000 years ago. It has survived as the most spectacularly successful adaptation in the evolution of life. Profound changes have taken place since the first primordial pooling of matter between bacteria, or blue-green algae, or whatever. The hundreds of millions of years between then and now have seen the unfolding of an incredible diversity. Among human beings this diversity shows up not only in behavior but in ideals: societies that insist on a very limited range of erotic acts versus those that revel in erotic riches; cultures dominated by prudes versus those governed by lechers; and all sorts of gradations.

Our own society has recently been exposed to tremendous ideological changes with regard to sex. In large part this has to do with two developments: the widespread use of contraception, and the breakdown of the traditional division of labor whereby men and women performed different but complementary tasks, and marriage was seen as a financial arrangement. This view of marriage now has less reality than ever before. More and more, sex has become the fragile basis of getting and staying married, or of living in some less ritually defined relationship.

Among human beings, nowhere has sex remained merely a physical act to relieve certain bodily tensions. It has been transformed within all human societies to become a basic area for morality and the organization of society. At an even greater remove from biology, it has generated themes that permeate religion and art and so participates in enormously complex symbolic systems.

This mingling of biology and symbolization in human sexuality can, I think, best be dealt with from the anthropological viewpoint — the fundamental assumption of and justification for this book.

Sex is clearly one of the important aspects of human life, but in the four million or so years that human (or humanlike) beings have existed, only within the past few hundred years have people started to study it objectively. Even some of the most fundamental and seemingly obvious facts of biology have been misunderstood. And as examples of misconceptions, we need not dwell on such oddities as the belief that some people are male one month and female the following month — a belief that has been reported from such divergent groups as the Tarascan Indians of North America and the Burmese (who say these individuals are being punished for illicit seductions in a previous life).

Early anthropology: artist's impression of an Australian society.

A 5th-century terracotta figurine of Baubo (below), the goddess who officiated as nurse at the ancient Greek Eleusinian Mysteries, shows the interdependence of religion, art and sexuality in many cultures.

Amazon Indians (above) may combine a simple life-style with complicated beliefs and tabus about sex.

Consider instead such commonplace matters as menstruation and paternity. At least 12 societies in the world hold that menstruation is caused by having sexual intercourse. This belief can probably be explained by the fact that most girls in these societies marry or are allowed to have sex before puberty. But surely some girls do not. Among the peasants of Tepoztlán, Mexico, this belief broke down when later marriages became the fashion, but even so is still held by older people. A man who accidentally discovered that his 15-year-old unmarried niece was menstruating, denounced her for not being a virgin and held her mother responsible for not guarding her.

Theories about how babies are made have great variety. Some societies, such as the Áranda of Australia, the Trobriand islanders off the coast of New Guinea, and the Yapese on an island in Micronesia in the Pacific, reportedly deny that men are necessary for procreation. Some anthropologists discount these reports, but there are other beliefs that are equally astonishing. The Buka of the Solomon Islands in the Pacific believe that a child is formed only out of its mother's blood — semen playing no role in procreation. But sticking a penis inside the woman is necessary: it somehow triggers the whole business of conception. As proof of the correctness of this belief, people told about a man in a neighboring village who developed an ulcer on his penis, which rotted away. Undaunted, the man made an artificial one of wood and continued to copulate with his wife, who gave birth to a number of children. Clearly, penetration, not ejaculation, was all that was required!

In a great many societies throughout the world it is believed that conception requires more than one act of sexual intercourse. The Wógeo of Papua New Guinea, for example, say that a foetus is made up of a combination of menstrual blood and semen. Copulation has to be repeated often so that the passage leading from the womb will be blocked up with semen to prevent the blood from escaping. The Yãnomamö of Venezuela and Brazil believe that for a child to grow strong, many men should copulate with the mother frequently during her pregnancy. This has its problems, since if she is discovered with a lover, her husband will almost invariably challenge him to a duel and will abuse her. But mothers apparently know their obligations and risk even the wrath of their husbands for the sake of their children.

The Ngonde of Malawi take the belief in the need for many acts of coitus one step further: if a woman should become pregnant after having had sexual intercourse only once with her husband, she would be accused of adultery — without any further evidence. On the other hand, the Mam of Guatemala may accuse a woman of adultery if she has

BELIEFS ABOUT PROCREATION, MENSTRUATION AND CONCEPTION

NORTH AMERICA
● POMO ●
■ NAVAHO ●
● CONTEMPORARY USA – SOME BLACK HOMOSEXUALS ■
▲ TEPOZTECANS ●
○ TZELTAL ●
▲ JAMAICANS ▲

EUROPE
TRADITIONAL • PRE-SCIENTIFIC WESTERN VIEW ●

AFRICA
□ BAMBARA ● • DOGON ■
▲ ANDAMANESE ●
□ MONGO ●
■ ILA ●
• TSWANA □

ASIA
• AINU □
• LEPCHA ▲
▲ TRUKESE ●
• YAPESE ●
TIKOPIA ●
▲ KWOMA ● HUA ■
KERAKI ●
● TROBRIANDERS
▲ TIWI ● • MURNGIN ▲
AUSTRALIA
• ARANDA ●

ANCIENT HEBREWS ●

▲ YÃNOMAMÓ ●
● TUKANO- • KUBEO
▲ APINAYÉ ▲
• TUPINAMBÁ ●
• TIMBIRA ▲
• BORORÓ ▲ ▲

SOUTH AMERICA

• ONA □

● BELIEF THAT SEXUAL INTERCOURSE IS NOT NECESSARY FOR PROCREATION

■ BELIEF THAT SEMEN IS NOT NECESSARY FOR PROCREATION

▲ BELIEF THAT MENSTRUATION IS CAUSED BY SEXUAL INTERCOURSE

○ BELIEF THAT MEN HAVE WOMBS

● BELIEF THAT FATHER ONLY CONTRIBUTES SUBSTANCE TO FOETUS (MOTHER GREENHOUSE)

■ BELIEF THAT MEN CAN GET PREGNANT

▲ BELIEF THAT CHILD CAN HAVE MULTIPLE FATHERS

□ BELIEF THAT CHILD CANNOT BE CONCEIVED WITH ONLY ONE ACT OF INTERCOURSE

copulated with her husband regularly for two or three years and does not become pregnant: they believe that having sex with more than one man prevents conception.

A society that recognizes that men are necessary for procreation and that one act of intercourse is enough to cause pregnancy may hold to other inaccuracies. The Kubeo of Brazil insist that a pregnant woman stop having sex altogether, because continued intercourse will pile up the number of foetuses within her and she may explode. Somewhat less dramatic is the conviction in a number of societies that twins are a sign of adultery.

All of these examples tend to be amusing to us in part because they are culturally remote. It is more upsetting to know that Westerners have held equally wrong ideas. In contemporary urban England, in many parts of rural America, Jamaica and Puerto Rico an earlier European belief that a woman must experience orgasm if coitus is to lead to conception, is still held. The fact is that women need not enjoy sex at all to get pregnant — as prim Victorian women who lay back, shut their eyes, spread their legs, and thought of England could readily attest.

A more serious matter is the belief held throughout most

Ignorance of the basic facts of sex has led to many inaccurate theories of conception and procreation among cultures of the world. The development of scientific technology may have eradicated many errors, but some superstitions have lingered, even in the West.

of western history (which has been discounted by educated people only within the last 200 years) that a woman is simply the greenhouse in which a man's seed grows to become a child. Of course, this myth was not restricted to the West: the Trukese of the Pacific and the Tupinambá of South America still believe it. Without scientific technology people will create such explanations not only to account for biology but probably also to justify some aspects of their society. For example, those societies that play down paternity tend to play up the woman's role in the culture and trace descent, inheritance and succession through women. The opposite is true when maternity is played down.

For the most part, ignorance about basic aspects of sex and the reproductive cycle can be blamed on the lack of microscopes and other such equipment. But ideology has also been a deterrent.

On the one hand, specific religious groups have tended to put down such study as immoral. On the other hand, there is even more persistent folk morality based on philosophically crude notions of what is natural (I am not referring to natural law, which is, however, related). Every culture has developed such ideas with regard to sex. Reference is made to the "order of things" or "nature" when such ideas are challenged. Now the interesting thing is that cultures do not always agree on what is natural. For example, we in the western world frown on polygamy, whereas it is the ideal in most societies: not only is it thought natural for a man to have more than one wife, it is expected of him if he can possibly afford it.

Consider the views of the Kágaba Indians of Colombia on what is natural. Unlike many peoples in the world they do not believe that incest will produce deformed or insane children. But if a man's rhythm during sexual intercourse is

Sex education in a Central African society. What is normal and natural in one group may be seen as "against the natural order" in another.

thrown off, this may cause harm to his children — and to himself and his partner. Furthermore, if the woman should even move, she might cause the whole world to tremble and fall from the shoulders of the four giant men believed to hold it up.

The Kágaba have other apparently unique beliefs. One is that people have copulated on every square centimeter of the earth and that semen has seeped through the ground everywhere. For more semen to penetrate the earth would in some way open up the gates of sickness and possibly destroy the world. Masturbation, therefore, is regarded as monstrous and even during sexual relations in marriage special magical stones must be placed beneath the sex organs to catch any seminal flow. Semen has a special importance in another way: if a forbidden sexual act has been performed, a semen sacrifice must be made to the spirit Heiséi, the master of sexuality and its aberrations. What this means is that the forbidden act has to be done all over again. To expiate incest, the guilty couple — whether brother–sister, father–daughter, or even mother–son — must repeat the offense so that the semen and vaginal secretions can be collected on a piece of cotton cloth and handed over to a priest to sacrifice. (There is said to be much incest among the Kágaba.) I know of no other society in the world in which expiation for a crime demands its repetition.

Certainly of all human behavior, sexual conduct on the face of it should be closest to the instinctual, with relatively little variation. The facts are different: even the way people copulate differs from one group to another. The missionary position (as it is informally referred to, with the partners prone and facing each other, the man on top) is generally taken for granted in the western world as the most natural in the repertoire. When the Bororó Indians of southern Brazil

The missionary position (top right) is regarded in the West as the most "natural." Christian missionaries even insisted that their converts should use only this position, hence its name. Early representations of intercourse show woman on top in a Mesopotamian cylinder seal (top left) and rear-entry (below) on an ancient Peruvian Mochica pot; but the missionary position is less common.

first heard about it, they were deeply offended. "What an insult against the one who is underneath!" exclaimed one Bororó man; another said in astonishment, "But what weight!" The Trobriand islanders are almost as uncompromising as traditional Westerners: they recognize two natural copulatory positions — neither of these is the missionary position, which they regard as impractical and improper. As one Trobriander reported of this position (to use the stilted translation given by the anthropologist): "The man overlies heavily the woman; he presses her heavily downwards, she cannot respond." The Zulu of South Africa judge it to be vulgar and unbecoming in a human being because they claim — quite inaccurately — that it follows "the manner of the animals."

The earliest representations of human sexual intercourse tend never to be the missionary position. The commonest may be with the woman on top, and this is found in one of the oldest representations known (about 3200 BC) from Ur in Mesopotamia. The same position is found in ancient Greek, Roman, Peruvian, Indian, Chinese and Japanese art. Rear-entry intercourse is also frequently shown.

Sex and class Within the same society there may be striking differences in sexual behavior and ideology. In the United States, Kinsey and his associates found that Americans in the 1930s and 1940s showed a very clear social class difference, and the differences even included instances of involuntary nocturnal emissions. Specifically, American men who had gone to college or who belonged to one of the professions started having nocturnal emissions earlier in life than blue-collar workers. Among the more educated males emissions continued longer and occurred 10 to 12 times more frequently. In general, less educated men tended to think of anything but the missionary position as perverse. They avoided and condemned as unnatural: masturbation, oral-genital sex, petting, deep kissing, mouth-breast contacts and the use of pornography as an erotic stimulus. When they had sex, they did so with a minimum of foreplay and nearly always wearing some clothing. On the other hand, promiscuous premarital intercourse with someone other than their future wife was regarded as normal and natural. The young man from a less educated background who had not had intercourse by the age of 16 or 17 could be characterized quite succinctly: he was either physically incapacitated, mentally deficient, homosexual, or earmarked for leaving his social class by going to college.

Better educated men showed a strikingly different pattern, stemming partly from the fact that they were willing to delay sexual intercourse (or experienced so many social pressures that they had to delay it) until fairly late in life.

Sexual behavior varies according to class, whether in contemporary America or in the India of the Kaama suutra. And the higher the class, the more elaborate the behavior.

Kaama suutra *sexual techniques were not widely studied outside the circles for which the book had been written.*

They made do with masturbation, petting and pornography. When they did begin intercourse, it was generally performed in the nude, with a great deal of foreplay and experimentation with regard to position. Premarital sexual intercourse occurred most frequently with their fiancées. In general, men of this class tended to react to a greater variety of erotic stimuli.

Since Kinsey's 1948 study, these class differences seem to have changed considerably. What is particularly interesting is that these distinctions seem to represent long-established patterns going back at least to colonial times and probably earlier. Aretino, an Italian living in the sixteenth century, describes how a lower-class woman taught her daughter to become a prostitute — this meant in part accepting the "perverted" behavior of her rich upper-class clients. In much the same way there is evidence that the exotic sexual techniques recorded in the *Kaama suutra* were known only to the social elite of India; these were mysteries that ordinary people did not know or even hear about, although devotees of the book regarded it as a religious revelation. Even the relatively simple and homogenous society of the Marquesans in the

The breast is an erotic image in many cultures, including that of the West; to other societies it is seen simply as a provider of food. Both themes are suggested in Roman Charity *by Giaocchino Serangeli, 1824.*

Pacific shows subcultural differences with regard to sexual behavior. And everywhere, the sexual behavior of the upper classes and ordinary people seems to show marked differences.

What seems obvious is that sex is to a very large extent learned and not totally biological. Sexual tastes are similar to food likes and dislikes, which are also acquired and vary from culture to culture. These tastes need not even be spelled out in strong tabus or admonitions. It does no good for most Westerners to discover that insects are a perfectly adequate source of protein. They simply will not rush out to catch a grasshopper or start breeding cockroaches to supplement the family diet. For both sex and food, elaborate rationalizations are constructed, sometimes of considerable symbolic intricacy.

As an example of the variation of symbolic values attached to a sexual act — as well as a tie-in with food — consider the sucking of a woman's breast. In many societies breasts are not considered especially erotic and they are thought of primarily as the source of a baby's milk. Among the Navaho Indians an adult man may sometimes suck on a nursing woman's breasts to relieve her of the pain caused by excess milk when there is no baby around to empty them. Orthodox Jews, on the other hand, specifically prohibit an adult from drinking the milk from a woman's breast. The Marquesans and the Kgatla-Tswana of southern Africa recognize sucking and kissing of breasts as standard foreplay — among the former, to excite the woman; among the latter, apparently the man.

Various patterns joining eating and sexual behavior are found throughout the world and cannot be accidental. It is useful to keep this in mind because sexual rules, behavior and expectations are for the most part less easy to deal with objectively than food and eating. But there is no reason why we should not at least try to deal with sex objectively, and no reason why sexual customs cannot be examined as are other customs, to find out when and where they originated, how they spread, and why they are maintained.

In part, that is what I have tried to do. In a more general way, I have attempted to document the culture of sexuality. In doing so I have hugged the facts pretty closely and avoided large-scale theorizing. Not that I am against such theorizing; it is merely that a lower level, less grandiose approach has its own merits and an indisputable fascination.

Of all the sciences, only anthropology studies man crossculturally. Every culture is taken as an experiment in survival and a realization of the human potential. This book assumes an anthropological perspective in exploring the richness and diversity of human sexuality in spite of its biological underpinnings. On the pages that follow I have tried to map that variety within its cultural contexts.

Two & THE WESTERN CULTURAL BACKGROUND

Almost all anthropologists are products of the sexually repressive Judaeo-Christian tradition, and this has colored their perception of the sexual customs of other cultures.

Adam and Eve: a medieval representation.

Sex and anthropology seem to go together in most people's minds. Bizarre erotic customs investigated by licentious PhDs in pith helmets, reveling in the honored field methods of observation as well as participation — this is a popular myth about the anthropological profession: it is not accurate.

Anthropologists may develop a certain objectivity about their own customs and it seems to be the case that they are sometimes even misfits in their own culture (maybe that inability to fit in is what pushes them into the study of all cultures). But the great majority are probably as embarrassed and guilty about sex as anyone else brought up in the Judaeo-Christian tradition. Initially, therefore, it is necessary for us to investigate that tradition in some detail in order to get a more dispassionate view of sex. Otherwise, we may be reduced to uttering moralistic judgments that will tell more about ourselves than the cultures we are studying.

I remember well my first field trip to Africa and my encounter with a Christian missionary who had lived for 20 years with a group I wanted to study. Within the first five minutes of our conversation, he blurted out with astonishment and horror: "These people marry more than one wife!" Twenty years had not lessened his moral outrage.

The Judaeo-Christian tradition encompasses quite a varied collection of beliefs about sexuality. For the most part, only conservative, orthodox views will be examined here, rather than those associated with the folk reality or with various liberalizing tendencies (these are examined in Chapter 11). For a generation that has experienced the "sexual revolution," the pill, Women's Lib and Gay Lib, some of the beliefs summarized here may sound quaint. However, these doctrines still hold enormous influence over a very large segment of the western world.

In the Judaeo-Christian tradition the ultimate justification for sexual intercourse is procreation. The only appropriate setting for sex is marriage, which is held to be divinely sanctioned. More specifically, the fundamental notion of Christian sexual morality (Jewish views sometimes differ) is that a man should ejaculate only within his wife's vagina. All other forms of sexual expression causing a man to ejaculate are tabu.

Many groups forbid the insertion of a penis into any bodily opening except the vagina, whether or not ejaculation

All activities have a *definite purpose, and the purpose of sexual activity is procreation: this belief pervades the Judaeo-Christian tradition.*

occurs, but others permit such behavior if ejaculation does not occur. Thus, some Roman Catholic moralists hold that a woman may legitimately perform fellation on her husband as foreplay, but that it becomes a mortal sin if he has an orgasm in the process.

The sexual response of men is the obvious focus for the moral code. What women do in the absence of men has not usually been considered of much consequence. For example, in the Bible there is no tabu on lesbian activity (although most groups in the tradition disapprove of it), but female bestiality is condemned — perhaps because it is presumably with a male animal. Female masturbation is virtually never considered, and at one point in the Middle Ages was tolerated if the woman did not achieve an orgasm in intercourse, which was believed to be necessary for procreation.

In contemporary western Judaeo-Christian practice, marriage is almost always monogamous except for a very few aberrant groups such as dissident Mormons (about 20,000 to 30,000 Mormons in the western United States are involved in polygamous marriages at the present day). Virtually all groups permit divorce (and remarriage) for one or another reason — almost always for a wife's adultery. The Roman Catholic Church insists on the indissolubility of marriage, but permits remarriage on the death of a spouse.

Premarital virginity is highly prized and generally expected of women and desirable for men, although a double standard permitting male experimentation has generally been tolerated and even fostered by western society if not by the religions themselves. Lifelong virginity is advocated as a possible sexual career — and conceded to be spiritually higher than married life — primarily among the Eastern Orthodox and Roman Catholics, but even among them marriage is the overwhelmingly common life-style. In a very few sects such as the Shakers, an American offshoot of radical Quakers, total sexual abstinence was required. New mem-

Polygamy, though common cross-culturally, is extremely rare in the Judaeo-Christian tradition. Some western American Mormons (right) still endorse the practice.

bers were recruited from non-Shaker families through conversion. Theirs was an exceedingly uncommon life-style,
both in the Judaeo-Christian tradition and cross-culturally.

Different social roles for men and women are believed to
be divinely sanctioned and to reflect the biological order of
things. A unisex society is regarded as undesirable. In particular, transvestism is condemned as a blurring of
categories. Interestingly enough, however, although there
are no male transvestite saints in the Christian tradition, a
few transvestite women, such as Joan of Arc, have been
elevated to the sainthood.

Until quite recently, nearly all groups within the tradition
have considered contraception to be the equivalent of murder. Abortion and infanticide are also condemned. The reality, however, has not always been in keeping with the ideal.

One of the fundamental themes found in western thought,
to make sense of the sexual moral code, is the notion of
"nature" — a basic assumption in Roman Catholic teaching
and also greatly influential throughout the rest of Christendom and even Judaism. According to this doctrine (originally
derived from pagan Greek philosophy, especially Aristotelian notions) all actions have an essential purpose — or
nature, in the technical jargon. The essential purpose of eating is to sustain life. The essential purpose of sexual activity
is procreation. To perform an act so that its essential purpose
— its nature — cannot be met, is to perform an unnatural act.
The notion of "nature" in this use is not really the same as the
romantic notion of nature involving animals and plants (or,
more familiarly, the birds and the bees) — though it is not
completely alien to it. But even if animals performed sexual
acts without reproductive relevance, this would not alter the
situation since the moral laws exist only for human beings.

Consider masturbation. Clearly it cannot meet the criteria
of legitimacy for sexual acts and so is both a mortal sin and
an unnatural act. It follows that all other acts that qualify as
the equivalent of masturbation — fellation, anal intercourse,
vaginal intercourse using some sort of contraceptive — are
sinful and unnatural. Masturbation, homosexual acts and
birth control are, therefore, equated. To change positions on
one of these would have far-reaching implications for the
system as a whole.

Changes have however occurred before in the sexual morality
of the Judaeo-Christian tradition. One of the most fundamental occurred relatively recently. In the 1930 Lambeth Conference of the Anglican Communion, previous condemnation of birth control was modified. The 1958 Conference
proclaimed the Christian obligation of limiting births and
sanctioned the use of artificial contraception. This ruling
applied to the Church of England, the Episcopal Church in

The western tradition emphasizes different social roles for men and for women, corresponding to the biological differences between the sexes. It frowns on societies where the categories are blurred.

Modifications through time

the United States, and various related groups. Apart from a few talmudic dispensations permitting women (but never men) to practice contraception, this was the first time in a more than 3,000-year tradition that sex was deemed to be moral even if procreation had deliberately been made impossible to achieve.

The consequences of making artificial contraception respectable in such an influential group have undoubtedly been tremendous. It may even have helped to bring about the acceptance of birth control in something like 70 percent of Roman Catholic households in the United States, in spite of papal denunciations. What implications the change will have on other aspects of the sexual code is not altogether clear, although some within the Anglican Communion have already taken a conciliatory attitude toward the activities of practicing homosexuals.

An examination of the history of Judaeo-Christian traditions shows a number of other important changes.

The Christian breakaway from the Jewish community in the first century AD also signaled a shift from the notion of ritual contamination to personal sin. A practical consequence of this has been the abandonment by all Christians of the *mikvah*, a ritual bath house where menstruating women and women who have given birth must bathe to remove their "polluting status."

Among Christians (except for the Eastern Orthodox), menstruating women have no special status, nor is it usually

Jewish women at a **mikvah,** *or ritual bath: from Kirchner's* Jewish ceremony, 1776. The mikvah *is one of the most important institutions of an Orthodox Jewish community. Menstruating women are regarded as unclean for seven days from the beginning of the period. Christianity shifted the emphasis from ritual contamination to personal sin, and thus did not take over the concept of a ritual bath.*

considered sinful for a man to have sexual intercourse with his wife during her period, but under Orthodox Jewish law sexual intercourse with a menstruating woman is strictly tabued at the present time.

The view about nocturnal emissions is comparable. The Orthodox Jewish position is that any depositing of semen outside of a vagina is unclean: semen, like menstrual blood, is polluting.

Because Christians have given up the notion of ritual pollution, nocturnal emissions are not generally considered to have any moral significance whatever. But this position was not entirely clear until St Thomas Aquinas argued that sin involves a conscious wilful act. Thus, nocturnal emissions cannot in themselves be considered sinful but masturbation must be and is regarded as a mortal sin. (The Orthodox Jewish position on masturbation comes from the view that it is a conscious waste of nature, in effect the murder of potential progeny. Consequently, some Jewish commentators have wanted it to be punished by death.)

An even more dramatic change with the independence of Christianity from Judaism was the adoption of monogamy. What seems to have happened is this: throughout the Graeco-Roman world (with a few exceptions such as the Jews) monogamy was the prevailing form of marriage at the beginning of the Christian era. Christianity did not introduce monogamy to the pagans; rather, it embraced a pagan social institution and abandoned Judaic custom.

In the matter of marriage, Christianity broke with its Judaic antecedents and, instead of the polygamy once general in Judaism, chose the system of monogamy practiced by the pagan religions of the Graeco-Roman world.

The adoption of monogamy by Christians in turn affected the customs of Jews living in Christian Europe. They accepted monogamy as obligatory following a ban on polygamy in AD 1030 by the eminent rabbi Gershom ben Judah. But this ban merely reflected social reality: Jews in Europe no longer practiced polygamy by that time but followed the Christian pattern. Jews living in the Muslim world, where polygamy is accepted, have preserved their own old custom, although they follow the Muslim (and talmudic, but not biblical) ban on having more than four wives at a time.

The changes discussed so far are obvious ones. Examination of both ritual and scripture suggest a number of other significant and somewhat unexpected changes. They are not accepted by all scholars and the orthodox will reject them outright.

Consider for example a detail in the Orthodox Jewish ritual of circumcision: the *metsitsah*. This is the custom of sucking off a drop of blood from the newly circumcised penis by the mohel (circumciser). Kinsey and a number of other scholars believe that it is a survival of an ancient phallic cult that required ritual fellatio. Although this explanation may seem farfetched, it is bolstered by the fact that sacred prostitutes (that is, prostitutes used in religious rites) were known to the ancient Hebrews from their association with the Canaanites. Several biblical condemnations of male sacred prostitutes (for example, Deuteronomy 23:17–18, where they are referred to as "dogs"; and II Kings 23:7, where they are linked to the temple in Jerusalem) prove that they existed among the Hebrews from probably before the tenth century to the Babylonian Exile in 586 BC, if not later. Although officially condemned, they seem to have been accepted in practice. Sacred prostitution has now entirely disappeared from the Judaeo-Christian repertoire. But that it once existed might help to link up the *metsitsah* to a phallic cult.

Differences and developments

Today there are different rules about incest in the various groups within the Judaeo-Christian tradition. An examination of the Bible shows that the rules changed even during the formation of the Scriptures.

As an example of the differences, Orthodox Jews permit marriage between uncle and niece but forbid it between aunt and nephew. They also permit marriage between full stepbrothers and sisters as well as between first cousins. Most of these marriages are totally forbidden by Christians. First cousin marriage is tabu for Eastern Orthodox Christians but is occasionally allowed in most other groups. Furthermore, traditional Jewish law has permitted and even encouraged marriage between a man and his deceased wife's sister and his deceased brother's widow.

Variations in incest rules between Christianity and Judaism indicate the different needs of the two cultures. Judaism's relatively lax incest laws reflect the structure of a close-knit community, whereas Christianity developed laws that opposed marriage ties between relatives at a time when it was seeking to enlarge its area of alliances.

Christians, however, were eventually associated with a larger international community in which marriage ties with relatives or in-laws were not profitable and there was everything to be gained from alliances farther afield; so the list of forbidden marriages increased. The rules have fluctuated considerably, so that at the present time it is possible for Roman Catholics to marry their first cousins (but only with a dispensation).

The Judaeo-Christian tradition also underwent changes in emphasis or philosophy. For example, Jews have traditionally tended to regard marriage as a moral necessity. But at the beginning of the Christian era there were a number of ascetic Jewish sects such as the Essenes who were in part associated with monasticism or played up celibacy. For Christians, the example of Jesus' own life elevated the unmarried state. This notion was encouraged by St Paul, who thought that marriage was a good estate but celibacy was better: for those who could not exercise self-control, it was "better to marry than to burn" with passion (I Corinthians 7:8–9). According to Augustine, a few centuries later, sex even within marriage was suspect and he doubted that in Paradise before the Fall Adam would even have had erections, since lust — concupiscence — had not yet entered the world. His doctrine is not the official view of the Church, which holds that sexual passion in itself is morally neutral.

The emphasis on celibacy in the Church was attacked by Luther and various other reformers, who tended to elevate the status of marriage; at the same time they denied that it was a sacrament and permitted divorce.

Three developments since the Reformation have been particularly repressive with regard to sex. The first of these was the rise of the Puritans in England in the seventeenth century. Although not opposed to sex within marriage, the Puritans were intolerant of adultery and fornication in a practical sense that was virtually unparalleled in the history

The theme of Lot and his daughters (below left), depicted by Lucas van der Leyden in 1530, may indicate an earlier period in the development of Judaism when a different set of incest rules was in operation.

of Christianity. It was they who developed (particularly in their American offshoot) an extraordinary paranoia about satanic sexual orgies which led to a methodical and widespread persecution of witches.

A second development, also in the seventeenth century, was the revival of Augustinian doctrines in the Roman Catholic Church under the label of Jansenism. This movement stressed the damage caused to human nature by original sin and the evils of lust. Although Jansenism was declared a heresy, much of its moral preoccupation with the dangers of sex lingered in Holland even after it had been officially disapproved, and it has particularly survived in Ireland, where fear and repression of sexuality is said to be astonishingly high, unparalleled elsewhere in the Roman Catholic world or perhaps anywhere.

The third development is more recent and only partially religious in nature: Victorianism. The extreme prudery of

The lusts of the flesh take form in a detail from the Bruegel woodcut Luxuria, (above).

The burning of witches (right), continued well into the 18th century. The persecution of women suspected of being witches often revealed sexual undertones.

Witches' Sabbath (below), by Francisco Goya (1746–1828), illustrates the western paranoia concerning satanic sexual orgies.

Brothels proliferated in the climate of Victorian England. Establishments such as Kate Hamilton's Night House (above) catered mainly for a middle-class clientele. The Victorian gap between public prudery and private license was so wide that it stimulated the first modern scientific investigations into the nature of sexuality.

the movement was accompanied by a belief in the dangers of the loss of semen — not in the Orthodox Jewish sense of pollution, but in the pseudoscientific belief that all ejaculation was debilitating and that sexual intercourse even within marriage was to be avoided as much as possible for the higher good of society. In other words, it espoused with a vengeance a doctrine of sublimation. This doctrine was to have profound results. In spite of its concomitant cult of the sexless woman, England developed an enormous cadre of prostitutes (some estimates go as high as 40,000 in London during the heyday of Victorianism). This discrepancy between the ideal and the real created the cultural climate for the beginnings of scientific sexology and the in-depth probings of Freud.

In some of Freud's writings Judaeo-Christian notions survive. The traditional idea of reproductive relevance was adopted by him (at least occasionally) as a measure by which to judge the normalcy of sexual acts. And it is a common criticism of psychiatry and psychology that Judaeo-Christian conceptions of sin have been translated wholesale into "pseudoscientific" notions of mental sickness.

But in spite of the awesomeness of the Judaeo-Christian tradition, it is clearly not an unchanging monolithic structure. It has made numerous responses to a number of outside forces, and is continuing to do so.

Throughout the history of the West, sexual infractions have not only been sins but very often crimes as well. The punishments for these crimes have been fines, imprisonment, torture or death. Regulations concerning marriage, divorce and incest (but not always other areas of sexual behavior) have been incorporated into all the western legal systems from Roman law — the earliest legal code considered here — through to English common law, the Napoleonic code, the Soviet socialist penal code, and the Model penal code proposed by the American Law Institute.

Western legal notions on sexuality

In Roman law, a small number of sexual offenses were, at least theoretically, punishable by death. The regulations varied over the years, but at one time or another the following were treated as capital crimes:

Adultery committed by the wife. A husband's adultery did not count as a crime at all. At times banishment or some lesser punishment was substituted.

Incest. Originally the death sentence was carried out by throwing the culprits from the Tarpeian rock near Rome. Later, banishment was the appropriate punishment.

Intercourse between a free woman and a male slave. Under the emperor Constantine, both were to be killed (the slave by burning). A free man had legal sexual access to his own slaves.

Romans apparently dealt with sodomy as a form of fornication, which in some instances was punishable by seizure of half of each guilty party's property. Under some emperors the penalties could be considerably more severe. But the Roman legal attitude to homosexuality is not clear, nor is it known whether the law reflected general sentiment. It would seem that institutionalized pederasty was, along with male nudity, considered an essentially Greek custom.

During the reign of Valentinian I, the fourth-century Christian emperor, men found guilty of sodomy are said to have been burned alive. By the time of the emperor Justinian (sixth century), the death sentence for homosexual acts was certainly on the books — although Justinian had offenders castrated rather than killed — and was officially retained throughout Byzantine history. In the Middle Ages in western Europe, the charge of sodomy seems to have been heaped on heretics and others who were going to be killed anyway, so the reality of the law here is not clear.

In Constantine's time (fourth century) rape was a serious offense: even the victims were liable to be punished for not preventing the rape by screaming for help. Thus a virgin who was raped might well be burned to death.

Virtually all these extreme punishments were paralleled in the Mosaic code. Both the Mosaic code and the Roman law permitted divorce. According to Plutarch, the earliest laws of the Romans (traditionally ascribed to Romulus) permitted only the husband to initiate a divorce and the sole grounds were that his wife had committed adultery, poisoned his children, or counterfeited his keys, presumably to get at the wine cellar. Drinking was thought to lead almost inevitably to adultery and in early Rome a wife accused of either drinking or adultery could be killed.

The divorce laws changed and other reasons for divorce were permitted. During the Empire, women were allowed to initiate divorce but apparently never on the grounds of a husband's adultery.

Fornication was an offense only if it involved upper-class women. A man might frequent prostitutes without being guilty of fornication, but no upper-class women were allowed sexual relationships outside marriage. The emperor Augustus exiled both his daughter and granddaughter for criminal fornication and forbade their burial in his tomb. Some upper-class women dared oppose this double standard by officially registering as prostitutes, who were not subject to such laws.

The emperor Tiberius, who succeeded Augustus, closed this loophole by making it illegal for a woman to register as a prostitute if her father, grandfather or husband was a Roman knight or senator.

Roman law also punished celibacy and childlessness by

Pederasty is a frequent theme in ancient Greek art, as in a red-figure vase showing foreplay between a man and a boy.

giving substantial privileges to people with many children; the unmarried and childless thereby suffered economic and social disadvantages.

The establishment of Christianity as the official religion of the Empire tended, at least in the West, to make sexual offenses and marital disputes a matter for ecclesiastical rather than civil courts. There were, of course, exceptions and local variants. In Spain under the Visigoths, for example, homosexual acts were punished with castration and death following secular court decisions, whereas in the British Isles penance was prescribed. According to one Welsh penitential, sodomy requires a four-year penance as opposed to a three-year pilgrimage for incest with one's mother. The sixth-century Irish penitential attributed to St Columban insists on a 10-year penance for sodomy committed by a clergyman or monk, but only a seven-year penance for a layman. In both instances, the only food the penitent is allowed to eat is bread and water, salt and dry vegetables.

In another penitential, the sixth-century *Book of David*, nocturnal emissions are regarded as sins; as a penance the sinner is required to sing seven psalms on rising and live on bread and water for a day. The book also stipulates that bestiality or fornication with a nun requires as much as a lifetime of penance.

The Reformation saw the secularization of many of the traditional religious sexual prohibitions. In England, ecclesiastical law on sex was converted in large part to common civil law. During the reign of Henry VIII, the notion of sin against nature was transformed into that of crime against nature so that in 1533 sodomy was made a crime for the first time, although this law was repealed by the first parliament of Edward VI, his successor. In 1548 sodomy was again made a crime, but this law was abolished once more in 1553 under Queen Mary. In 1563 the law was re-established under Queen Elizabeth and remained (with some modification) until its repeal in 1967. The punishment varied but from time

Sexual offenses in the
Middle Ages often came under the jurisdiction of the Church rather than the secular courts. "Sodomites" were burned alive in Spain by order of the Inquisition (above), and a contemporary picture by Pedro Berruguete shows the method.

Sexual activity between
members of religious orders. Though often not strictly enforced, medieval punishments for such offenses were very severe.

A contemporary woodcut illustrates the burning to death of monks accused of sodomy, dated 1578.

to time included death or life imprisonment.

The domination of the English parliament by the Puritans led, in 1650, to the Act of May 1, according to which adultery and sodomy were punishable by death, and fornication by three months' imprisonment and the posting of a bond to guarantee good behavior. The Restoration of Charles II in 1660 saw the repeal of all sex laws except those dealing with the practice of sodomy.

The French Revolution provided the first major break with western tradition. The early revolutionaries removed the death penalty for sex crimes soon after taking control of the country and in 1792 made divorce legal and dependent on mutual consent of the parties. (The latter rule was eventually changed and divorce was abolished altogether in 1816 after the restoration of the monarchy.) In 1810, an important revision of the laws appeared: the Napoleonic code. The most significant feature of this, from the point of view of sex crimes, was that sexual behavior in private between consenting adults was decriminalized and bestiality was no longer considered a crime. Certain acts continued to be punishable but only if they involved an outrage of public decency, violence, or happened to be committed with a minor or an incompetent.

Many western countries (with the notable exception of England and other common-law countries such as the United States) followed suit, at least in the abolition of the death penalty, which was generally on the books for bestiality and homosexual acts but was seldom actually meted out. The dropping of these harsh penalties had the effect in some areas of creating a greater willingness to prosecute such crimes. But there has been a movement toward the decriminalization of consensual sexual acts between adults in private since the enactment of the Napoleonic code.

In 1917, the Soviet Union started what has been called a sexual revolution. Incest, bigamy (and polygamy), adultery, homosexual acts and bestiality were expunged from the penal code. Abortion was legalized in 1920, and so was divorce by consent. Only civil marriages were recognized and the distinctions between concubinage and marriage, as well as legitimacy and illegitimacy, were legally dropped. Social changes within the Soviet Union, however, resulted in the re-emergence of what had previously been attacked as bourgeois morality. In 1934, new laws against homosexual behavior were passed. In 1935–36, abortion was made illegal and divorce laws were made more severe: substantial fees were introduced and each divorce was registered on internal passports. By 1944, the only recognized ground for divorce was the political disloyalty of the spouse. Some of these changes are directly attributable to the losses accompanying collectivization (a minimum of 10 million) and the enormous number of casualties in World War II (30 to 40 million). Nevertheless, legal abortions and birth control were re-established in 1955–56.

At present the only form of marriage allowed in the Soviet Union is monogamy and incest is considered to be a crime.

Although the general trend in the West has been to decriminalize adult consensual private acts, in some areas the laws against at least some of them are still severe. The most consistent opponents of liberalization in the twentieth century include some of the modern Communist governments and various conservative religious groups. Earlier in the century the Fascists and Nazis also both took an anti-liberalizing position.

The goals of the sex law reform are still championed by a number of small groups. In large part liberalized views put forward in the recommendations offered by the Bellagio Conference of 1963 have been adopted in the Model penal code for the American Law Institute and essentially accepted by the Association Internationale de Droit Pénal during the Ninth International Congress on Criminal Law held at The Hague in 1964.

Folk wisdom in the western world has often been as misleading as religion and the law have been repressive. Superstitions recorded by Pliny in ancient times are still believed by some people. The astonishing thing is that superstitions and misinformation are not restricted to the uneducated. Studies of medical students' knowledge about sex, for example, show that they seem to be no better informed than their nonmedical contemporaries. A report by Greenbank

In 1917 the Soviet Union legalized a whole range of sexual acts previously classed as offenses. But the USSR has since brought back, and even strengthened, many of the old laws. By 1944, the only recognized ground for divorce was political disloyalty.

Western folk notions on sexuality

Masturbation or "onanism" led to "failure of intelligence, nocturnal hallucinations, and suicidal and homicidal propensities," according to a leading 19th-century psychiatrist. Illustrations from The silent friend *(1853) illustrate two of the practice's supposed deleterious effects.*

revealed that half of the 1959 graduates of a Philadelphia medical school believed that mental illness is frequently caused by masturbation. A more extraordinary finding is the fact that one out of every five *faculty* members of that school believed the same thing.

Members of the medical profession have even manufactured their own kinds of sexual myths. A notable example is Dr David Reuben in his enormously popular book *Everything you always wanted to know about sex (but were afraid to ask)*. It is a sort of hip catechism of sex — but without the benefits of revelation, or sometimes even the most basic information.

The most striking error in the book may unfortunately be the one best remembered. He puts in a plug for Coca-Cola as a contraceptive: all you have to do is shake up a bottle and fizz the liquid into the vagina after intercourse and you are safe. He forgets to add that such a procedure might lead to salpingitis, peritonitis, or even gas embolism, causing death. All things do not go better with Coke!

A thoroughgoing study of sex myths and superstitions has not yet appeared. Some involve quite fundamental errors. A case in point is the whole notion of biological relationships as *blood* relationships. This is scientifically false: what is involved are genes, not blood. Nevertheless, it is a dominant theme in the western folk idea of conception.

A number of less farfetched myths or folk tales have appeared in the West and survive in various places. A few are given below, arranged according to topic.

Menstruation is associated with an enormous number of superstitions. The general belief of the Graeco-Roman world (as described by Pliny) included some of the following notions: contact with a menstruating woman will turn new wine sour, blunt the blade of an iron knife, rust bronze and iron, cause ivory to lose its luster and trees and plants to become unfruitful. Should a menstruating woman look in a mirror its brilliance will be blurred. If such a woman sits under a tree its fruit will fall off. A dog that laps up menstrual blood goes mad and its bite becomes incurably poisonous.

All of these notions are false with the possible exception of the adverse consequences on plants. There is some evidence, though this is controversial, that menstrual blood contains a toxin that has an injurious or at least an inhibiting effect on flowers, sprouting seeds and plants in general.

Many of these ideas or similar ones have survived in various parts of Europe and the New World. Thus, eastern European Jews believe that the touch of a menstruating woman can stop the process of pickling (a folk idea with no biblical support at all). According to a belief reported from North Carolina, if a woman bakes a cake while menstruating, it will not turn out well. In some parts of the English-speaking world, girls are advised not to wash their hair while menstruating or to pick fruit (which would go bad).

Menstrual blood has not always been avoided. In the Middle Ages in Europe it was sometimes used as a medicine for sufferers of leprosy, and it has occasionally been assumed to be a powerful aphrodisiac. Louis XIV of France apparently believed in its aphrodisiac powers; he reportedly was introduced to this idea by his mistress the Marquise de Montespan.

Avoiding intercourse during menstruation may be due to a superstition about the dire consequences of such an act. Although some risk of infection is admitted by a few scientists, there are no clear dire consequences at all. From the point of view of birth control, intercourse during menstruation is safest because it is unlikely to lead to conception.

The widespread belief that a woman's least fertile time is midway between periods may be related to the ancient doctrine that menstrual blood is the basis for the female contribution to an embryo.

The size of a penis or vagina is frequently believed to be correlated with other anatomical characteristics. For example, a frequent correlation is made between the size of a man's penis and that of his nose, feet or hands. It is also generally believed that tall men have large penes. No scientific information exists confirming these correlations. A similar unverified statement, but one less frequently made, is that a woman with a large mouth has a large vagina.

Other related notions involving anatomy include the following: a woman whose vagina is dry during intercourse has been unfaithful. Women with small breasts are poor risks in bed. The genitals of Oriental women lie farther back than those of European women and therefore Oriental positions for copulating are different from the European ones. A small, straight forehead denotes unbridled lust, and small ears a certain sexual flair. But cold feet suggest that a sexual encounter will be unpleasant or unsuccessful.

A very widespread notion found in cultures throughout the world is that the bigger a man's penis, the more effectively he will sexually satisfy a woman. The researches of Masters and Johnson suggest that this simply is not the case. Sexual adequacy seems to be unrelated to the size of a man's penis since a vagina can generally adjust to the size of any intromitted penis. Their researches further indicate that the size of the vagina is also of no special consequence in arousing men. An English schoolboy rhyme suggests another point of view:

Genitals and
other body parts

An ancient Egyptian *figurine indicates that the Egyptians, like most other cultures, regarded penis size as very important in sexual and procreative matters.*

Long and thin goes right in
And doesn't please the ladies.
Short and thick does the trick
And gives them all the babies.

Sexual acts and fertility

Anti-erection appliances of
the 19th-century betray the
obsessive concern of many of
those societies with
masturbation and
"spermatorrhea." The four-
pointed ring (below) was fitted
round the penis, and the
"erection detector" (bottom)
rang a bell in an adjoining
room if an erection occurred.

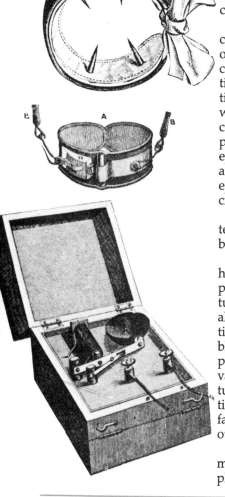

Sexual activity, particularly when it is believed to be excessive, has been said to cause a number of disorders, including elephantiasis, blindness, swollen gums, bad breath, weak legs, whitening of the hair and baldness (particularly if one picks an old partner). All coital positions except the missionary or other standard positions are thought to be harmful. This is quite a common notion. Rabbinical commentators, for example, have held that coitus performed while standing leads to convulsions and prevents impregnation; while sitting, to delirium; on the bare floor, to sickly children; and in other unacceptable positions, to diarrhoea.

On the other hand, sexual intercourse is sometimes credited with various beneficial effects, and has been seen as good therapy for certain types of epileptics, depressives and various other mental patients. It is said to restore skin texture. One unfortunate but widely held view is that intercourse with a virgin is a cure for syphilis.

Some people have associated female orgasms with conception; they are in fact irrelevant. Following the same train of thought, it has been said that sad or weeping women cannot conceive, nor women with too much passion. Prostitutes are generally believed to be infertile because of multiple partners. There is, however, some evidence that women who are raped seldom conceive from the rape incident — though the reason is not clearly understood. One possibility is that the rapists may not actually have ejaculated: a high number of them are believed to suffer from a condition known as ejaculatory incompetence (or retarded ejaculation). Another is that the chemical intolerance created by fear in the woman has a contraceptive effect.

Fellation is believed erroneously to cause rotting of the teeth (of the fellator). Swallowing the ejaculated semen has been said to cause a woman to grow a moustache.

The most extraordinarily elaborate notions about the harmful effects of masturbation have been perpetuated, in part, as a pseudoscientific legacy from the nineteenth century. The practice of male masturbation was associated with all of the following: insanity, infantile paralysis, rheumatism, acne, epileptic fits, bed-wetting, round shoulders, blindness, melancholy, impotence, hair growing on the palms of the hands, idiocy, hypochondriasis, tuberculosis, various skin diseases, asthma and suicide. Female masturbation was said to cause rickets, hysteria, hermaphroditism, painful menstruation, jaundice, stomach cramps, falling of the womb, painful childbirth and sterility (among other calamities).

Masturbation is now known to cause none of these maladies and to be totally harmless from a psychological and physiological point of view.

Three ✑ HISTORY OF THE STUDY OF SEX

Sexual repression and prudery have both hampered and stimulated the development of sexology. The scientific study of sex may have begun as a reaction to Victorian hypocrisy.

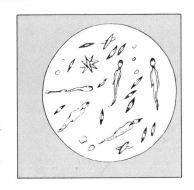

Human sperm as drawn in 1703 by Leeuwenhoek, the first man to observe and describe spermatozoa.

The history of the study of sex is characterized by two major ironies: first, scientific sexology began in the Victorian era, when the mere mention of sex was strictly tabu; second, professional anthropologists for the most part have been too embarrassed to add much to such a study.

Prior to the Victorian era there were very few sexologists. Paul Gebhard has described the centuries following Aristotle's groundbreaking work as a period of "unrelieved ignorance and silence."

Perhaps the peculiar prudishness and sexual repression associated with the Victorian period helped escalate serious thinking on the subject: the discrepancy between the ideal and the real was too great to go unnoticed. But there was also the emergence of empirical science, the growth of medicine and psychology, a weakening of belief in traditional religions and moral codes in general.

Sexologists of this period were persecuted in a number of ways. Their professional status was nearly always in jeopardy and personal attacks centering on speculations about their own sexual problems were common. Books and articles of even the highest scientific respectability were often banned if published, and actually getting published was a serious problem. Havelock Ellis's work is a case in point. Edward M. Brecher has characterized Ellis's erudition as breathtaking, but Ellis's books were banned in his native England and had to be published in Germany. On the other hand, Richard von Krafft-Ebing was accepted in spite of the highly detailed accounts of sexual behavior and fantasy he presented. But then, as Brecher has said, Krafft-Ebing was more respectable simply because he characterized sex "as a loathsome disease"; he deplored pathology and perversion (and wrote the juicier portions of his books in Latin).

I shall discuss aspects of the second irony in more detail later. The only thing I want to stress at this point is that both before and after the Victorian period, very few people have studied sex at all and many saw fit to condemn any such study, whatever shape it might take.

The ancient Greeks are a case in point. They speculated about certain aspects of sexuality and used religious myths to explain the origins of certain sexual practices. For example, there were at least two myths accounting for the origin of pederasty, which they considered an essentially Greek institution. According to one, Orpheus turned to the love of boys because of his grief over the loss of his wife,

Dionysiac phallic ritual. The ancient Greeks included obvious sexual themes in their religion, but did not produce any extensive study of sex.

Monsters from the Nuremburg Chronicle illustrate the Middle Ages' unrealistic expectations about human variability, including sexual variability.

Eurydice. Another explains pederasty as the invention of Thamyris, the son of Philammon and the nymph Argiope, who was captivated by the beautiful youth Hyacinthus.

But there are no down-to-earth accounts of Greek sexual behavior or studies of sexual practices comparing Greek with Persian behavior, or even one Greek group with another. Herodotus, the fifth-century Greek historian often called the father of history (and geography and anthropology), is a partial exception. Furthermore, he suggested a theory of sexual behavior that is perhaps the first anthropological theory of any kind recorded in human history. He set up the hypothesis that peoples living in warmer climates tend to be sexually more active and less restrained than peoples living in colder areas. In 1980, G. P. Murdock tested this hypothesis with a sample of 126 societies and found, amusingly enough, that it was confirmed—this after 2,400 years! (Actually, what Murdock confirms is that the rules for behavior differ according to climatic zones, rather than actual behavior, which is not the same thing.)

Until the Renaissance most travelers' accounts included fictitious stories of monsters with ears so big they could be used as umbrellas, or people with misplaced eyes or genitals. Traditions of this kind existed even in Columbus's day, so that his writings may sometimes be unreliable.

A general exception to this is Marco Polo's account of his travels in the early fourteenth century where he occasionally writes about sexual customs. For example, he talks of virgin deflowering in Tibet; sex hospitality among the Kaindu (perhaps the Ningyuen in modern Sichuan) and the Kamul or Hami (who lived north of the Gobi desert); the couvade in the province of Zardandan (in Yunnan); and various sexual superstitions, such as the belief found in some parts of Cathay (modern northern China) that a stain made by the blood of a virgin cannot be removed from cloth by any amount of washing.

This is in the western tradition, if one may call it that, of ethnographic sexology. In India, a much more sophisticated and informative tradition developed, which culminated in the *Kaama suutra* (*The precepts of pleasure*) by Vaatsyaayana. This dates from about AD 200–400, but probably represents a continuation of much earlier traditions.

A number of other similar manuals were derived from or inspired by the *Kaama suutra* and continued its format. These include the *Koka shastra* by Koka Pandita, which possibly dates from the twelfth century, and the *Anangga rangga* (*Theater of the love god*) by Kalyaanamalla from the fifteenth century. The important thing is that these books were respectable in Indian society and the *Kaama suutra* in particular was considered a revelation of the gods.

This tradition moved from India to the Islamic world,

where it produced a number of treatises, the most famous of which is known in English as *The perfumed garden*, written by an Arab, Nafzaawii, possibly in the sixteenth century. One of the interesting ethnographic aspects of this work is the recognition of 25 coital positions as peculiarly Indian (11 others described are within the Arab tradition).

There was really nothing approaching such sophistication in the West until the translation and publication of the *Kaama suutra* and *The perfumed garden* in the 1880s. The closest thing to a sex manual of coital positions about which we have reasonably accurate information is a series of paintings by Giulio Romano from the sixteenth century. These paintings represent 16 coital positions. In 1524, Romano had engravings made of the entire series and tried to distribute them in Rome. Pope Clement VII found out and was outraged that an artist who had been employed by the Church should have been involved in such a scandal. The engraver was actually arrested, Romano threatened with arrest and the pictures confiscated. In 1559, the *Index of prohibited books* was established, and whatever sexology or pornography existed was driven underground.

Even sex in plants was a suspect topic. Some 100 years later, in 1676, Sir Thomas Millington first proposed that plants had sex. When Carl Linnaeus published an essay on it in 1759, there was a scandal and some clergymen wanted his books to be banned.

An astonishing source of information about the sexual repertoire of the Middle Ages comes, however, not from sex manuals but from the penitentials, the handbooks that stipulated how much penance should be meted out for particular sins. In a sense, they represent the *Kaama suutra* in

The Kaama suutra (The precepts of pleasure) *was regarded in India as respectable and, indeed, divinely revealed.*

The erotic studies of Giulio Romano *(1525–1535) are the closest western parallels to the Kaama suutra until comparatively recent times.*

Aristotle (384–322 BC),
considered by some the father of
western sexology.

Leonardo da Vinci's
drawing of sexual intercourse.
The shape of the man's scrotum
suggests a standing position.

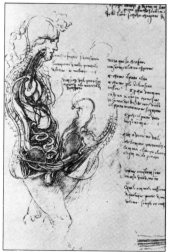

reverse, or *The perfumed garden* for sexual negativists.

The ancient Greeks were more interested in theories about the mechanism of reproduction and the origin of sex as a phenomenon than in sexological ethnography. Some of their ideas on these matters were current until recently. The most influential thinker was undoubtedly Aristotle, whose views were adapted hundreds of years later by Avicenna and St Thomas Aquinas. Aristotle has been considered the father of western sexology. Unfortunately, in spite of his concern with fundamental problems, he proposed some erroneous answers that have become entrenched in western thought. For example, in *Generation of animals* he proposes that the contribution of a woman to the development of an embryo is merely the substance needed for its growth, and he identifies it with menstrual blood. This was, however, only one view held by the Greeks. A theory referred to as the doctrine of the two seeds was held by Hippocrates as well as by a later (second-century) writer, Galen. This doctrine proposes that a woman contributes to the formation of the embryo through her vaginal secretions, thought to be the female equivalent of semen. Aristotle's view seems to have prevailed because it coincided with biblical views and supported the outlook of a patriarchal society.

A number of contributions to the knowledge of sexual physiology were made over the centuries, and even Leonardo da Vinci was concerned with such questions, as his anatomical drawings show. Important names in the study of sexual anatomy include Andreas Vesalius, a sixteenth-century Belgian, and a contemporary of his, Gabriel Fallopius, who is famous for his description of the fallopian tubes and the clitoris.

In spite of this increase in knowledge, radical changes in thinking about sexuality only became possible with the invention of the microscope in the seventeenth century. With its aid, Antonie van Leeuwenhoek discovered spermatozoa in the semen of insects, dogs and man in 1677. The mammalian egg was discovered in 1827 and the human egg in 1829 by Karl Ernst von Baer. In 1875, Oscar Hertwig became the first scientist to observe the very moment of fertilization, in sea urchins.

The laws of genetics were discovered in the 1860s by an Austrian monk, Abbé Gregor Mendel. Curiously, his findings remained unknown to, or ignored by, the scientific community until after 1900, when they were independently rediscovered by three other researchers: de Vries from the Netherlands, Correns from Germany and Tschermak from Austria. Even more recent investigations into hormonal secretions and chromosome patterns have led researchers to a study of maleness and femaleness more profound than could have been imagined in the previous centuries. The development of surgical techniques made transsexual operations reasonably successful. Although some sort of sex reassignment may have been attempted in the nineteenth century, the most famous instance gained international notoriety in 1952: an American ex-soldier, George Jorgensen, became Christine Jorgensen after treatment in Denmark. Since that time hundreds of sex-change operations have been performed and attempts at producing functioning genitalia have had practical as well as theoretical results.

Sexology as a discipline also developed out of a number of social reform movements in the nineteenth century, including attempts to repeal or change sex laws in the western world, particularly with regard to birth control and homosexuality. The most important pre-World War II organization involved in the study of sex developed in conjunction with the first homosexual emancipation lobby: the *Wissenschaftlich-humanitäre Komitee* (Scientific Humanitarian Committee) founded by Magnus Hirschfeld in 1897. In 1919, Hirschfeld founded the *Institut für Sexualwissenschaft* (Institute of Sexual Science, or Institute of Sexology) in Berlin. Although it had a close association with the Committee — they were both housed together — the Institute concentrated on the whole range of sexual behavior and offered counseling for all sorts of sexual problems.

In the field of sexology, the Institute made important contributions, not the least of which was the model of what such an institute could be like. It accumulated impressive archives of ethnographic and biological material and amassed an enormous library open to scholars from all over the world. It also collected the sex histories of more than 10,000 people who made use of its facilities. By 1923, the importance of the Institute was officially recognized by the Prussian government and was renamed the *Magnus Hirschfeld Stiftung* (Foundation). Hirschfeld himself was an indefatigable worker and wrote several enormous volumes on sex, which remain classics in the field.

The Committee, on the other hand, was not only involved in lobbying for the reform of antihomosexual legislation, notably Statute 175 of the German criminal code, it also attempted to gather reliable information about the incidence of homosexuality and bisexuality in Germany.

In 1904, questionnaires were sent to 5,721 Berlin metal workers. Unlike a previous attempt with students the year before, there were no lawsuits this time and about 49 percent of the total sample answered. On the basis of these replies, Hirschfeld concluded that 94.3 percent of the males were exclusively heterosexual, 2.3 percent were homosexual and the rest bisexual. Although the percentages for non-heterosexuals seem small, they suggested that more than 1,000,000 Germans were homosexual—a finding that was

Magnus Hirschfeld
(1868–1935), a tireless scholar and advocate of sex law reforms, founded the Institut für Sexualwissenschaft *in Berlin in 1919, the most important scientific center for the study of sex before the* Kinsey Institute.

Sexology in Germany grew out of attempts to reform the law and was dominated by the work of Magnus Hirschfeld. These developments ended with the coming to power of the Nazis.

astonishing at the time and politically of some importance.

In 1921, Hirschfeld convened the first International Congress for Sexual Reform, held in Berlin. Out of this developed the World League for Sexual Reform, which at one point had a membership of 130,000 (counting membership in organizations affiliated with the League). Other conferences of the League were held in Copenhagen (1928), London (1929), Vienna (1930) and Brno in Czechoslovakia (1932). Some very eminent sexologists were members of the League, including Havelock Ellis and Wilhelm Reich. The disbanding of the League was in large part the outcome of the destruction of the Institute by the Nazis in 1933. Its incomparable library of more than 10,000 volumes was publicly burned, its anthropological and biological material destroyed and at least some of its workers sent to concentration camps. The justification for this destruction by the Hitler regime was that the Institute was *undeutsch*.

In the United States, which was eventually to become the major center of sex research, the attempts to establish a comparable institute met with serious resistance. In 1921, the distinguished biologist–psychologist Robert Yerkes tried to establish a Committee for Research in Problems of Sex within the National Research Council. Although this proposal was eventually accepted by the Division of Medical Sciences (after having been refused by the Division of Anthropology and Psychology!), most of the research findings of projects sponsored or approved by the Committee were never published owing to a lack of funds. If they did appear, they did so without sponsors. A precedent for the scientific study of sex within the United States had been set, however, and was to culminate in the official establishment of the Institute for Sex Research at the University of Indiana in Bloomington in April 1947 (in November 1981 it was renamed the Alfred C. Kinsey Institute). In fact, Kinsey and his co-workers had been doing research on sex since 1938.

The findings of the Kinsey Reports and of other research projects carried out by the Institute are referred to constantly throughout this book, but two of the most important conclusions, from an anthropological point of view, were that sexual morality and the sex laws of society do not necessarily correspond with how people behave, and that the behavior of individuals varies enormously within a society.

In spite of the flood of criticism that nearly overwhelmed the first two volumes published by the Institute, *Sexual behavior in the human male* (1948) and *Sexual behavior in the human female* (1953), they remain the standard references on the subject. Kinsey considered a sample of 100,000 would be adequate, but when he died only 18,000 interviews had been completed. The major criticisms launched against Kinsey concerned sampling and statistics. However, his findings

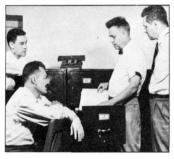

Alfred Kinsey (1894–1956) here shown with members of his team (from left: Martin, Gebhard, Kinsey, Pomeroy). Kinsey's work, although severely criticized by many of his contemporaries, is undoubtedly the most important ever done on human sexual behavior.

tend to be confirmed by more recent surveys. One reason for this is Kinsey's attempt to avoid the exclusive use of volunteers, who might present some sort of bias, and to obtain 100 percent group interviews—that is, interviews with all the people in a certain group, for example a law school, fraternity, rooming house or Sunday school.

In reviewing the literature, Kinsey deplored the lack of reliable reporting by anthropologists. There still remains virtually nothing even remotely approaching a Kinsey Report for any non-western society. Anthropologists, however, tend to be quite free with their criticism of the work of the Kinsey team.

Margaret Mead, for example, was extremely critical of the second volume, and described the first as "puritanical." But whatever that might mean, it is nothing compared to what Pomeroy calls her "shocking" proclamation that the sale of *Sexual behavior in the human female* should be restricted because "the sudden removal of a previously guaranteed reticence has left many young people singularly defenseless in just those areas where their desire to conform was protected by a lack of knowledge of the extent of nonconformity." She was joined in this view by a virtually international group of Christian clergymen of various denominations, as well as a few rabbis. The critics did not dispute the factualness of the report, but for the most part attacked its moral message.

The attack was so virulent that the Rockefeller Foundation under Dean Rusk withdrew its financial support from the Institute. The United States Customs began seizing material addressed to the Institute, and a member of the United States House of Representatives urged that Kinsey's books should be barred from the mails.

Fortunately, in spite of all this opposition, the National Institute of Mental Health took up the funding of sex research on an unprecedented scale and the Institute itself was maintained for many years. In 1978, the NIMH funding for the Institute's important information services was dropped—ostensibly the money was to be used to support new ventures rather than those that were well established. As a result, the Institute has been forced to curtail many services.

During the whole history of sexology, information has been acquired by questioning rather than by observation. One exception was the nineteenth-century traveler Sir Richard Burton, who probably based his reports of sexual practices on first-hand experience—including his accounts of Near Eastern boy brothels (the vividness of his descriptions so horrified his widow that she burned all his unpublished manuscripts).

In 1966, however, Dr William H. Masters and Mrs Virginia E. Johnson published an epoch-making book, *Human sexual*

Dr William E. Masters (1915–   ) and Mrs Virginia Johnson (1925–   ), sex therapists whose groundbreaking work on sexual dysfunction has led to a more profound understanding of sexual function as well.

Havelock Ellis (1859–1939), a scholar of vast erudition who tried to put sexology in a firm cross-cultural perspective. His own interest in the study of sex he quite consciously explained in terms of personal problems arising from his own highly repressive background.

response, which was based on direct laboratory observation of sexual activity performed by 694 persons (382 women and 312 men) between the ages of 18 and 89. This meant observation of more than 10,000 male and female orgasms.

The book was the result of work done over a 12-year period, largely at the Reproductive Biology Research Foundation in St Louis, Missouri. The goal of the research was primarily therapeutic: to find the simplest cures for impotence, frigidity and other sexual dysfunctions that apparently plague an enormous number of men and women in the western world. But in carrying out the research, basic information about sexual response in general was collected. For example, Masters and Johnson confirmed Kinsey's earlier assertion that the existence of a clitoral as opposed to a vaginal orgasm is a myth. This distinction — which, as we have seen, may go back to Aristotle—was proposed by Freud in 1913 in his *Die Disposition zur Zwangsneurose* (Collected Works, vol. 8). The distinction has been retained as orthodox psychoanalytic theory.

Reaction to Masters and Johnson's work was mixed. Some found it morally deplorable—in part because of the use of "marital surrogates" (prostitutes) at various stages of the research. Others hailed it as a giant step toward the solution of serious marital problems. Anthropologists have tended or pretended to be uninvolved. Mariam Slater recalls that the response of her anthropologist colleagues to Masters and Johnson at an annual meeting of the American Anthropological Association, before the publication of their book in 1966, seemed to be for the most part either embarrassment or (feigned?) indifference. And at a showing of some of their extraordinary slides and films, only five women anthropologists dared to appear and the men made adolescent jokes. This unfortunate reception of their work apparently so offended Masters and Johnson that they decided never again to return to anthropological conventions — a decision, if true, one hopes will be abandoned.

There are, of course, problems with their study that they themselves concede. All the people they observed were American, none was Oriental, most were Caucasoid. Clearly what anthropologists could do is to try to improve the sample by studying nonwhite, non-western subjects. So far this has not even been considered.

Masters and Johnson have been attacked in a similar vein but in a different key by the prominent women's liberationist Germaine Greer. She describes their research as producing "dull sex for dull people" (*The female eunuch*).

A specifically anthropological approach to sexology has been uneven in the making. On the whole, it appears that most professional anthropologists have not concerned themselves with the topic, and the closest they have come has been in chapters on marriage customs.

The nineteenth century saw the development of encyclopaedic inventories of sexual behavior, unfortunately at times uncritical and sometimes even approaching a Ripleyesque "believe-it-or-not" point of view. One of the earliest of these was by Friedrich Carl Forberg, who ransacked Greek and Latin literature and art for every scrap of erotica. His main publication appeared in 1824: *Manual of classical erotology (De figuris Veneris)*. On the basis of his research, he concluded that the Ancients knew of at least 90 erotic postures (48 referred to heterosexual coitus; the others included coitus with animals, group sex activities and various noncoital acts). A comparable study for all periods of the western world was made less than 100 years later by Edward Fuchs.

For cultures outside the West, a number of sexual compendia were made early in the twentieth century by Eduard Westermarck, E. Crawley and some others. The most important early work in cross-cultural studies was that of Havelock Ellis, who admitted that at the age of 16 he resolved that the main business of his life was to spare the youth of future generations the trouble and perplexity which ignorance of the true facts of sex had caused him.

The essential theme of Ellis's work is that people differ sexually and that diverse cultures at various times have capitalized on these differences. Sex is clearly a physiological imperative, but society can dominate its expression in incredibly powerful ways.

At the same time that Ellis was collecting data to document diversity, Freud (another Victorian who defied convention to study sexuality, but on different terms) tried to set up a universal model of the steps of sexual maturation. Freud believed that culture could have only a superficial effect on what was basically a matter of biology. Relatively few anthropologists have taken an orthodox Freudian view. Since Freud was a theoretician and therapist rather than a sex researcher, he will not be specially considered in this historical sketch.

Ellis's work remains unparalleled except for a cross-cultural study by Clellan S. Ford and Frank A. Beach: *Patterns of sexual behavior* (1951). This study had the benefit of the Human Relations Area Files, a compilation of anthropological data for nearly 200 societies. In this book I have tried to update their account by going through the most recent, expanded form of the Files.

Unfortunately, the Files are only as good as the information provided by field workers, government officials, missionaries and travelers. More information has been provided by officials, travelers such as Sir Richard Burton and even missionaries such as Henri Junod, than by

Margaret Mead *(1901–1978). Although Mead is internationally linked with the study of sex in non-western and western cultures alike, she really worked with problems of sex roles rather than sex. She was highly critical of Kinsey's work and was perhaps his severest critic among anthropologists.*

professional anthropologists. The most detailed sex information has been acquired about Oceania and Africa, and most of the field workers were either trained or stimulated by Bronislaw Malinowski (1884–1942). His best known work has the racy title *The sexual life of savages* (which the book does not live up to although he provides a good deal more information on copulating positions and practices than many of his colleagues). Kinsey regarded Malinowski as a prude and thought that he was afraid of sexuality—which seems to be an accurate judgment. But Malinowski deserves praise for making the study of sex respectable in anthropology.

The other major anthropological figure associated with the study of sex is Margaret Mead. Actually, she provides relatively little information about sex itself and is more concerned with such matters as sex temperament and sex roles.

The work of anthropologists with regard to sex has been a mixed bag. Malinowski made sex research respectable for anthropologists but was apparently too embarrassed to carry it off successfully. Margaret Mead became famous for studying sex but actually didn't.

A common view of her work by professional anthropologists is that she seems to have found in a society what she herself wanted—or needed. As we have already seen, she was opposed to much of Kinsey's work and in particular was against the use of statistics in studying primitive societies. In a sense, she felt the aim of anthropology was to get at the ideal pattern of a culture, such as the natives themselves perceive it. She believed that the natives would strive towards accommodating that ideal, which could be thought of as the grammar of that culture: cultural slips of the tongue—realized in deviant behavior—were of less interest to her.

Unfortunately here we have the dilemma that Kinsey confronted: the ideal versus the real. The anthropologist must ultimately know about both. But he sometimes fools himself into thinking that the ideal will correspond in some direct way with the real.

A striking case is found in the studies of the Highlands of New Guinea, where the ideal is often said to be that menstruating women are contaminating and dangerous and that men will do all they can to avoid contact with them, much less have intercourse with them. The recent field work of Gillian and David Gillison demonstrates that the reality is much more complicated. In fact, the huts to which menstruating women are confined are sometimes sought out by men as places of assignation.

In more recent years, a number of anthropologists have become increasingly interested in sex research. For example, sessions at the American Anthropological Association annual meetings have occasionally been devoted to the subject. The first such meeting of major importance took place in 1961 in Philadelphia, when human sexual behavior was the exclusive topic of a plenary session. It is to be hoped that more research will be carried out with regard to sex and that a greater refinement of field techniques will lead to truly significant studies.

Four ❧ EVOLUTION OF HUMAN SEXUALITY

Human sexuality is the result of millions of years of evolution. But although based on an ancient heritage traced through mammals, it has become a unique human phenomenon.

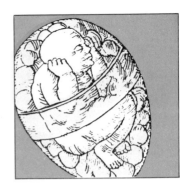

Jacob Rueff's **De conceptu et generatione hominis** *(1554) assumed production of an embryo from the father's semen and the mother's blood.*

Given the theory of evolution, the scientist can say with confidence that human sexuality and certainly human sexual anatomy are part of man's ancient biological heritage. In short, sex did not begin with man nor was it reinvented independently by him. So the speculations found in folklore and mythology have been dropped in one sense and pushed back in another to earlier nonhuman forms that were our ancestors.

For example, if we try to figure out why a woman has breasts on her chest, rather than near the groin like cows, we cannot restrict our theorizing to human females alone: having two milk glands on the chest is the pattern for chimpanzees, gorillas and monkeys — in fact all primates (as well as bats and hyenas). Why should this be, since this pattern does not hold for all mammals? With four-legged mammals there are three patterns: a dozen or so milk glands arranged in pairs running down the whole length of the trunk of the body (as in pigs, rats, dogs, cats); four or so milk glands at the hind-leg end of the trunk (as in cows and horses); two to four milk glands near the forelegs, corresponding to the human chest area (as in elephants).

There are two separate questions involved here. Why should there be different numbers of teats or nipples? And why should there be different locations for them? For the first question there is a reasonably simple and convincing explanation: the number of milk glands reflects the number of offspring normally born at one time. Pigs and dogs give birth to litters and have many milk glands; horses, elephants, and human beings give birth to very few offspring (usually only one) and have few glands.

There are less convincing explanations for the position of the nipples. The human and general primate pattern of having them on the chest has been most often explained by reference to the fact that the ancestral primates probably lived in trees and held their young by a forearm pressed against the chest while climbing on a branch. Nipples on the chest might therefore have made nursing easier.

Referring to another aspect of human sexuality: just as human breasts could be dealt with for the most part in terms of the larger problem of primate breasts, there is no need to think up ingenious explanations for the basic fact of human copulation — inserting the male penis into the female vagina. It is simply the general pattern for all mammals and has to be understood as part of man's mammalian heritage.

Fertilization in the mouth. The female African mouthbrooder takes into her mouth the eggs she has produced and, with them, the sperm ejaculated by the male.

To be sure, other ways of bringing sperm and egg together have been evolved—though never through the nose or the navel, in spite of the folkloristic fantasies frequently found. For example, in a certain kind of fish, the African mouthbrooder, the female deposits her unfertilized eggs in the water and then catches them up in her mouth. The male waits nearby. He has red spots on his anal fin that look like eggs. The female tries to take these into her mouth, but when she opens her mouth, she takes in sperm ejaculated by the male instead. Fertilization takes place in her mouth rather than in her sexual organs.

The origin of sexual reproduction

Sexual reproduction involves a transfer of genetic material from one organism to another of the same species. Distinct sexes may not even be involved in sexual reproduction at all. Consider the paramoecium, a one-celled animal that normally reproduces merely by splitting itself in half—a nonsexual form of reproduction called binary fission. It multiplies rapidly because it splits in half about every eight hours. Occasionally, however, one paramoecium joins with another and they lie side by side: the cell membranes break down in the area of joining and the paramoecia exchange genetic material. Eventually the fused pair will divide into a number of daughter cells, each of which is now distinct from the ancestral couple. This process of fusion, called conjugation, is sexual reproduction without anything that even remotely approaches a traditional male/female distinction.

Many forms of nonsexual reproduction occur (fission is simply one of them). It is generally assumed that at least some of them are older than sexual reproduction. But even in the simplest organisms we now realize that an exchange of genetic material is basic to their survival.

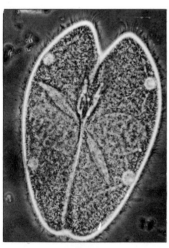

Conjugation in the paramoecium: two individuals lie side by side exchanging genetic materials and then break apart into new "daughter" individuals.

Some organisms are not known by direct observation to reproduce sexually. This is true of bacteria. And ever since it was first discovered, the amoeba, a one-celled animal, has been observed under the microscope by literally thousands of scientists for about 200 years and has never been seen to reproduce in any way other than by splitting in two. At one point the amoeba was believed to be the prototype of the ancestor of all animal life so that it more or less followed that nonsexual reproduction preceded sexual reproduction. But even though amoebas have never been observed conjugating, they probably do so because otherwise it is extremely difficult to explain why the descendants of an original amoeba sometimes contain different genetic material not found in the ancestor.

The evolutionary significance of sexual reproduction and sexuality

Why should sex have developed at all? And why should it have become the dominant mode of reproduction among all higher plant and animal forms?

The usual explanation is that it has a tremendous advantage in ensuring the survival of a species in a changing environment. Fission, on the other hand, guarantees the production of new forms that are identical to the parent form: in a sense, an original amoeba does not die but is continued in identical copies when it reproduces by fission only. But if an original form cannot survive when the environment changes, identical copies of it will fare no better. The payoff is extinction.

In sexual reproduction, differences are emphasized. The new forms are not identical with a single parent but have inherited unique combinations of traits from both. It is more likely then that at least some of the offspring produced sexually will be able to survive.

In spite of the tremendous evolutionary success of sexual reproduction some of its drawbacks are obvious (others are more obscure). Consider an obvious one: there is a relatively long period of helplessness in the life history of an animal produced by sexual reproduction; for example, the larval stage in insects and the embryo/foetus/newborn stages of mammals and particularly of human beings, where such helplessness lasts many years.

Another drawback is the time, energy and frustration brought about in seeking and securing a new mate. Perhaps human beings can appreciate this disadvantage most clearly of all living beings because of the romantic and social trappings that have been added on to their sexuality. Inability to find a mate spells reproductive failure. It may also ensure psychological chaos.

This drawback to sexual reproduction has been called by a recent school of biologists, the sociobiologists, "the cost of mating." What sociobiologists are trying to do is to calculate, like an accountant going over the books of a business, what the "costs" are of the various strategies of reproduction.

Anthropologists tend to dismiss sociobiology as inadequate to explain human behavior. But the approach raises many interesting questions. We shall soon see where this economic model of sexuality leads.

Before we do so, let us consider yet another cost of sexual reproduction which is also obvious: if the original form is a success, any departure from it may not be. The genetic reshuffling that goes on because of sexual reproduction may in fact be dangerous and even lethal: the offspring of the healthiest stud bull may be sickly or die because the bull has passed on some hidden deleterious gene. The same is true for all animals that reproduce sexually, including man. This drawback is known as the "cost of recombination."

George C. Williams has argued that sexual reproduction will have the most value and provide the most benefits if millions of offspring are produced and scattered or dis-

An amoeba splitting apart in binary fission.

One advantage of sexual reproduction over others is that it enables species to adapt to a changed environment. But even so, sexual reproduction has drawbacks.

persed into new environments. Among these many offspring there may be some that will be able to fit into the changed ecology. Sex, then, is adaptive for oysters, whose young are carried along indiscriminately by sea currents, and for elm trees, whose seeds are scattered by the winds.

But human beings are neither oysters nor elm trees. Sex may not be as much of a benefit as is usually assumed either for human beings or for the less prolific organisms in general. Possibly the recent interest in cloning could be taken to reflect an unconscious desire to return to an amoeba-like kind of existence.

There is at least one more cost that has been recognized by sociobiologists; and with it the investment model or accountant metaphor is most clearly pointed up. The technical expression for this is "the cost of meiosis." It refers to the fact that in sexual reproduction both parents pass on only half of their genes to an offspring. This may not seem to be much of a loss, but it is crucial to sociobiological thinking and the reason for its rejection by most anthropologists —at least when applied to human beings.

The point is that genes, not individuals, are played up in this model. The Darwinian notion of the survival of the fittest has been somewhat reinterpreted. It is no longer seen in terms of a specific *individual* reproducing himself but rather in terms of a *gene* perpetuating itself. In fact, sociobiologists tend to look at people (or snails, worms, lizards, ostriches, giraffes—you name it) as tools used by genes to replicate themselves. This may not be the most exalted way of viewing mankind, but there are certain advantages in it.

With this in mind, one can argue that it might even prove to be good reproductive strategy for a given individual *not* to reproduce—if by so doing his genes are more likely to be successfully passed on through his kinsmen.

Sexual reproduction makes sense for oysters and elm trees but possibly not so much for human beings. A recent way of looking at evolution suggests that our genes act like accountants trying to figure out if it pays to reproduce or if it makes more sense to make sure a relative does so instead.

One of the big virtues of this reinterpretation is that it can make sense of something that Darwin could not: why some animals have developed castes of nonreproducing individuals, such as the sterile workers among bees, ants and termites. What traditional Darwinians had to think of as dysfunctional can be shown to have a very real function in the sociobiological scheme of things. In the same way, it also makes evolutionary sense of those human beings who do not normally reproduce, whether for social or for other reasons: celibate priests, monks, nuns and exclusive homosexuals. All these individuals by not reproducing but by otherwise playing useful roles in society may be helping to ensure that their genes found in the offspring of relatives (nephews, nieces, etc.) will survive. Therefore, real evolutionary fitness cannot be equated with the successful reproduction of a single individual—as in the traditional Darwinian view—but with his success combined with that of his relatives: in other words "inclusive fitness."

There is, however, a problem here for sociobiologists since inclusive fitness strictly refers only to immediate kinsmen (brothers, nieces, etc.) and fitness would probably not include even second, let alone third, cousins. For human beings, we would probably have to invoke some wider notion of group affiliation—which sociobiologists do not want to do and which they apparently need not do with nonhuman animals.

Whatever the ultimate merits of sociobiology, it seems likely that a considerable amount of human behavior involving sex and reproduction can make sense in terms of a model developed for the animal kingdom as a whole.

Furthermore, it is true that sexuality in human beings is a mixed blessing involving some benefits but also considerable difficulties and problems. We are, however, stuck with it. We are as likely to change the nature of our sexuality as we are to develop gills to breathe underwater without diving equipment, or wings to fly without an airplane.

Internal fertilization was a development necessary to permit animals to live on land. Different techniques for internal fertilization were developed by different animals.

Animals as different as woodlice, periwinkles, octopuses, scorpions, spiders, sharks, turtles, kangaroos, dogs, lions and human beings have evolved different and in some cases totally dissimilar ways of placing sperm inside the female so that eggs can be fertilized internally.

Internal fertilization and the anatomy of sex organs

A very common form of internal fertilization requires the male to deposit his sperm directly into the female's body by putting part of himself into her genital opening. This is of course the human way, and the way associated with all mammals and many reptiles. Various parts of the body other than the penis have been used to deposit sperm inside the female. For example, lobsters, crabs and shrimps have a modified leg serving the same function. Squids and octopuses use a specialized arm; in a few species this arm snaps off in the process of fertilization.

The penis of mammals has a single channel running through the urethra, and a single opening for depositing sperm. Lizards and snakes, on the other hand, have paired organs that are like pockets (often with spines like thorns). During copulation they are pressed together like claspers but turned inside-out and used separately. When not in use, they retract into the tail. When erect they stand out to either side: which one is used depends on which side of the female the male finds himself.

Kangaroos and other marsupials have a forked penis, which has two openings to fit the double vagina of the female, which is also unique in the animal kingdom.

The development of internal fertilization had dramatic consequences for the evolution of animals: it led to life on land. Both eggs and sperm need a moist or liquid environment; without this, they would dry up and perish. Internal fertilization provides an appropriate environment which is also usually safer than water. Other aspects of internal fertilization, however, could count as drawbacks. For example, it requires finding a very specific mate. Although courtship practices exist among some spawning animals, courtship increases in importance as a necessary consequence of internal fertilization. The cost of mating mentioned earlier becomes even greater. This is obvious particularly in species where a male will try to mate with many females. In such a species only something like 25 percent of the males reproduce at all and only one percent of the males sire the great majority of offspring.

Furthermore, with internal fertilization, females cannot possibly produce very many eggs: few offspring are produced and parents (particularly the mother) make a considerable investment in their survival.

In some widely differing species internal fertilization is accompanied by what seems to be an attempt by the male to guarantee his own investment and to secure what has been called "paternity certainty." Human beings have had to improvise with various cultural innovations such as chaperones or actually sewing up the vagina (infibulation), or locking it up with a chastity belt. But some animals such as cockroaches, garter snakes, wombats and rhesus monkeys have evolved a kind of internal chastity belt. After copulation, the male deposits some sort of secretion to plug up the genital opening of the female. This "mating plug" has been described by David Barash as a male calling card, indicating that the female is already taken.

In dogs, foxes and wolves another development has taken place that has also been suggested as ensuring paternity certainty: the penis swells inside the vagina during copulation so that the male is locked to the female, sometimes for as long as half an hour. This genital locking makes sense for dogs because they are promiscuous, but not for monogamous foxes. Some other animals such as kangaroos copulate for hours at a time without genital locking. But this sort of behavior all too clearly has its dangerous side too. It is lucky that wolves get locked up this way and not sheep.

Rumors about less functional kinds of genital locking pop up every once in a while concerning human beings. Such locking is then referred to as *penis captivus*, "the captured penis." I well remember a vivid account told me several years ago of the peculiar circumstances associated with the death of Francois Félix Faure (1841-1899), president of France. Even the most sober historians assume he died in the presence of a woman not his wife. But the version I heard added that he actually died in a *maison de tolérance* while copulating and the prostitute he was with got so hysterical

A chastity belt, *the cultural equivalent of a mating plug in various animals*

that her vaginal muscles contracted round the dead man's penis. She had to suffer the further ignominy of surgical separation. But this is almost certainly mythical: many people have died in comparable circumstances without requiring nekroamputation.

The *penis captivus* theme is not limited to the western world. The Marshallese of the Pacific believe that incest between brother and sister (less commonly between parent and child) brings about a disease called *rue*, in which the woman develops muscle spasms that trap her partner's penis inside her. Among the Yao of Africa, a husband who must leave home for a while will put a knife into a sheath and hang it in his hut. If his wife commits adultery in his absence, she and her lover will be locked together until someone draws the knife from the sheath.

Although this theme is widespread, no factual basis for it exists among human beings.

The sex organs of human beings are similar to those of other mammals and of primates in particular. All primates have a penis that hangs free and is not attached to the belly, as it is in other mammals. The human penis is virtually unique among primates in lacking a small bone (the penile bone). The few other primates that lack it are the tarsiers and some New World monkeys (we have no evidence at all as to whether ancestral forms of man such as *Homo erectus* or *Australopithecus* types had it or not). In gorillas this bone is about three-quarters of an inch (2 cm) in length, and one inch (2.5 cm) in diameter. It is widely found among mammals in general, including shrews, hedgehogs, rodents, whales and bats.

There are a few other differences in the male sex organs among primates. For example, among some of the prosimians, the testes are withdrawn seasonally into the body; in all other primates, they lie permanently in the scrotum. The scrotum itself is variously colored, making it easy to differentiate between species.

The female sex organs differ in several ways. In New World monkeys, for example, the clitoris is quite large; the spider monkey in particular has such a long clitoris that it resembles a penis and (at least for the human observer) makes it difficult to tell the difference between the males and the females. Of all primates, only human beings have a real hymen. Its exact function or evolutionary advantage is unclear. Among many societies an intact hymen has significance far out of proportion to its biological usefulness.

In general, the vaginal opening in nonhuman primates is farther to the rear than in human females. The human position seems clearly to be associated with changes in the body because of walking on two legs, and this has encouraged frontal entry coitus.

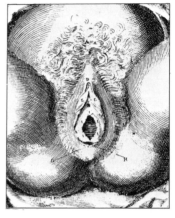

The hymen is a uniquely human feature that has taken on tremendous social significance in many Old World cultures and their overseas descendants.

The sexual anatomy of human beings and other primates is so similar that the same basic repertoire of sexual techniques is shared by them, with one notable exception: human males are rarely capable of bending over far enough to perform fellation on themselves. It has been estimated that fewer than four percent of all men are able to do so. But among male chimpanzees autofellation is reportedly commonplace and all are apparently able to perform it.

Sexual differences Biologically it is not absolutely necessary that differences (besides those in genitalia) should actually exist between males and females. In the simplest animals living in water, males and females are identical except for the sex cells. Fertilization takes place externally. Sex cells are simply ejected into the surrounding water: no need to find a particular mate, no pressure to fight off rivals or to attract a partner.

Even in higher animals, there is sometimes no noticeable difference between males and females and even the genitalia are fairly ambiguous, as among hyenas. But for the most part the development of internal fertilization (which requires attracting a mate) has led to an elaborate evolution of secondary sex characteristics. These characteristics usually involve size, body shape, or color—sometimes all three.

Darwin assumed that these characteristics had a significant value: they either aided the individuals to mate more frequently or to choose more fertile mates. This is the essence of his theory of sexual selection. For example, he explained the brighter plumage of male birds as an attraction for females. In general, it is the male in the animal kingdom that is the more prepossessing of the sexes with regards to both decoration and size. An example of this is the bull sea lion, which may weigh as much as seven times the average cow in his harem.

Among deep-sea angler fish, the male attaches itself to a female and then shrivels up, becoming little more than a sac of reproductive tissues.

Sometimes, however, the differences are dramatically reversed, as in the case of the deep-sea angler fish: the male becomes permanently attached to the female's body and shrivels up so that he is virtually reduced to a glorified sex organ — his only biological function being to produce sperm. It is a sobering thought that the hulkiest football player or the most muscle-bound weight-lifter is reproductively no better biologically than the wizened male deep-sea angler fish. Within an evolutionary framework, males can be thought of merely as devices for impregnating females.

Recent biological theorizing has tried to make the Darwinian notion of sexual selection clearer. In particular, attempts have been made to explain why females tend to be shy and coy and less striking in appearance than males. The major explanation for these tendencies is in terms of what is called "parental investment strategy." Females tend to "invest'' more in their offspring than males. For one thing, sperm are cheap. And even with regard to size of sex cell, eggs are bigger than sperm. Generally it is the female who takes care of the young (if any care is shown to them at all).

Consequently, according to the theory of parental investment strategy, females will be choosier than males when it comes to finding mates. That implies that males may have to develop all sorts of displays to catch the coy female's attention and at the same time be bigger and stronger to fight off other males. Among human beings, all things being equal, this should mean that bigger muscles and possibly bushier beards would pay off in gaining feminine favors. But being a good hunter or owning a Rolls-Royce or a yacht would seem to be an even more effective display than having the body of a Greek god—depending on what culture you live in. Culture will out.

Females as a rule, then, do not develop display tactics or surpass males in size or strength. But sometimes they do. In those species where this occurs, it is the male that takes care of the young. Among sea horses, for example, it is the male who carries the fertilized eggs until they hatch. True to the theory, it is the female sea horse that is bigger and more brightly colored and it is the male that is coy and reluctant and must be courted.

Adam and Eve, by M. Grunewald. *Differences between the sexes are less pronounced in humans than in many other species. The males tend to be somewhat larger.*

When males mate with several females and set up harems (as is true of sea lions, antelopes and hamadryas baboons), the differences between the sexes tend to increase. Most typically, the males become even larger and more aggressive —presumably because there is even greater competition for females. But this increase in the differences between the sexes may have serious consequences: sometimes the males become so different that they cannot live with the females and juveniles. The reason is that a larger individual usually has need of a different diet and requires a different kind of area to live in.

One of the most extraordinary examples of this is a close relative of man: the orangutan. An adult male orangutan normally weighs almost twice as much as an adult female and there is very little interaction between them. Even sexual encounters between males and females are infrequent and have been described as rape by some observers, perhaps because extreme sexual differences have forced them to live apart and they have to seize sexual opportunities as they present themselves.

Nearly 4,000,000 years ago, the earliest ancestors of mankind were walking upright on two legs. Doing so was to change sex in profound ways for their descendants. Other developments have also modified human sexuality. Here we shall consider some of the distinct aspects of this sexuality.

One of the more dramatic changes linked to the development of upright posture and walking on two legs is frontal entry intercourse. Human beings are almost the only higher animals who regularly use frontal entry: rear entry is practically universal among other mammals (including primates), as well as among reptiles and birds.

Primates other than man sometimes practice frontal entry, but it is exceedingly rare and never the commonly observed position. For some primates a number of positions have been noted — among orangutans, called by some the "sexual athletes of the primate world," copulation may even be performed while hanging from a tree and last an hour or more. Among gorillas, too, which according to Desmond Morris are the "least sexy primate" (he considers man to be the "most sexy"), a wide range of positions have been observed, though seldom in the wild.

Copulation positions of gorillas observed in captivity.

Virtually all of these positions are used by human beings as well.

The development of frontal entry as associated with the change in posture makes sense because of changes in the relative placement of the vagina along with other aspects of pelvic geography. A number of other distinctively human sexual traits have also been linked to upright posture. Some of these may fall into the category of the farfetched, but let us consider a few that have gained a certain popularity.

Women are the only female primate to have permanently large breasts. According to Desmond Morris in *The naked ape* (elaborating on a somewhat different theory proposed by Wolfgang Wickler), breasts are buttock substitutes.

In most primates, a female who is in heat presents herself sexually to a male by exposing her buttocks to him. In some primate species such as baboons, macaques and chimpanzees, the skin around the anus and between the anus and vagina swells and changes color. For example, among baboons the "sexual skin" is usually black, but in heat changes to pink. In other words, the area around the buttocks is a sexual key to female receptivity and presumably also acts as an attractant to the male, although sexual odors seem to play a greater role. With upright posture and frontal entry, this area no longer plays a crucial role. Human beings have no sexual skin at all (although there may be premenstrual swelling of hands, feet, belly and breasts all at the same time).

It is maintained that the shape of breasts has therefore evolved as a kind of sexual mimicry: to evoke memories of buttocks — hence their erotic appeal to men. However, breasts are not considered especially erotic in all human cultures. Therefore, the alleged motivation for their "emergence" is poor.

A more plausible explanation for the development of breasts has to do with the human female's loss of body hair, in addition to upright posture. The fat deposits around the milk glands serve as insulators of a sort and possibly also as energy reserves.

Female orgasm has also been linked to upright posture, walking on two feet, and frontal entry intercourse. It is generally believed that among all nonhuman primates female orgasms simply do not occur. But if such orgasms are distinctively human, why should they have evolved at all? One line of argument goes as follows: for primates who do not walk upright and who practice rear-entry intercourse, there is little danger that semen will drip out of the vagina after being ejaculated into it, even if the female should walk away immediately. But if a woman stands up and walks away right after intercourse, it is quite likely that the semen would simply ooze out. Loss of semen in this way might be considerable and even maladaptive. It is argued, again by Desmond Morris, that orgasm produces a sort of fatigue that ensures that the woman will probably not jump up before the sperm has traveled a sufficient distance inside her.

The argument may have a certain appeal until one realizes that frigid women—that is, women who do not get orgasms—can produce and have produced many children. Moreover, there is the probability that other female primates get orgasms without using the missionary position. It seems likely that female orgasms have another evolutionary advantage: they probably ensure that the male will ejaculate.

Erect posture has played a large part in discussions of the sexuality of women, but hardly any in those about the sexuality of men. Even Desmond Morris has refrained from doing so in spite of the fact that he has called man (in the nongeneric sense) the sexiest of the apes because he has the

Among baboons, color change in the sexual skin of the buttocks (top) indicates female sexual receptivity, often followed by rear-entry coition (above). Some researchers believe that for human beings breasts are buttock substitutes.

largest penis among all the primates. The male gorilla, which can weigh up to 200 lb (about 90 kg), has a penis perhaps two inches (5 cm) long at most. It is so small that it is hidden in the surrounding fur. Unlike its human or chimpanzee counterpart, it does not just hang normally but projects stiffly. The human penis generally measures about four inches (10 cm) and considerably longer ones occur— the maximum reliably recorded so far is 14 inches (35 cm). No one, as far as I know, has seriously pursued the possibility that the size of a human penis has anything to do with the change of the angle of insertion during intercourse because of frontal entry—or the loss of a penis bone, or the nonexistence of genital locking (though increased length might be a compensation, associated with paternity certainty).

The only theories suggesting a function for a larger (especially thicker rather than longer) penis have to do with an apparently wider vagina. I have been unable to find detailed reliable information about vaginal openings in the various primates, but it seems clear that there must be something larger or at least more accommodating about the human vagina because of the large skulls of human infants.

Recently, upright posture and walking on two rather than four feet (or two feet and two knuckles, as gorillas and chimps do) have been tied up with explaining two profound changes in human sexuality: the development of long-term sexual bonds rather than general promiscuity, which tends to be true of primates, and the development of year-long sexuality rather than the normal mammalian pattern of breeding seasons, or copulating only when the female is in oestrus.

Long-term bonds are fairly rare among mammals. Monogamy is even rarer. Among primates, only gibbons and marmosets are monogamous. For mammals in general, the list is not much longer: beavers, foxes, badgers, mongooses, hooded seals (but not fur seals), possibly also rhinos, roe deer (but not usually other deer), and hyraxes (small animals closely related to elephants, which are not monogamous).

With regard to seasonal sex, it should be realized that most animals engage in no sexual behavior at all during most of the year: about 90 percent of all mammals and animals mate seasonally. Mice are a common exception to this, and the same thing is generally true of species that live in the tropics and most domesticated animals such as dogs, cats, cows and pigs (but not sheep). Possibly human sexuality could be interpreted as a consequence of domestication, as some other human traits are: for example, loss of body hair.

Some primates have breeding seasons. Japanese macaques mate nearly always during winter months, and macaques in a monkey colony off the coast of Puerto Rico restrict mating to the period between July and January.

Male and female differences in appearance and sexual behavior have been associated with differing investment of time and energy by the sexual partners in bringing up the offspring.

Chimpanzees, on the other hand, seem to mate throughout the year. Rhesus monkeys kept indoors under constant conditions do not show any mating seasons, which must be triggered in part by diet and light differences.

It has sometimes been suggested that human mating has seasonal aspects — at least in some groups — but this is much disputed. Among mammals, the seasonality in breeding tends to be timed so as to ensure the best period for birth. Spring is in many ways an optimal period for many mammals and autumn matings are the rule, for example among deer and sheep. With animals that have a longer period of gestation, such as horses, the mating occurs before autumn. Bats mate in the fall but store the sperm for several months before fertilization; once fertilization occurs, gestation is short and birth occurs in the spring. Among human beings births occur throughout the year, though there is seasonal variation. This variation may be cultural, however, since Europe and North America have peak periods for births at different times of the year.

The theory relating upright posture and walking on two feet to significant aspects of human sexuality stresses the human trait of food sharing. The remarkable thing is that of all the primates, it is only the basically monogamous ones that regularly share food: marmosets, gibbons and human beings. Furthermore, human infants go through a very long period of helplessness. It is much longer than that of chimpanzees; and even chimp babies have to be looked after for the first four or five years of their lives. Chimps, who do not share food except in mother–child pairs, can raise only a single infant at a time.

Copulation of rhinos—*one of the few mammalian species to practice monogamy.*

Owen Lovejoy has recently proposed that if an early human mother had had to raise a child unaided by food sharing with her mate, there would have been tremendous problems in reproducing fast enough for human groups to thrive, particularly since fossil evidence suggests that early human beings died young, generally by about the age of 30. To reproduce successfully and in sufficient numbers, a female could not space her children 8 to 10 years apart, but would have to reduce that period considerably. Lovejoy thinks this was possible only because of food sharing. Food sharing in turn was possible because human beings began to walk on two feet, thus freeing their hands to carry food back to a home base. Lovejoy's model is that the mother basically stayed put with the kids, and the father "brought home the bacon." The father was willing to do so, because human sexuality somewhere along the way must have stopped being bound up with female oestrus and he could be sexually rewarded throughout the year. Even the great variability of appearance among human beings—much greater than among chimps or gorillas—plays a part here, since it probably adds to the tightness of pair bonding among mates.

This model accounts for a great many things: for example, long-term heterosexual bonding, the nuclear family, and the sexual division of labor. Lovejoy first proposed the model because of theoretical difficulties associated with a recently discovered apparent ancestor of man known as *Australopithecus afarensis*, who lived between 3,000,000 and 4,000,000 years ago in East Africa. The usual explanation, which linked upright posture and walking on two feet to enlargement in the size of the brain and increased intelligence, could not apply to this new find because its head was perfectly apelike and showed no brain increase. Consequently, there must have been some other advantages or effects. Hence, Lovejoy's own model. Unfortunately, the theory seems to ignore the fact that in all societies of the simpler hunting and gathering sorts it is the women who gather and contribute most of the food for their families. This may not demolish the theory, but it makes it less compelling.

Sex is closely tied in with dominance and submission in human beings as well as in other animals— although not necessarily in the same ways.

One last thing with regard to upright posture. This has to do with homosexual behavior. It is true that homosexual acts involving both males and females are fairly common in nonhuman animals. But most of these incidents have been reported from zoos; accounts from the wild vary.

The general view of many anthropologists, biologists and sexologists is that human homosexual response represents merely a continuation of a mammalian heritage. In at least one aspect, however, this cannot be entirely correct. In most mammals, there would seem to be a virtually automatic mounting response to an individual who "presents" himself: that is, crouches and assumes the female position to show sexual availability. In many instances the "presenting" behavior is only minimally sexual and apparently expresses submissiveness rather than passion. Similarly, mounting is an automatic response to a behavior rather than to a sex. The whole dimension of homosexual behavior as an automatic response seems to be lost among human beings perhaps because of the loss of the presentation position with the general switch to frontal entry intercourse. Of course, much sexuality has retained dimensions of submission, dominance and status.

It has been argued that rape, the most clear-cut instance of domination, is a purely human phenomenon — again because of the loss of female oestrus and the switch to frontal entry. But this is less obvious, and the facts suggest that rape occurs in other species as well. Among mallard ducks, for example, gang rapes of a female occur, often resulting in the female's death since she may have her head held under water until she drowns.

Five ✺ SEX TECHNIQUES

The sexual acts have been classified
by several societies before the growth of
modern sexology,
notably in the *Kaama suutra*.

There are exactly 529 possible positions for sexual intercourse, according to the Indian sexologist Yashodhara,
a commentator on Vaatsyaayana's *Kaama suutra*.
Vaatsyaayana inflates the number considerably by including
different arm and leg positions and sometimes other
relatively inconsequential details. Take, for example, his
description of the *dhenuka* position ("congress of a cow," as
it is translated). The main characteristic of this position is
that the woman stands on her hands and feet in imitation of
a cow and that the man penetrates her from the rear like a
bull. Vaatsyaayana adds: "In the same way can be carried
out the congress of a dog, the congress of a goat, the
congress of a deer, the forcible mounting of an ass, the
congress of a cat, the jump of a tiger, the pressing of an
elephant, the rubbing of a bear, the mounting of a horse.
And in all these cases the characteristics of these different
animals should be manifested by acting or producing
sounds like them."

Multiplication of sexual positions in this way has been
called the *Kaama suutra* fallacy. I shall not perpetrate it here.

A more basic problem is to find out what people do sexually. For the most part we can only ask because human
beings, unlike other mammals, seldom copulate in public.
This means that they have to be told what to do. In several
societies, verbal instruction is aided by sexual apprenticeship. A man may take his son to a brothel to be initiated
into the heterosexual adult world—a pattern reported for
much of Latin America. In Polynesia, teenage boys were
traditionally assigned to older married women who were
charged with their sexual training. To my knowledge, no
anthropologist has undergone such an apprenticeship—
and recorded it.

The terms used to describe sexual acts have not been completely standardized, and the traditional terms are neither
adequate nor satisfactory on all points. The term "sodomy,"
for example, has been used with so many different meanings
that it is not clear what a particular writer may be referring
to. It has referred to sex with animals or sex involving anal
penetration or even other sexual acts (often unspecified).
The term should be avoided as much as possible, and prefer-
ably altogether.

The term coitus also presents a problem. Specifically it
refers to the act of inserting a penis into a vagina (as does the
less precise term intercourse). It is also commonly used to

Sex position from the Kaama
Suutra

Temple sculpture from
Khajuraaho, India, showing
the dhenuka *(cow) position.*

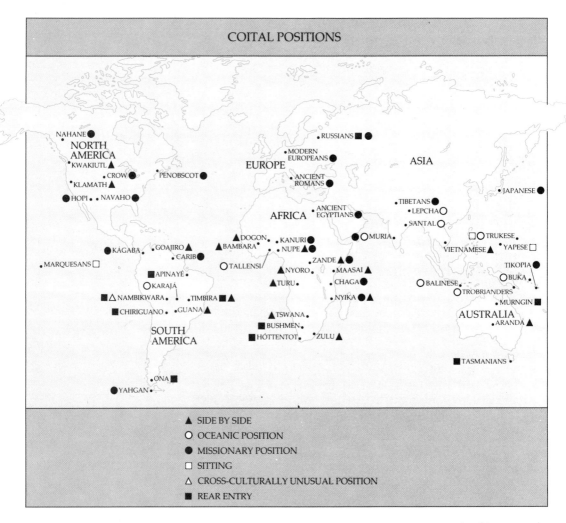

COITAL POSITIONS

▲ SIDE BY SIDE
○ OCEANIC POSITION
● MISSIONARY POSITION
□ SITTING
△ CROSS-CULTURALLY UNUSUAL POSITION
■ REAR ENTRY

Map of coital positions. describe the insertion of the penis into any bodily opening or fold, so that we find expressions such as anal coitus (placing the penis into the rectum), interfemoral coitus (placing the penis between the partner's thighs), intermammary coitus (holding the penis between a woman's breasts). Most of these activities could more accurately be classified as techniques of petting: as preliminaries to vaginal penetration, or substitutions for it. I have therefore coined another term, to *forate*, and suggested to the Kinsey Institute their adoption of it. I define it technically as follows: to insert the penis into some nonvaginal opening or other body fold. The term is derived from the Latin *forum* "open space."

In some instances, only obscene words exist for specific acts and these are hardly suitable for scientific discourse. For example, quite recently in the United States among a few sadomasochistic homosexuals (more rarely heterosexuals) the practice has developed of inserting a hand or arm — sometimes as far up as the elbow — into the rectum or vagina of a willing partner. Very seldom do people try to insert feet, though this also happens. This may be the only sexual practice invented in the twentieth century and was not noted in any of the Kinsey reports. Paul Gebhard, the

Japanese woodblock print *from about 1680 showing gantizing with a foot. The man, a young samurai, is the second figure from the right.*

present director of the Kinsey Institute, has told me that statistically its incidence in the 1940s and before was negligible. It is totally unreported from other cultures, ancient or modern. The earliest written reference to it I know of is in James Joyce's *Ulysses* (1914), in what is almost a stage direction: "Bello bares his arm and plunges it elbow deep in Bloom's vulva." From the sixteenth century comes a curious scene in Michelangelo's *The Last Judgment* in the Sistine chapel: one of the damned has begun his punishment by having a demon's hand thrust up his anus. Whether this is a sexual joke desecrating the sanctuary where popes are traditionally chosen or merely Michelangelo's imagination without any reference to secret sexual obsessions is not known. Some Japanese erotic drawings occasionally show unlikely combinations of feet (or toes or heels) and vulvas. Again, their relation to reality remains unclear. Since the 1960s, however, there seems to have been a tremendous increase in this practice. Subsequently a club called TAIL (Total Anal Involvement League) was formed; it has a current membership of about 1,500 men. When the act is discussed it is almost invariably referred to as fist-fucking. Another similar club exists called Fist-Fuckers of America, which holds annual meetings. Its initials, FFA, are the cause of some amusement since the uninitiated sometimes think they refer to the First Families of America or the Future Farmers of America. The term is unsatisfactory on several counts.

To remedy the linguistic situation, I have suggested to the Institute that they should adopt the verb *gantize*, which I define technically as follows: to insert a nonpenile extremity (such as an arm or leg or part thereof) into the anus, less commonly the vagina. The term is derived from the French *gant* "glove" and the idea is to suggest that a hand is inserted into the anus much as into a glove.

The pages that follow present a classification of coital (and some foratal) positions that are known to occur in different cultures of the world. Only three dimensions are used in this classification: general posture — lying, sitting, squatting, standing; position vis-à-vis partner — face to face, rear entry; dominance — man on top, woman on top, side by side.

Of the many combinations that even these few dimensions could create, only a few are singled out in the anthropological record as culturally recognized positions.

Both partners lying, face to face, man on top

This is the so-called "missionary position." According to Montegazza, the natives of Tuscany refer to it as the "angelic position" (*la posizione angelica*); a metaphor at the other extreme is reported from some Arabic-speaking groups who call it "the manner of serpents." The sixteenth-century Tunisian sexologist Nafzaawii lists it first in his catalog of

The missionary position as shown in Rembrandt's Ledakant, *c.1646. Note that although the couple are alone, they are at least partially dressed.*

coital positions in *The perfumed garden*. He notes that it is a particularly good position for a man with a long penis.

Although by no means found or approved of in all societies, the missionary position is nevertheless the most common in reports from other cultures. It occurs among such diverse societies outside Europe as the Japanese, Tibetans (Asia); Chaga, Kanuri (Africa); Crow, Navaho (North America); Kágaba, Yahgan (South America). Among traditional Christian groups, moralists have defined it as the only appropriate or natural position for sexual intercourse because, according to St Paul, women should be subject to their husbands; the husband must, therefore, assume the dominant position in copulation. It is not for nothing that it is called the missionary position: Christian missionaries have felt it incumbent upon them to spread its use to societies where other positions predominated.

The major advantage of the position is that it is good for ensuring impregnation, since sperm will not readily escape from the woman's vagina. The major drawback is that it may not be as satisfying to the woman as other positions.

A number of variants of this position occur, mostly affecting where the woman places her legs. She may keep her legs apart and flat or wrap them around the man's waist, or she may place her ankles on his shoulders. For the most part, anthropologists have not provided enough detailed information on these points to enable us to draw such fine distinctions. Often it is pointless to do so, since these variants may be assumed within the same copulatory act.

In the western world this has sometimes been considered an "unnatural" position and the man who prefers it has been suspected of being a latent homosexual. No convenient label exists, but one possibility is to call it the Ur position, because the earliest representation of it was found in Ur in Mesopotamia. Although this position figures prominently in ancient art, at present it is nowhere the preferred or most common one. As a secondary position it seems to be fairly commonly reported, but in one sample of nearly 200 societies, fewer than five percent are stated as practicing it. Among these are the Murngin (Australia); Crow, Hopi (North America); Marquesans, Ponapeans, Pukapukans, Trobrianders, Trukese, Wógeo (Pacific). The main advantage of this position—generally recognized by the peoples who use it—is that it gives the woman greater satisfaction than possibly any other. The main disadvantages are that it is poor for impregnation and the man's penis may keep

Man lying,
woman squatting,
face to face, woman on top

A satirical scene by Rowlandson (left) *showing intercourse with woman on top.*

An early representation (above) *of woman on top from Mesopotamia.*

slipping out of the vagina during the up-and-down movements performed by the woman.

Both partners lying, face to face, side by side The Marquesans call this position "the gecko-lizard manner." No convenient label for it exists, but since it is reported from quite a few African societies, it might well be called the African position. It is the preferred (or only recognized) position in the following African societies: Bambara, Basongye, Dogon, Maasai, Nyoro, Tswana, Turu and Zulu.

In several societies it occurs as a secondary variant, thought to be particularly suitable when the woman is pregnant. This is the case, for example, among the Zande (Africa), Crow (North America), Trobrianders (Pacific), Murngin (Australia), Lepcha (Asia), and Goajiro (South America). According to Noël Berckmann, it is the preferred position among the Vietnamese for a very practical reason: their beds are made of bamboo slats. To use the missionary position (which he calls *la position de l'amour classique*) would probably result in the skin being scraped off the man's knees. Unfortunately Berckmann's account comes across as so unscholarly that it is hard to know what to believe.

The advantages of this position include the fact that both partners usually find it restful; it is particularly pleasant when one (or both) of the partners is tired, sick or old. It can also be used during the last months of pregnancy. Its major disadvantage seems to be that some men find it difficult to achieve entry at all. According to Nafzaawii, continued use of this position leads to rheumatic pains and sciatica. No reliable data support his assertion.

Rear entry Reliable accounts of all positions in this category are so rare that further specifications as to squatting, standing, etc., turn out to be superfluous for our purposes. In Marquesan, rear entry of any kind is referred to as "horse intercourse," or "stick the bottom"; in Arabic it is known as "after the fashion of a bull." Nafzaawii lists a number of Indian positions requiring rear entry; animal names again predominate: one is "after the fashion of a ram," another is "coitus of the sheep," a third—described as the easiest of all methods—is simply "coitus from the back."

Rear-entry coitus seems to be used most commonly for brief encounters in the woods—illicit interludes that may require a quick getaway. In this situation the man usually stands behind the woman while she bends over or rests on her hands and knees. Such is reported for the Crow, Hopi (North America); Buka, Dobuans, Kwoma, Marshallese, Marquesans, Wógeo (Pacific); Lepcha (Asia). According to Berckmann, this is a common alternative to the major position among the Vietnamese and is actually performed on a bed rather than standing.

Early travelers' reports frequently included graphic accounts of rear-entry intercourse among the most technologically primitive peoples, for example the Tasmanians and the Bushmen of South Africa — suggesting that they are so primitive that they retain the basic mammalian position. It turns out that modesty, not bestiality, explains the prevalence of this form among most groups where it is the primary position: to copulate in this way (lying side by side under a covering) in the presence of others round a campfire permits the couple to entertain the fiction that no one else will know they are copulating.

Rear entry is most frequently mentioned for South American Indian groups, including the Apinayé, Chiriguano, Nambikwara, Ona and Timbira. It is also reported as extremely common among contemporary Russians, who consider it highly erotic and refer to it as *rákom* "(in the manner of) the crayfish."

In spite of the stigma of bestiality that often accompanies this position, there are advantages to it, most notably the fact that it can be performed during the last stages of pregnancy. It can also be good for impregnation. Disadvantages include the difficulty some men experience in entry as well as in keeping the penis in the vagina.

Chinese rear-entry position *known as the "Leaping Tiger."*

This is frequently known as the "Oceanic position" because it predominantly occurs in the Pacific. Nafzaawii describes a position that seems to be a variant of the Oceanic position, called "with the toes cramped."

Man squatting, woman lying, face to face, man on top

The man usually squats or kneels between the spread legs of the woman, who is lying on her back. He draws her toward him so that they embrace each other while squatting. Variants of this position are reported from the Balinese, Buka, Kusaians, Lesu, Trobrianders, Trukese (Pacific); Santal, Cencu (or Chenchu), Lepcha (Asia); Sirionó, Karajá (South America); and Tallensi (Africa).

This position achieved a certain notoriety in western intellectual circles because it figured prominently in Malinowski's much quoted description of the Trobriand islanders in *The sexual life of savages*. Although Malinowski was quite the gentleman (he was actually a Polish aristocrat as well as being a university professor), he is said to have entertained his colleagues at staid academic parties by demonstrating this position.

One benefit of the Oceanic position is that it can be carried out with a minimum of bodily contact—which encourages young people to have sex with ugly or older partners. On the other hand, as Malinowski has expressed it: ". . . where love exists, the man can bend over the woman or the woman can raise herself to meet him and contact can be as full and intimate as is desired."

The Tallensi list another possible advantage or disadvantage. They point out that the position the woman is in, vis-à-vis the man, enables her to push him over with a kick.

Man sitting, woman squatting, face to face, woman on top

This position is the preferred one in only a handful of cultures, including the Yap and Palau in the Pacific; it also occurs as a variant among the Trukese and the Marquesans. Nafzaawii discusses a similar one he identifies as Indian and calls "pounding on the spot."

Usually the man sits with his legs stretched out. Among the Pukapukans (Pacific), the man folds his legs under him and the woman faces him with her legs on his thighs.

Sitting in a chair figures prominently in Chinese erotic art but seldom occurs in other cultures. In fact the oldest known Chinese erotic painting depicts coitus in a seated position. An advantage of this position is that it is restful and the man can delay ejaculation because motions do not involve sharp pelvic thrusts. Disadvantages include the fact that it may not prove to be vigorous enough.

LIFE IS A JEST
AND ALL THINGS SHEW
I THOUGHT SO ONCE
BUT NOW I KNOW IT

Intercourse with the man sitting *(left) is recommended in Chinese Daoism.*

Standing intercourse *(above) is often associated with hurried sex as in this image from Rowlandson.*

Among most cultures of the world any kind of standing position for coitus seems to be associated—if mentioned at all—with brief and often illicit encounters. The Fijians, for example, use it exclusively for premarital or extramarital affairs. Standing positions are common in Chinese erotic paintings—perhaps because they frequently depict illicit interludes. Nafzaawii mentions several Indian positions where at least the man has to stand: "belly to belly" and "driving the peg home" (in which the woman wraps her legs around the man's waist and her arms around his neck; she steadies herself by leaning against a wall). This second position is similar to what is called *avalambitaka*, "suspended congress," in the *Kaama suutra*, but here it is the man who leans against a wall while the woman sits on his clasped hands. She throws her arms around his neck and hugs his waist with her thighs. She is the one who moves, by shifting her feet, which are touching the wall the man is leaning against.

Anthropological accounts of standing coitus seldom include such gymnastics. Among the Trukese, for example, people occasionally stand during a quick daytime encounter, with one leg of each partner supported by a tree stump. They are also said to practice a variant where the woman rests her foot on the man's shoulder. The description is not clear and leaves a great deal to the imagination.

Occasionally other coital positions are mentioned for a particular society. A truly exotic example is the "flying fox" position, in which the copulating couple hang from a beam with their legs free. There is a single reference to it in the sexological literature. It is recorded for Fiji but seems likely to be part of the folk fantasy. But even sexual fantasy is cultural in part and will be mentioned when relevant.

Other variants and idiosyncratic techniques are mentioned in the chapters dealing with specific cultures.

Few noncoital erotic techniques have been mentioned in anthropological studies. What is known can be briefly summarized here: interfemoral foration and genital apposition —that is, placing the penis between the partner's thighs or against the vagina without penetration—are reported from various cultures such as the Tuareg of the Sahara and the Pukapukans of the Pacific, but are traits mainly associated with black Africans.

Anal foration (or sodomy) is rarely mentioned as a heterosexual technique, though it does occur, for example among the Mangaians during menstrual periods. On the other hand, it seems to be the most common homosexual act among primitive peoples. In many New Guinea societies anal foration is absolutely obligatory for young men as part of the puberty rites: it is generally believed that boys will not grow properly unless they have received the semen of older

The "African position" —*side by side.*

Chinese technique using swing (right).

Homosexual scene from Turkey (below).

Fellation and cunnilingus from an Indian temple, 11th century AD (bottom).

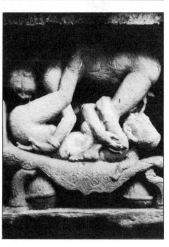

men. Various positions occur involving both face to face and rear entry, but they are seldom discussed in any of the anthropological accounts. Only a few recent western sex manuals for male homosexuals explore the possibilities.

Other kinds of foration are even less frequently discussed. An exception is again provided by the Mangaians, who practice a number of different kinds of foration including placing the penis between the woman's breasts or in an armpit. These variants occur primarily when the woman is menstruating because menstrual blood is thought to cause venereal diseases.

Oral–genital acts are reported most from high civilizations and from parts of the Pacific and Africa. From the scanty information that exists, it appears that mouth–penis contacts are more common than mouth–vulva contacts. In the United States both are more frequent with those who have been to college than with the less well educated. In particular, American male homosexuals are said to be orally, rather than anally, oriented; but fellation even among American heterosexuals is believed to have become quite common since the 1950s. The French call this preoccupation *le vice americain*. Mouth–penis contacts are sometimes distinguished as fellation (or fellatio), in which the person applying the mouth is the active partner and sucks, licks, moves up and down on, and even bites the penis; or irrumation, in which the person whose penis is being stimulated makes coital thrusts in and out of the partner's mouth, which is literally a vagina substitute. A similar distinction for mouth–vulva contacts (cunnilingus) is not made.

Soixante-neuf or sixty-nine is simply simultaneous fellation and cunnilingus. Reports of it are scattered and few, but it is depicted on ancient Peruvian pottery and in art from other erotic high cultures. Soixante-neuf figures as part of the normal erotic training program of Mangaian youth.

Information on bestiality, masturbation, deep kissing and various other sexual acts is seldom adequate. They are discussed in the chapters on specific cultures.

Six ❧ PHYSICAL TYPES

Variations attributed to race, geography,
temperament and even sex itself indicate the
complexity of human sex roles as well as the
anatomical differences.

In spite of the enormous casual interest in such matters as racial differences in sexual anatomy — particularly the length of penes and the size and location of the vaginal opening—very little serious work has been devoted to the matter. From the information available it seems that actual physical variation in sex organs in human beings is of little physiological consequence and may occur within the same group to the same extent. The only truly unique characteristic I can think of is reported from the Bushmen of southern Africa. Among them the flaccid penis often looks as though it is in semi-erection, but no known physiological consequences follow from this.

The greatest amount of information available about variation in sex organs deals with the size of the penis. The studies are unsatisfactory in many ways and are not consistent. In the findings of a Dr Robert Chartham reported in *Simon's book of world sexual records* (1975), the consistently greatest size of the erect penis is found among Englishmen with a length of 10½ inches (26·7 cm); Negroes—not otherwise defined — are attributed 7½ inches (19 cm); Frenchmen, 7¾ inches (19.7 cm). I gather that Dr Chartham is himself English. His findings are not in accord with the assertion of an early twentieth-century sexologist, writing under the pen name of Dr Jacobus, that the largest penes of any human population are found among Arabicized Sudanese Negroes, with recorded dimensions of 12 inches (30 cm). He describes such an organ as a "terrific machine—more like that of a donkey than of a man."

The most extensive data on penile size was gathered by the Kinsey team for over 6,000 American men, both white and black. It remains unpublished. Unfortunately, the data refers merely to penis size and gives no indication of other body dimensions, such as height (although it does specify whether the individual is college educated or not). It would have been interesting to find out if folkloristic fantasies correlating nose length or size of hand to penis length had any basis in fact. The subjects measured themselves, so that there may be some inaccuracy in the figures. (Length is given to the nearest quarter inch and to the nearest centimeter): The smallest penis was 1½ inches (3.8 cm), found among whites—the smallest among blacks being 2¼ inches (5.7 cm). The largest, 6½ inches (16.5 cm) was also found among whites—the largest among blacks being 5½ inches (13.97 cm). The most frequent penile size for blacks, 4½ inches (11.4 cm) was a

Female physical type: the *Indian ideal.*

Bushman *with habitual semi-erect penis.*

The Dorset giant *(probably 2nd century AD, England) suggesting great concern for penis size.*

'The penis of "Long Dong" Silver.' If the photograph is not doctored, this may document the longest human penis ever recorded.

Variation in age of maturation and duration of active sexuality

little bigger than that for whites, 4 inches (10.2 cm).

These figures do not include absolute extremes. For example, men with a flaccid penis 14 inches (35.6 cm) and possibly more in length exist among both white and black, although they would seem to be quite rare. Some porno magazines have reported the existence of a man ("Long Dong" Silver) with a 19-inch (48.3 cm) penis. To my knowledge this measurement is unconfirmed by any reputable researcher.

Variations in female genitals have also been reported but no reliable statistics exist. Measurements are hard to make. One variation is the so-called "Hóttentot apron," found among Hóttentots in southern Africa. It is not clear that this condition, which involves very long labia minora, is really natural and not induced by stretching, as in many societies throughout the world.

The older anthropological literature differentiated a number of breast shapes in human populations, such as conical versus hemispheric, and noted variations in the formation of the nipple and the areola (the colored area round the nipple), but precise measurement is hard because no natural boundaries are readily found. Very little comparative information is available.

With regard to female sexual maturation, it is clear that populations vary, but for the most part there would seem to be as much if not more individual variation as there is ethnic or racial variation. Some scholars believe that in the past 100 years the onset of menstruation has decreased by about four years. In 1860, menstruation began at about 16 to 17. In 1960, the age had gone down to 12 to 13. This pattern is found in Great Britain, the United States, Norway, Denmark, Sweden, Finland and Germany. However, statements from the ancient Romans as well as from medieval Arabs show that girls generally became mature between 12 and 14. Among Orthodox Jews, girls traditionally were married shortly after puberty, at about 13.

At the present time Cuban girls, and Chinese girls in Hong Kong, have the earliest recorded average age of onset of menstruation: a little more than 12 years. In some parts of the world, the average age is over 15—as among Greenland Eskimo and South African Bantu, not to speak of the Bundi of New Guinea, where the average age has been reported as 18.8 years. It has been suggested that we are not dealing with racial or ethnic variables; rather with dietary and sociocultural considerations that were fairly close to those of nineteenth-century England.

It is generally asserted that girls in warmer climates menstruate earlier than those in cooler climates and that climate has other effects on the menstrual cycle. Parkes mentions a study of 192 American army nurses transferred from the

United States to New Guinea, where the tropical jungle heat was said to have had the effect of shortening their average menstrual cycles from 27.7 days to 26.9. But here there are problems with the way in which the data were collected so that this particular study can hardly be thought crucial (if even significant). Ashley Montagu maintains that higher temperatures and humidities delay the onset of menstruation and in general retard development of reproductive functions. He cites data on American girls born and brought up in the Panama Canal zone who also began to menstruate later than girls in the United States. The variables are many, the studies few.

The onset of menstruation is usually taken to mean the onset of fertility, but this seems to be untrue and a case is generally made for what is called adolescent sterility. This means that there is a period after menstruation begins (perhaps as long as four years) during which conception is not possible for most girls. The reason for such a period has been attributed to the delayed secretion of a hormone produced by the pituitary gland called the luteinizing hormone.

But this does not mean that no girls can get pregnant during this period. In Great Britain in 1971, about 4,000 girls under 16 were known to become pregnant. A girl of 12 had a therapeutic abortion (her lover was 13). The youngest mother ever recorded was an eight-year-old Peruvian girl, Lina Medina, whose child was delivered by Caesarean section. This girl was unusual because she began to menstruate at five months. (Her child was raised as her sister.)

The variability of the age at which menopause occurs is even greater than that for the onset of menstruation, although 50 is generally taken as the maximum age. However, an American woman is said to have given birth at 57.

The data for the sexual maturation of boys are not as clear as for girls. There really is no event in a male's life that is truly comparable to menstruation. Information available about first ejaculations (however produced, including nocturnal emissions) suggests that there is an enormous variation even within a single population. Kinsey found a range from the age of 8 to 21, but noted that 50 percent of his sample had their first ejaculation at about 13 years and 10 months. He also found that there was no significant difference between whites and blacks in this matter. Information about other groups is simply lacking.

Even the age of the first appearance of pubic hair or onset of change of voice does not seem to vary considerably, though there is said to be a difference of almost two years in the development of pubic hair in Israeli boys of Near Eastern and European backgrounds. In the United States it has been reported that virtually no difference exists between white and black boys on this score.

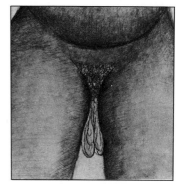

Hóttentot woman *with so-called Hóttentot apron, which may not be natural but artificially stretched.*

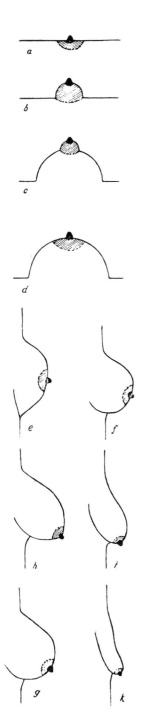

Breast types: *an early 20th-century formulation.*

Intensity of sexual interest and even the duration of sexual activity may differ from one group to another, but when it does, it seems likely to be cultural rather than biological or racial. As to the period of sexual activity, for the most part we must rely on anecdotal accounts. One of the fullest of these is given by Sula Benet for the Abkhasians, a people living in the Caucasus in the south of the Soviet Union. They are among a number of other Caucasian groups famous for their remarkable longevity. According to the official census for 1954, there were 100,000 ethnic Abkhasians living in the Soviet Union and 2,144 of them were 90 or older. Several were more than 100. Benet has indicated cultural factors that may account for this longevity and among other things points out that only 79 of the people over 90 lived in urban nontraditional areas.

The Abkhasians have no notion of "dirty old man"—or "dirty old woman," for that matter. They believe that regular sexual relations should start late in life. Abstinence in youth is held to prolong sexual potency and promote general physical and psychological well-being. Many men are said to retain sexual potency far above the age of 70, and at least one man is known to have sired a child at the age of 100: doctors obtained sperm from him when he was 119 and he still maintained his sexual interest and potency. Unfortunately, no hard and fast figures are available for these assertions of vigorous old Abkhasian men. It is interesting to compare Kinsey's findings for American men: 75 percent of his sample were potent at 70 but only 20 percent at 80. Alan S. Parkes notes that a certain American farmer almost came up to Abkhasian standards: he produced 16 children during his first marriage, and a seventeenth by a second wife in his ninety-fourth year. It is perhaps the fact of longevity rather than sexuality in old age that is so extraordinary among the Abkhasians.

One of the assertions of early travelers (including Marco Polo) was that primitive men differed from the civilized in that some groups had a rutting season. The closest thing to this that has been reliably reported for any human group involves variations in seasonal birth rates. Mammals tend to give birth in an optimal time for ensuring the survival of the offspring, and there might be tendencies of this sort among human beings as well. For example, Ethel Nurge found that in rural Germany more babies were born in that period of the year when there is less work to be done—presumably this would be of survival value because the infant would be better tended. The highest birth rate occurred in March; however, although November has virtually the same workload as March it has a significantly lower birth rate, so deterring factors must be more complicated than mere workload. A number of other factors come to mind: for example, intercourse may be most frequent during times of greatest leisure (in summer vacations in western cultures; or even during massive electrical blackouts in cities when there is literally almost nothing else to do).

Obviously, temperature and climate enter into the picture as well, since copulating at 50°C (122°F) awash in a pool of sweat, or at minus 10°C (14°F) when one is freezing to death, does not present a very enticing situation. But things are never quite that straightforward. Even fairly plausible suggestions must be checked carefully. For example, the lower conception rate in wintertime in Europe is sometimes explained partially in terms of hot, heavy underwear worn by men, which presumably reduces their fertility, in much the way that this is done for some domestic animals by enclosing the scrotum in an insulating bag. But Parkes relates the following incident that indicates that human testes may have become desensitized to heat. While he and a fellow biologist were in India, they went to a restaurant in Delhi where the cooks, wearing only loin cloths, squat on top of special cauldron-shaped ovens, *tandoors*, with the top open at floor level, half-full of redhot charcoal. This situation was clearly more drastic than heavy underwear. Parkes's companion, curious about the reproductive consequences of working in such conditions, asked one of the cooks whether he had any children. "Oh yes," was the reply, "a large family." The man had been working at the job nearly all his life: "like my father before me, and his father before him." Another problem with the underwear theory is that the conception rate is reversed in the United States.

Although stories about human rutting seasons are found, there are no reliable accounts of a biologically based sexual periodicity in human groups.

For one society where there has been extraordinarily high concentration of births in the spring, a cultural explanation rather than a climatic or biological one would seem to make at least partial sense. The group is the Yurok of California. Alfred L. Kroeber suggests that the concentration of births in the spring among them should be attributed to a preoccupation with shell money and the tabus associated with it. The curious factor is the belief that if sexual intercourse is performed in the house where the shells are kept, the shells will leave that house. A man never sleeps in such a house with his wife; rather, he sleeps in a separate "sweat-house." It is only during the summer months when the couple can sleep together outdoors in comfort that they normally copulate. And so births tend to occur in the spring. Although there are elements of the implausible in this explanation—most notably in the fact that year-long sexual receptivity goes unrequited for an extraordinarily long period of time—nevertheless it helps to explain an otherwise unlikely occurrence.

Arctic winters and high altitudes may have a significant bearing on reproduction and even sexuality.

Among the Eskimo, a comparable seasonality for copulation has received much attention, but the pattern is practically the reverse of the Yurok situation: there is a very low conception rate during the summer.

Again, positing a rutting season seems unwarranted, but some sort of climatic explanation is possible. There is some evidence that the reproductive cycle is seriously affected by the six months' daylight and six months' darkness alternation of the Arctic. Dr Cook, the ethnographer accompanying the first Peary North Greenland expedition, reported that menstruation was generally suppressed during the winter period of day-long darkness. This is not, however, confirmed by other reports: a Dane living in Greenland who married an Eskimo woman found she had no apparent change in her menstrual cycle throughout the year.

In any event, it is clear that the sexuality and reproductive abilities of human beings are affected by climate and geography, although precisely how is not clear. One of the most famous instances of such effects concerns altitude. In 1545, the city of Potosí was founded in Bolivia. It is one of the world's highest cities, its altitude being 13,045 feet (3,976 m) above sea level. No child was born to Spanish settlers until 53 years after the foundation of the city. But the native Indians had made high-altitude adaptations (comparable in some sense to their barrel-chestedness to facilitate breathing) and did not suffer from sterility.

In spite of occasional examples of this sort, for the most part evidence suggests that human sexuality varies more within a group than across groups and that the variation across groups can by and large be ascribed to cultural rather than biological differences.

Sex, physique and temperament

The ancient Hindu sexologists attempted classifications of human beings according to physical type and temperament and tried to suggest which combinations were the most desirable. For example, in the *Kaama suutra*, men are classified as to size of penis, and women as to depth of vagina; both are further classified as to degree of passion and also by the amount of time they take in coitus. No attempt seems to have been made to correlate these various components but best-partner combinations were suggested.

Ancient Hindu classifications of physique and temperament tended to see the sex organs as all determining.

In a later Hindu erotic manual, the *Anangga rangga*, a correlation between temperament and penis size and vagina depth is made. For example, a man with a large penis (described as one that in erection is 12 finger-breadths long) is called a Horse-man in both books. But in the *Anangga rangga*, both his physique and temperament are predicted from this one feature.

The classification of women is more complicated because vagina depth is the basis for one typology but this is superimposed on another dealing with total appearance and character. The genital typology talks of the Deer-woman, with a depth of six fingers; the Mare-woman, nine fingers; and the Elephant-woman, 12 fingers. The last of these is decidedly the worst, being unclean, noisy, gluttonous in the extreme, wicked and utterly shameless. The other classification sets up four types of women. Of these, the most desirable is the Lotus-woman, who is beautiful, courteous and pious. Her neck is so delicate that the saliva can be seen through it. Her vagina represents an opening lotus-bud and her vaginal secretions are "perfumed like the lily which has newly burst." The other types are the Art-woman, the Conch-woman and yet another kind of Elephant-woman —again the worst of the lot with her coarse body, choked voice, slouching walk and insatiable sexuality.

This kind of classification is interesting in itself but hardly contributes to a scientific understanding of a relationship between physique, temperament and sexuality.

The scientific classification of physique dates back to Hippocrates (c.400 BC). The most important recent work in trying to create an adequate typology is surely that of William H. Sheldon in the 1940s. He isolated three components of extremes in general body type: endomorphy (round, soft, fat); mesomorphy (square, hard, massively muscled); ectomorphy (thin, fragile, delicate).

These components show up in the genitalia as well. (Unfortunately, nearly all typologies of physique deal primarily with males; Sheldon's work is no exception and a comparable study for females is not available. Hence the bias of the following discussion.) An endomorph has a penis that is short and small and sometimes almost completely hidden within the pubic hair; it seems to be practically undeveloped. The foreskin is frequently "too long"—whatever that means. Undescended testes are common. A mesomorph is described as nearly always having genitalia that are compact and "well developed"—again, whatever that means. The scrotum is said to be relatively thick and firm. An ectomorph has genitalia that seem overdeveloped in comparison with the rest of the body. The penis is characteristically quite long. The scrotum is also typically long and permits the testicles to hang loosely. The left testicle is usually lower than the right. We must take Sheldon's word for all these assertions since the photographs he provides block out the genitals altogether.

With regard to his observation on the relative heights of the testes, it has more recently been shown that in right-handed men the right testis tends to be higher whatever the physique type. The opposite holds true for left-handed men. This has nothing to do with actual weight of the testis, since the right testis is heavier and of greater volume.

Concerning differences in the degree of sexual interest, the ectomorphs are described as being intermittently over-

Types of woman according to the classification of Hindu sexologists. Lotus-woman (top), Conch-woman (middle), Elephant-woman (bottom).

come by an overwhelming sexual drive and to experience the most intense sexual ecstasy. Although people who are endomorphic tend to need companionship most strongly, sex is not their most pressing need. Mesomorphs tend to be matter-of-fact about sex and fairly unimaginative.

Sheldon also sets up three main components of temperament: viscerotonia (love of eating, indiscriminate amiability, need of people when troubled); somatotonia (love of exercise and physical adventure and lust for power, competitive aggressiveness, need of action when troubled); cerebrotonia (inhibited social behavior, emotional restraint, need of solitude when troubled).

His correlation between physique and temperament is the crucial and most controversial aspect of Sheldon's approach. For one thing, it takes no account of cultural influence. Consider, for example, the case of Boris, who is written up in some detail as a subject showing extreme somatotonia as well as mesomorphy. For us the crucial parts of his history are the sexual aspects. He seems to have become fully mature physically at 14, and in fact was sexually experienced at that age. He is described as sexually well endowed, with large testes and "fairly massive penis of moderate length and well-developed corona." Since the age of 16 (he was 21 at the time of interviewing), he has not had a nocturnal emission. Sexual intercourse is described as a matter-of-fact business for Boris and he is not sexually stimulated by pornography of any kind or by the thought of a girl. Intercourse is an exercise lasting from 10 minutes to half an hour. Although Sheldon's description does not include this information specifically, Boris seems not concerned with foreplay or sexual experimentation.

Sheldon's classification of physique and temperament failed to consider cultural variables

The sexual picture Sheldon draws of Boris is totally consistent with the definition of somatotonia, apparently generated from Boris's basic mesomorphy. But this picture of Boris's sexuality rings a cultural bell that Sheldon could not at the time of writing (1942) be aware of. Everything about Boris's sexuality, from rarity of nocturnal emissions to nonstimulation by pornography and early coital experience is essentially what Kinsey found to be the pattern associated with noncollege-educated, working-class people (which actually was Boris's background)—Kinsey's "lower level." Culture rather than physical constitution may be the key element here.

This sort of thing is one of the main problems of Sheldon's work: lack of a cultural perspective. Very little work has been done to revise his scheme using cross-cultural testing and data. But Sheldon, in spite of this perspective, has created a typology that is flexible enough to be used in a considerable number of different situations — such as the study of sexual behavior.

How many sexes?

"... There are more than five sexes, and only the Demotic Greek distinguishes among them."

So wrote Lawrence Durrell in his haunting novel *Justine*. Recent work in genetics suggests that in at least some ways Durrell may not be far wrong.

Since the 1960s especially it has become clear that the genetic combinations are more complicated than was assumed earlier. In human beings, there are usually but not invariably 46 chromosomes (not 48 as was previously believed). These chromosomes are arranged in 23 pairs. Determination of the sex of an individual depends on the presence of chromosomes labeled X and Y. Like all mammals (but unlike birds, which reverse the pattern) the presence of two of the same chromosomes (XX) produces a female, two different chromosomes (XY) a male. A YY pattern does not occur. Whatever the physical appearance of an individual, these patterns are now taken to define the sexes so that, for example, in sports competitions, unusually robust "women" are given chromosomal tests (to prevent men from posing as women to gain an unfair advantage).

But other chromosomal patterns occur, such as X, XXX, XXY and XYY. The last pattern (known as XYY-trisomy) has gained much publicity because a high incidence of this pattern has been found among persons—all apparently males — convicted of crimes of violence or sex. In France and Australia, courts have taken XYY-trisomy as grounds for lessening punishment or even acquittal in criminal cases, but there is no positive evidence that there is a causal connection between this condition and any criminal acts at all. People with the XYY pattern have been described as having a kind of "supermaleness," being tall and aggressive.

"Superfemaleness" has sometimes been attributed to people with XXX (X-trisomy or triple-X syndrome), but these all appear to look and act like ordinary women. They experience puberty and are usually fertile.

A single chromosome (X) condition—symbolized as XO —is known as Turner's syndrome and is thought to be quite rare. An individual with such a syndrome looks like a physically immature female. Ovaries are absent or rudimentary. Unless treated with female sex hormones the person does not undergo puberty or experience a sex drive. Individuals with a single Y chromosome have not been found. Turner's syndrome is the only known condition in which a single chromosome pattern is not lethal.

The XXY pattern is known as Klinefelter's syndrome. Persons with such a syndrome appear to be men. They are tall and thin with small genitals; some develop breasts. Such men are sterile and usually sexually inactive. A number of rare variants are generally included under Klinefelter's syndrome: XXXY, XXXXY, XXYY, XXXYY.

Human sperm as seen under the microscope. The X-bearing sperm has the larger, oval-shaped head; the Y-bearing sperm has the smaller head and larger tail.

In a sense, these 10 chromosomal patterns could be defined as separate sexes. Interestingly, they seem not to account for hermaphrodites, transsexuals, transvestites or homosexuals who have in folk taxonomies sometimes been regarded as constituting separate sexes over and above males and females.

In spite of the various unusual types mentioned above, and the numerous sensational accounts to the contrary, there are no real human hermaphrodites in the sense that both male and female reproductive capacities exist in the same person at the same time or even at different times in his life history. This is also true of all primates and indeed of all mammals. It is only in lower forms that we find both types of hermaphroditism. For example, simultaneous hermaphroditism exists among earthworms. To copulate, an earthworm only needs to find another mature earthworm. They lie in close contact next to each other and simply exchange sperm through grooves in their bodies.

Real hermaphrodites—individuals containing simultaneously both male and female reproductive capacities—do not in fact exist among human beings.

A different system is followed by a large shell-less snail called the seahare. Seahares do not exchange sperm, but while one seahare mounts another, a third may mount the top one. The number of seahares involved in such copulations may be seven or eight and sometimes the one at one end swings round to mount the one at the other end, forming a true hermaphrodite daisy-chain.

Sometimes with this sort of hermaphroditism, self-fertilization takes place and no partner is needed. The tapeworm is an example of this and for it self-fertilization is almost a necessity because quite frequently only one tapeworm exists in the host animal's body. Self-fertilization is exceedingly rare in the animal kingdom (though fairly common among plants).

Some animals change their sex at different times of their life as a natural process of maturation. Such sequential hermaphroditism is found among oysters and a number of other marine animals such as the hagfish (which has many sex changes during its life) and the cleaner fish, whose sex changes are triggered by social conditions: when the one male fish in a group dies, the largest female assumes his role and actually changes sex.

Among human beings, the term hermaphrodite has been used to refer to an individual whose sexual anatomy is ambiguous and who is in a sense sexually "unfinished" rather than containing equally functioning sets of sexual organs. In different societies, the reaction to such individuals has varied considerably — from awe to disgust. Among the ancient Greeks and Romans, babies born with ambiguous sex organs were usually killed.

Human "hermaphrodites" have traditionally been differentiated as "true hermaphrodites" or "pseudo-hermaphrodites," and virtually all general sexology text-books have preserved this distinction. Traditionally, true hermaphrodites have some traces of both ovaries and testes, either separate or combined. Usually, the external appearance shows masculine sex organs but feminine breasts. Some hermaphrodites of this sort menstruate.

Pseudo-hermaphrodites have only ovaries or testes but not both, but because of hormonal factors the individual may have the appearance of the opposite sex. For example, an individual with female sex organs may have a clitoris so enlarged that it is taken to be a penis; and the folds of the labia may be fused to such an extent that they are taken to be a scrotum.

Experts such as John Money maintain that this distinction between true and pseudo-hermaphroditism is unjustified and that it is based on "the mistaken belief that only the gonads revealed the truth."

The situation is further complicated by the existence of a number of people of unambiguous gonadal, chromosomal, hormonal and anatomical sex who nevertheless feel that they are genuinely members of the opposite sex. They consider themselves women trapped in the bodies of men, or vice versa. Such people have been reported from a number of cultures, but until recently had to assume the role of trans-vestites or else be castrated. They are now called trans-sexuals, a term coined by D. O. Cauldwell in 1949, and have received a flood of publicity because of sophisticated operations that have recently been developed which change the anatomy quite successfully, though reproductive function-ing has not yet been achieved.

Jan Morris (née James Morris), a postoperative trans-sexual, has described transsexualism as "not a sexual mode or preference. It is not an act of sex at all. It is a passionate, lifelong, ineradicable conviction, and no true transsexual has ever been disabused of it."

The earliest reference to transsexuals in any sense may be in classical mythology — Venus Castina is said to be the goddess who is concerned with and sympathetic to the yearnings of feminine souls locked up in male bodies.

The Emperor Nero is said to have ordered one of his ex-slaves, a young man called Sporus, to undergo a sex-change operation. Nero had previously kicked his pregnant wife, Poppaea, to death. Filled with remorse, he sought someone who looked like her to take her place. Sporus was the closest look-alike. After his operation, the two were married with all the traditional trappings, including a bridal veil and a dowry. Sporus lived as a woman from that time on.

In the West, surgical technology to effect a reasonable facsimile of the opposite sex was reported by the end of the nineteenth century. One of the first known postoperative

The English writer James Morris who, after a successful career as a reporter of such super-masculine exploits as Hillary's scaling of Mt Everest, underwent a transsexual operation to become Jan Morris.

The Hindu god Shiva as
Ardhanaarisvara—the
male–female Lord

transsexuals started out as a woman, Sophia Hedwig, whose operation and treatment in 1882 brought her a penis of sorts, a beard and the name Herman Karl. The most famous instance is that of George Jorgensen, who in 1952 became Christine Jorgensen, as I have already mentioned. Since that time several thousand transsexual operations have been performed and greater surgical finesse had been developed. There were over 2,000 transsexuals (mostly men wanting to be changed to women) in the United States in the 1970s.

Some societies recognize intermediate "sexes." One group that has recently been written up with regard to this is found in Oman (controversy exists as to how best to describe the situation). This culture observes the custom of purdah, prohibiting women from socializing with men who are not related or married to them. The curious thing is, however, that there is a group of men known as *xaniith*, who may intermingle freely with women as though they themselves were female. Unni Wikan regards them as transsexuals, but none has gone through any transsexual operations or been castrated. Some eventually return to a masculine role and are then forbidden to mingle freely with women; most of these maintain their masculine role till death, while others drift back and forth between sex statuses. It is unknown for women to assume a comparable role.

The *xaniith* dress neither as women nor as men, but as some intermediate category. Whereas both men and women cover their heads, the *xaniith* go bare-headed. They eat with women in public but unlike them do not wear a mask. Wikan suggests the *xaniith* does not become fully assimilated to the woman's role precisely for the sociological reason that he is what no Omani woman should be: a prostitute—and for a *xaniith* to dress like a woman would be to disgrace womanhood. In a sense, the *xaniith* functions to mark off more clearly the roles of men and women by being what they should *not* be. Wikan found them fairly numerous; in a town of about 3,000 adult men, there are about 60 *xaniith*—one in every 50. Although it is regarded as shameful to be a passive homosexual, *xaniith* are tolerated. And it is said that they are the best singers.

Clearly *xaniith* constitute a range of people who may be either impotent, homosexual or transvestite from a western point of view, but who are conceptualized in a way different from any of these western categories.

In dealing with homosexuality in western cultures, it has sometimes been argued that they constitute a third sex. Not many people share this view at present. Karl Heinrich Ulrichs, a self-proclaimed homosexual and one of the first leaders of the German homosexual emancipation movement, produced a theory (between 1865 and 1875) that homosexuals indeed constituted a third sex and that to persecute them was therefore unjust, cruel and pointless. The belief that homosexuality is at least congenital (if not associated with a third sex) seems to be a dogma encouraged in the Metropolitan Community Church, a gay Christian denomination that has arisen in the United States as an off-shoot of the Gay Liberation movement.

Hindu culture is also described as recognizing a third sex. This is a hodgepodge, including hermaphrodites as well as eunuchs of various kinds. Those most like males wear false beards and try to act like other men; those most like females wear false breasts and try to act like other women; inter-mediate types assume either form. They appear to be pros-titutes who are willing to provide a variety of sexual acts.

In the light of the fact that in several societies "third sexes" are frequently prostitutes, it is interesting to note that in the western world a great many postoperative transsexuals (male to female) also are known to function, for a while at least, as prostitutes.

A Crow Indian sex-reversal shaaman from the 19th century.

Sexual superiority

"Everywhere, in every known culture, women are con-sidered, in some degree, inferior to men." This is a state-ment by an anthropologist who happens also to be a woman, Sherry Ortner. Her view is challenged by some profeminist anthropologists, but seems to be generally true in a number of ways including actual denial of authority and power to women and symbolically viewing women as polluting. For example, menstrual blood is frequently thought to cause sickness, but semen is regarded as giving health and vigor.

Another way in which women are seen as subordinate to men has to do with the fact that female sexuality is fre-quently controlled by men but not the other way round. A woman's adultery is almost always a serious offense; this is seldom true for a man. Furthermore, in all societies the traditional tasks performed by women tend to have less prestige than those performed by men.

An astonishing theory proposed by Émile Durkheim sug-gests that the increasing complexity of society has been ac-companied by a decline in women themselves: they have become weaker and their brains smaller, leading to a greater dependence on men. Although the earliest men and women were basically equal in physical and mental capacities, civilization and its need for a tight interdependent family unit created the passive, inferior woman subject to her hus-band. In a sense, Durkheim's view is the opposite of a more recent one by Ashley Montagu.

Montagu argues that women are superior to men in most ways. He carries this position even to the point of down-grading the Y chromosomes, whose presence is necessary in the production of a male. He calls the Y chromosome "really a sad affair; in fact, it isn't really a sex chromosome at all."

Hence, the male can be considered "a sort of crippled female, a creature who by virtue of the fact that he has only one X chromosome is not so well equipped biologically as the female."

Men are subject to a number of unfortunate or undesirable conditions simply because they are male. Genetically, at least two different things are at work. First, the Y chromosome carries genes for at least four undesirable conditions that never occur in women at all since they have no Y chromosomes. Fortunately, the drawbacks to these conditions are more aesthetic than anything else: barklike skin; dense hairy growth on the ears; nonpainful hard lesions of the hands and feet; and a form of webbing of the toes (fusion of the skin between the second and third toes).

The case for the natural superiority of women over men.

Second, men suffer biologically because they have only one X chromosome, which may carry harmful genes that are not blocked by the Y chromosome. Women are sometimes subject to these conditions, but the chances that they will suffer are far fewer because both their X chromosomes would have to have the same deleterious gene. Some of these sex-linked conditions are of no particular consequence, for example, a lock of white hair on the back of the head, double eyelashes, red–green colorblindness and various forms of baldness—including congenital baldness. But others can be quite serious indeed, including haemophilia, a kind of glaucoma, mitral stenosis (a heart deformity), wasting of the eye (optic atrophy), wasting of the muscles of the legs (peroneal atrophy), retinal detachment and thromboasthenia (a blood defect). Over 30 conditions of this sort are known.

Even statistics of life *in utero* make a case against male superiority. Montagu estimates that at the moment of fertilization for every 100 female embryos there are about 120 to 150 males. The reason for the considerably greater number of males at this time seems to reflect the advantages of the smaller size of the Y chromosome as compared to the X: the Y has greater mobility and speed, enabling it to arrive at the egg consistently earlier. But in spite of the enormous difference in sex ratio at fertilization, at birth the proportion is about 106 males to 100 females. Throughout life women survive better than men. In the first year of life, the death of one girl is matched by the deaths of three boys. By 21, the ratio is one to two. The life expectancy of women is always greater than that of men.

Montagu not only argues that femaleness is biologically sounder than maleness but that femininity (nurturing, sensitivity and lack of aggressiveness among other things) is normally preferable.

Such is not the cross-cultural consensus, however. The view in most societies would be more in accordance with the sentiments of the Orthodox Jewish male, who thanks God daily for not having been born a woman. What most societies emphasize as valuable is the greater size and strength of men generally, in comparison with women. This is reflected in the fact that men throughout the world more readily beat their wives than the other way round. Most important of all, throughout the world, whatever the social organization of a particular culture, overt institutionalized power is in the hands of men. Women, of course, can always tap informal sources of power, and a domineering wife can no doubt exert considerable influence over a milksop husband. Even in cultures where the organizing principles of the social structure focus on women, as among the Iroquois Indians, power is still vested in men. The Iroquois trace descent through women, men move in with their wives (rather than the other way around), and succession to political office goes through women. Nevertheless, real power is in the hands of men.

In present-day society with widespread contraception and the development of a technology that reduces the need for physical strength, hard and fast boundaries between men's and women's roles make less sense than at any other time in human history. It is no wonder, therefore, that women's liberation movements should have developed in such a society. The main thrust of the ideology of Women's Liberation — that the options and rewards open to men should be available to women — came in a society where women have long been competing for jobs in the economic marketplace traditionally monopolized by men. The social reality had changed and significant numbers of middle-class women were already going out to work *before* the rhetoric of Women's Liberation proclaimed that this should be so. In this instance we see a basic principle at work: values follow from social reality — though they may in turn loop back and influence society, at least to make it more consistent.

Descent, inheritance, succession and marital residence are organized around women in some societies, but in none are these traits combined with female dominance.

Another point to be considered here is an aspect sometimes related to notions of male dominance; the widespread custom of killing more girl babies than boy babies in societies where infanticide is customary. In a sense, female infanticide offsets the biological advantages of natural female hardiness. But from a reproductive point of view, very few males are really necessary to ensure the production of a new generation since a single male can mate with large numbers of females and sire hundreds of offspring.

In some nonhuman species only a few of all the males actually do reproduce. One estimate is that in species where males try to get several partners, perhaps only the fittest 25 percent mate at all and that the top one percent may sire many more offspring than the other 24 percent. Hence, from a reproductive point of view, male rather than female infanticide might make sense since most males are reproductively superfluous. But there are military considerations.

The fact is that males are always in control of weapons and are regularly involved in warfare. Therefore in the maintenance and defense of a society men are indispensable. According to an argument proposed by William Divale and Marvin Harris, women's very fertility may pose a threat to a group: overpopulation. The most efficient way of providing for the survival of a group at a particular stage of development may very well be to cut down on the number of women, while preserving as many men as possible. Harris has in fact called the development of preferential female infanticide "a remarkable triumph of culture over nature." The theory offered is at present hotly debated in anthropological circles.

Are women closer to nature than men, or vice versa?

The position of men and women in society has been compared by Claude Lévi-Strauss to the basic dichotomy he recognizes between nature and culture. Men as hunters, for example, provide the raw meat (nature) which women must cook (culture). In a sense, women in all cultures could be said to try to tame the rawness of men's natures. In fact, much of Ashley Montagu's argument for the superiority of women can be seen in Lévi-Straussian terms: woman—as civilizing agent, as ennobler, as tamer — is of necessity superior to man.

I think it is interesting that Lévi-Strauss's very comparison has been challenged by Sherry Ortner, following Simone de Beauvoir. She believes that the analysis should be the other way round. Women are closer to nature physically. Being tied to a menstrual cycle (natural time rather than cultural time) they are controlled by nature and more intimate with it. The English idiom "Mother Nature" is indicative of this sort of tacit conceptualization; "Father Nature," or some comparable male image, simply does not exist in any language as far as I know. Men, on the other hand, try to control nature and even bend it; they are the products of, as well as the contributors to, culture.

This analysis would help in part to explain the widespread use of male puberty rites that make boys into men — frequently by genital or other mutilations sometimes thought of as breaking ties with mother, and/or the learning of special cultural information such as secret languages or ritual secrets. In a sense, too, it points out that male dominance, though real, has to be propped up, suggesting that it is essentially quite frail.

These polar interpretations (Lévi-Strauss's and Ortner's) point to the complexity and importance of the role of the sexes over and above actual anatomical differences.

Seven & PHYSICAL ATTRACTIVENESS

*Beauty may be in the eyes of the beholder,
but the beholder is culturally conditioned to begin
with, so that variations
will always exist in ideal types.*

*A*sk a Northern [American Indian what is beauty [in . . . *A*a woman and he will answer, a broad flat face, small eyes, high cheekbones, three or four broad black lines across each cheek, a low forehead, a large, broad chin, a clumsy hook nose, a tawny hide, and breasts hanging down . . .

So wrote Hearne in 1796 after many years of encounters with American Indians still living in traditional cultures. His account was quoted by Darwin in 1871 in a detailed examination of what people look for in sexual partners. In all the years since Darwin's work, anthropological investigations into ideas of physical attractiveness have tended to stagnate on the anecdotal level provided by Hearne. The general lack of interest by anthropologists in the topic is unfortunately symptomatic of the way they deal with anything having to do with sex. Only here, prudery cannot account for failure to deal with the matter. Even collecting photographs of people considered attractive (and unattractive as well), in terms of their own standards, has seldom been attempted, though Malinowski did so as early as 1929, in his famous book about the Trobriand islanders called *The sexual life of savages*.

In anthropological studies of physical attractiveness, anything at variance with contemporary western tastes invariably gets played up. A cross-cultural survey of notions of beauty is sure to include such "oddities" as a preference for cross-eyes (Mayans), flattened heads (Kwakiútl), black gums and tongue (Maasai), black teeth (Yapese), joined eyebrows (Syrians), absence of eyebrows and eyelashes (Mongo), enormously protruding navels (Ila), pendulous breasts (Ganda), gigantic buttocks (Hóttentot), fat calves (Tiv), crippled feet (Chinese), and so on. Because of the nature of the information we have, we can do very little else. Such differences are in themselves astonishing and certainly interesting. It is possible that in every culture (there have been at least 100,000 different cultures since the time of the Neanderthals) some detail or other has been singled out as particularly entrancing in its standardized fantasies of beauty. The facts of variation are intriguing enough.

But it seems almost inconceivable that people are not born programmed to find some things more attractive than others. A healthy appearance almost certainly is one of them. The only counterexample I know of is the claim by Tessman, writing in 1913, that women among the Fang of Africa actually prefer men with leprosy for adulterous love

Paleolithic "Venus."
*Ideal type, realistic portrayal
or fertility idol?*

A Trobriand island beauty
*(top) according to local
standards. A woman not
considered attractive by local
standards (bottom). These
photos, published by
Malinowski in 1929, are the
only studies of native standards
of beauty made by any
anthropologist.*

Ghanaian canons (below) of female beauty.

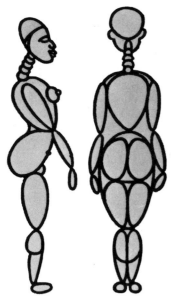

affairs. I'm afraid I can hardly take this claim seriously: there is no evidence from anywhere else in the world that lepers or others with comparable diseases like ringworm, yaws, or tertiary syphilis rate high in attractiveness. On the contrary they are almost inevitably shunned or even tabued, as among the Balinese.

The whole question of physical attractiveness is very complicated. Perhaps all societies play up some notions of attractiveness that have significance in choosing a sex partner. But since in most societies nearly everyone marries and reproduces, the evolutionary importance of these criteria for good looks (which is what Darwin was after) is not clear.

In western society, the criteria of attractiveness have often been so specific that very fine rankings based on physical beauty can be achieved — the basis on which all beauty contests rest.

In other cultures even talking about physical attractiveness may be tabu. I know of only one culture where this seems to be true: that of the Hasidic Jews.

In yet other cultures, specific detailed criteria may be lacking. I remember talking to certain northern Nigerians, several years ago, trying to find out what they thought a beautiful woman should be like. Although I did not do so systematically, the few answers I received astonished me at the time. A truly beautiful woman must walk in a sort of languorous way, they said. She must be deferential to a man (in their society, good wives would kneel when greeting their husbands in the morning). But I noticed that they were hard pressed to specify anatomical details such as being slender, having big breasts or special facial characteristics. After some prompting they were willing to say she should

Before and after pictures of a girl from Calabar, Nigeria, who has undergone a fattening process to make her more desirable as a bride.

have a fairly long neck. When I asked about facial features and virtually insisted on some sort of reply, one man said in exasperation: "Well, she certainly shouldn't have a nose like yours!" (which is a relatively nondescript Caucasoid type).

This experience brought vividly to mind one of Darwin's conclusions about physical attractiveness: people generally admire (and even try to exaggerate sometimes) the physical characteristics they are used to. In fact he saw this tendency as a major cause of social differences. One of the more striking generalizations he makes along these lines is that in populations where the men have little facial hair, whatever hair exists is disliked and often removed; whereas beards are greatly admired in hairier groups. Darwin's generalization has its problems however. Ever since Alexander the Great ordered his soldiers to shave their faces so that the enemy could not grab their beards in hand-to-hand combat, the western world, although hairy, has had its glabrous centuries.

More recently, Dale Guthrie has suggested that beards have a symbolic value and that they tend to be found in societies where social inequality is stressed. A clean-shaven chin, on the other hand, would be more appropriate in a democracy. The facts don't bear this out in any compelling way. But I'm sure beards can have very symbolic connotations. And I am equally sure that the present widespread fashion for beards in the West is in some part a male reaction to the Women's Liberation movement — if only because it defines boundaries in an otherwise unisex world.

In many instances, the anthropological reports suggest that in various cultures, the total gestalt of a person is considered, not just some isolated criteria — at least for a marriage partner. It is not only a beautiful face (whatever that might mean) that is considered in a wife, but more importantly whether the woman looks able to bear many children or is known to be a good worker.

It is almost impossible to specify any cross-culturally valid notions of physical attractiveness, though a few do exist. Donald Symons suggests that good teeth, clear eyes, and a firm gait almost certainly are universally attractive if only because they indicate health. He does not believe, however, that any particular body build could by the same token be universally desirable. In some situations, depending on diet and the possibility of food shortages, fat may indicate both health and high social status; in other situations, exactly the opposite may hold true. The individual picks up what fatness means in his particular social group and acts accordingly. In some societies, for example, fat women are prized and (as in some West African groups) women are even placed in a "fattening hut" before marriage, where they are made to gorge themselves in order to gain as much weight as possible. In other societies, fat is anathema. In the 1980s

Notions of physical attractiveness differ widely around the world, but presumably play a key role in selecting a sex partner, and therefore in reproduction. But the evolutionary importance of these criteria is still uncertain.

Some physical traits are universally considered repulsive.

in the western world, this would seem to be the case. The dictum attributed to the Duchess of Windsor that "one can neither be too rich nor too thin" summarized the economic and aesthetic philosophies of a great many people in our society. Nevertheless, there is considerable personal variation and some people are attracted only to the fat.

One generalization that can be made is that men are usually aroused more than women by physical appearance. This would seem to be true whatever sexual orientation is involved. For women the world over, male attractiveness is bound up with social status, or skills, strength, bravery, prowess and similar qualities.

But this male concern with good looks in the ideal partner does not mean that even women defined as ugly cannot find male partners in the real world. In an anthropological study of a brothel in Peru (the only large-scale study of this sort), Primov and Kieffer found that physical appearance was seldom of prime importance in determining the popularity of a particular prostitute, even though the men were paying and could be choosy. The prostitutes themselves were unanimous that the most important professional asset was the ability to get along well with the customers and to be a good and sympathetic listener.

Outside the brothel, men the world over seem willing to accept "any port in a storm" — which is how Holmberg characterized the behavior of Sirionó men, who have fairly clear-cut standards for female beauty. Such willingness to put up with less than the ideal relates to what sociobiologists see as the major male reproductive strategy found throughout the animal kingdom. Sperm are cheap. Copulation, therefore, will be attempted as long as there is some potential mate.

Clear-cut standards for female beauty exist in most cultures; but it seems likely that male reproductive strategy in human beings, as in other animals, requires copulation (and therefore reproduction) so long as there is some potential mate, attractive or not.

Although specific universals of physical attractiveness are hard to discover, it is fairly easy to list traits regarded as disgusting and sexually repulsive (they can perhaps all be related to the criterion of health mentioned before). Poor complexion and excessive acne and pimples, for example, are almost always considered negative qualities.

Bodily filth, bad breath and body odor are also almost universally mentioned as repulsive. Odors associated with the genitals are sometimes especially singled out as disgusting. For example, among the Marquesans very scrupulous attention is paid by males to cleaning beneath their foreskins. Girls are started on treatments a few weeks after birth to ensure that vaginal odors will be suppressed and that the vagina itself will be kept tight and free from superfluous vaginal secretions.

The generally adverse reaction to genital odors found cross-culturally is of considerable interest because in many mammals odors are part of sexual communication, and function as what are known as pheromones. For example, among some primates, vaginal odors indicate whether the female is sexually receptive. It is known that many chemical substances given off in sexual secretions have odors detectable to human beings; the question is, do they function like the sex attractants of moths or are they without any aphrodisiac properties whatever? The answer is not clear. But one experiment which required participants to smell tampons taken from women at different points in their ovulatory cycle found the participants unable to tell when the women were most fertile. Some commentators on western culture have decried the widespread use of deodorants because they may destroy biological attractants of various kinds. But in very few cultures do we find evidence that genital odors are natural attractants.

Individuals may be conditioned, however, to finding body odors of various kinds sexually arousing. Morris Opler reports that an Apache said that he would stick a finger into a woman's vagina and smell it as a method of combating temporary impotence. In our own society, certain people are into sniffing soiled underwear, and various homosexual publications occasionally include advertisements for filthy, smelly jockstraps. This is interesting because the odor is clearly unrelated to ovulatory cycles and suggests that other conditioning factors are at work; possibly in this instance a locker-room mystique has been eroticized.

Yet another generalization about sexual attractiveness can be made in relation to grooming. In virtually every society some form of grooming prevails and the individual who does not follow the convention is considered unattractive — all other things being equal. There are exceptions to this generalization. Prophets, for example, are often shaggy, disheveled and otherwise unkempt, but because of a personal magnetism they may exert a profound sexual attraction on their followers.

Medieval bath-house.
Cleanliness was not always considered as next to godliness.

In this connection it should be noted that the early Christians were highly suspicious of the grooming habits of the ancient Greeks and Romans. In particular, the Christians were opposed to the institution of public baths largely because they were assumed to be a hotbed of illicit sexual activity. The noted anthropologist Alfred Kroeber has traced the history of cleanliness in the western world and found that for much of the Christian period a feeling developed that being scrupulously clean was not being too good a Christian — especially for a man — and smacked of the sensuousness of paganism. The current cliché that cleanliness is next to godliness would have been rejected as dangerous nonsense.

This view persisted for about 1,000 years, through the early Middle Ages until the 1400s, when people once more began to enjoy washing and public baths were opened. There was less piety than in previous centuries, perhaps because of greater contact with foreign cultures.

In the 1500s Protestants and Catholics alike called for a return to an ascetic ideal and demanded the suppression of the baths. Kroeber suggests that "if we of today had personally met sovereigns like Elizabeth or Louis XIV, we should probably have been aware of their body odor."

In the seventeenth and eighteenth centuries, the revival of cleanliness occurred with the rise of the middle classes. Europe and America are still in this cycle in which hygiene is venerated.

A custom associated with the baths of the ancient Mediterranean and continued in the modern baths of Turkey and other areas in the Near East was the removal of body hair by special attendants. Various methods of depilation were and are used, including shaving, plucking, hair removal creams, waxing and a method still in use in the Near East involving the unlikely sounding combination of sugar and lemon juice heated until they caramelize. Women in these societies depilate their entire bodies, removing even pubic hair. Men

Among many Brazilian groups, the ideal is a completely hairless body for both sexes (except for hair on the head). In some groups even eyelashes are removed.

normally remove hair only from their armpits, though sometimes more extensive depilation is practiced. These conventions were dropped by Christians, perhaps with the abandonment of the classical bath system.

When some of the returning crusaders tried to revive female depilation, they were quite unsuccessful. Female pubic hair is almost universally regarded as erotic in the West, although, strangely enough, in western art idealized bodies, both male and female, have nearly always been glabrous. This convention probably represents petrified Graeco-Roman tastes and has as little reality now as the Greek profile found on classical statues had even among ancient Greeks (the archaeologist Schliemann was dismayed to uncover graves of Greeks whose profiles were "less than Greek"). But this too has implications: we cannot derive knowledge of reality directly from artistic conventions.

In classical statues body hair is shown only in such subhuman forms as satyrs or comical bacchantes. In idealized human forms, men are hairless except for pubic hair (always represented in the typical feminine pattern) and woman are totally hairless — as well as vulvaless. By the Renaissance, even men lose their pubic hair in art, though not in reality.

Presumably as a looping back to these artistic conventions, some men in the West are sexually aroused only by women with hairless pudenda. A famous example is John Ruskin (1819–1900), who had led such a sheltered life that he was shocked to discover his wife had pubic hair and refused to consummate his marriage.

16th-century European woodcut showing woman removing pubic hair— apparently a fashion of the time.

The custom of removing hair from various parts of the body can be found on every continent. In particular, there is a vast expanse in the Old World where both men and women remove pubic hair as well as hair from the armpits. This ranges from the Zulu in southern Africa to Muslim groups in India and Pakistan, and includes many Bantu-speaking peoples as well as the Amhara of Ethiopia. Among Jews in the area, only women are allowed to remove body hair; men are specifically forbidden to do so.

The Bantu Ila have the unusual custom that a bride must pluck out all of her husband's pubic hair the morning after the consummation of the marriage. She must start at the crack of dawn and remove all hair from her husband's chin as well. Later that morning, an old woman comes to inspect the job and fingers the naked man's genitals and chin to see that everything is smooth.

Throughout the world, if there is a custom of depilation it will almost always apply to women — though it may also apply to men. In virtually no society that has so far been reported do men, for example, remove pubic hair if the women do not. The only exceptions to this generalization

The Bath of Psyche,
by Lord Leighton (1890). Western art traditionally idealizes the hairless body.

that I know of are the contemporary Bororó of South America and the ancient Egyptians (who drew in pubic hair in paintings of women but not of men).

This tendency to depilate women more readily than men could be interpreted symbolically in at least two ways. It could be a way of making women more like children and hence not as threatening to men. Or else it could be an attempt to make women less like beasts — an interpretation that would support Lévi-Strauss's view that women are closer to "culture" than to "nature."

At present, the Anglo-American style of female depilation of the whole body except for pubic hair is spreading throughout the western world. Resistance to it has been championed by some women's liberationists but is apparently ineffectual.

Male body depilation has not caught on in the West. A study by Veneris and Roll (1970) found that in a group of American college students of both sexes from two schools in Illinois, male body hair was not considered attractive to either men or women, but it was associated with being more masculine and virile. A hairy arm was seen, for example, as "more masculine, harder, larger, more virile and stronger" than an otherwise identical hairless arm. And all these features are of more consequence than good looks in assessing male attractiveness.

The last general category to be discussed here is skin color. An occasional fantasy that white people have had is that a light-colored skin is universally more highly prized than a dark skin. The cross-cultural evidence makes it clear that such is not the case. An American Indian group, the Pima, dislike light-skinned people. Among the dark-skinned Wógeo the light coloring of Europeans — especially blondness — is regarded as almost shameful and reminiscent of albinos, who are considered unattractive. They think that the skin coloring of Europeans is more than enough justification for wearing many clothes to hide it. The Trobriand islanders also regard albinos with distaste; on the other hand, a very dark brown complexion is considered a decided disadvantage — a truly attractive skin may be compared to "white flowers, moonlight, and the morning star."

In some Polynesian groups, however, both men and women attempt to bleach their skins.

The attractiveness of a light skin coloring sometimes has obvious sociological reasons — often it is associated with social prestige for one reason or another. For example, in many of the Islamic emirates of West Africa, such as the Hausa and Nupe of northern Nigeria, men tend to marry "light"; the taste in light-skinned women must at least partially be the result of contacts with Arabs and also with the often light-colored Fulani groups who conquered many of

Fashion plate of a woman
*with parasol to prevent getting
a suntan. Today's standards
for skin color have changed
with massive employment in
factories rather than in fields.*

these emirates before the middle of the nineteenth century.

That notions of attractiveness can be rooted in other social situations is well illustrated by color preferences in the western tradition. Until recently paeans to the beauty of women played up the whiteness of skin and compared it glowingly to snow, ivory or some other appropriate white object.

Until a generation or two ago, ladies of quality in the western world carried parasols to avoid a suntan, which was identified with farm workers toiling in the fields. But the status significance of a suntan (first sanctioned by Coco Chanel in the 1920s) has been reversed: parasols are now out and a suntanned body is considered sexy. What has happened? Laborers have mostly moved out of the fields and into factories. But the rich can fly to Acapulco, Mykonos or wherever is fashionable and sport suntans throughout the year.

A greater concern for good looks in women rather than in men is a characteristic of all societies, but what constitutes good looks varies considerably.

Take, for example, general body shape. From the point of view of one of the main functions of women — the bearing of children — wide hips to permit easy delivery should be desirable. In the great majority of societies for which there is adequate information, this is true. Ford and Beach in their classic cross-cultural survey, found only a few societies that prefer slim women, notably the Dobuans (who consider fatness in either sex to be disgusting) and the Tongans (whose women actually diet to avoid getting fat bellies). But even these societies seem to go along with the dictum that women should have a broad pelvis and wide hips. The Yakut of northern Siberia are the only society mentioned by Ford and Beach who dislike such women — to which we can of course

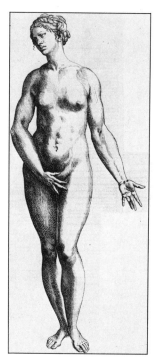

__European female ideals__ of the 16th century (above) and of the 20th — Jane Russell (right). Slender waists are a minority preference cross-culturally, seen here in a Japanese and an ancient Cretan example.

add modern western and Japanese society. It has been suggested that the modern western taste has serious biological consequences since the ideal type of woman may have problems in the delivery of her babies, and this type is being selected for reproduction.

The Mangaians are an example of a society where wide hips are seen as exceedingly desirable. Donald S. Marshall reports that Mangaian men are almost fixated on hips and genitalia. Breasts, ankles and legs are not considered especially erotic. What the Mangaian fantasizes about is a fairly plump girl with big hips who can rotate and swing in hula-like dancing as well as during copulation. Such a girl is spoken of approvingly as a "bed with a mattress."

In many societies, outright fat is considered desirable in a woman. Among the Marquesans, a truly flattering description of a girl is simply *tau tau!* (fat), and the male admirer who makes such a comment may flex the biceps of both arms to indicate the voluptuous chunkiness of the girl in question — not to indicate his own muscularity. Girls with heavy shoulders, hips, buttocks and legs are believed to have the most endurance and vitality during sex.

Among Hóttentots and related African groups, women have developed a unique accumulation of fat in the buttocks called steatopygia. One explanation offered for this peculiarity is that it is an adaptation to a desert environment, not unlike a camel's hump. In *The descent of man* Darwin cites Sir Andrew Smith as asserting that steatopygia is highly prized among these people. Smith once saw a woman who was considered a beauty and who was so immensely developed behind that when seated on level ground she could not rise, and had to push herself along until she came to a slope.

In many societies, breasts are not necessarily thought of as erotic but what constitutes beautiful breasts are clear enough. Among the Marquesans, for example, large breasts

The European fashion of the corset (far left) and of the bustle (center). A supposed cross-cultural interest in buttocks has been suggested by comparing the bustle shape with the steatopygia found among Hóttentot women (above), but the former is out of fashion and the latter not necessarily prized among Hóttentot males.

are considered an asset but are rarely mentioned along with the other idealized traits. For the most part, long pendulous breasts generally associated with old women are not considered to be very attractive, although at least two groups, the Zande and Ganda, idealize such breasts.

The American preoccupation with what has jocosely been called "pneumatic" breasts has been linked by Geoffrey Gorer in his book *The American people* with an unsuccessful attempt at finding a nourishing mother. This somewhat Freudian interpretation is mentioned here only because Whiting and Child, in their cross-cultural study of child-bearing practices (*Child training and personality*), reveal that in their entire cross-cultural sample, American society is probably the most strict and unrewarding orally toward children; so Gorer's interpretation gains a certain credence.

In some societies there are specific criteria for beauty associated with the female genitals — thus belying Freud's dictum that sex organs are not at all beautiful. Among the Mangaians, men are very much concerned with the size, shape and consistency of the *mons veneris* and of the degree of sharpness or bluntness of the clitoris. Among the Marquesans a flat *symphysis pubis* is desired. A fat vulva is highly prized among the Sirionó. A large clitoris is reportedly preferred by Easter Islanders, and elongated labia minora are of great interest to Dahomeans, Kusaians, Marquesans, Ponapeans, Thonga, Trukese and Venda. In all these groups attempts to lengthen the labia are made, usually by simply stretching them.

Among the Kgatla-Tswana long labia minora seem to have extraordinary erotic value, and are sometimes referred to as "the exciter of the bull." With the onset of puberty Kgatla girls start pulling their labia and sometimes will ask a girlfriend to help. If the labia do not get longer as quickly as desired, the girls resort to magic. They kill a bat and cut off its wings, which they then burn. The ashes are ground up and mixed with fat. Each girl makes little cuts around her labia and smears the bat-ash ointment into the cuts. This is done so that the labia will become as big as the wings of a bat.

Such a remarkable preoccupation with a physical detail is matched by the opposite side of the coin: surgical removal of the labia as a precondition for marriage.

The American mania *for large breasts has been linked by some psychologists to bottle-feeding children and their resulting oral deprivation. Photograph (above) of Jayne Mansfield.*

The attractive man (cross-culturally)

Darwin in his discussion of the development of the differences of appearance between the sexes, suggests that males who put on the most spectacular displays are preferred by females. The most brightly colored male birds have an advantage and are the most likely to be chosen as mates by relatively drab looking females, thereby reproducing themselves. Similarly with mankind, Darwin suggests (*The descent of man*) that beards were developed "as an ornament to charm or excite the opposite sex," and that in effect facial and bodily hairiness were assets. In reply to this, the physical anthropologist Ernest A. Hooton has pointed out a probably ethnocentric bias on Darwin's part here. Many of the features that Darwin singled out as part of human masculine display recall the fact that he boasted a bushy beard, tufted eyebrows "and a somewhat Neanderthaloid physiognomy." Hooton fantasized that the protohuman female (in Darwin's reconstruction of the earliest human groups), instead of waiting around while hairy-chested males fought over her, might well "sneak off into the bush with some sinuous and smooth-cheeked precursor of the modern gigolo" (*Apes, men and morons*, 1937).

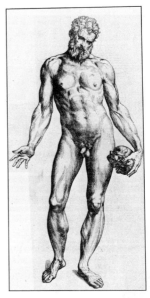

The notion of physical "display" as a major element in masculine attractiveness can be doubted, if only because it seems quite likely that nonphysical characteristics, primarily social status and wealth, or possibly even some personality trait such as valor or dependability, are ultimately more attractive to women than good looks. Among the Toda of India, for example, women reportedly find men especially attractive who are good at catching buffalo at funerals (a prestigious ritual act). A recent survey of English women's tastes revealed that they preferred men who had a slight paunch to those with a trim athletic body — presumably the aesthetic ideal. The reason why may be that a paunch suggests a certain social position, being able to afford to eat luxurious foods and not having to do manual labor. A paunch goes well with a Rolls-Royce.

According to G. Charles-Picard the ancient Oriental high cultures even held the body-beautiful goal of their Greek contemporaries to be an abomination. Dignity and wealth were preferred to strength and athletic prowess. Men, therefore, chose to cultivate a portly figure and to cover themselves in ample robes rather than follow the Greek ideals of muscular symmetry and heroic nudity. Similarly, the pre-World War II *shtetl* Jews of Eastern Europe idealized the pale, emaciated, etherealized man whose pallor was to be taken as a sign of studiousness and spiritual vigor. But babies and women were primarily considered beautiful only if round and rosy.

Ideal type of man *in the 1530s (top) and in the 1960s (above) – the French actor Alain Delon.*

One of the common ideals for masculine good looks in the contemporary western world is the combination of broad shoulders and narrow hips. Alice Brues has suggested that this aesthetic standard may reflect a holdover from an age of archery, and believes that a case can be made for assuming that a dominant tool or weapon (such as the bow) in a culture may give a selective advantage to individuals having a physique best adapted to its use.

For many societies, there are criteria for male genitalia. Almost invariably a big penis is much admired. Among the

Sirionó, for example, it is thought that a man's penis should be as large as possible. Among the Hausa, men boast in their praise songs (a kind of personal advertisement) that they are "breakers of vaginas," both because of sexual prowess and penile size. Curiously enough, contrary to most other societies, the ancient Greeks seem to have idealized a small penis and identified large ones with passive homosexuals. Even more curious is the following assertion from the *Anangga rangga*, the medieval Indian sex manual: "The man whose Lingga (penis) is very long, will be wretchedly poor. The man whose Lingga is very thick, will ever be very lucky; and the man whose Lingga is short, will be a Rajah."

In the United States, fear of inadequate penis size is one of the most frequent sources of sexual anxiety for men (as reported by an analysis of letters to *Sexology* magazine), and several devices have been offered for sale — usually a type of suction pump — to increase the size. At least some of these devices are dangerous because they can rupture blood vessels and may cause fatal blood clots.

The *Kaama suutra* suggests another method for enlarging the penis that is both painful and dangerous. The man is advised to rub it with bristles from certain insects that live in trees, and then rub it with oil for 10 nights. After that he

The **Kaama Suutra** *advocates not only complicated sexual gymnastics but also a painful method of penis enlargement.*

should again apply the bristles. The whole procedure should be repeated until a swelling is produced. He should then lie down with his penis hanging through a hole in the cot. This is said to produce lifelong effects and is attributed to certain Dravidian people.

The human body has been altered in several ways to make it conform to aesthetic, social or erotic ideals. Methods used include: cutting; burning; insertion of foreign objects (lip plugs and penis bars); staining (as in tatooing or body painting); compressing; distending and enlarging.

The cultural motives for such alterations may have little to do with physical attractiveness. For example, in various societies ranging from the Plains Indians to the highlanders of New Guinea, a finger, or less commonly a toe (as in Fiji), is hacked off after the death of a near kinsman as a sign of grief. In large areas of Africa, tribal or other local allegiance is indicated by facial cuts varying in design. Religious motivations are sometimes involved, as among the Skoptsý (a nineteenth-century Russian Christian sect), who cut off women's breasts. It has been said that Germans joined fencing clubs primarily to get scars on their faces from wounds acquired in duels: these scars had a tremendous prestige value in some circles and possibly had erotic connotations.

The variability of alterations from culture to culture (as well as from time to time in the history of particular cultures) seem to be largely unpredictable — although certain patterns emerge. Kroeber, who was skeptical about notions of evolution in human culture, nevertheless believed that one could talk about cultural progress in some instances, including the decline of physical mutilations.

Yet although the more severe and dysfunctional alterations have in fact been given up, the resurgence from time to time of various alterations as part of the general fashion makes it seem implausible that such alterations will be abandoned altogether. At present, for example, in the United States there has been an upsurge in ear piercing among women — sometimes with multiple piercings of each ear; a fashion also adapted by some men. Nose piercing, unheard of only a few years ago, has a certain limited vogue — presumably in imitation of Indian or African models.

A number of alterations involving the head are reported in the cross-cultural literature. Attempts at molding the actual shape of the head in infancy, either by flattening with a board or lengthening by tiering bands around the back of the head, occurred in many parts of the world, including various parts of France as late as the twentieth century.

Piercing of cheeks occurs but is fairly rare, but the piercing or perforation of ears, noses and lips is quite common. One of the most extraordinary examples is the use of lip plates by

Duelling scars (top) *were formerly considered highly desirable in certain German student circles. In some parts of Africa cheek scars (above) were traditional decorations (as in this example from Ethiopia).*

Criteria of attractiveness:
Head flattening was considered
beautiful among various
Northwest Coast Indians
(above and right). A Bira
woman from Zaire (below)
wears an enormous lip disc,
which for unknown reasons
once became fashionable in
Central Africa. Women of
Padaung, Burma (below right),
with stretched necks.

women in the Ubangui-Chari region of Africa, notably among the Sara. It is sometimes suggested that the Sara started the lip plate fashion in order to make their women so unattractive that slave raiders would not be interested in capturing them. Nevertheless, the fashion caught on and tastes among the Sara themselves changed. At present, the fashion has changed once again and it seems that the use of lip plates is dying out.

Teeth have been blackened, reddened, knocked out, dug out, filed, chipped and drilled (and filled with decorative objects). Many of these customs are clearly dysfunctional but nevertheless they have a wide distribution and a considerable history. Among the Nilotes of East Africa, two or more (up to six!) of the lower front incisors are removed, usually at puberty. In some groups an instrument resembling an icepick is used to dig out the teeth, without the benefit of anaesthesia. Other groups knock the teeth out. Some evidence exists that the custom of tooth excision goes back to the Mesolithic: a skull found on the Blue Nile, referred to as the Singa skull, is also missing its lower front incisors and is sometimes taken to be an ancient relative of modern Nilotes. Because of western influence, the custom has begun to disappear.

One of the best known nongenital alterations is the foot-binding practiced by upper-class Chinese women from the eleventh century AD until the twentieth century. It probably originated as a symbol of a woman who has no need to work and so became a form of conspicuous waste to indicate wealth. But very early the bound foot took on highly erotic connotations, and was referred to approvingly as "golden lily" foot. Traditional Chinese erotic drawings usually show women completely naked except for socks covering tiny deformed feet. The effect on someone outside that sensibility might be that such drawings are vaguely comical rather than erotic; but the passion for bound feet in Chinese culture reached the proportions of a national fetish. But although enormous numbers of traits from Chinese culture spread to Japan, the fashion for foot-binding did not.

Common methods of decorating the skin include tatooing, painting, cutting and less frequently burning. Cicatrization is generally found among dark-skinned people, perhaps because tatooing does not show up so well. In Japan, tatooing is the only physical mutilation of any importance. Japanese tatooing clubs have existed for some time and both men and women often tatoo their entire bodies. Tatoos are also associated with the criminal underworld. Perhaps for this reason they play a conspicuous role in certain domestic Japanese sadomasochistic pornography. In several Polynesian groups, such as the Maori, tatooing can also be quite extensive and elaborate.

Covered and naked bound feet of a Chinese woman. Bound feet became the national fetish of China and remained so for several centuries.

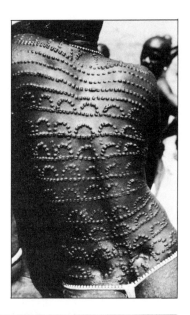

Beauty contests

Tatooing and cicatrization:
Extensive tatoos were once universal among Samoans (right), and so popular in some Japanese groups that a prize example (above) was preserved after the owner's death. Elaborate scars or cicatrices (top) decorate the back of a woman from the Kordofan in the Sudan.

In some societies, the designs are erotic, but occasionally the mere fact of tatooing or cicatrization on the body is regarded as erotic. Among Bala women of Zaire, the cicatrices extend from the chest above the breasts down to the groin. Cicatrices are erotically important to Bala men, who will avoid intercourse with a woman who lacks them.

Other kinds of alterations are relatively rare. Neck stretching is practiced by Padaung women of Burma with the aid of coiled brass neck rings. A length of 15 inches (38 cm) can be attained. Bands are sometimes tied around arms and legs so tightly that they may become pronouncedly enlarged. Practices of this kind are found in various parts of Africa, South America and Melanesia.

The earliest known beauty contests occurred among the ancient Greeks, and both men and women were honored for their looks. According to Athenaeus, a chatty writer from the third century , contests for masculine good looks were the most common and usually had religious connotations.

The Romans did not hold beauty contests of any sort, and the coming of Christianity — which abhorred glorification of the body — saw the end of any contests that still existed.

Beauty contests were revived as a totally secular institution in the twentieth century and the emphasis shifted towards preoccupation with contests for women. Male beauty contests have not caught on in modern times, perhaps because there is some sort of traditional stigma associated with a man overly concerned with his appearance.

The whole idea of beauty contests came under attack by women's liberationists in the 1960s as relegating women to the status of sex objects. This view did not make much impact on large portions of the US population, and these events are regularly televised.

To my knowledge, no real female beauty contests have been developed independently in any non-western culture. But some developments come close. Each year, for example, Havasupai Indian men are said to agree informally on the one or two most attractive girls of the season. These unofficial "Miss Havasupai" become prize catches and are put under more than usual sexual pressure from the men.

Only one non-western culture has developed male beauty contests independently: the Bororó Fulani of the Sahel in

Male physique and beauty contests: *Steve Reeves (above) won the Mr Universe title in 1950. Bororó Fulani men (below) decorate themselves in their annual male beauty contest.*

Africa. These contests are part of yearly ritual dances known as *gerewol* and seem to approach the ancient Greek contests in their symbolic function. The standards used in judging are totally different from those in western physique contests. From a western point of view, they reward effeminacy. The faces of the contestants are frozen in a tight-lipped smile, with eyes almost popping to expose the whites as prominently as possible. The contestants are concerned that their make-up and ornaments should be just right.

Genital modifications "They practice circumcision for the sake of cleanliness, considering it better to be cleanly than comely." This rather curious remark was made by Herodotus in the fifth century to explain why the ancient Egyptians circumcised. It represents the beginning of scientific speculation about why circumcision — or, for that matter, any surgical modification of the sex organs — occurs. Controversy continues today as to the origin and benefits of such customs.

Whatever the reason, people in many different societies have felt and still feel that the genitals should be altered in one way or another by cutting, piercing, hacking, or slicing, or by inserting objects into them.

Some alterations have become relatively well known because of the flood of handbooks about erotic miscellanea. A Burmese custom of inserting tiny bronze bells under the penis was made famous by David Reuben in *Everything you always wanted to know about sex (but were afraid to ask)*. At one point details such as this would have been buried in learned treatises, but in this instance an arcane bit of anthropological knowledge swept the United States and

Circumcision as performed in ancient Egypt, about 2300 . The relief suggests that boys were circumcised in groups as in many modern-day African societies.

The maps opposite show types of male genital alteration (top) and of female genital alteration (bottom) as found in societies around the world.

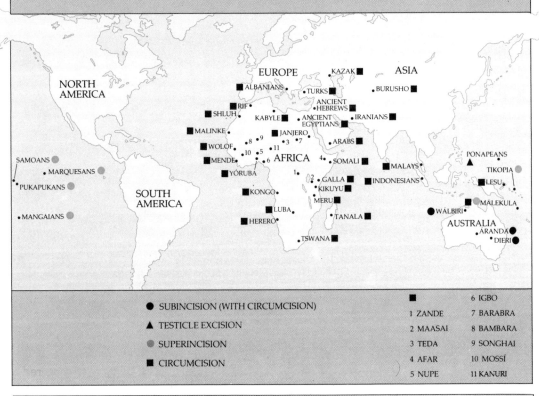

MALE GENITAL ALTERATIONS

- ● SUBINCISION (WITH CIRCUMCISION)
- ▲ TESTICLE EXCISION
- ● SUPERINCISION
- ■ CIRCUMCISION

1 ZANDE	6 IGBO
2 MAASAI	7 BARABRA
3 TEDA	8 BAMBARA
4 AFAR	9 SONGHAI
5 NUPE	10 MOSSÍ
	11 KANURI

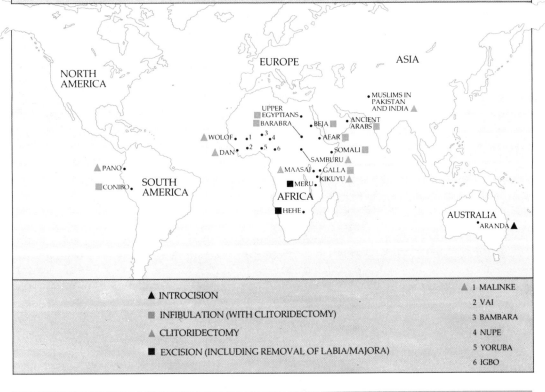

FEMALE GENITAL ALTERATIONS

- ▲ INTROCISION
- ▪ INFIBULATION (WITH CLITORIDECTOMY)
- ▲ CLITORIDECTOMY
- ■ EXCISION (INCLUDING REMOVAL OF LABIA/MAJORA)

1 MALINKE
2 VAI
3 BAMBARA
4 NUPE
5 YORUBA
6 IGBO

apparently became the basis for the phrase "Come ring my chimes," popularized on television in the late 1960s.

Among the Trukese of the Pacific, it was the women who exploited sounds erotically. Until recently, some Trukese women made holes in their labia and inserted objects that tinkled when they walked with their legs a little apart. The anthropologists who studied Truk were unable to determine exactly what these objects were, but they were said to have been retained during coitus.

A comparable genital modification, only noiseless, is reported from the Dayaks of Borneo. They insert a metal rod, called an *ampallang*, into the penis. The rod has balls or brushes fixed to the ends and is worn transversely through a perforation in the end of the penis. It is like a built-in

Circumcision ceremony as performed by Aborigines from West Arnhem Land, Australia.

"French tickler," a device sometimes used in the West for the same purpose but which is simply fitted onto the penis and is removable.

Mutilation of the male genitals is both more frequent and more varied than that of the female.

The most common mutilation is, of course, male circumcision, whereby the foreskin is totally removed. It is estimated that about half of all the men alive in the world today are circumcised. Egyptian representations of circumcised men (and even of the act of circumcision) date back beyond 2000 BC. Because in most areas where circumcision is performed a stone rather than a metal knife is used in the actual surgery, some theorists posit a Stone Age origin. In any event it is a very ancient custom.

Circumcision is religiously required of all Jewish males,

and it is customary among Muslims (although not enjoined in the Koran). Slight differences in the manner of circumcision occur between these groups. It is common throughout most of the Middle East and Africa, but there are several areas where it does not occur, notably among the southern Bantu such as the Zulu, and among Nilotic groups of East Africa. Hunting and gathering groups such as the Bushmen do not practice it either, though Pigmies do in imitation of their taller neighbors. There is doubt as to whether circumcision was ever developed by American Indians, but it may have been found among the Totonác of Mexico and the Moche of Peru (the facts are not clear). It is not found among Orientals or traditionally among Christian Europeans or Americans. Egyptian and Ethiopian Koptic Christians practice it, in imitation of their Muslim neighbors.

Circumcising babies is normal among Jews and in the West, but in most societies, including traditional Islamic ones, circumcision and the other genital mutilations to be discussed later are performed after the age of six, often at or around puberty. A striking exception is presented by the Konso of Ethiopia, who use circumcision not to mark the beginning of sexual maturity but the end of sexual life: men may be in their 60s or older when the surgery is performed and they often become transvestites, being as it were in a sexual limbo.

In many societies in the Pacific, the foreskin is not totally removed, it is merely slit lengthwise. Making such a slit is known as superincision or supercision. Among the Marquesans the operation is performed without an anaesthetic (as is also the case with all traditional genital mutilations) by stretching the foreskin tightly over a piece of bamboo.

Superincision is almost entirely restricted to Polynesian groups. The major cultural explanation for the custom is that it promotes cleanliness and reduces the odor from smegma, considered altogether disgusting and the cause of insults of a very serious nature. Among the Mangaians, if the superincision is not well done and the foreskin hangs the wrong way, below the shaft of the penis, it is also considered a very serious matter.

Carving of Angolan circumcision rite.

Case of silver-mounted instruments used in the Jewish circumcision rite (or milah), dating from 1801.

The medical value of circumcision is in dispute. But to assume circumcision was first begun for hygienic reasons is undoubtedly wrong.

Wooden statuette from *Sudan used as magical protection against castration.*

Subincision is a mutilation of the penis not involving the foreskin. A single cut is made on the ventral side of the organ from one end to the other, through to the urethra. As a result, the penis can be flattened out. One of the consequences of this mutilation is that a man cannot direct his flow of urine and usually squats while urinating. In a similar way, it has been speculated that semen will not flow and will therefore not be effective. The evidence suggests otherwise, however, because in all the societies in which subincision occurs, it takes place before marriage and legitimate children are produced. One of the curious things about subincision is that with a single exception, the Samburu (a group in Africa), it occurs only in areas where there are kangaroos or closely related animals. This fact has been used with some success to explain the existence of the custom. I shall discuss this in more detail later on in the chapter.

Bleeding the penis without altering its shape is rare but has been reported from the Maya of Mexico and is still performed regularly by the Wógeo, who live on an island just north of New Guinea. The Wógeo bleed themselves in this way because they believe that contact with women leads to infection and diseases that can only be prevented by bloodletting. One might imagine that this custom would drive men en masse into homosexuality. The remarkable thing is that although it is not condemned, homosexual behavior almost never occurs.

Only four societies in the world are believed to practice (or have practiced) the removal of one testicle: hemicastration, also called semicastration or monorchy. Two of these societies are in Africa, one in Ethiopia: the Janjero, a subgroup of the Sidamo; the other in southern Africa: the Hóttentot, who are said formerly to have cut out one testicle to prevent the birth of twins (thought to be especially bad luck). The other two are in Micronesia in the Pacific. The best documented account comes from the Ponapeans, who live on an island in the Caroline group in Micronesia. The operation used to be performed between the ages of 14 and 16. More recently, with the decline of the custom, it was performed at a later age. At present, the custom has practically died out. To perform the operation on oneself seems to have been considered especially brave. The last instance of a reported attempt at self-castration occurred during the Japanese occupation and was not successful; the operation had to be completed by a Japanese surgeon. Traditionally it was also considered a good thing to remove the remaining testicle fairly late in life as a demonstration of loyalty to a chief, particularly in time of war. It is said that the chiefs and other nobles often managed to avoid the removal of even one testicle. We cannot be sure about this because it was forbidden for a commoner to remark about the omission.

Varieties of castration:
Farinelli (left), a famous
castrato singer of the 18th
century; the goddess Cybele
(right), depicted on a 3rd-
century Roman altar with her
devotee, Attis, was worshiped
by castrated priests.

Total castration has been inflicted on various people for various reasons. The Roman priests of the goddess Cybele were eunuchs dressed as women. Although the Koran forbids castration, Islamic societies have made use of eunuchs castrated by Christians: the keepers of harems have almost invariably been castrated slaves. In Byzantium, China, and a number of African despotic kingdoms, eunuchs were occasionally elevated to important positions such as that of vizir or general to avoid dynastic rivalries. The biblical injunctioń, now widely challenged, that women should keep silent in churches (I Corinthians 14:35) was observed so strictly in the Roman Catholic Church at one point that women were not even allowed to sing in them and this led, especially in Italy, to the employment of the castrati (castrated male singers). Papal decree abolished the custom in 1878.

Nipple excision — cutting off the nipples of adolescent boys (to my knowledge, never off girls except occasionally among the Skoptsý, a Russian religious sect) — has been reported from at least one society, the Janjero. In addition to hemicastration, they also circumcise and take male genitals rather than scalps as war trophies. The custom of taking genitals as trophies is more widespread than might be imagined. Even in the Bible we hear that David was required to collect the foreskins of 100 Philistines killed in battle (I Samuel 18:25).

Female mutilations have recently become the subject of considerable political concern because they are seen as techniques to rob women of practically all sexual fulfillment. Only two are normally mentioned, clitoridectomy and infibulation (terms used very loosely), but there is at least a third: vaginal introcision (cutting of the perineum). This is found exclusively among certain Australian aborigines.

Clitoridectomy refers to the removal of the clitoris and sometimes other parts of the female genitalia.

Clitoridectomy occurs much less frequently than male circumcision. It is fairly common throughout Africa, but seems to be the custom only where male circumcision occurs. The Falashas, the black Jews of Ethiopia, observe clitoridectomy, unlike other Jews, presumably in imitation of neighboring

Defeat of the Philistines by the Israelites. *King Saul commanded David to collect the foreskins of 100 slain Philistines; he collected 200.*

groups. This practice has been reported from various other groups, particularly from certain Islamic peoples. A single group of American Indians has been reported as practicing it, the Pano of Ecuador, but the report may be dubious. Clitoridectomy has been used sporadically in the West both as a therapy to overcome frigidity, nymphomania and lesbianism as well as a punishment for "excessive" masturbation. Success on all these counts seems to have been nil. It is sometimes maintained that clitoridectomy reduces sexual pleasure in women and that it most probably started as a custom to accomplish just that. Very little clinical information is available, but the one study that is at all scientific (by Marie Bonaparte) found that removal of the clitoris did not lower sexual excitement and that masturbation was as effective a means of sexual stimulation as before surgery. However, informal accounts by men who have copulated with women who have not been declitorized as well as with those who have, suggest that clitoridectomy has a drastic effect and lowers female response considerably.

The various procedures known as infibulation are even more restricted geographically. Eastern Africa is the main center of infibulation, particularly among the Kushitic-speaking people of the Horn such as the Somali and the Galla. It has also been reported from various other Islamic groups. The term Pharaonic circumcision is sometimes used for infibulation, suggesting that it was practiced by the ancient Egyptians, but this seems to be unwarranted. One variety of infibulation, the commonest, involves sewing the labia majora together with only a very small opening to allow for urination. In all forms of infibulation, parts of the clitoris and labia minora are also removed.

Knife used in Central African clitoridectomy ceremonies.

The Conibo of Peru seem to be the only American Indian group to have developed a kind of infibulation — and this quite independently of northeast African groups. The Conibo variety had the unique feature that a clay dildoe — apparently an exact replica of her fiance's penis — was inserted into the girl's mutilated vaginal opening.

A kind of infibulation was practiced on men by the ancient Greeks and Romans. The Greeks tied the foreskins of athletes over the glans. Among the Romans, musicians, actors and similar people actually made a hole in the foreskin and a fibula (a ring or clasp) was inserted.

There are many theories to account for these various practices, and some have already been mentioned. The rationale for infibulation seems fairly straightforward: the prevention of intercourse by a sort of built-in chastity belt. Sporadic examples crop up even in modern Europe. In Portugal recently a jealous woman was reported as having infibulated her lover with two gold clasps. After five years, the man was reduced to seeking medical aid.

Why the other mutilations are carried out is less obvious. The usual explanations for circumcising in the West (apart from religious rules) have been hygienic or other medical reasons. These considerations are based on the following facts. An uncircumcised man sometimes develops blisters on his foreskin because of repeated intercourse and occasionally the foreskin itself tightens up, a condition known as phimosis. The most striking factor is the incidence of cancer of the penis, which accounts for less than two percent of all the cancers of men in the United States, but in China for about 18.3 percent. Circumcised men almost never develop cancer of the penis. Only one case has ever been reported in a Jew. Indian Muslims, who practice circumcision, rarely if ever develop such cancers, whereas the non-circumcising Hindus have an incidence of about 10 percent. In addition, the wives of uncircumcised men have a significantly higher incidence of cancer of the cervix. Whether the level of personal cleanliness is the important factor here rather than the mere presence or absence of a foreskin is a matter of some dispute, but these details have been advanced as cogent arguments for circumcision. Nevertheless, they can hardly have led primitive peoples to originate or even perpetuate the practice, lacking as they did scientific methodology and notions of causality. In fact, the general conditions under which circumcision and other mutilations are traditionally performed — unsterilized stone knife with no anaesthetic — make a hygienic explanation of origin not very plausible. In any event, people may develop useful techniques for the wrong reasons.

Kangaroo-penis envy may underlie the subincision practices of some Australian societies, where the effect is to create a close resemblance to the two-headed kangaroo penis. Kangaroos are observed to copulate for up to two hours.

The orthodox Jewish explanation for circumcision is merely that it shows a bond between God and Abraham and his descendants (Genesis 17:10-11, 14). No other scriptural reason can be cited.

Two outrageous but possibly true explanations for subincision exist. According to one, it reflects vagina envy in boys (comparable to the Freudian notion of penis envy in girls — more specifically, menstruation envy since blood figures prominently in subincision rituals and old wounds may be reopened). This explanation has been proposed by the psychoanalyst Bruno Bettelheim.

The menstruation-envy theory of subincision has recently been challenged by a competing kangaroo-penis envy theory. According to the kangaroo version, subincision attempts to imitate the kangaroo penis, which is distinctive because it is two-headed (in technical jargon, bifid). A number of arguments support this theory, hilarious as it has seemed to some who accept with a straight face the notion of menstruation envy. Subincision is found only in areas where kangaroos or other marsupials with bifid penes live. And the anatomical similarities between subincised men and kangaroos are impressive: the urinary stream emerges at about the same place; the urethra is exposed, urination requires squatting; the penis is widened, and resembles quite closely the two-headed kangaroo penis. Perhaps most important is the fact that the Australians practicing the mutilation say that they do so in imitation of kangaroos and other marsupials. An additional factor seems to be envy of the sexual prowess of kangaroos, who can copulate for up to two hours at a time. It is interesting that this theory was proposed by two different groups of anthropologists independently.

Other scholars have argued that genital mutilations are not associated with any specifically sexual motivation but are arbitrary social rituals serving the same function in a puberty ritual as, say, the pulling of teeth, a custom having fairly wide distribution. In aboriginal Australian initiation rites, for example, various physical operations are practiced

Before clitoridectomy; Buli girls line up wearing small bells against evil spirits.

that differ from one part of the continent to another, but are in a way functionally equivalent. Thus, we find circumcision (and sometimes subincision) especially prominent in central and northwestern Australia, pulling teeth in New South Wales, yanking out body hair south of the Murray River, and cutting elaborate scars on the body in South Australia and eastern Queensland. Occasionally, a group may have more than one kind of operation involving the imposition of a foreign type of mutilation upon a culture already practicing another kind. The Nilotes of East Africa literally dig out two to six lower front teeth and their Kushitic neighbors practice circumcision and clitoridectomy. The Maasai, a Nilotic group heavily Kushitized, have the best of both worlds by

After clitoridectomy: a young Bwaka girl from Budjala.

Genital modifications often carry a high symbolic value. The ancient Greeks, for example, would not allow circumcised men to compete in athletic contests.

requiring all three operations. Yet other scholars have tried to find correlations between specific genital mutilations and the way children are brought up. It has been suggested, for example, that noninfant circumcision is an attempt to separate a boy from his mother's influence and to help create a strong masculine identity. Elaborate male coming of age ceremonies involving circumcision are often found in societies where the child is closer to his mother than his father, or where the father is away a good deal of the time. In societies where circumcision occurs boys and girls tend to be treated differently and their differences are maximized or at least stressed. This can be seen even in the puberty rituals for girls which often involve clitoridectomy. But their ceremonies tend to be informal, private and matter of fact.

Superincision, on the other hand, is associated with a different upbringing pattern: boys and girls tend to be treated alike and their differences minimized. The menstruation-envy theory seems to hold here, at least in the imagery of the superincising cultures themselves. The same term, for example, may be used for menstrual bleeding as for bleeding from the superincision opening, and the tabus associated with the menstrual period may also apply to men while they bleed from their wounds.

But it must be admitted that the motivations for these mutilations remain obscure and require considerably more investigation. What is not obscure is the very great symbolic value often attached to them. This is perfectly illustrated by Colin Turnbull in his book *The lonely African*. He tells of an English missionary working in what was then the Belgian Congo, who at one point abducts a boy about to undergo ritual circumcision as part of an initiation rite. The missionary, fearful of both the unhygienic and pagan aspects of the rite, has the boy circumcised in a western-type hospital. The boy's relatives — even though they are Christians — are furious, and the missionary attempts to explain to his congregation that circumcision is not required of Christians and that he himself is not circumcised. Dumbstruck, the congregation abandons him (only their enemy neighbors are known to be uncircumcised). He is alone except for his most trusted convert, who asks him if it is true:

"When I answered yes, he spat at me, his filthy spittle clinging to my clothes as I stood numb with shock, and said, 'That is what we think of the uncircumcised.'"

The convert went back to his own village and completely renounced Christianity.

Eight ✥ CLOTHING AND MODESTY

*Clothing may imply modesty
—and also sexuality. Nudity is associated
with lust in some cultures, and
with purity in others.*

Masked Englishwoman, *17th century.*

Nudity and unbridled lust go hand in glove — at least this has been the view of orthodox Jews, Christians and Muslims. It is not necessarily the personal experience of Westerners who saw "streaking" as a welcome comic relief to Vietnam War protests or of health addicts promoting therapeutic nudity. In other societies, nudity has other, sometimes totally different meanings.

For the traditional Zulu of South Africa, for example, willingness to expose the body is sometimes taken as a proof of sexual morality. They believe that sexual looseness produces flabby bodies. In certain rituals, unmarried girls are supposed to dance naked (more precisely, dressed only in beads with breasts bare). Because of European influence, many girls have taken to covering their breasts in these rituals to the great consternation of older non-Christian Zulu, who see it not as an expression of modesty but as a way to cover up evidence of sexual misconduct.

The Tonga of the South Pacific similarly had a ritual dance in which a high-born virgin had to dance naked. This was not viewed as licentious but rather as a symbolic way of proclaiming her chastity.

A very few groups have forbidden total nudity in all situations, even when a person is alone. The Mormons require the faithful to wear a sacred garment at all times, even when copulating. This piece of clothing (called the "temple garment" by Mormons, but commonly "jet suit" by unsympathetic non-Mormons) is something like a decorated white long john. It is first worn by women when they marry, and by men when they are "sealed" in the temple (a rite preparing them for missionary activity). The motivation for wearing the temple garment seems not to be prudery but the belief that it is a form of supernatural protection — something like a body-covering religious medal.

It is sometimes alleged that certain ultra orthodox Jews are so prudish that they copulate through a cloth with a hole in it. At least 100 Jewish informants have told me that they have heard of this custom. As far as I can discover, this assertion is pure myth and totally untrue.

There is at least one society, however, that actually required sex to be performed in a similar way: the Menomini Indians, who made use of a soft deerskin blanket with a hole in the middle.

Occasionally, Christian groups have sprung up that championed or tolerated nudity. Several groups appeared in

"Streaking," or public *stripping, developed as a form of protest in the 1970s.*

the second century who preached that the perfection and sinless condition of Adam before the Fall had been re-achieved with Christ through baptism so that nakedness was the preferred state. They were persecuted wholesale and by the end of the fourth century all the groups had died out. A similar group of nudist Christians sprang up after the Middle Ages in Germany and Holland: the Adamites. They too were short lived. Occasionally Christian ascetics might include nudity in their self-denial, as with the early desert eremites or the early Franciscans, but these are relatively idiosyncratic. The use of nudity as religious nonviolent protest has been developed by the Dukhobors, a Russian Christian sect founded in the eighteenth century. Most of the present-day members (about 20,000) live in Canada, where an extremist subgroup (the Sons of Freedom) occasionally protests against taxation and compulsory education by burning down government buildings as well as

The Dukhobors, a religious sect originally from Russia but now mainly found in Canada, may show disapproval by removing their clothes.

their own houses and also by parading in the nude.

In other religions and cultures, nudity plays quite a different role. It is frequently regarded with reverence and is considered the appropriate state for confronting the divine. The fear of ritual pollution associated with dirt on clothes prompted pre-Islamic Arabs to offer sacrifices naked. In the Hindu–Sikh–Jain–Buddhist traditions, nudity often has overtones of the highest piety. Vardhamaanaa Mahaaviira, who died about 468 BC and was one of the founders of Jain-ism, preached not only nonviolence and vegetarianism but instructed all his ascetic followers to walk about totally naked as an act of the utmost religiosity (laymen, however, were permitted to wear clothes).

A particularly interesting Hindu ritual is the Sinhasta or Lion festival held every 12 years at the holy city of Naasik. One of the high points of the festival is catching sight of the naked saadhus (holy men) who have congregated in the city to bathe in the sacred Godaavari river. Other pilgrims clamor around them; women who are otherwise quite proper rush forward to touch the saadhus' fingers as "they march past . . . in their naked majesty and glory," as Masani puts it. The origin of this naked procession is somewhat surprising and reminiscent of the Dukhobor protests. According to the saadhus themselves, the cult of nudity started in the seventeenth century when some Hindu holy men in Junaagadh were molested by fakirs (Muslim holy men). The ruler of Junaagadh refused to interfere and so the saadhus took matters into their own hands. One night they stripped stark naked, smeared themselves with soot and charged the fakirs, who were frightened out of their wits by the sight.

Nudity is regarded with reverence in many societies. It may indicate ascetism, with overtones of the highest piety. Or it may be used as a scare tactic in battle.

Going to battle naked (by otherwise clothed people) is a scare tactic reported from a number of diverse areas. Marco Polo in the thirteenth century reported that the people of Malabar "go to battle all naked with only a lance and a shield." The same practice was apparently a standard strategy of the Gauls in pre-Roman France and of the Picts in Scotland, who either painted their naked bodies blue or were elaborately tatooed. At least some ancient Greek warriors are believed to have gone forth in battle naked except for helmets, shields and sandals.

Nudity is sometimes an essential ingredient in initiation rites. One of the more extraordinary examples of this comes from a description of the ritual swearing of the "Batuni" oath, which bound a Kikuyu man to the Mau Mau rebellion against British rule in Kenya. Josiah Kariuki, writing of his initiation, said that when called he took off all his clothes and squatted facing his initiator. He was given the thorax of a skinned goat and was told "to put my penis through a hole that had been made in it and to hold the rest of it in my left hand in front of me." The oath to the death was then sworn. Clearly the function of nudity here was to create an atmosphere of appropriately chilling awe.

Obviously, then, nudity in itself cannot be equated with concupiscence in any simple-minded way. The modern nudist movement, which began in Germany at the end of the nineteenth century, always tries to underplay the sexual connotations of nudity.

Nudism was also popularized by the Wandervogel movement in Germany, a romantic youth group not unlike the boy scouts, which was frequently beset by charges of immorality and in particular homosexual licence. To counter

__Modern nudism__ was inspired by advocates of "clean living."

such charges, later organized nudism has played down all aspects of overt sexuality both in its propaganda and in practice at nudist camps. Family nudism is encouraged and single men have usually had a hard time gaining admittance to the camps. The result, in the words of Albert Ellis, the prominent sexologist (who is not a nudist): "Nudist communities are much more in danger of being distilleries of antisexualism than factories of rampant sexuality. . . ."

It has been conceded by various apologists for nudism that the movement attracted some peculiar types. But however peculiar these converts to nudism are, they are not the key to answering questions about the relationship of nudity or clothing to sexual behavior simply because they were not brought up in a nudist culture.

The question remains: what happens to the sexuality of people raised in societies where all the people normally expose their sex organs all the time?

A fairly detailed account of modesty training among a traditionally naked people is given by John W. M. Whiting for the Kwoma, who live just north of the Sepik river in Papua New Guinea. Modesty is stressed from childhood. Boys are scolded and even beaten for looking at female genitals. The same tabu continues throughout life except with respect to the genitals of a lover or wife. When he reaches puberty, if a boy stares at a girl's body he is suspected of having made a sexual advance; to stare at her genitals may invoke insults and threats from the girl's relatives. The proper behavior for a boy or man in the presence of a woman is to fix his eyes on the ground or to sit or stand with his back to her whenever he is in her presence. Furthermore, if he meets a woman walking, they may not speak until they have passed each other.

A girl for her part is trained not to assume "immodest" postures. Even little girls are scolded for doing so, but in adolescence the criticism may become severe. A proper girl should not sit with her legs apart or knees drawn up, but should stretch her legs out close together with knees unbent. She should never bend over when men are present unless she is wearing a net bag (which functions as an article of clothing as well as a receptacle for carrying objects). This bag hangs from the forehead down the back and may reach almost to the knees. If a girl does not observe these rules she is branded as a loose woman and greatly reduces her chances of getting married.

Such rules of modesty persist throughout life, to be broken only by the old. The old may even embrace someone of the opposite sex — an act totally forbidden to others except among spouses, lovers and with infants.

A matter of particular embarrassment among the Kwoma is getting an erection in public. Even in boyhood, an erection is a cause of considerable humiliation and any female who sees a boy with an erection is expected to hit his penis with a stick. Whiting noted that the training must have been very effective because he never saw a man with an erection and only once observed a little boy with an erect penis.

In his important early survey of modesty in different cultures, *The evolution of modesty* (1899), Havelock Ellis concluded that modesty was far more entrenched among primitive peoples than among those who were more highly developed, and furthermore that modesty continued to be more intense among lower-class people than among "the more cultivated classes." The second observation has in part been confirmed by the later researches of Alfred Kinsey and his colleagues in the United States. They found that in the 1940s (older) working-class people tended to wear some clothes when copulating, and that the men did not even go bare-chested before their wives; modesty required that they should at least wear undershirts.

Among the cross-cultural evidence that Havelock Ellis gives are the following: Tocantins reported that although the Mundurucú women of Brazil are completely naked, they are so skillful at avoiding any indecorous postures that it is impossible to tell when they are menstruating. As for the Dinka, among whom the men go naked and the women wear only a pubic covering, Lombroso and Carrara in the 1890s wrote of how astonishing the intensity of modesty was among these people: no Dinka man would permit examination of his genitals; no Dinka woman, of her breasts. One woman who permitted examination of tatoos on her chest was clearly upset by it for two days.

Writing some 50 years later, Franz Kiener compared the "high" sexual morality of the Luo of Kenya, among whom

Dinka men of the Sudan. *Lack of clothing does not preclude an intense sense of modesty.*

In some societies the man goes naked and the woman is clothed.

the men lived in total nudity, with the "loose" neighboring Baganda, who were traditionally covered to the neck.

A recent study by William N. Stephens tries to relate degrees of modesty to stages of human social evolution. The most intensely modest peoples turn out to be peasants who also attach great importance to premarital chastity in women. Virtually only peasant societies require that women cover their breasts, although there are a few exceptions such as the Bali, Dahomey, Naayar, Mohave and Ojibwa. Stephens attributes the peasant obsession to a particular kind of authoritarian, patriarchal family structure, which is the rule among such societies. He associates this family structure with the rigid class structure of feudal kingdoms. The political democracies of industralized societies seem to be associated with more democratic family structures and these, in turn, he correlates with more relaxed attitudes to sex restrictions.

Although Stephens' causal model has attractive features, modesty does not invariably go along with chastity. For example, among societies where even women's breasts are covered (his highest criterion for modesty in this scheme), the Tepoztecans and Yadaw are said to have ineffectual rules against premarital intercourse for girls, whereas the Shavante, who rank very low in the modesty scale (the women go naked), have very strict rules against both premarital and adulterous relations for women.

Intensity of feeling about modesty seems to vary according to certain levels of society; peasant societies seem to be the most intense of all.

A more recent study by Gwen J. Broude and Sarah J. Greene has summarized the evidence on behavior and ideology among traditionally nude societies in comparison with others: there would seem to be as much variation as among clothed groups. The number of naked groups considered, however, was small. Of a sample of 186 societies, only six practiced adult male nudity. Of these only four were said to have comparable female nudity. This small sample shows that the concerted effort by Christian missionaries and others to stamp out nudity throughout the world has been quite successful. Even 100 years ago, a considerably larger number of people practicing nudity could be found. Be that as it may, in both behavior and belief, the existing naked societies show almost as wide a range as do clothed groups.

So far nudity has been equated with exposure of the genitals. Some people, however, do not hide their sex organs, but may wear headdresses, arm bands or strings around the waist. In a number of societies, skins or cloaks may be thrown over the shoulders as a sign of rank or for protection while the genitals remain uncovered. This is true of the Nuer leopardskin chiefs, California Indians, and other Indians from the Great Basin. Exposure of the shoulders, however, was not considered immodest. In all societies, modesty is almost always associated with the genitals, although it may be extended to other body parts, so that intense feelings can be aroused by having nose plugs removed (as among some Brazilian groups) or lip plugs (Alaskan Indians) or socks (Chinese). But it does not happen the other way around. Thus, we do not expect, nor do we find, societies in which normal women are intensely modest, for example, about their hands but not about their vaginas. The Naaga, a head-hunting group from India, are a frequently mentioned counterexample. This exception was first reported by Ibn Muhammad Wali in his history of the conquest of Assam (1662 to 1663), retold by Havelock Ellis and repeated verbatim in virtually every subsequent book on fashion and clothing. According to this account, Naaga women covered only their breasts because "it was absurd to cover those parts of the body which everyone has been able to see from their births, but that it is different with the breasts, which appeared later, and are, therefore, to be covered" (Ellis). But Masani, writing in 1934, puts the situation in a more readily believable light, saying that Naaga women wear necklaces and an apron — and sometimes not the apron. But necklaces are merely decorations, and decorations of even the most elaborate sort are sometimes found among naked people to indicate ritual or social status. An even more thoroughgoing description of the present-day Naaga by von Fürer-Haimendorf along with photographs he has taken suggests that although the necklaces are elaborate, they hardly hide the breasts. In fact, totally naked women can sometimes be seen among the Naaga and they apparently feel no embarrassment even if menstrual blood appears on their thighs. Usually, however, they wear narrow skirts that just cover the genitals.

An almost identical and equally unlikely story is told about a group in Thailand in the vicinity of the Mekhong. There, too, the women are said to go around bottomless but

Naaga women supposedly considered exposed breasts to be immodest, but not exposed genitals. Recent research shows that breasts too are not always covered.

"Heroic" nudity was an ancient Greek custom imitated by the Romans in art but not in life.

not topless, and for the same reason: that breasts were the one part of their body they did not have since childhood. A few other somewhat unexpected fashions have been reported, notably an early Egyptian male kilt that covered the buttocks but exposed the genitals, a style for working men in the Old Kingdom recorded in art. A similar anomaly occurs in the representation of ancient Greek hoplites (a kind of foot soldier), who are often shown with helmet, breastplate and greaves (leg coverings) but with genitals exposed. No obvious military advantage comes to mind for this outfit. In both the Egyptian and Greek situations we are probably dealing with an accepted nudity, although the styles in question are cross-culturally rare.

Greek nudity was proverbial in the ancient world. The Etruscans and Romans found it distasteful but copied Greek styles in their art: it did not correspond with the reality of dress any more than modern nudes in painting and sculpture correspond to how people look in New York or London. The Greeks themselves were conscious of the uniqueness of their custom of "heroic nudity," at the Olympic games and elsewhere. Initially, they wore a *perízooma* (something like a bathing suit) in athletic competitions. But traditionally the change came when Orsippus of Megara won the footrace by allowing his *perízooma* to fall off along the way.

A cross-cultural tendency with regard to nudity is that men either equal women in bodily concealment or wear less, seldom the opposite. The ancient Greeks, for example, did not generally tolerate nudity in women (except in Sparta); the statues of young women are invariably draped in long garments. The same tendency can be observed on so-called nudist beaches in America: the men are totally naked but their women companions are usually only topless. A number of reasons have been suggested for such a phenomenon. Perhaps the most striking is a psychoanalytic one: it is that women prefer to remain covered in order to hide what they lack — a penis.

In countries where part of the population has traditionally gone naked changes are sometimes difficult to enforce. The elite in these groups have usually been trained in the West or are very westernized and may want to end nudity because it is "primitive" or "immoral." Such has been the case with the Turkana of Kenya since the 1960s; they have resisted attempts by the central government to get them to wear clothes. Nudity became a symbol of Turkanahood and so not something to be given up lightly.

Tanzania launched the same sort of harassment against the seminaked Maasai in 1968 (Maasai men cover their bodies with red ochre and wear a loosely draped blanket, which does not always hide the genitals). Maasai men were forbidden to enter the town of Arusha unless they wore trousers. An enormous debate was thereby unleashed. Maasai in neighboring Kenya were outraged by the cultural pogrom the Tanzanians had attempted. Interestingly, at the

The Maasai custom of *wearing only a blanket, which may not conceal the genitals, has been attacked in the name of "modernism."*

same time, Tanzania forbade the wearing of miniskirts. The move against the Maasai was taken in the name of modernization and national integration; the move against miniskirts as a rejection of western decadence.

Nudity is clearly a complex matter and may become a symbol having little to do with concupiscence.

Clothing frequently does not diminish sexuality but enhances it, and is often deliberately designed to entice. In saying this, I am not even considering the psychoanalytic view that clothes can function as sexual symbols (for

Clothing and Sexuality

Clothes may increase rather than reduce sexual drive, particularly in highly clothed, prudish societies.

example, the modern tie is frequently cited as a phallic symbol).

In those areas of the world where women go topless, breasts are not singled out as particularly attractive, whereas in the West and particularly the United States, breasts form the focus of much sexual fantasizing and attraction. A female researcher of my acquaintance went to a certain island in the Pacific in the late 1950s, wearing conservative western clothes of the time. The women of the island customarily go about topless but with wraparound skirts reaching to the ground. My friend noticed that although native men paid no attention to the bare breasts that were everywhere to be seen, they ogled her ankles. Her social position was in doubt because exposing her legs was considered reprehensible. She went native in dress and had no more problems on that score.

A somewhat similar account (which has become quite famous in the sexologist literature) also suggests that hiding the body is itself erotic. It was mentioned by Havelock Ellis and drawn from the autobiography of the celebrated philanderer Casanova (1725 to 1798). When he was in Rome, Casanova went to a public bath in which he was bathed by a naked girl attendant. After the bath, the girl expected Casanova to have sex with her, but to his own surprise he found he was not attracted to her. He concluded that his nonsexual comportment with her while she was naked had reduced her attractiveness.

Other accounts also support this view, at least in part. Young men I interviewed in Síssano on the north coast of New Guinea told me that they found the breasts of young girls very erotic; older men did not. But it was only within the past two generations that young girls (but not older women) covered their breasts at the insistence of the Catholic missionaries. Clearly one can find anecdotal accounts that support the idea that the wearing of clothes promotes concupiscence rather than reduces it. Along these same lines, clothing fetishes (sexual interest in articles of clothing) are fairly common in prudish, highly clothed, advanced societies but are almost nonexistent elsewhere.

One of the obvious functions of clothing is to exaggerate the distinction between the sexes. A true unisex style of dress and adornment is rare in the world's cultures. The use of codpieces, penis sheaths, epaulettes or padding to broaden the shoulders, play up certain aspects of male anatomy; the use of crinoline hoopskirts and décolleté have emphasized feminine characteristics. An especially explicit fashion for women has been called the erotic style. It is characterized by such features as transparent materials (gauze, tulle), tight-fitting clothes and garments that only partially cover the body (décolleté, cutouts, side vents).

Strangely, in medieval Europe, the Virgin Mary is occasionally represented in one version of the erotic style — with cutouts for her breasts (a fashion never worn by contemporary women). Another style that has been identified as essentially masculine is the so-called aggressive style, characterized in part by noisy materials such as creaking leather or clanking metal.

The various recent changes in the status of women in the western world, bringing them closer to men both economically and socially, have led to the widescale use of trousers for women and the emergence of a fairly general unisex style. Mario Bick, in an unpublished paper "What's on, what's coming off," has suggested that an erotic style is not essentially a feminine style but one associated with a certain position in what he calls the "sexual marketplace." For Bick, the sexual marketplace has little to do with marriage but is essentially "the arena in which premarital and adulterine sexual relationships are contracted."

In his analysis of European peasant society, he says that women are on display before marriage and tend to wear colorful clothing and expose their hair. After marriage, their dress tends to become drab and their hair is generally hidden under some sort of kerchief, indicating that they are not technically available for adultery. But married men, Bick finds, are more decoratively dressed after marriage in peasant society: they then become the "objects" in the sexual marketplace, displaying themselves so that "consumers" will be attracted. In the royal courts of Europe, the sexual marketplace was open to everyone and men and women were equally on display.

With the breakdown of arranged marriages in the western world, women became virtually always the objects, in competition for men who until recently represented economic security as well as sex partners. Hence it is the women who have consistently been more flamboyant (except for a few periods such as the 1920s and today, when women have become more economically independent).

In most societies, says Bick, it is men who are nearly always more gaudy. But recently in the West their clothing has been uniformly drab and regimented. This drab masculine style has been called the "great renunciation" by J. C. Flugel, the psychoanalyst of clothing. If Bick is right, this label seems to be quite accurate. Fashion for men is changing and Bick suggests that the sources for the new fashions are lower-class black ghettos and the gay world, where men are competing in a special sexual marketplace. Among blacks, it is frequently women who are economically the more stable and so, in a sense, able to be the consumers. Among homosexuals in anonymous settings such as gay bars, appearance is virtually the only criterion of attractiveness.

Medieval depictions of the ***Virgin Mary*** *sometimes show her clothed in a dress with cutouts for breasts—an erotic style not worn by women of the time.*

A prostitute dressed in a nun's habit works in an Italian street.

Bick's analysis, which is meant to account for a vast array of details of style, has several attractive features but seems not to be totally true cross-culturally or even within western society. And it certainly goes against what sociobiologists would predict.

Drab versus gaudy clothing in the West can, for example, be associated with the development of local forms of cloth manufacture and dyeing. Jane Schneider has set up a contrast between sartorial "penguins" and "peacocks." The Italian Renaissance was a heyday for peacocks: fashionable men wore brightly colored clothes as varied as those of women. But the dyes were expensive and had to be imported from the Orient. Eventually a superior black dye was developed in Europe and this became the preferred color not only for economic reasons but also as an expression of nationalism. Black even ousted white as the traditional European color of mourning. Black became at once a symbol of piety, frugality and elegance. It also developed erotic overtones: black stockings and underwear, for example, were identified with prostitutes. On the one hand, the ideal nun wears black garb; on the other, so does the ideal sadomasochistic dominatrix (both sadomasochists and leather fetishists tend to opt for black leather clothing or accessories, particularly boots). Although the nun and dominatrix may share a number of characteristics — notably an image of strictness and discipline — they are clearly at opposite ends of an erotic reality. Probably we are dealing with some sort of symbolic reversal.

Homosexual clothing conventions tend to vary considerably. There is no inherent "homosexual style" of dress, and what would be identifiable as such a style in one society at any given time may be interpreted differently in others. At present in the United States the use of a single earring or ear stud by men is thought of as a "gay" style. But it is also worn by many black heterosexual men in the United States and even by white heterosexuals who are into various counterculture movements (such as punk rock).

In some cultures, homosexuals are identified with transvestites and there is no terminological difference between them. But homosexuals are seldom transvestites in the western world. According to the evidence we now have, western transvestites tend to be more often heterosexual than homosexual.

The kinds of clothing conventions homosexuals have used in the western world vary. Green cravats were an ingroup sign among Parisian homosexuals during the nineteenth century. I have been told that in some sections of New York in the 1950s or 60s, the wearing of a green tie on Thursdays was taken as a sure sign that the person wearing it was homosexual. In *Sexual inversion*, Havelock Ellis seems to suggest some sort of psychological or even instinctual basis for preferring green, but this can hardly be taken seriously if only because he reports that at the end of the nineteenth century, male prostitutes in New York and Philadelphia almost invariably wore *red* ties, and it was assumed that any men wearing such ties were homosexual. Bullough notes that the Chicago Vice Commission in 1909 found that the numerous male homosexuals there (estimated at 10,000 or more) also made use of the red tie convention to identify each other. Bullough comments: "This leads to a question of whether homosexuals had adopted red as a color in Chicago or whether they wore red because Havelock Ellis told them it was the thing to do."

In the 1960s another set of conventions was developed among a subgroup of male homosexuals: the sadomasochists. These conventions distinguish sadists from masochists by having the former wear keys, chains, earrings, occasionally also handcuffs on the left; and the latter wear the same items on the right. What is curious is that even masochists have started wearing "hardwear" on their left because it is felt to be chic or at least more "manly" to be sadistic. The symbolism used is exceedingly interesting since it almost certainly represents a reversal of what is nearly a cultural universal. In most societies it is the *right* side that is regarded as the more masculine or prestigious and in

Yahgan Indians of Tierra del Fuego, *whose ancestors must have migrated the entire length of the Americas, wore no clothes in spite of the harsh climate.*

many languages the right hand is called the "male hand."

Clothing, then, can obviously be an integral part of various expressions of sexuality. It has probably exerted an influence on sexuality from its very inception at least 400,000 years ago. By 100,000 years ago, clothing of various sorts and a knowledge of sewing and tailoring existed among several peoples in different parts of the world. But the use of clothes must have been abandoned at least once (and possibly more than once). Ancestors of the American Indians migrated across the Bering Straits at least 20,000 years ago undoubtedly with clothing for protection against the cold. But they may have used clothing as the Eskimo and other contemporary Arctic peoples do, for warmth outdoors unaccompanied by a sense of shame at its absence indoors. When the Indians reached farther south, the indoor/outdoor distinction was dropped and with it clothes. The most southerly group of Indians, the Yahgan of Tierra del Fuego, did not reinvent this distinction. Although they lived in a severely cold climate, they went about naked. Darwin saw snow melt on the skins of Fuegians. He offered a large piece of cloth to one of the natives for protection, but instead of using it to cover

Traditional Islamic societies such as in Muscat require females to wear the veil from the onset of menstruation until old age.

his body the Fuegian tore it into strips and gave each of his fellow tribesmen a piece for decoration.

The earliest references to the veil occur in the ancient Mesopotamian *Epic of Gilgamesh*, parts of which date from as early as 2000. In it a goddess is described as "covered with a veil"; and night is metaphorically referred to as a "veiled bride" suggesting the custom found in many societies and still in use in the Judaeo-Christian tradition.

In modern times, the habitual wearing of a veil is primarily associated with the conservative Islamic world. In traditional Muslim society, veils are worn by girls after the onset of menstruation and up to old age. Women may uncover their faces only before other women, children, husbands or close male relatives. Not only the head and the lower part of the face but also most of the body should be covered. Some veils are so extensive that the whole body is hidden.

The Islamic custom developed out of pre-Islamic fashions in Arabia, when the use of veils was optional. The ancient Hebrews also used veils: covering the head with a large shawl such as is usually shown in traditional Christian representations of the Virgin Mary. St Paul's injunction to women to cover their heads when they pray or prophesy (I Corinthians 11:5–15) presumably refers to the use of such veils. The general Roman Catholic practice of requiring women to cover their heads in church (at least during Communion), was made optional only in the mid-1960s.

The use of veils for women was borrowed by upper-class north Indian Hindus in the period of Muslim domination. Occasionally groups on the fringe of Islamic cultures have adopted the veil and reinterpreted it in a totally non-Islamic way. A striking example of this comes from the African country of Chad, where some non-Muslim women have adopted veils though they still go bare-breasted.

A number of attempts have been made to get Muslim women to abandon the veil. Kemal Atatürk made use of the veil optional in Turkey after he took over the government in a coup following defeat in World War I. He discouraged the wearing of veils but realized that total abolition would be too scandalous for most Turks. On the other hand, in November 1923 the wearing of the traditional Turkish head covering for men, the fez, was totally forbidden as part of a general westernization policy.

In 1935, Riza Shah outlawed the veil in Iran. A little more than 10 years later, when he was forced into exile, the veil reappeared overnight. In 1978 to 1979, during demonstrations against the Shah, even profoundly westernized women readopted the veil as a symbolic rejection of the regime. On the other hand, when the postrevolutionary

The Tuareg of the Sahara *are one of the few societies in which men wear the veil, whereas women go unveiled.*

government insisted on the use of the veil, there was a massive protest demonstration by these same women.

The general Islamic justification for veiling women is that it shields men from their dangerous sexuality rather than because of some extraordinary sense of modesty. It has been noted by travelers that women brought up with a tradition of veiling when caught unawares by strange men tend to cover their faces even if otherwise naked.

In a very few societies, men normally wear veils, the best example being the Tuareg of the Sahara. The Tuareg probably originated in Tripolitania and were at one time Christian. They converted to Islam after the eleventh-century invasion of North Africa by Beduin Arabs, who displaced them and forced them into the desert. The remarkable thing is that unlike other Muslim groups, women do not go veiled. It is not clear why the men do so instead. In any event, the male veil (or mouth muffler, *tagilmust*) has become symbolic of social distance between men and is not even removed while eating; special spoons with long curved handles that can go under the veils are used. The greater the social distance, the higher up his nose a man's veil will go.

Men sometimes wear veils for special reasons, very often religious or magical in nature. In the Bible, Moses and Elias are both described as veiling their faces in the presence of God (Exodus 3:6; I Kings 19:13), and Moses was also believed to have covered himself with a veil when he came down from Mount Sinai bearing the Ten Commandments. This is surely similar to customs found in certain traditional kingdoms of black Africa whereby the king, regarded as divine, is virtually isolated and concealed by curtains because his glance is considered dangerous. According to Westermarck, in Arabia handsome men used to veil their faces against the evil eye, especially in large gatherings of people. Male transvestites have frequently adopted the use of the veil in Muslim countries.

The wearing of masks is similar although a different part of the face may be covered. In western Europe, the custom is said to have been introduced by Venetian courtesans and is recorded as early as 1295. Samuel Pepys notes that in the England of his day (1664) "ladies hide their whole faces."

In the 17th century fashionable Englishwomen sometimes wore masks, a custom introduced into Western Europe in 1295.

The penis sheath, the codpiece and foreskin tying

In some societies, men wear no clothing other than penis sheaths or other kinds of coverings for the penis variously called phallocrypts or penis wrappers. These seem almost never to be used for contraception and are generally removed both for urinating and during copulation.

Phallocrypts are of particular interest because on the one hand their users almost always identify modesty with covering the head, or glans, of the penis, but on the other hand, these devices are often so large and so elaborate that they must surely draw attention to the genitals rather than hide them as the term phallocrypt (penis-hider) suggests. In the New Hebrides, for example, the custom was for a man to go naked except for wrapping his penis in many yards of calico, winding and folding it until a bundle 18 to 24 inches (45-60 cm) long and two inches (5 cm) or more in diameter was formed; it was then decorated with flowers. The testicles were left naked. Gourd penis sheaths up to two feet (60 cm) in length are reported from a number of areas; they were sometimes decorated with bird feathers, beaks, animal fur or tails and attached to the body at an angle suggesting a gigantic erection.

A number of theories accounting for the various fashions of penis confinement have been given: for example, they might indicate that men are sexually available in those societies where women are the sexual "consumers," as in

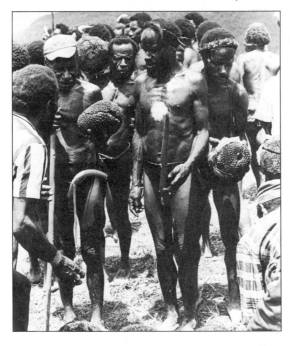

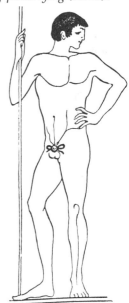

The ancient Greek custom of penis tying (below).

some places in New Guinea where fears of menstrual pollution inhibit male sexuality (in accordance with Bick's theory mentioned earlier); they might involve aggressive display much like that found among baboons and other primates who are sitting guard over the group territory (a theory proposed by Wickler in 1966); they might be concerned with "status sex" and the greater the angle of the pseudo-erection displayed the more dominant and aggressive are the people in question (a theory proposed by Desmond Morris in 1969 and derived from Wickler's views);

Elaborate penis sheaths are worn (left) in many societies in Vanuatu (the New Hebrides).

The medieval codpiece, invented in the late 14th century, was discarded as indecent some 200 years later.

or there might be some sort of positive correlation between circumcision or other genital mutilations and the use of penis sheaths.

None of these theories receives total support from the cross-cultural data. Native explanations tend to be practical and neither sexual nor aggressive (although the real reasons for the fashion may be repressed). Explanations given are, for example, that penis sheaths are protection against insects or thorny bushes or that they prevent fish from biting off the penis while a person is wading. These explanations are not particularly compelling if only because an equally vulnerable area of the body — the testicles — is exposed and in many instances the construction of the penis sheath offers very little protection.

The essence of the function of the penis sheath is covering the glans, and for this reason it has been likened to foreskin tying found in such diverse cultures as those of the Amazonian Indians, Marquesans and ancient Greeks.

Another fashion penis sheaths have been compared with is the European codpiece, the origins of which are obscure, but which was first invented in the late fourteenth century. This fashion continued until the late sixteenth century, when it fell out of style and was considered indecent. It survived in some rural areas until the seventeenth century. Codpieces started out as a means of ensuring decorum when jerkin and doublet became shorter and hose tighter. Later on they became a matter of display and approached the spectacular qualities of some penis sheaths, being stiffened, padded, decorated with embroidery or bows and so large that they were used as pockets or purses (it has been said that men could hide oranges or spoons in them). In design they often resembled an erect penis, but there was considerable local variation.

Penis sheaths have been made in a variety of materials, even in the same community. In Vanuatu (the New Hebrides), for example, the penis might be wrapped in grass, tapa (bark cloth) or cotton cloth; or placed in a horn or within a bamboo sheath. Leaves, grass, shells, gourds, wool, ivory, nuts, horns, leather and basketry have been common materials. A recent Zulu style found in South Africa makes use of aluminum for glans cups. In various parts of New Guinea the following recent materials have been utilized in addition to traditional ones: toothpaste containers, Kodak film containers, opened sardine cans. With the onslaught of western styles, penis sheaths and foreskin tying are no longer obvious in many areas because of the adoption of trousers. But, nevertheless, it seems that many peoples still wear them under their western clothes.

Nine ✥ MARRIAGE AND INCEST

Since marriage of some sort is the setting for much (probably most) sexual behavior throughout the world, it is important to realize the great variety of forms marriage has taken.

S everal kinds of marriage may be recognized within a single society. An extremely complex situation occurs among the Dahomey of Benin in West Africa. They permit 13 different kinds of marriage each depending on a different economic arrangement. In ancient Rome, at least two types of marriage were distinguished: free marriage, in which the wife and her property did not come under the power of her husband; and marriage with *manus* (literally "hand," referring to the hand of the husband), in which the woman's status was changed so that she was legally the equivalent of her husband's child and was adopted into his family.

But there is no need to go so far afield. In the contemporary western world, there is traditional monogamous marriage defined either by a religious or civil ceremony (or both) as well as common-law cohabitation. Although the living arrrangements may be identical, money interests and the legitimacy of children are different in the two situations. The much publicized legal battle in 1979 between the American movie star Lee Marvin and a woman he had lived with for several years but never married, illustrates the difference well. In spite of the social acceptability of their relationship (at least in the circles they moved in), legally she was not entitled to alimony (the money settlement she did get was facetiously termed "palimony"). In some circles even homosexual unions are sometimes referred to as marriages. This is not legally the case, though various proposals have been made for the legal recognition of such unions.

In some societies it is the custom to arrange marriages between living people and the dead. The best known example of this is contemporary American Mormons, who believe that being married is a necessary condition for being saved and going to heaven, and that dead unbelievers can be saved by posthumous marriages with Mormons. Among traditional Chinese groups, if a couple betrothed as children both die, they are married anyway in a kind of heavenly marriage, in part to placate their ghosts.

All of these ritual joinings and others like them have been called pseudomarriages. But even if we do not consider them in defining marriage cross-culturally there are other problems. The definition given by a basic reference book *Notes and queries in anthropology* (1951), put out by the Royal Anthropological Institute, is useful in a rough and ready way, but even the following definition is too specific to apply in all societies:

Incest depicted: a 16th-century German woodcut.

Marriage takes many different forms around the world. Among the North American Kwakiutl, in addition to the usual marriage between a man and a woman, a man could also "marry" the arm or leg of the chief, if the chief's son was not available.

Lee Marvin, American movie star who became embroiled in a law suit defining his legal obligations to the woman he lived with for many years but never married.

Marriage is a union between a man and a woman such that the children born to the woman are recognized as legitimate offspring of both partners.

If we are concerned that marriage (and with it its minimal domestic realization — the nuclear family) should be a universal category, then this definition will not do.

The classic counterexample dealing with the first part of the definition ("a union between a man and a woman") is found among the Naayar of India. Before she began to menstruate, a Naayar girl is supposed to go through a four-day ceremony that links her to a man who has been described as a ritual husband. A special pendant is tied around her neck indicating that, in a sense, she is married. But this does not mean that she is going to settle down and form a family with her "husband." On the contrary, it means that she is now free to have as many lovers or "visiting husbands" as she likes. These men come to her room in the great house where she lives with her mother's family. Her lovers do not live with her, they merely spend the night. Any children born after the marriage ceremony are legitimate, but if the woman has a baby before the marriage she is punished. In short, the ritual husband is totally peripheral to her family unit, though essential for legitimizing children.

An interesting relationship exists between the Naayar and the Nambuutiri Braahmans, who belong to a higher caste. Among the Nambuutiri Braahmans, only the eldest son is allowed to marry and raise a family. His younger brothers instead arrange alliances with Naayar women. For the Braahmans such alliances do not count as legal marriages and the resulting children are not considered legitimate. For the Naayars, however, they are a source of prestige and the offspring are legitimate.

Because of the Naayar, Kathleen Gough has proposed a definition of marriage that is considerably more general than the one quoted earlier from *Notes and queries*. But her definition also emphasizes the notion of legitimacy, the second part of the *Notes and queries* definition. However, a rule of legitimacy is also not a cultural universal.

The Caribbean is a case in point. This is an area of the world where the rule of legitimacy is lacking. An unusually high percentage of children are here born to unmarried women: between 53 and 56 percent of the births are "illegitimate" in Guatemala, Jamaica and Trinidad; 67 percent in Martinique. Leyburn maintains that "there is less marriage in Haiti than anywhere else in the world." It is true that upper-class groups in these areas follow the western rule of legitimacy, but the other groups do not. There is no stigma in being illegitimate. The people who are not upper class and who do marry — they sometimes do this when their children are grown up — do not do so to legitimize their children, but to hold a large party (*fête*), thereby meeting their social obligations and expressing group solidarity. To hold such a *fête* even after one's children have grown up is prestigious among these groups. To get married in a church at any time without a *fête* is deviant and despised. Nevertheless, people may get married for different reasons; certain jobs such as school teacher, for example, are open only to married parents.

A contemporary Mormon polygamous family, composed of one husband and several wives and their children. The official position of the Mormon Church no longer advocates polygamy in any practical sense, but sees it as a spiritual ideal.

The Naayar of India and many groups in the Caribbean are examples that suggest that marriage and the nuclear family are not human universals.

Clearly there are many problems in getting a cross-cultural definition of marriage. I shall not belabor the point further but use the term "marry" in the following pages in an informal and practical way.

In western society, the only form of marriage legally recognized is that between one man and one woman at a time: monogamy. The great majority of people in the history of mankind have lived in monogamous marriages and the great majority of people in the world today are monogamous. The preferred form of marriage, however, in most societies is, and has been, a kind of polygamy in which a man is married to several women at one time, technically known as polygyny. Nearly half (44 percent) of all the societies in Murdock's *Ethnographic atlas* — a compilation of information on 862 cultures throughout the world — regard polygamy as the norm, and 39 percent permit it along with monogamy. Only 16 percent insist on monogamy. (The remainder have other arrangements.)

Furthermore, even though monogamy is the reality (but not the ideal) for most people, an enormous number of them have more than one spouse in a lifetime. Liberalization of divorce in the West has resulted in multiple marriages, often called serial monogamy. According to the *Guinness book of records* (1979), the greatest number of such serially monogamous marriages is 20, entered into by Mr Glynn de Moss Wolfe, an American. Serial monogamy is also reported

Polygamy in a West African society: a Nigerian musician and his wives.

for other monogamous groups such as the Hopi Indians and the Siwans of Egypt.

Having more than one wife at a time is generally considered shocking and immoral in the West. In most parts of the world, however, it is a sign of being successful, rich, even powerful; such a man might well be considered a good match and accumulate still more wives. Usually there is a ranking system among the co-wives so that their status is reasonably defined. To offset favoritism, traditional polygamists normally institutionalize some form of rotation system so that a man must spend an equal amount of time with each wife. In spite of these safeguards and considerations, much ill will may exist between co-wives. In Hausa, the very term for co-wife is *kíishiyáa*, which means "partner in jealousy." Nevertheless, Christian missionaries who try to break up polygamous families have reported that the women object most to the imposition of monogamy.

All the men in a society cannot have many wives only because the sex ratios are fairly equal: one does not find normal populations with two or three times as many women as men. The number of women available depends in part on the absolute number of wives permitted. In some the number is enormous — at least for kings and noblemen. King Solomon is described in the Bible as having 700 wives and 300 concubines. A chief of the Bakuba and Bakete tribes in Zaire, called Lukengu, had 800 wives according to the *Guinness book of records* (1964). But the all-time record seems to be the 3,000 wives of one of the Monomotapa kings in what is now Zimbabwe.

In some societies, such as that of the Tiwi of Australia or the Zande of central Africa, the older, richer men take up all the marriageable women of whatever age and younger men must delay marriage until their 30s and 40s or until they "inherit" their fathers' wives (all except their own biological mother). A kind of widow inheritance is known from the Bible: a widow was supposed to marry one of her dead husband's brothers. This custom is found in a number of societies throughout the world.

For a woman to marry a number of men at the same time — a form of polygamy known as polyandry — is very rare: only four societies in the *Ethnographic atlas* permit polyandry. Societies permitting polygamy are roughly 100 times that number. This makes sense in light of an interpretation of marriage offered by Claude Lévi-Strauss, that it is the "gift" of women exchanged between men. He formulates the reality of the situation thus: "Men exchange women; women never exchange men." Marvin Harris adds that sex (through such marital gifts) is used in most societies as a reward for male bravery: "No battle-hardened headhunter or scalp-taker is going to settle down to connubial bliss in the company of four or five of his boon companions under the tutelage of a single woman . . ."

True polyandry involving a stable household where a

For a man to have more than one wife was the Old Testament norm and is the ideal, if not the norm, in most societies in the world.

For a woman to have more than one husband is unusual and condemned in most societies. Such a marital setup is never the mirror image of a man with many wives.

A Toda woman from southern India may have several husbands.

woman's husbands all share the same residence is unusual and found mainly in the Himalayas. Such households almost always involve a number of brothers who share a wife. One of the major advantages of such a system is that it prevents the breaking up of family wealth or property.

All forms of polyandry are exceedingly rare at present and it seems likely that it was always so. Consequently nearly all anthropologists reject a suggestion by J. F. McLennan, a nineteenth-century ethnologist, that polyandry was the normal form of marriage at one stage in the development of human social organization.

In the African forms of polyandry (found in a limited number of groups in Nigeria), the husbands do not live together. They are not brothers and the wife circulates from one household to another. Furthermore, both polyandry and polygamy occur, so that some men have several wives living with them in the same household — unlike the women, who never have several husbands living with them.

A 'her variety of polyandry characterizes the preferred and ...ost common form of marriage among the Pahaarii of northern India. Their custom requires a very high bride-price, a gift given by the groom's family to the bride's family. Because of this great expense, brothers normally pool resources and acquire a wife in common. Later, when they can afford other wives, they will again acquire them in common. This is not really polyandry but what is called group marriage (less commonly, polygynandry). The Pahaarii are apparently the only society in the world in which group marriage is the cultural norm.

An even more extreme form of group marriage, known as complex marriage, was practiced for a short time by the Oneida community, a utopian Christian religious group founded by John Humphrey Noyes in Putnam, Vermont, in 1841. The group moved to Oneida, New York, in 1847. In this society every man was the husband of every woman and every woman the wife of every man. This aspect of the society evoked considerable hostility from the surrounding communities. In 1879, Noyes recommended that the complex marriage system should be abandoned.

In almost all societies — whatever form of marriage is permitted — a marriage can be ended by divorce. The traditional western Christian view that marriage is indissoluble is practically unique, Hinduism being the only other important tradition to take the same position. Hindus have even frowned on the remarriage of widows. Until the practice was outlawed by the British in 1829, the prestigious way for a widow to mourn for her husband was to burn herself to death on his funeral pyre, a custom called *satii*.

In some groups, such as the ancient Scythians (as reported by Herodotus) or the Zande of modern times, some of the wives or concubines of a king are killed at his death and buried with him. This custom is rare cross-culturally. In 1971, a mass grave was found in Yugoslavia dating about 1800 BC. In it, the body of a man (presumably a chief) was surrounded by the bodies of 15 women who were believed to be his harem.

Satii (or suttee): the custom that required a Hindu widow to burn herself to death on her husband's funeral pyre.

The Kubeo of South America require a boy to copulate with his mother to mark the beginning of his official sex life. This is the only instance in the world that I have heard of, of compulsory mother–son incest. Marriage between them is forbidden, however.

Among the Tutsi (or Watusi) of East Africa, a cure for the impotence that a bridegroom may experience on his wedding night requires that he copulates with his mother.

These are the only well-attested rules for all the cultures of the world promoting mother–son matings. A number of dubious or unreliable reports suggest that even mother–son marriages are possible in some societies, but they cannot be taken seriously.

A tabu on mother–son marriage can safely be cited as a cultural universal. Moreover, any form of approved, institutionalized incest is decidedly rare, and more commonly incest tabus are extended beyond the nuclear family to larger kinship groups.

The great social and cultural importance of incest regulations has not escaped anthropologists and other social scientists. The pioneer thinkers Sigmund Freud, Lewis Henry Morgan and Claude Lévi-Strauss, approaching the subjects from totally different perspectives, suggest that human social organization as we know it today began with the conscious institution of incest tabus. In the Freudian

Cleopatra, the descendant of generations of brother–sister marriage, also married her brother.

model, one of the prices one has to pay for being civilized, one of the prime discontents of civilization, is the suppression of the satisfaction of incestuous urges. But Freud was partially wrong: this is not restricted to civilized man. Even the otherwise promiscuous chimpanzee would be given a good slap by his mother if he attempted to copulate with her. Mother–son matings have rarely, if ever, been reported by field observers of any of the primates. Nature has its discontents, too.

Any examples of institutionalized incest have occasioned great interest. The most common exceptions to universal tabus on incest involve brother–sister marriage practiced by the royal families of ancient Egypt, Hawaii and the Inca, among others. Cleopatra is the classic example: she was simultaneously her husband's sister as well as his wife. Unfortunately for her young husband-brother, Cleopatra had him murdered when he was 15 in order to pursue some nonincestuous unions with Julius Caesar and Mark Antony: politics rather than a horror of incest seems to have been her primary motivation.

Half-sibling, occasionally also full-sibling, marriage was legal and fairly common in the ancient Near East and was found among the ancient Persians (at least among the upper classes) and probably the ancient Hebrews at one point. The ancient Greeks also permitted it, though Roman law forbade it altogether. The Lakher of southeast Asia permit the son and daughter of one mother but two different fathers to marry. Elsewhere, when half-sibling marriages are permitted, this would most likely be forbidden.

In Bali, both full- and half-sibling incest is forbidden with one interesting exception. It is assumed that the twin brother and sister have already been intimate in the womb. With an appropriate ceremony of purification, they are allowed to marry each other when they grow up. The Aymará of South America also permit twins to marry. The Marshallese of the Pacific believe that twins have indeed committed incest in their mother's womb, but unlike the Balinese, feel they must therefore kill at least the boy.

The Lamet of southeast Asia permit brother–sister marriage if the couple has been brought up in different households: they are then not viewed as members of the same sociological family. Similarly, the Nuer of East Africa feel that incest has not occurred if the relationship is not known (unlike the ancient Greeks, as seen in *Oedipus rex*). Interestingly, the same argument applies in a recent and as yet unresolved legal proceeding in Sweden. A government official discovered by accident that a man and woman who were married were brother and sister, and therefore under Swedish law the marriage was null and void. When the couple was confronted with the matter, it turned out that they did not know they were related because they had been separated as children and had lost contact with one another. The couple decided to challenge the law. Their argument is that even though they are biologically brother and sister, sociologically they are not, and therefore they should not be forced to separate.

Father–daughter incest is occasionally tolerated or institutionalized but doing so is very rare, much more so than brother–sister unions. (As a matter of fact, however, father–daughter incest is the most common form of incest in the modern western world.) The Persian emperor Artaxerxes was said by Plutarch to have married his own daughter, and the Egyptian pharaoh Amenhotep III is known to have married at least one daughter: his son Akhenaten several. The Roman situation is unambiguous. Here nuclear family incest was totally forbidden, but a few royal instances that went unpunished existed; Caligula committed incest with his three sisters, and even married one, Drusilla. Another sister, Agrippina, was rumored to have had sex with her son also, the emperor Nero. This was not something traditionally permitted to the royal family in Roman eyes.

The rules about marriage between cousins vary considerably throughout the world, and often involve distinctions for which there are no words in English or most European vocabularies.

More widespread and of great importance in anthropological theorizing are restrictions on cousin marriages. The majority of societies in the world today prohibit marriage to any kind of cousin. In Murdock's *Ethnographic atlas* a wide-ranging sample of 762 cultures throughout the world, about two-thirds forbid cousin marriage.

In the Judaeo-Christian tradition, considerable variation has occurred with regard to the question of cousin marriage. The Bible does not prohibit cousin marriage of any kind, and Jews have allowed it throughout their history. But under Pope Gregory "the Great" (AD 590–604) marriage between third cousins was forbidden. A little more than a century later, Pope Gregory III (AD 731) forbade marriage even between sixth cousins.

These fairly extreme rules were changed by Innocent III in the fourth Lateran Council in 1215, when marriage beyond third cousins was permitted. Modern Roman Catholic marriage laws date from the Council of Trent (1563): second cousin marriage is permitted, and sometimes even first cousin marriage (but special permission is required).

The living law can change. Two interesting examples are known from outside Christendom. The emperor Claudius petitioned the Roman senate to change the incest laws so that he might marry his niece, Agrippina, who has been mentioned before as being involved in other incestuous unions. The senate made the required change, but according to Suetonius, a contemporary of Claudius', there was no great rush by uncles and nieces to get married.

The second historically attested change occurred because the prophet Muhammad received a special revelation permitting him to marry Zaynab, the wife of his adopted son, Zayd. Custom prohibited marriage between a man and his son's wife, and up until that point an adopted son counted as a blood son. From then on inheritance laws were to differentiate between adoptive and blood relatives.

To return to the question of cousin marriage. The marriage laws of the western world take into account only such distinctions as first and second cousin; but other societies observe different ones. For example, 20 percent of the *Ethnographic atlas* sample prohibit marriage between a man and his father's brother's daughter and his mother's sister's daughter but permit it between a man and his mother's brother's daughter. A few societies are even more selective and insist on only one kind of cousin as a possible spouse. Less than four percent (32 out of 762) of the *Ethnographic atlas* samples permit and encourage marriage between a man and his mother's brother's daughter. Less than one percent (4 out of this 762) require marriage between a man and his father's brother's daughter.

But the question remains: why should any rules about incest exist at all? This is a perennial topic among anthropologists and a variety of answers have been proposed. For the most part, anthropologists (but not sociobiologists) reject the idea that incestuous matings have been tabued because the children of such matings may be deformed, insane, sterile or markedly unhealthy in other ways. Such results are not inevitable; primitive peoples have no knowledge of genetics and explain misfortunes in terms of witchcraft or similar supernatural events; and the marriage laws of a society may exclude some close relatives but permit others equally close (as we have just seen with cousins).

Theories more popular with anthropologists to account for incest rules have played up a number of different, quite diverse considerations. For example, incest rules force people to get ties with other families that are important socially, economically and politically (a view championed by Edward Burnett Tylor, the first professor of anthropology at Oxford and in the world, whose position can be summed up in his motto "marry out or be killed off"). Or, tolerating incest would create jealousy in the family and disastrous role confusion (associated with Bronislaw Malinowski; summed up in the words of an American song from the 1940s, "I'm my own grandpa"). Or, early childhood association kills off sexual interest (the "familiarity breeds contempt" theory, associated with Edward Westermarck and directly at variance with Freudian notions). Or, modern incest tabus simply spell out what in prehistoric times was improbable for a number of factors including longevity, e.g. people then

Some societies do not count a union as incestuous unless the couple know they are related. Oedipus was unlucky not to be born into such a society.

Sharing milk (in some sense) is considered by certain societies to be just as much a ban to marriage as sharing blood.

seldom lived beyond 30, making parent–child marriage unlikely (a theory proposed by Mariam K. Slater, partially
summed up by the sentiment "the old ways are best").

Traditional approaches to incest are at least equally varied
in non-western societies. The !Kung of southern Africa give
no explanation for such tabus at all: it is simply so horrible
they refuse to theorize about it: "Only dogs do that — not
men," they say. And, "it would be dangerous, like going up
to a lion." The Yapese of Oceania also think incest is something animals do, not human beings. But they regard it as
impractical rather than horrible, and betray no sense of deep
revulsion. However, they believe that a woman who has
committed incest can never bear children.

The Kágaba of South America think incest has no biological effects whatever, and will certainly not produce deformed or retarded children. The Comanche Indians seem to
lack an idea of incest altogether: they consider incest neither
a crime nor a sin, but impossible. The Tallensi of West Africa
condemn brother–sister incest intensely but find the idea of
mother–son incest incredible and ridiculous because a
grown man's mother is inevitably thought of as an unattractive old woman.

A cross-culturally common explanation for tabuing incest
assumed that kinsmen share the same blood, and that mixing
this blood together is harmful. Though scientifically untrue
(blood is not even involved in fertilization), this belief is still
held by many Westerners — including, to my surprise, many
of my own students. In some societies, other shared substances are believed to render individuals inappropriate as
mates, so that in addition to what we can call "blood" incest
(the usual kind), at least two other kinds exist.

(1) Milk incest: people who have drunk milk from the
same wet nurse may not marry. This tabu is found in the
Koran and is absolutely binding on all Muslims. (Malayan
Muslims get round the rule by a ritual pardoning.) Milk
incest may have been an ancient Mediterranean custom and
is still found among Eastern Orthodox Christians, southern
Italians and various Spanish groups. It may also have been
more general in all of Christendom. We still find expressions
like "milk brother" in French and German, although milk
incest is not recognized among them at present.

Another kind of milk incest occurs among certain groups
in the Transkei of South Africa: if a man drinks milk from the
cattle of another family line, he may not marry a woman of
that family.

(2) Name incest: a person may not marry someone who
has the same personal name as one of his parents or siblings
(a common surname is not in question here). This rule is
found to my knowledge only among the Bushmen of
southern Africa and Orthodox Jews.

*The !Kung Bushmen of the
Kalahari Desert do not
speculate about incest: it is too
horrible and dangerous.*

Other kinds of incest exist that are symbolic extensions of parent–child relations:

(3) Spiritual incest: among Roman Catholics and Eastern Orthodox Christians, godparents are thought of as spiritual parents. Consequently, it is tabu to marry one's godparent and in some groups even the children of godparents. In Latin America, the *compadrazgo* (godparenthood relationship) has been elaborated to an extent rare in Europe.

(4) Teacher–student incest: among the Balinese it is forbidden to marry the daughter of one's teacher; among the Vietnamese it is forbidden to marry his widow.

(5) Master–servant incest: among Albanians of Martanesh, a servant could be condemned to death for seducing the daughter of his master because in a sense his master was his "father" and he had committed incest.

(6) Midwife incest: among the Semang of southwest Asia, a man may not marry the midwife who assisted at his birth, nor may his father marry her. The Zande of Central Africa have a similar rule, but it apparently does not apply to the man's father.

The extension of incest tabus in these ways readily fits in with Tylor's model that it is impractical to marry into groups one already has ties with. But even so, I do not think this proves that incest tabus necessarily began because people realized the practical consequences of setting them up.

Premarital virginity According to Marco Polo, "no man [in Tibet] would ever on any account take a virgin to wife. For they say that a woman is worthless unless she has had the knowledge of men." He maintains that foreigners were besieged to sleep with un-

Virginity of the bride *(but not of the groom) is important in many societies. A Chinese woodcut illustrates the display of the blood-stained bedsheet.*

married girls and to give them some trinket as a sign that they had a lover. Although this description may be inaccurate or exaggerated, reports from contemporary societies suggest it could be true. Clearly, premarital virginity is not a universal value.

On the other hand, in many other societies there is a mania for virgins, and premarital virginity is highly prized, but almost always in the female only. Many societies have devised various tests for determining whether a bride is a virgin at her first wedding. In a sample of 141 societies, Broude and Greene found that 36 required brides to be virgins, and meted out severe punishments for those who failed virginity tests. On the other hand, an almost equal number of societies, 34, were found to approve of girls having premarital sex. An additional 29 societies tolerated premarital sexual behavior in girls if they were discreet. Broude and Greene offer no information about attitudes toward premarital sex on the part of males. The general impression one gets from the ethnographic literature is that males are usually expected to have had some sexual experience before marriage.

Almost everywhere, men are usually permitted to have sex before marriage, but attitudes about women doing so vary.

In the western world, controversies exist as to the value of virginity. Of course, some positions are merely repetitions of the traditional Judaeo-Christian moral code. But there are various arguments that have a more general significance. Some theorists have argued that cultural evolution is largely an outcome of diverting sexual energy into socially desirable goals. Havelock Ellis, for one, suggested that "it is impossible to say what finest elements in art, in morals, in civilization generally may not be rooted in an autocratic impulse . . . arising from the impeded spontaneous sexual energy of the organism and extending from simple physical processes to the highest psychic manifestations."

The Freudian theory of sublimation, which is perhaps the most important nonreligious argument for sexual abstentions of any kind, was first written in 1905 in *Three essays on the theory of sexuality*. Briefly, sublimation is the doctrine that psychosexual energy (libido) can be directed away from sexual gratification to nonsexual ends. Freud viewed the diversion and desexualization of such energy as one of the most important ways that civilization was achieved, the prime example mentioned as an instance of sublimation being artistic activity.

The authors of *Sexual behavior in the human male* considered the question in some detail. Kinsey, Pomeroy and Martin assumed that "if sublimation is a reality, it should be possible to find individuals whose erotic responses have been reduced or eliminated, *without nervous disturbance*, as a result of an expenditure of energy in utterly nonsexual activities."

What are the facts?

Two groups were considered by them, together totaling over 4,200 males who had either unusually low rates of sexual activity or were consciously trying to sublimate. Kinsey and his co-workers were unable to find any clear-cut cases of successful sublimation.

There is another line of argument. Since sublimation has been regarded as one of the great civilizing factors, if the theory makes any sense there should be some sort of cross-cultural confirmation of this.

The most ambitious attempt to get cross-cultural support for such a theory — not couched entirely in Freudian terms, however — is that by J. D. Unwin in his book *Sex and culture* (1943). This is a serious contribution to the subject, and one of the first cross-cultural anthropological studies on a truly massive scale designed to test any hypothesis.

Sexual restrictions may possibly produce, if not a higher level of culture, at least a greater degree of cultural complexity.

What Unwin specifically tries to establish is that the mental level of a culture is directly correlated with the number and severity of impediments that the society places in the way of sexual contacts.

An impartial examination of Unwin's data shows that a correlation of some sort exists between the classes of culture he sets up and the impediments to sexual contact. Unwin's study is based on an analysis of some 80 non-European societies, ranged on a cultural scale whereby the mental level of a society can be deduced.

Unwin believes that his data show that sexual restrictions produced a higher level of culture. He argues that a cultural advance must depend upon a factor that produces thought, reflection and social energy. The compulsory check of sexual impulses is that factor. He grants that continence may produce morbid symptoms in some individuals, but he insists that when sexual opportunity of a society is reduced almost to a minimum (particularly for women before marriage) the resulting social energy produces "great accomplishments in human endeavor" and "civilization." When the compulsory continence is of a less rigorous character, lesser energy is displayed, and lower level cultures result.

A later study by a professional anthropologist, G. P. Murdock, corroborates a good deal of what Unwin discovered. Murdock's study of 400 societies generally goes along with Unwin's finding that the stricter the rules for premarital sex behavior, the greater the degree of cultural complexity of a society. But Murdock gives a different explanation for this finding. For example, he says that in advanced societies practicing intensive agriculture, a high level of self-discipline and industriousness is expected: the young must spend a considerable amount of time acquiring needed skills and discipline and cannot be allowed to indulge themselves in unrestricted sexual freedom. In simpler hunting and gathering societies, the same rules do not apply. The

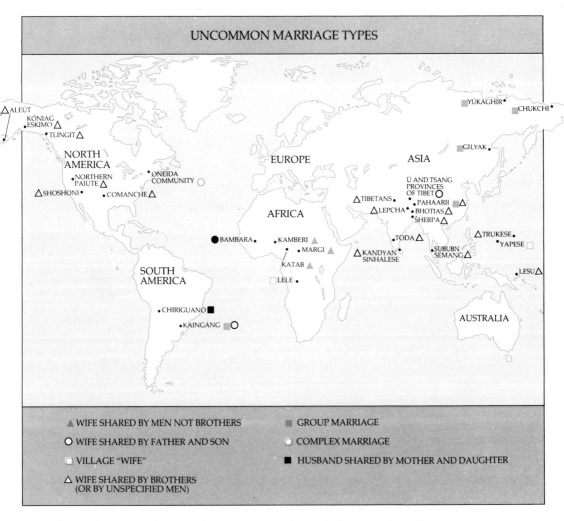

UNCOMMON MARRIAGE TYPES

ALEUT
KÓNIAG
ESKIMO
TLINGIT

NORTH
AMERICA

NORTHERN
PAIUTE
SHOSHONI
COMANCHE

ONEIDA
COMMUNITY

EUROPE

AFRICA

BAMBARA
KAMBERI
MARGI
KATAB
LELE

SOUTH
AMERICA

CHIRIGUANO
KAINGÁNG

YÚKAGHIR
CHUKCHI

GILYAK

ASIA

Ú AND TSANG
PROVINCES
OF TIBET
TIBETANS
LEPCHA
PAHAARII
BHOTIAS
SHERP'A

TODA
KANDYAN
SINHALESE
SUBUBN
SEMANG

TRUKESE
YAPESE

LESU

AUSTRALIA

▲ WIFE SHARED BY MEN NOT BROTHERS
O WIFE SHARED BY FATHER AND SON
▫ VILLAGE "WIFE"
△ WIFE SHARED BY BROTHERS
(OR BY UNSPECIFIED MEN)

▪ GROUP MARRIAGE
◉ COMPLEX MARRIAGE
■ HUSBAND SHARED BY MOTHER AND DAUGHTER

fewer the skills demanded, the fewer the sexual restrictions. But if this is so, how can we account for the spread of permissive standards in contemporary American society?

The answer Murdock suggests is not altogether compelling. He finds a relationship between permissiveness and the fact that a newly married couple establish their own place to live without reference to the families of either the bride or groom. In cultures where a bride must live with her husband's family, on the other hand, there is also a demand for virginity in the bride. When people know they can eventually escape from the control of their parents and kinsmen, they are more apt to establish permissive rules. This is precisely the case in contemporary America.

Murdock concludes his article with the observation that if a fully permissive code of premarital sexuality is achieved in the United States and elsewhere in the civilized world it would mean that there would be "a reversal of the long-term direction of cultural evolution, at least with respect to premarital sexual morality."

One of the problems in Unwin's and Murdock's discussion is that they talk about morality and codes of permissiveness as opposed to what people really do. But the

Map of uncommon marriage types.

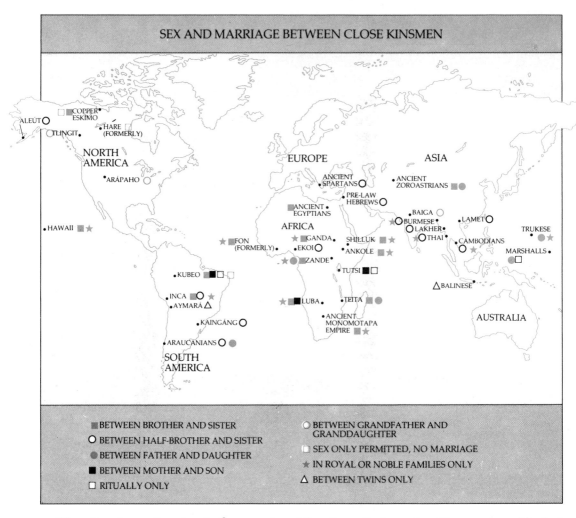

SEX AND MARRIAGE BETWEEN CLOSE KINSMEN

BETWEEN BROTHER AND SISTER
BETWEEN HALF-BROTHER AND SISTER
BETWEEN FATHER AND DAUGHTER
BETWEEN MOTHER AND SON
RITUALLY ONLY

BETWEEN GRANDFATHER AND GRANDDAUGHTER
SEX ONLY PERMITTED, NO MARRIAGE
IN ROYAL OR NOBLE FAMILIES ONLY
BETWEEN TWINS ONLY

***Map showing rules about
sex and marriage between close
relatives.***

theory of sublimation deals not with moral codes but behavior. There is no necessary correlation between the two. Murdock suggests — quite accurately, it seems to me — that American society in the 1940s and before would have to be characterized as having restrictive premarital sex norms, in contrast to the 1960s, when there was a tendency toward permissiveness. Nevertheless, some scholars maintain that behavior has remained relatively constant, although a greater freedom to talk openly about sex may generate a belief to the contrary. John L. Gagnon and William Simon, former senior research sociologists at the Kinsey Institute, state that "the evidence is that very little has changed in American sexual patterns over the past four decades." Whatever the truth of this assertion, we must emphasize again that what people say sexual behavior should be need not necessarily have anything to do with what the people themselves actually do. The Kinsey report was not controversial for nothing.

How then can we explain Unwin's and Murdock's findings? Perhaps there are factors that neither has considered.

Consider simply the factor of age of marriage. It is surely one thing to tabu premarital promiscuity if the average age of marriage is 15, quite another if it is 25. Westerners tend to forget that Biblical standards of premarital virginity presuppose very early marriage: about 13 for girls (as practiced among Orthodox Jews until quite recently). Christian tradition has the Virgin Mary becoming the Mother of God at 14 — and age was not the miraculous part of this event.

From a survey by Ludwik Krzywicki, it would seem that members of hunting and gathering societies tend to marry soon after puberty, at about 15. Note that it is these societies that are always listed as being among the most permissive, although the marriages are overwhelmingly monogamous. Moni Nag's latest cross-cultural survey of societies with relatively recent data tends to confirm a tendency toward early marriage for women (at 18 or younger) in most societies; of 48 societies in his sample, 37 had early marriage.

Why then strict rules about sex before marriage? Murdock's suggestion of the need for a greater concentration on acquisition of skills in more complex societies has a certain plausibility. Surely someone in constant pursuit of sex partners simply has not adequate time to learn many other things. This does not confirm the theory of sublimation, however, only the very obvious fact that one seldom can do two things at one time. It would be equally reprehensible, by the same token, for a youth to spend all his time reading and rereading *Bambi*.

What is more important with these tabus is their economic implications. They may simply boil down to attempts to ensure legitimate inheritance and succession. Because inheritable property and high social status are negligible in hunting and gathering groups, there would be little motivation at that level to develop elaborate rules for establishing such legitimacy, but there would be a great deal of interest at higher levels. Contemporary American society does not go against these economic interests: because of effective contraception, legitimate heirs can be guaranteed in spite of actual promiscuity.

The cultural differences in permissiveness and restrictiveness do not, as we have seen, provide a convincing case for sublimation. The question, however, is more profound than a cross-cultural test might suggest. What is needed is detailed information about the energy levels and cultural accomplishments of individuals. It is quite plausible to assume that high levels of cultural productivity could go along with comparably high levels of sexual performance, which the careers of artists such as Boccaccio and Fragonard might suggest. Certainly, the prodigious Bach, with his incredible musical output as well as 20 children, was not sublimating all the time. These are admittedly isolated examples. However, of the six most active males in the Kinsey sample — men with maximum orgasm frequencies

Early marriage in hunting and gathering societies is common, as with this Amazon Indian group.

Johann Sebastian Bach and some of his numerous offspring. He could not have been sublimating all the time.

during 30 continuous years, ranging from 10.6 to 33.1 weekly orgasms — two were physicians, one an educator, one a lawyer and one a scientific worker.

Societies vary to a certain extent with regard to which sexual behaviors are prohibited as well as in the severity of the punishments handed out. A striking example of this is rape. In western society at present even the most ardent liberalizers of the sex laws are opposed to rape and want it punished as a serious crime. The Model penal code sponsored by the American Law Institute proposes that all sexual acts performed in private by consenting adults be decriminalized, but retains rape as an offense — presumably not because of its sexual nature but because it involves violence and is nonconsensual. However, the Judaeo-Christian tradition nowhere singles out rape as a sin. It is forbidden in the Bible when committed against a betrothed or married woman. Even then the victim may have a hard time proving her case because if she was raped in a city she was expected to call for help and prevent it. This sort of reasoning was incorporated into the laws of Rome under the Christian emperor Constantine.

In two societies — the Marshallese and the Baiga — rape is reportedly the preferred form of sexual activity and goes totally unpunished. A number of societies similarly ignore rape altogether; these societies are fairly numerous and include the Copper Eskimo, Kaska, Mundurucú, Trumai, Navaho, Hadza, Lepcha, and Trobiand islanders.

In most societies, however, rape (particularly of a married woman) is one of the most serious sexual offenses. Death is regarded as the appropriate penalty for rape among some societies, severe punishment among others, and still others ridicule the rapist or impose a token punishment. The spectrum is fairly wide.

Attitudes about rape vary considerably throughout the world, from approval to total disapproval. The Bible does not single out rape as a sin but suggests true rape is impossible in a city.

Again, the same sort of variation is found with regard to male homosexual acts. In some societies they are universal and compulsory, as among the Étoro. Among the ancient Hebrews and Aztecs they were punishable by death.

The most frequently tabued and most severely punished sexual acts are incest, abduction and rape. The least frequently mentioned and most lightly punished infractions include premarital promiscuity and intercourse with the person one is betrothed to. Adultery (particularly by a woman) is generally a serious offense but seldom considered as serious as rape or incest. Punishment may typically include public ridicule, disgrace and divorce. However, in some societies people guilty of adultery may be killed along with their lovers. The Jívaro of South America permit a betrayed husband to kill or multilate the genitals of his adulterous wife and to slash her lover's scalp. A woman found guilty of adultery among the Vietnamese might formerly be thrown to a specially trained elephant, who in turn threw her into the air with his trunk and when she had landed, trampled her to death.

The more people a sexual infraction involves, the more severely it is punished. Solitary masturbation, for example, may be considered reprehensible but is seldom punished in any way but through ridicule. The suggestion in the Jewish tradition that death is appropriate for masturbation (being a total "waste of nature" and hence the most reprehensible of sexual crimes) is decidedly at variance with cross-cultural judgments. Generally, sexual acts involving a married person are more serious than other acts, perhaps because marriage in most societies is not only a union of two people but also of two kin groups. Thus, adultery is more serious than premarital promiscuity; rape of a married woman is more serious than rape of an unmarried girl.

The actual punishments used for a particular sexual offense may vary considerably from society to society. The Ganda of East Africa, for example, traditionally punish incest by drowning the offenders; the Vietnamese and Aztecs by strangulation. Among the Cayapa of Ecuador, anyone guilty of incest was formerly punished, say informants, by being suspended over a table covered with lighted candles and slowly roasted to death.

Rape occurs as a form of punishment in a number of societies for a woman's adultery. Among the Cheyenne, a man who discovered that his wife had committed adultery invited all the unmarried men in his military society (except his wife's relatives) to a feast on the prairie. This means that the woman is raped by each of these men in turn. A woman who survived being raped by 30 to 40 men had the unending burden of the disgrace. Gang rape as a means of social control is reported from several other societies.

Rembrandt's **Woman taken in adultery.** *The biblical punishment was stoning.*

Multilation of one sort or another is used by a number of groups as punishment for adultery. Fairly common throughout the world has been cutting off the nose of an adulterous wife. A Freudian explanation for this is tempting; since adultery in men is seldom punished and often expected, cutting off a woman's nose (a phallic symbol) can be seen as equivalent to castration. Nose-cutting was practiced by Plains Indians such as the Comanche and Blackfoot. Similar punishment was meted out in England in the time of King Canute, who ruled from 1017 to 1035: a woman caught in adultery was to have her nose cut off as well as both her ears. In twelfth-century Naples, adulterous women and procuresses had their noses slit (elsewhere in the Holy Roman Empire under Emperor Frederik Barbarossa, cutting off the nose was a punishment for whores). The cutting off of an adulteress's nose was recommended in ancient

Zande adulterer punished.

Mesopotamian legal codes; her lover could either be castrated or put to death. This same custom of nose amputation in ancient India prompted what may be the first known attempt at plastic surgery.

The Zande punish the wife's lover by very severe mutilations; the ears, upper lip, hands and penis — but not nose, interestingly — might all be cut off the man unlucky enough to be found out. If caught in the act both he and the woman could be killed. Among the Ashanti, adultery in a wife required compensation to the husband by the lover; but adultery involving the wife of a paramount chief required that she should undergo an excruciating, long-drawn-out surgical death.

Among some Zulu groups, adultery could be punished with death, but flogging the offenders with thorny bushes also occurred, and the adulterous wife was sometimes punished by having cacti thrust into her vagina. The Igbo punished adultery by a chief's wife by forcing her to copulate publicly with her lover and hammering a stake some five feet long through his back until it came out through her body.

Burning an adulterous wife to death seems to have occurred at some time among the ancient Egyptians. Both the Hebrews and Aztecs killed such a woman by stoning. According to the Koran, a woman convicted of adultery or fornication should be killed by being locked inside a room until she dies (the severity of this sentence mitigated by the necessity of four witnesses to an adulterous act before a verdict is reached). In point of fact, stoning has been the traditional punishment in Muslim countries.

Among the ancient Romans, seducers of married women were occasionally castrated. Other more unusual punishments have also been recorded. According to Juvenal and Catullus, the lover of a married woman who was caught could get the hair on his buttocks burnt off with red-hot ashes, or the head of a certain fish covered with spines shoved up his anus. The Emperor Aurelian punished one of his soldiers for having seduced his innkeeper's wife with a punishment considered so terrible and unprecedented that the whole Roman army was said to be seized with fear: the guilty soldier was tied by his feet to the tops of two trees that had been bent over; suddenly, the trees were let go so that he was literally snapped apart.

Punishments for sexual crimes have grown increasingly less severe in the West. Nevertheless there are certain broad categories of acts that are universally tabu and generally punished with severe penalties: incest and acts involving violence and a lack of consent among the parties concerned.

Ten ✥ PROSTITUTION

*Prostitution is today regarded as,
at best, a necessary evil in most societies.
Yet it may have originated as a
sacred rite.*

A medieval brothel

The history of "the oldest profession" is not well documented. Marx and Engels argued that prostitution — along with adultery and cuckoldry — was invented when matriarchal societies were overthrown by patriarchy. There are problems with this view.

In any event, prostitution is known to have been widespread and generally accepted in the ancient Near East. The Babylonian Code of Hammurabi from about 1700 BC contains a reference to "beer houses" kept by women. These beer houses may have been brothels; at any rate, they were not respectable. According to this code women dedicated to the worship of a god were to be killed if they even entered such a place for a drink. Otherwise there was legal indifference to prostitution.

The same attitude was true of the ancient Hebrews. For the most part, no moral judgment of any kind is passed on the secular prostitutes mentioned in the Old Testament. The story of the two harlots seeking a judgment from King Solomon concerning the custody of a child indicates, if nothing else, that they were allowed access to the king like other subjects. Nor do the clients of prostitutes come under censure in biblical stories. The Book of Judges (16:1) describes Samson's visit to the whore in Gaza without any reprimand even though Samson had the status of Nazirite: a man dedicated to God from the womb.

On the other hand, although tolerated, prostitution was not respectable. The Mosaic code forbade priests from marrying harlots and the daughters of priests from becoming harlots (Leviticus 21:7–9) — the penalty for the latter was death by burning. But even with the coming of Christianity and its often antisexual biases, toleration of a sort persisted. Augustine maintained: "Suppress prostitution and capricious lusts will overthrow society."

Babylonian prostitution is recorded in the Code of Hammurabi, 1700 BC.

Usually people look for two things before they speak of prostitution. First, there must be a payment (normally immediate) of money or valuable materials in return for sexual services. Second, sexual services must be made available to individuals in a relatively indiscriminate way.

In some situations, even using both criteria, there are borderline areas. In pre-Islamic Arabia and today among some Muslims, particularly Shi'ites (who are found predominantly in Iran), there is a kind of temporary marriage. Most but not all Muslim moralists have denounced it as simple prostitution. The "marriage" is contracted for a limited time, often only for a night, sometimes with a minimal "dowry" and no legal claims by the woman after the contract expires. But children of such unions are regarded as legitimate.

It might very well be that within a particular culture there is simply no notion of prostitution at all. This is true of the Trobriand islanders. Among them, men constantly have to give small presents to the women they sleep with. Someone from another culture might, therefore (but unjustifiably), conclude that prostitution is universal among the Trobrianders. Certain early travelers seem to have made comparable judgments on cultures they did not understand well. There are, however, many borderline cases of prostitution, as in some forms of sex hospitality.

Temporary marriage, practiced in some Muslim societies, is denounced as disguised prostitution by orthodox Muslims.

It has been said that prostitution was introduced to many parts of the world by European travelers, colonialists and military men or that it had been brought about by a breakdown of traditional morality which was due to the coming of the Europeans. The classic example of European influence is that of Polynesia. Tahiti is a case in point. In 1767, Captain Samuel Wallis witnessed women "prostituting" themselves to sailors for the price of an iron nail. The length of the nail was in proportion to the beauty and charm of the woman.

In the New World before the coming of European settlers, prostitution is sometimes said to have been practiced among the high cultures of the Aztecs, Maya and Inca. Francisco Guerra says that male homosexual prostitution also occurred in some areas of Central America. Again we do not know what the natives thought.

In native North America the picture is even less clear, although some early accounts report the existence of prostitution. Captain John Smith in 1624, for example, wrote that among the Indians (coastal Algonkians) "they have harlots and honest women; the harlots never marry, or else are widows." Other early information about the North American situation from white commentators suggests extensive prostitution in the contacts between colonists and Indians, but not necessarily because of a native tradition of prostitution. Prostitution may, however, have existed among the Kwakiútl, Nootka, Bororó, and Araucanians.

In Black Africa, prostitution would seem for the most part to result from social upheavals that occurred after contacts with the Europeans. The Chaga of Tanzania have been cited as a classic example of a society with no tradition of prostitution that has developed a complete European model of it, including the town brothel. Among certain Central and West African kingdoms, however, prostitution may be considerably older and, if not native, then perhaps derived from North African (Arabic) models. The Banyoro of Uganda were described by all early European travelers as having an organized corps of about 2,000 prostitutes under the control of the king. They were regarded as his servants but plied their trade quite openly in the market places of large towns.

Among the Hausa of West Africa (predominantly northern Nigeria and parts of Niger), prostitution is quite formalized. A head prostitute is officially recognized and installed in a public ceremony in which she receives a turban from the local chiefs as a symbol of her office. Hausa prostitutes not only form a deviant subgroup within the society because they are prostitutes, they are also the devotees of a pagan possession cult known as *bòoríi*, even though they are nominally Muslim. In the Hausa kingdom of Abuja, they are joined in support of this cult by yet another group of powerful and relatively independent women: the women of the royal family.

Prostitution is believed to have been introduced by Europeans into some parts of the world, such as Polynesia. But it has also developed independently in many societies.

North African prostitution represents a continuation of ancient Near Eastern patterns with local variations. The extent to which prostitution was practiced seems to have been extraordinarily high, if we are to believe the accounts of early commentators. An estimate of the number of prostitutes in Algiers in 1830 has been made at 3,000 out of a total population of about 30,000 — that is one out of every five women (presuming that there were about 15,000 women).

Before the French occupation, most Algerian prostitutes were under the control of *mezouars*, officials given the right by government to collect taxes from prostitutes. The *mezouars* were also empowered to force prostitutes to work and functioned virtually as pimps. One of the *mezouars'* duties was to hold a prostitutes' festival once every two years to which all the men of Algiers were invited.

In rural Algeria, prostitution was of a somewhat different type since the girls stopped once they had accumulated enough money to make up their dowry. Similar dowry prostitution has been reported from ancient Armenia, Cyprus and Etruscan Italy. A study by Florence Goldhammer of contemporary prostitution on Aruba, an island in the Caribbean, suggests the same sort of pattern.

In Muslim Egypt, prostitution was traditionally associated with entertainers, particularly dancers known as *ghawaazii*. They married mainly within their own distinctive ethnic group, which was possibly allied to the gipsies. Like the gipsies the men were often blacksmiths or tinkers. They acted as procurers for their wives and as their musical accompanists. Figures given by Lane suggest that one out of every 25 people in Egypt were *ghawaazii* in the 1830s. They enjoyed social acceptance if not respectability and some of them who accompanied pilgrims to Mecca were permitted to count their trip as a pilgrimage and take the much coveted title of *haajii*. In June 1834, the Egyptian government outlawed female dancing in public and prostitution.

North African dancer–prostitutes (above) sometimes discontinued their trade once they had accumulated enough money for a dowry. Egyptian ghawaazii *dancers (above right) formed a distinctive ethnic group.*

The latent disapproval of prostitution found in Islamic and Christian societies presents a marked contrast to the attitude found in ancient India. In the *Kaama suutra* an important section is devoted to what the successful prostitute must do. The author discusses, for example, 27 ways for her to obtain money from her customer or patron, including lying about such incidents as pretended theft or loss of her jewels, or pretending to be sick and making up items for doctor's expenses.

Another source for ancient Hindu attitudes to prostitution is a book on how to govern a kingdom: the *Artha-shaastra* by Kautilya, a kind of Indian Machiavelli, living perhaps as early as 300 BC. The book was lost for several centuries and only rediscovered in 1905. One chapter is devoted to how prostitutes should be regulated. The king should employ a superintendent of prostitutes. There should be at least one main court prostitute receiving a yearly salary of 1,000 *panas* and a rival prostitute getting half that salary. The daughters, sisters or even mothers of such prostitutes must substitute for them if they go traveling or die. Some of their nonsexual functions should include holding the royal umbrella and fan, attending the king seated on his throne or in his chariot, and spying on visiting foreigners.

In spite of the institutionalization of prostitution, it was not an honorable profession. In line with Hindu doctrine of the transmigration of souls, it was believed that a person was reborn as a whore because of some transgression in a previous life. But following the teachings of the *Mahaab-haarata*, however, someone who is a whore must be a good whore in order to be reborn to a higher life.

Buddhism held the same view of prostitution and prostitutes, but offered the option of achieving grace in one's present life by renunciation. There are many instances of a prostitute achieving holiness through becoming a nun in Buddhist literature. A famous example of this is the story of Ambapaali, who gave the Buddha a mango grove. She became a nun and achieved a state of grace. In spite of such stories, Buddhists view prostitutes as threatening to the spiritual life.

The Muslim conquest of India did virtually nothing to change the status of prostitutes. Although the Koran requires that prostitutes be punished and forbids the faithful to marry them, nevertheless public prostitution flourished under Muslim rulers and large red-light districts were part of the more important towns.

Certain castes and tribes traditionally practiced prostitution. Among the Bediyas, for example, all the women became whores and the men had to find wives from other groups. The Kolhatis, nomadic acrobats from Bombay, permitted their women either to marry or to work as prostitutes. The Harni and Mang Garuda criminal castes were also associated with prostitution, and robbed their customers with regularity.

The Indian system of prostitution extended to Java, which has long been influenced by India: in particular, the close association of prostitute and dancer, the terms for both being synonymous. This system did not spread to neighboring islands in what is now Indonesia. In nearby Sumatra, for example, prostitution seems to have developed in response to the European whaling enterprise.

Prostitution in China is traditionally said to have been initiated by a woman, Hung Yai, more than a millennium before the beginning of the Christian era; but the first reliable

Erotic Indian sculpture, as at an 11th-century Khujaraaho temple, may be linked with the practice of prostitution.

Indian courtesans were not *subject to disapproval in ancient India.* historical reference to it is much later, stemming from the Jou dynasty (650 BC), during which the minister Gwan Jung officially established red-light districts for merchants. Interestingly, this was also the dynasty during which China became one of the most technologically advanced countries in the world: large-scale irrigation, iron plows, writing — and chopsticks — were introduced. Brothels for the general public came much later during the Tang and Sung dynasties (AD 618–1279). Attempts to contain prostitution in specified wards of a town failed and the prostitutes infiltrated other areas, with the result that another kind of brothel developed — one that provided various kinds of entertainment as well as prostitution.

In China, the attitude toward prostitution has been ambivalent. Confucians, for example, found the practice evil. But prostitution flourished. According to Marco Polo, in the thirteenth century, there were more than 20,000 female prostitutes in the suburbs of Peking (then Cambalac), the capital of Kublai Khan, but none in the city. Marco Polo suggests that most of these were for the benefit of foreigners, but this is doubtful.

Throughout Chinese history, prostitution has had certain special features. Distinctively Chinese, for example, were the "floating brothels" — boats docked in a riverine red-light district.

Not until the Communist takeover of China was the basic fabric of Chinese prostitution shaken. From the evidence that exists it would seem that prostitution has in large part been eliminated.

The descriptions of prostitution in Japan suggest that it was well integrated into, and institutionalized within, the Japanese social system. In the Shinto religion, there is even a recognized god of prostitution, Inari, who is also the god of rice, a fertility deity whose association with prostitutes resembles ancient Near East sacred prostitution practices.

There seems to have been much greater acceptance of prostitution in Japan than even in China. Although modern governments after World War II have modified the traditional pattern and in many cases outlawed it, nevertheless the continuing social acceptance of prostitution is reflected in the demands for fringe benefits sometimes made by trade unions in Tokyo (at least as late as 1958) so that employees may be guaranteed an allowance to visit bars in order to consort with bar girls (the modern equivalent of the traditional whore).

The early history of prostitution in Japan is not clearly known. Englebert Kaempfer, writing in 1727, suggests that brothels both public and private were first established in the twelfth century under the Shogun Yoritoma to placate his soldiers for their participation in his long and strenuous military expeditions. But prostitution probably existed in Japan long before that. In 1617 one of the most famous red-light districts in the world was established: the Yoshiwara (literally "meadow of happiness") district of Tokyo. It took 10 years to build. Before that time, there was no fixed place set apart for brothels. By 1889 there were 156 brothels in the Yoshiwara with 3,000 prostitutes.

One of the main sources for Japanese prostitutes was destitute parents willing to sell their young daughters, usu-ally between the ages of 10 and 20, to a bawd or proprietor of a "tea house" for a specific number of years. Girls were brought up to regard compliance in such matters as fulfilling the duty of obedience to parents. In any event, prostitutes were expected to be entertaining in a number of ways — not

Chinese prostitutes date back to at least 650 BC.

A "cage" brothel in Tokyo's Yoshiwara district, where a red-light area was established in 1617.

only sexually — and consequently had to start early and work through a period of instruction and apprenticeship.

There was a hierarchy within the ranks of prostitutes, the lowest being the *pan-pan*, street walkers who accepted customers of any social class; the highest were the *tayu*, whose clientele was restricted to the well-born. Occasionally, prostitutes were bought and subsequently married.

The eighteenth century saw the rise of the geisha. The term refers to anyone possessing a skill, and was first used of men skilled at riding, fencing or shooting who were attached to the courts of feudal lords. Female geisha were women who had skills in dancing and singing. They eventually became confused with prostitutes, who tried to imitate their accomplishments. In 1872, the government enacted legislation to make sure that only real geisha were employed at geisha houses. There has been a partial resurgence of the geisha as an institution since the 1930s. Geisha were never common prostitutes if only because their sexual favors were not granted indiscriminately.

In the 1950s various aspects of prostitution (but not technically prostitution itself) were made illegal: soliciting, procuring, incitement to prostitution. Brothels have since been closed. What has happened is comparable to what has occurred in the West: the development of new forms of prostitution involving call girls and bar girls with few of the stabilizing elements associated with the traditional highly structured institution.

In the western world, prostitution has existed since antiquity on a large scale. There have been many attempts to regulate it by licensing, requiring special clothing or setting aside various wards for red-light districts. Since the nineteenth century attempts have been made at eradicating the phenomenon altogether. A number of factors have contributed to the recent development including the emancipation of women, the evolution of egalitarian romantic marriages, and the rise of humanitarian movements of various kinds.

The first known western regulations are to be found in Solon's establishment of state-run brothels in Athens in 594 BC. Prostitutes of one form or another had existed earlier than this in Greece but without legal definition. The prostitutes in such brothels were usually slaves, but there were also women who had been sold to the brothels by their fathers or brothers for having committed fornication.

In the hierarchy of prostitution that existed in ancient Greece, such prostitutes were at the bottom. They were badly paid civil servants who had few civil rights and had to wear distinctive clothing. Some of these restrictions were relaxed after Solon's time, but the social status of the common prostitute was never high. Above them in rank were the flute players, who were specialists in dancing, gymnastics and fellation. They were mainly foreigners from Asia Minor (modern Turkey). The hetaerae were the most famous of the prostitutes. They were comparable to the Japanese geisha in that they were "companions to men" because of their intellectual and cultural training.

Roman society was quite different and did not continue the hetaera tradition. There were women who were similar in some ways but seem not to have had the accomplishments of the Greek courtesans.

The Romans were the first to register prostitutes in Europe. The overwhelming majority of whores, however, were unregistered. Registration had profound consequences for the social status of a woman. Once she was included on the roll and given a license, it was impossible for her to be removed from it. For the most part these women were slaves, although under the emperor Augustus, because his laws against fornication were so strict, some highborn women tried to register themselves as prostitutes to avoid severe punishments. Further legislation under Tiberius prevented them from doing so and under Caligula a tax on prostitutes was introduced.

The prostitutes' dress was regulated by law, although some are known to have flouted these and other rules quite openly. They were forbidden to wear the *stola*, the normal dress of freeborn women. They had to dye their hair yellow or red (some authorities also say blue) and were forbidden

Geisha girls of Japan were culturally trained, as well as skilled in dancing and singing. They were never common prostitutes.

Ancient Greek prostitution ranged from the hetaerae (above), who provided intellectual as well as physical stimulation, to the common prostitute (below), whose social status was very low.

to wear purple clothes, jewelry and shoes. They normally wore sandals and clothes with a flowered pattern, but some wore transparent dresses. Brothels were common, and Roman moralists such as Cato who were otherwise incensed about the moral decay they saw around them, praised men who satisfied their lusts in brothels rather than with respectably married women. In competition with the brothels and sometimes synonymous with them were the public baths. Some baths were frequented only by prostitutes or loose women and their clients. Prostitutes plied their trade in many places, including the space provided by the arches forming the basements of theaters and circuses. The word *fornicate* is, in fact, derived from the Latin word for these arches — *fornices*.

The rise of Christianity in Europe saw the development of a great ambivalence toward prostitution. The Council of Elvira in AD 305 excommunicated all prostitutes. However, at other times even the Church saw fit to profit from them. It is said that in 1309, the Bishop of Strasbourg kept a brothel. Pope Clement II required any person found guilty of prostitution to leave half her property to the Church. On the other hand, from time to time, pogroms of various kinds were launched against prostitutes. The emperor Charlemagne, for example, enacted laws with severe penalties including capital punishment. In the thirteenth century, they were expelled from France by Louis IX (St Louis). There was, however, no consistent policy except perhaps a general toleration of a necessary evil. In reality prostitution flourished in Europe. Some brothels are known to have been enormously elegant. Protestant countries tried to suppress prostitution but only drove it underground. The vast African slave trade in the New World led to widespread black prostitution organized by whites.

Under the Roman emperor Augustus, high-born ladies sought to register themselves as prostitutes to escape the severe laws against fornication.

A Roman prostitute *(above left) from Pompei, Italy. Medieval brothels (left) flourished, although official attitudes were hostile.*

By the end of the seventeenth century, because of the epidemics of syphilis that swept through Europe in the preceding century, the regular medical inspection of prostitutes began. It became a feature of nineteenth-century state-regulated brothels in France and elsewhere.

In the nineteenth century, a movement for the eradication of prostitution developed. In 1869 in England, a campaign was started to launch an international movement to abolish state-regulated prostitution. By the 1940s the Russian Communist government declared that they had eliminated brothels as well as prostitution. How real this elimination was, however, is not known.

Prostitution in the 19th century:
Lobby loungers *of Regency London (right), an illustration by Cruickshank. Toulouse-Lautrec, the painter of prostitutes (right, below), photographed with a model beside his* Au salon *(1895).* The Procuress *by Felicien Rops (below) illustrates the late 19th-century emphasis on the evils of prostitution.*

In France, state regulation ended in 1946 due largely to the urging of a national heroine, Marthe Richard. This merely meant the closing of state-controlled brothels (*maisons de tolérance*) which — no matter how despicable they were made out to be — made life somewhat less oppressive for the prostitutes who were not rehabilitated under the new legislation. Marthe Richard has since changed her mind about the desirability of the abolition.

What has happened is that brothels in all their variety are being closed although the reality of prostitution goes on. In the United States, where prostitution is nearly everywhere illegal, attempts have been made by some militant prostitutes to have it decriminalized and a labor union for prostitutes recognized. Although there is a greater sense of sexual liberation than ever before in western culture, prostitution continues to survive.

Male prostitution has existed from ancient times and is referred to in the Bible (Deuteronomy 23:18–19; a male prostitute is there referred to as a "dog"). Quite predictably, it often occurs in social situations in which women are dramatically absent — among migrant laborers, for example, working in mines or on plantations where the sex ratio may be one woman to 100 men or more. Junod mentions that in Johannesburg in 1915, in the all-male compounds of the copper mines, young boys called *tinkhontshana* worked as prostitutes and received about one dollar for a night's work. The men in these compounds reportedly preferred the boys to female prostitutes, who spread venereal diseases (whereas the *tinkhontshana* were believed not to). Junod characterizes male prostitution as a "regular institution" in the Johannesburg mining community.

Very little attention, however, has been paid to the subject. Possibly this has to do with western ways of conceptualizing sexual careers. The structural equivalent of female prostitution in the western scheme of things is not male prostitution but male homosexuality: female prostitution or male homosexuality constituting the traditionally most despicable sexual statuses. Male prostitution and female homosexuality are somehow more remote or unimportant or unexpected, as shown by the use of the word "prostitute," which normally refers to women, and "homosexual" to men.

Male prostitution has almost invariably been homosexual, although male prostitutes in the modern western world frequently conceptualize themselves as heterosexual. *In many parts of the world,* Heterosexual male prostitution, where women pay men for *particularly in the Near and* sexual services, exists but is relatively rare and practically *Far East, male homosexual* unstudied (rarer still is homosexual female prostitution). *prostitutes have tended to* The use of male prostitutes by women is virtually never (if *be transvestites. But among* ever) reported for primitive societies. *self-avowed western*

Homosexual male prostitution is reported from a great *homosexuals, transvestite* many societies. It existed in ancient Greece but was *prostitution is apparently* discouraged. Solon, who created state-run female brothels *almost nonexistent.* in the sixth century BC, feared male prostitutes because he presumed that anyone who sold his body for money would be ready to betray his country without even giving the matter much thought. Thorkil Vanggaard argues that homosexual relationships were so idealized by the ancient Greeks that male prostitution was considered especially contemptible. Whatever the motivation, the men who had been prostitutes in their youth were not granted full civil rights as adults. This was possibly due not to some extraordinary romanticism about homosexuality but because male prostitutes were frequently prisoners of war who had been sold into slavery. The same seems to have been true for the Romans, who did not register male prostitutes.

Transvestite homosexual prostitutes in Singapore.

Among the Greeks and Romans, male prostitution seems to have been essentially pederastic — that is, involving teenagers and even younger boys. But transvestites were sometimes involved and occasionally also eunuchs. Elsewhere in the world, particularly in the Near and Far East, transvestites are the more numerous.

The most extensive report by a modern anthropologist on such prostitution is by Unni Wikan for certain towns in Oman. She reports that male prostitutes have much lower rates than their female counterparts: 1 rial Omani (about £2 or $3.20), whereas a woman would charge 5 rial. Female prostitutes are not only expensive but also rare (they may, in fact, be mainly foreigners and their very existence is concealed).

Comparable transvestite male prostitutes called *washoga* have been reported for Mombasa and other East African coastal areas among Muslim groups.

One of the earliest reliable accounts of Near Eastern transvestite prostitutes comes from G. W. Lane's *An account of the manners and customs of the modern Egyptians* (1833–35). He mentions two kinds, the *xawal* (which he writes as *khawal*) and the *gink*. Of the latter he says almost nothing except that the word itself "is Turkish, and has a vulgar signification which aptly expresses their character." They were male transvestite dancers of non-Egyptian background, mostly Jews, Armenians, Greeks and Turks. The *xawal* were also dancers and were considered less offensive in some respects than their female counterparts, the *ghawaazii*. The *xawal* often wore a veil but their other clothing was a mixture of male and female styles, although their mannerisms and overall style were more feminine than masculine. They were native Egyptians. Henriques suggests that they may have had their heyday after 1834, when female dancers were declared illegal. The present status or even existence of the *xawal* is not clear.

In ancient China, transvestite male prostitutes had developed their own guilds or trade unions as early as the Southern Sung dynasty (AD 1127–1279). This was a tremendous change from the previous Northern Sung dynasty (960–1127), when male prostitutes were threatened with heavy fines and 100 blows with bamboo rods.

In Japan, male prostitution was also largely transvestite. It became fairly common in the seventeenth century with the early development of the Kabuki theater, in which young men played the part of women. Some of the places where they could be hired were the grounds of religious shrines (which suggests a kind of sacred prostitution).

Male brothels have been reported from many countries over the centuries. In eighteenth-century England they were known as "molly houses." One in particular became famous because the proprietress, Margaret Clap (known as Mother

Clap), was brought to trial in 1726 for running the place and sentenced to two years in prison. In nineteenth-century Victorian England, male brothels flourished. The best known of these, located on Cleveland Street in London, became embroiled in a tremendous scandal. The authorities pressed charges and the prosecutors pursued several high-ranking people including H.R.H. Albert Victor (Prince Eddie), the son of the Prince of Wales (later Edward VII), and Lord Somerset, a confidant of the Prince of Wales.

In the present century, although some brothels exist, most male prostitutes either work the streets or more frequently operate from specialized gay bars or other homosexual meeting places. Unlike female prostitutes, they function independently, without pimps. A call boy system also can be found in large cities, although little is known of it. In various gay newspapers in the United States, but less often elsewhere, personal advertisements for models, escorts and masseurs are frequent: they are barely disguised code terms for prostitutes. Male prostitution is tolerated in many countries and even legal in a few, such as West Germany.

A comparison of contemporary western and nonwestern forms of male prostitution reveals extraordinary differences. Non-western prostitution nearly always involves either young boys or transvestites. In the West, transvestite prostitution has apparently become specialized for clients who may not even conceptualize themselves as homosexual and who prefer to think they are being serviced by real female whores. Among self-avowed homosexuals, transvestite prostitution is almost nonexistent if the advertisements in the gay underground newspapers are representative. Thus, of 360 advertisements in one issue of such a newspaper (*Advocate*, 12 July 1978), not one suggested that the available prostitute was even remotely transvestite. On the contrary, adult supermasculinity was the most frequent drawing card.

What these advertisements indicate is a remarkable transformation in the nature of male homosexuality in the West during the past two centuries.

Victorian homosexual prostitutes: the arrest of Boulton and Park (1857).

Sacred (or temple) prostitution refers to a number of different customs in which sexual acts are performed as part of a religious rite or with persons who are regarded in some sense as sacred, or associated with a sacred place.

The most famous description of sacred prostitution is found in Herodotus, writing in the fifth century BC. In his account of the Babylonians, he describes two kinds of sacred prostitution and these have become the prototypes for related phenomena throughout the world. In one, a woman performs a single act of prostitution and never does so again. The other involves dedication to the services of a god or temple for a period of time, perhaps for life.

Sacred prostitution

In describing the first kind, Herodotus says that every Babylonian woman must have sexual intercourse with a stranger in the temple of Mylitta (a variant of Ishtar or Astarte, a goddess Herodotus equates with Aphrodite) once in her life. As soon as she has taken her seat in the sacred enclosure, she may not return home until a stranger throws a silver coin into her lap and she goes off with him. Once the women have fulfilled their obligation they return home and never prostitute themselves again.

In Heliopolis (now Baalbek) in Lebanon, the function of such temple prostitution was primarily that of defloration: women could not marry before they had performed this ritual. This custom survived in Heliopolis until the fourth century AD, when it was prohibited by the emperor Constantine. He destroyed the temple of Astarte and erected a Christian church in its ruins.

The second kind of sacred prostitution can be found in Herodotus' description of the precinct of Baal in Babylon. It contains an enormous tower on which are built several other towers, one on top of the other. In the topmost tower there is a richly adorned temple literally taken to be a dwelling of the god. This chamber is occupied by a woman specially chosen by the god as his bride. Herodotus remarks in passing that he does not believe that part of the story but notes a resemblance to similar customs observed by the Egyptians.

Apparently the Babylonians also had long-term sacred prostitutes dedicated to the goddess Ishtar, who offered their services to worshipers during fertility ceremonies. The god Marduk was also attended by sacred prostitutes.

Sacred prostitution existed among the Hebrews for a considerable period of time, at least from the thirteenth century BC until the Babylonian Exile in 586 BC. It was, however, officially associated with polytheism and idolatry and was condemned as an abomination, although profane prostitution was tolerated.

Ishtar, Babylonian goddess of sacred prostitution.

Male prostitutes both sacred and secular also existed among the Hebrews. King Rehoboam, son of King Solomon, tolerated male sacred prostitutes, and as late as King Josiah (who died in 608 BC) they were reported to be living in the temple itself in Jerusalem (II Kings 23:7). Transvestite male prostitutes existed in ancient times in Canaanite temples and were described as devotees of Ishtar at Erech in Syria.

In both Christianity and Islam sacred prostitution was never officially countenanced. Curiously, several Christian female (but no male) saints had originally been whores — including SS Mary of Egypt, Pelagia, Theodotea, Afra of Augsburg (who had even set up a brothel before her conversion). In folk Christianity, Mary Magdalene has frequently been thought of as a fallen woman, although there is no biblical justification for this. In spite of official views, medieval French prostitutes, who were organized into trade guilds, adopted her as their patron saint.

Before Mohammed, sacred prostitution was known to have existed among the Arabs when on pilgrimages to the Kaaba. The name of one such woman, who lived shortly before the Prophet, is known: Kharqaa of the Banuu 'Aamir tribe. She is said to have considered herself "one of the pilgrimage rites." Some of the women from her tribe used to perform the ritual of walking round the Kaaba naked, reciting obscene verses. Even after Islam, sacred prostitution probably survived in various areas.

The Near Eastern complex of sacred prostitution was found throughout western Asia and in ancient Greece. Sacred prostitutes were known at the temples of Artemis at Ephesus, Aphrodite at Corinth and Dionysis in Sparta.

A second important area of sacred prostitution is India, where the practice is essentially a southern, Dravidian, one. Both the Near Eastern and the Indian institutions were linked to a fertility cult of a great mother goddess, so they may belong to some single cultural unit.

The earliest references to Hindu temple prostitutes, the *devadaasii*, seem to be no earlier than the ninth or tenth centuries AD. But prostitutes associated with religious shrines probably go back much further and may have existed in the Harappaa culture (in what is now Pakistan), which is as early as 3000 BC!

In more recent times, the *devadaasii* constituted a caste of women who were in attendance on the god of the temple to which they were attached, and prostituted themselves to

Indian dancer figurine
(above) from Mohenjo-Daro, c 3000 BC: perhaps the earliest example of sacred prostitution. Votive figurine (below left) of a Babylonian temple prostitute.

Mary Magdalene depicted as a "fallen woman." There is no biblical justification for this view.

Temple prostitutes of India, called devadaasii, sang and danced for the god's pleasure. They were regarded as his wives or representatives.

priests and public alike. A *devadaasii* was either the daughter of a *devadaasii* or was dedicated at the age of 12 by her mother as a special act of devotion. The girl was regarded as the wife of a god or of the representative of the god. In a Portuguese description from the sixteenth century, she was described as having to deflower herself ritually on a *lingga* (a sacred phallus). She sprinkled the blood from the broken hymen over the *lingga* and the stones on which it rested.

Large temples might have as many as 100 sacred prostitutes in attendance. But in the twentieth century, mainly because of attacks on the institution by Hindu reformers, they have fallen into disrepute and have begun to disappear.

The third area of sacred prostitution is West Africa, where it has been reported for the Ewe, Igbo, and a number of groups in Ghana. Any direct historical tie between West African practices and those of the Near East is not obvious. Sacred prostitution existed, however, in northwest Africa at Carthage and there may be some sort of link.

The Ewe type of sacred prostitution (now defunct) has been described by A. B. Ellis, a nineteenth-century traveler. According to him, sacred prostitution occurred only in association with the worship of Dang-gbi, the python god. Such prostitutes were thought of as the wives of the god, as well as priestesses. These women underwent a three-year initiation. If any woman, free or slave, single or married, publicly simulated possession, she could immediately join the novices. Because she was inviolable in this state, becoming a sacred prostitute could be seen as a kind of asylum from a bad husband or master. During the three-year training period, the prospective brides of the god were allowed to prostitute themselves to anyone. But once they were finished with their training, they were theoretically supposed to submit only to actual worshipers (although this rule seems to have been largely disregarded). Any children they might bear were considered to be offspring of the god himself. The status of such women seems to have been high; because a god had driven them to it, they were not reproached for prostituting themselves.

Other West African groups had similar institutions, most probably derived from the same cultural source, whatever that might be. Priestesses among Twi-speaking groups, for example, could not marry because they belonged to the god they served, but sexual license was not tabu and Ellis reports "custom allows them to gratify their passion with any man who may chance to take their fancy."

There is a possibility that prostitution in general began as a sacred rite and only later became secularized. Today sacred prostitution has virtually disappeared.

Eleven & CURRENT DEVELOPMENTS

Contraception and the women's movement are key developments in twentieth-century western sexuality. But the so-called sexual revolution has hardly touched western commitment to the family.

In 1948, the first of the Kinsey reports was published (*Sexual behavior in the human male*).

In 1952, George Jorgensen gained international notoriety through a sex-change operation and became a household name as Christine Jorgensen.

In 1955, the American Law Institute recommended in its Model penal code that all laws concerning private sexual behavior between consenting adults be abolished. (These recommendations were enacted into law by Indiana in 1961, Connecticut in 1969, and New Jersey in 1979 — the only states in the United States to do so).

In 1956, "the pill" was developed by Gregory Pincus and his associates as the first effective oral contraceptive.

In 1957, the Wolfenden report was published urging that private homosexual acts between consenting adults no longer be considered crimes in Great Britain. (These recommendations were made law in 1967 in England by the Sexual Offences Act.)

In 1960, the United States Supreme Court relaxed the traditional notion of obscenity and what was formally regarded as illegal pornography gained wide distribution.

In 1961, the first legally tolerated films with frontal nudity were shown in the United States.

In 1963, Betty Friedan published *The Feminine mystique*. This is generally considered the beginning of the modern Women's Liberation movement.

In 1965, the United States Supreme Court legalized the sale and use of contraceptives in all of the United States.

In 1966, Masters and Johnson published the first of their books on sexual functioning (*Human sexual response*). Their work prompted the spread of sex therapy centers.

In 1967, various test cases throughout the United States ruled that children produced by artificial insemination with a donor were legitimate if the husband had agreed.

In 1968, Pope Paul VI issued his encyclical *Humanae vitae* reaffirming traditional Catholic morality and condemning all forms of artificial birth control, including the pill.

In 1968, J. B. Gordon of Oxford succeeded in cloning a frog. By the 1980s, Russian scientists were attempting to revive the long-extinct species of mammoth through cloning, using mammoth cells from an animal preserved by freezing in Siberia.

In 1969, a police raid in the Stonewall Inn in New York sparked the Gay Liberation movement.

Call Off Your Old Tired Ethics. *The emblem of a labor union for prostitutes called COYOTE.*

Christine Jorgensen, *a former American soldier who changed sex after surgical operations in Copenhagen, Denmark, in the early 1950s.*

The first test tube baby, *Louise Brown, was born in England on 26 July 1978.*

In 1969, Denmark dropped all laws against publication or sale of pornography — the first western country to do so.

In 1970, the United States Presidential Commission on Obscenity and Pornography recommended that laws prohibiting the publishing or dissemination of pornography should be dropped. (President Nixon rejected the report as "morally bankrupt").

In 1973, the United States Supreme Court sharply curtailed government regulation of abortion.

In 1974, the American Psychiatric Association stopped labeling homosexuality as a mental illness.

In 1977, a major anti-gay rights backlash began gaining prominence for its leader Anita Bryant.

In 1978, the first test-tube baby was born, in England.

By 1980: The world's population had gone beyond 4,000,000,000 (by 2013, this figure will probably double).

One out of every three couples in the world was using some sort of artificial contraception or had undergone sterilization.

About 40,000,000 abortions were performed a year (more than half illegally). This involved about one out of every four pregnancies in the world.

The book *The joy of sex* by Alex Comfort (first published in 1972) had sold over 7,000,000 copies. The book *Everything you always wanted to know about sex (but were afraid to ask)*, by David Reuben (first published in 1969), had more than 8,000,000 copies in print.

Legislation on various aspects of sexuality or related fields such as adultery, fornication, contraception, abortion, homosexual acts, and pornography were becoming more liberal throughout the West and other industrialized parts of the world. In several Muslim countries, however — notably Pakistan and Iran — there was by the end of the 1970s a return to traditional Islamic laws involving the death penalty

Iranian women of the 1970s *adjust to the wearing of the* chador, *required by a fundamentalist government.*

for adultery, prostitution, and homosexual acts — as well as a return to the veil for women.

What has just been outlined are some of the more important aspects of the social setting for modern-day sexuality.

One of the major realities that have helped to shape a significant change in values has to do with the threat of overpopulation. It was Thomas Malthus (1766–1834) who first pointed out that human population always tends to outrun food supply. But in his 1798 work *An esssay on the principle of population as it affects the future improvement of society*, the only solution offered was sexual abstinence. Various followers of Malthus felt that this was an unrealistic approach to so serious a problem. A worldwide effort to promote birth control was launched in 1900 with the foundation of the International Neo-Malthusian League. Its goals met with almost unrelieved opposition on the part of governments and Christian religious groups, until 1930 when the Lambeth Conference of the Anglican Communion cautiously accepted birth control. In 1958, another Lambeth Conference came out strongly for the morality of birth control because (it was argued) there could be nothing moral about allowing children to be born who were to die as a result of malnutrition, disease, and the other scourges of overpopulation. From that point on, liberal Protestant groups became vociferous not only for the toleration of birth control but also for the moral obligation of family planning.

Politically, since 1960 there had been a radical change in government policies throughout the world regarding birth control. In 1960, only India and Pakistan supported family planning programs, but by the 1970s, over 60 other countries had launched their own family planning program.

A massive birth control policy has been adopted by the Chinese, whose population in 1979 neared the 1,000,000,000 mark. The government is experimenting with a number of means to achieve zero population growth by the year 2000, including raising the legal age of marriage, encouraging married couples to have only one child and experimenting with a pill to be taken by men. This pill contains gossypol, a substance derived from cottonseed oil. Gossypol came to the attention of Chinese health officials because of various symptoms discovered among peasants in Hebeh Province in the 1950s including heart problems but, more strikingly, infertility, apparently caused by an ingredient in the cottonseed oil used locally in cooking.

In the industrialized West, artificial contraception is practiced by over 80 percent of the total population. The consequences of the role of women in such societies is obvious: they need not devote themselves all their lives to

Population and birth control

Roman Catholic doctrine on birth control opposes artificial contraception, but it is practiced by the great majority of Catholics in western cultures.

bearing and caring for children. It is in such an environment that Women's Liberation movements flourish and by their success contribute to the further acceptability of birth control. Contraception and the women's movement are probably the two most important developments in setting the sexual scene in the twentieth century.

Until the 1960s, the most common form of population control was abortion. Even now, one out of every four pregnancies results in an abortion. In the Soviet Union, France, Austria, Italy, Portugal, and Uruguay the percentage is even higher; and in Japan it is higher still.

The social reality behind the widespread use and acceptance of contraception and abortion has serious implications for much of traditional western, specifically Roman Catholic, morality. It is not only Roman Catholics that are affected, but also certain Protestant fundamentalists, Mormons, and Orthodox Jews. In many instances they oppose the same development but not for the same reasons. Roman Catholics, for example, have traditionally been opposed to birth control in terms of the doctrine of natural law, but Mormons have a different reason. They believe that the souls of all future people already exist and are simply waiting to be born. The practice of birth control deliberately keeps these souls without a body.

Developments in the Roman Catholic Church are of particular interest. The Church has officially tended to hold out against any change in its traditional teachings on sexuality, marriage, and abortion. But its traditional and well-publicized position on sexuality is at variance with social reality even in predominantly Catholic countries such as France and Italy.

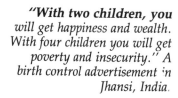

"With two children, you will get happiness and wealth. With four children you will get poverty and insecurity." A birth control advertisement in Jhansi, India.

It is in the area of birth control that its teachings have been most seriously threatened, at least in western Europe, the United States and other developed nations — by the great majority of Catholics, both nominal *and* churchgoing. In the 1950s, for example, some 80 percent of Roman Catholic women in the United States conformed to the Church's teaching that forbade all forms of contraception (outside of the rhythm method). By 1975, 90 percent of Roman Catholic women married for less than five years were using forbidden contraceptive methods. And this, only a few years after the proclamation by Pope Paul VI, in his encyclical *Humanae vitae*, which reaffirmed the traditional tabus on artificial contraception including the pill, sterilization and abortion.

Quite clearly, traditional Catholic morality is most sorely threatened by its official stand on birth control. Although there has been tremendous pressure to change this stand, no pope in modern times has been willing to do so.

The official teaching is ignored by increasing numbers of Catholics. Although shortly after Paul VI's 1968 ruling many priests who failed to accept the ban were threatened with disciplinary action and (in one instance at least) were called schismatics and told to leave the Church, and even though some people actually left the Church, nevertheless no substantial numbers of people deserted. What has happened instead is that Catholics in increasing numbers feel that the Church has no right to meddle in their private lives.

The birth control issue has all sorts of interesting repercussions for Catholic morality in general. Since the traditional ban was based on the idea of natural law, to permit mechanical birth control would mean that the justification of sexual acts in terms of potential reproduction would have to be given up. But this would destroy the traditional arguments for the bans on masturbation and homosexual acts — a radical change to say the least.

A number of significant statements assailing the traditional moral code have been made by various Catholics, but they have not been excommunicated for making them. The famous Dutch catechism is a case in point. Not only does it say that birth control is ultimately to be treated as a matter of conscience, it suggests that although Christian marriage is indissoluble, the Church should not abandon divorced and remarried individuals but should make the sacraments available to them. As for homosexuality, the catechism declares that the biblical condemnation of homosexual acts (in Genesis 19 and Romans 1) has nothing to do with people who are exclusively homosexual in their erotic interests and are therefore guiltless. Rather, the condemnation is directed against people who experiment because of cultural fashion even though they are able to function heterosexually.

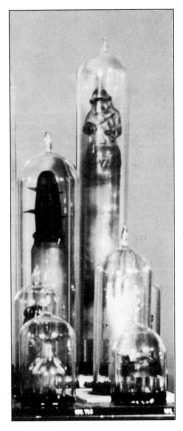

Part of the condom collection at the Kinsey Institute for Sexual Research, Bloomington, Indiana.

An even greater tolerance of traditionally forbidden sexual behavior is shown in a publication called *Human sexuality: new directions in American Catholic thought*. It was produced by a team headed by Father Anthony Kosnik and sponsored by the Catholic Theological Society of America. It appeared in 1977. Referring to sexuality as "God's ingenious gift," it departs from traditional views by denying that some sexual acts are intrinsically immoral (e.g., masturbation, adultery, and homosexual acts) and suggests that sexual practices are moral if they are "self-liberating, other-enriching, honest, faithful, socially responsible, life-serving, and joyous."

The Catholic Theological Society of America has urged greater tolerance of traditionally forbidden sexual behavior, and refers to sexuality as "God's ingenious gift."

In 1979, the Vatican condemned this book. No sanctions however were leveled against the authors of the report.

Throughout the West, the legal requirement that marriage was indissoluble was by the 1980s given up in virtually all countries, even in predominantly Catholic ones. Notable exceptions include Ireland and Poland. Furthermore, there is a trend toward living together without a marriage ritual to define the relationship. In the United States for example, in the period from 1970 to 1978, the number of unmarried couples living together had increased by 117 percent. Although this is an enormous increase (especially so for people under 25, for which the number has increased by eight times), the absolute number is not great, being just 1,100,000 households as opposed to 48,000,000 with traditional husband–wife households.

Furthermore, since the 1960s, in the United States at least, divorce rates have dramatically increased while those for marriage have decreased. In the 12-month period ending in March 1974, there were 925,000 divorces, an increase of some 200,000 over the estimated 703,000 divorces in all of 1973. In the 20 to 24 age bracket, the number of women who remained single jumped from 28 percent in 1960 to 39 percent in 1974; for men it has grown from 53 to 57 percent.

The birth control issue, based on the idea of natural law, has many interesting repercussions for Catholic morality in general.

The causes of these extraordinary changes in the basic structure of western society are complicated. One cause that at present remains fairly minor but may increase tremendously in significance is the government regulation that penalizes traditional structures. In the United States, a widow and a widower living on social security benefits must give up some of their income if they marry because benefits are smaller for a married couple then for two unmarried people. A similar situation exists with current tax laws and has been referred to as "sin subsidy." It's cheaper for two working people to live together unmarried.

A considerably more significant development bringing about changes in western behavior is the massive adoption of effective contraception, which prevents modern marriage from being tied to the production of children. In particular the use of the pill as well as intra-uterine devices, which are all "intercourse independent," have made it possible for women to decide without the knowledge or even cooperation of men if and when they have children.

Another reason for change was the development of a drug-oriented counterculture in the 1950s and 1960s — typified by the Woodstock concert (actually held in Bethel, New York) in 1969. There are several sources for this counterculture. In a sense it represented a development of earlier movements such as the bohemianism of the 1920s and existentialism following World War II. But it also had a rationale in terms of the grim reality of a persistent threat of the hydrogen bomb and, in the United States especially, the highly unpopular Vietnamese War. The counterculture had many facets: the hippie movement, the anti-Vietnamese War movement, the civil rights movement, and in particular the drug culture which saw large numbers of middle-class young people throughout the West flouting laws with the secure conviction that the laws were wrong. The 1960s saw an emergence of new life-styles among the young middle class that were tied in part to radical politics. In the 1970s, the radical politics diminished in importance and were separated from the life-styles. But the new life-styles tended to spread to the working class.

The counterculture not only accepted premarital sexuality casually but also public nudity, abortions, and homosexuality. A sort of "deviant chic" arose. The hippie movement in particular stressed a romanticized return to nature, and the abandonment of what was considered a bankrupt puritan capitalism. Communes and tribal families were created and regarded as solutions to the "unnatural" (in a romantic rather than Aristotelian or scientific sense) conditions created by middle-class nuclear families. Although a few communes persisted into the 1980s, for the most part these developments passed away with the hippie movement.

But what has not passed away are other social changes such as co-ed dormitories and "swinging." Wife swapping among friends has given way to the more anonymous encounters in establishments such as Plato's Retreat, developed in the late 1970s, where heterosexual couples (not necessarily married) go to explore the sexual field. In January 1980, a New York cable TV station (the infamous channel J) actually presented a copulation contest on the air from Plato's Retreat: a woman wanted to beat all existing records. I believe the number of men she copulated with was 52 (there was no known record, so she won by default).

Another development that is quite extraordinary from a historical perspective is the Gay Liberation movement in the late 1960s and early 1970s in the United States. Although other societies have been tolerant of homosexual behavior and it had acquired a certain chic in the western counterculture,

Ernst Röhm (left), head of the Nazi SA, whose murder in 1934 precipitated Nazi persecution of homosexuals.

nevertheless this movement was the first in which sexual orientation became the basis for political organization.

The result of this politicization has been a change from what was even in the late 1960s a secret and, in some commentators' views, an impoverished subculture, to a fairly public "satellite culture," with spin-offs into the heterosexual world. What is certainly remarkable in most cities in the United States is the public display in newspaper stands of homosexual newspapers, the probable presence of several gay bars, gay student clubs at college and universities, and possibly even a gay church (or at least a church that permits gay groups to meet there). There was literally nothing comparable in the 1950s, and it is astonishing that they should exist to such a wide extent in the United States, because at least some homosexual acts are almost everywhere still considered as crimes. In France, where private homosexual acts between adults have not been crimes since the time of Napoleon, such a satellite culture does not exist or is only now beginning — probably as an American influence. Clearly legal toleration does not always produce social creativity.

Attempts at changing anti-homosexual laws are not something new. They were started in the 1860s in Germany by Karl Heinrich Ulrichs. The main strategy of the German movement was to modify the laws (notably paragraph 175 of the penal code) through petition and education. Magnus Hirschfeld and his Scientific-Humanitarian Committee actually compiled a petition of more than 6,000 names of prominent professionals to present to the government. The names included those of Albert Einstein, Thomas Mann, Herman Hesse, Stefan Zweig, Karl Jaspers, Arthur Schnitzler, Franz Werfel, Richard von Krafft-Ebing — leaders of the German-speaking intelligentsia. Several prominent foreigners also sent their unsolicited backing — including Leo Tolstoy and Emile Zola.

The movement came to special prominence several years later under the Nazis. Although the Nazis had been ideologically anti-homosexual from the start, the beginning of intense persecution began on 30 June 1934, "the night of the long knives." On that date Ernst Röhm, the leader of the Storm Troopers (SA), was assassinated along with dozens of SA officers. This assassination was clearly political since Röhm's homosexual interests had been common knowledge at least since 1925, when his association with a male prostitute became public. What happened was that Röhm eventually got into serious conflict with Heinrich Himmler, the head of the Blackshirts (SS) and the Gestapo.

A new and much more severe law was issued, Paragraph 175a. The new law added the following to the already existing offenses: kissing, embracing, having unacceptable fantasies, and being listed in the address book of a homosexual.

Homosexuals were imprisoned, tortured, castrated and killed under the Nazis. The exact number of those killed is not precisely known. Current estimates vary between 220,000 (a figure suggested by the Protestant church of Austria) and 500,000. It is interesting that these actions against homosexuals are rarely mentioned in commentaries on the holocaust and have gone virtually unnoticed until the appearance of the play *Bent* by Martin Sherman produced first in London, and then in New York, in 1979. In West German courts, it has been ruled that homosexuals cannot be granted any form of restitution (unlike Jews and political prisoners) because they were punished for criminal not political offenses.

Hirschfeld's bust paraded by Nazi stormtroopers *during the burning of his priceless collection of books.*

Bent, *a play produced in 1979,* *first drew attention to the fate of homosexuals in Hitler's Germany.*

The Gay Liberation movement in the United States is usually dated as beginning the Friday night of 28 June 1969, two days short of the thirty-fifth anniversary of "the night of the long knives." The triggering event was a police raid on a gay bar in New York, the Stonewall Inn. The extraordinary thing about the raid was that the clients fought back. The police were pelted with beer cans and bottles along with chants about gay power.

About a month later, the Gay Liberation Front (GLF) was formed. Its radical character was apparent even in its name, taken in conscious imitation of the Algerian revolutionaries and of the Viet Cong. Demonstrations and marches became the order of the day.

In England, a more staid approach paid off in 1967 with the enactment into law of the recommendations of the Wolfenden Report. Denmark, West Germany, and Canada followed suit. But what has happened in the United States is not decriminalization of homosexual acts in spite of the wide variety of attacks on the legal system. Rather, *de facto* toleration of homosexuality and of a gay life-style has spread — but without the guarantees of law. The United States Supreme Court has upheld the legality of certain laws against homosexuals, although there is a widespread view that laws dealing with private sexual acts between consenting adults are religious and therefore unconstitutional.

In conscious imitation of the Gay Lib movement, a Masochist Liberation group was formed in 1971, called the Eulenspiegel Society. It soon changed from a group exclusively catering to masochists to one that included sadists as well, and of any Sexual Minorities (which is what the abbreviation SM means in Eulenspiegel Society publications). The group is predominantly heterosexual, but has functioned in several ways as part of the gay subculture. For example, an Eulenspiegel contingent regularly marches in gay parades in New York. The change from a predominantly masochist liberation society to a sadomasochistic social club came about partly through homosexual members, some of whom were able to play both masochistic and sadistic roles.

In spite of the fragmentation, and real lack of change of the anti-homosexual laws throughout most of the United States, in some areas homosexuals have developed an impressive political clout. This is most obvious in San Francisco, where it has been estimated that 20 percent of the 335,000 voters may be homosexual. In a recent election for mayor (1979), a homosexual ran third and swung his vote over to another candidate who won. Although the successful candidate (Dianne Feinstein) said no deals had been made, she agreed to appoint a homosexual to the police commission and to appoint homosexuals to other city boards and commissions based on proportional population representation — surely a first in human history.

In a number of ways, gay rights have tended to increase even though laws may not have changed. Avowed homosexuals have in some instances been allowed to adopt children. But attempts to legalize homosexual marriages have been unsuccessful. Although at one point the right to marry was sometimes held up as a goal of gay liberation, the decline in heterosexual marriages has seen a decline in the interest in homosexual marriage.

Reaction to the movement by various religious groups has been very uneven. The Southern Baptists have consistently been opposed to extensions of gay rights. Other groups have recognized as legitimate the right of homosexuals for sympathetic treatment. The question of ordaining known homosexuals to the ministry has been particularly vexing. The ordination of a homosexual woman priest in New York in 1977 by Bishop Paul Moore Jr. caused a furor in the ranks

A gay "marriage" was contracted by these two citizens of Rotterdam, Holland, in 1967, allegedly under the supervision of a Roman Catholic priest.

of Episcopalians. In 1979, The House of Bishops of the United States Episcopal Church decided that it was not appropriate to ordain a practicing homosexual. But in the same year, the Church of England produced a report *recommending* that homosexuals should not be barred from the priesthood and even admitted that homosexual relationships could be justified, though the report rejected the institution of homosexual marriage.

In the 1940s René Guyon called for a comparably radical change of the sex laws everywhere and maintained that the Judaeo-Christian sexual ethic went contrary to reason and health. His proposals required that "no person shall be molested, persecuted, or condemned by the law for having voluntarily engaged in sexual acts or activities of any kind whatever."

A similar approach, though spelt out in more detail, is provided by the Swedish reformer Lars Ullerstam writing in the 1960s. He did not even consider homosexual rights since he took it as a matter of course that civilized countries would recognize them. Ullerstam's proposals took a different tack. He wanted to set up theaters that exhibitionists could perform in. He suggested mobile brothels to accommodate the sexual needs of bed-ridden hospital inmates and severely paralyzed individuals, and called upon idealistic youth to help service these brothels. He thought the least we could do for paedophiles was to supply them with child pornography.

An entirely different aspect of changes involving sexuality in recent times had to do with technology in one way or another. For example, in 1978, the first publicized "test-tube" baby was born: Louise Brown. She was actually conceived in a petri dish (rather than a test-tube) from an egg cell removed from her mother, fertilized by a sperm from her father. This accomplishment, achieved in a British hospital under the direction of Dr Patrick C. Steptoe and Dr Robert G. Edwards, occasioned considerable controversy and brought forth ominous charges of Hitlerian or Frankenstein possibilities. On the other hand, many childless couples immediately wanted to avail themselves of the possibilities, and a test-tube baby clinic was planned for the United States shortly after the announcement.

Artificial insemination, which often involves the donation of sperm from a man other than a woman's husband, had been practiced for some time before this. At least 100,000 individuals who are products of artificial insemination are said to exist in the United States at the time of writing. Sperm banks exist in many places throughout the western world and the practice of inseminating a woman whose husband is sterile with semen from an unknown donor is reasonably common (exact statistics are unavailable). The use of a surrogate mother, on the other hand, to take the place of a

Button indicating support of the Gay Liberation movement (top). The Greek Lambda letter was chosen by early "gay libbers" because they believed it was a chemical symbol indicating a catalytic agent, hence an activist who would promote social change. The lesbian movements also sported buttons (above).

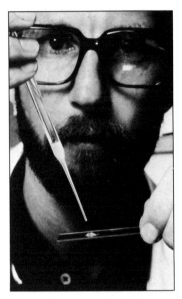

Artificial insemination by anonymous donor (AID) allows women with sterile partners to have children. There are believed to be as many as 200,000 children of such unions in Europe and America.

sterile wife is exceedingly rare. Such solutions are generally discouraged because of legal, social and psychological complications — as are requests for the insemination of single and/or homosexual women, but presumably they occur.

An even more extreme development involves clones or rumors of clones. Although successful cloning (the exact replication of an individual from a cell of the original's body) has been done on simpler animals such as frogs, no attested human examples are known — although a book became a bestseller in the United States for alleging that a prominent businessman had undergone successful cloning.

The extraordinary technological finesse involved in these matters is probably outdone in the recent development of penis and testicle transplants and similar surgery, especially in association with transsexual operations. In changing a male to a phenotypic female, the penis and testicles are amputated and an artificial vagina is constructed — sometimes from the tissue of the penis itself. In changing a female to a phenotypic male, a penis is sometimes constructed from skin flaps. Although natural erection is impossible, various devices that have been used in treating men who are impotent for physiological reasons have been applied. One of the most recent of these is a tiny hydraulic system that permits voluntary erections by pumping fluids from the abdomen into the belly.

Transsexual operations are of course the most spectacular examples of technological changes affecting sexuality. In spite of the fact that such operations are drastic and irreversible, by 1980 an estimated 4,000 people in the United States had undergone the procedure and sex-change operations had spread to medical centers around the country. The procedure had become so acceptable that by 1978, the United States Department of Health, Education and Welfare established a policy permitting people to have sex-change surgery paid for by Medicare (at least one actual case of this has been reported: a 31-year-old man confined to a wheelchair by a rare bone disease received $5,000).

Contemporary sex research — Since the publication of the Kinsey report, sex research has become a totally legitimate academic enterprise. Even outside of academia, a tremendous audience exists seeking out reliable information about sexuality and sex. But in spite of the general acceptability of the topic, many special-interest groups have helped in part to stifle government and private foundation support for sex-oriented research. For example, the Kinsey Institute had lost most of its funding by private and government agencies by 1977.

Several studies have been made since Kinsey's pioneering work. But the fact remains that with some rare exceptions such as the *Rapport Simon* (for France), we simply lack basic information about sexual behavior for the vast majority of cultures. It is unlikely that this situation will be dramatically changed within the next few years because of general opposition by governments to such projects.

Several years ago, when I was planning on doing such a study and wanted especially to contrast the behaviors of people living in groups that had very permissive norms with neighboring groups that were very puritanical, I faced such opposition. Margaret Mead wrote to me that my project simply would not be tolerated by the government in question. If such studies were to be done, they might have to be done secretly under the protective shield of a totally innocent project — for some anthropologists and sexologists, such deception would be morally and ethically indefensible. Laud Humphreys's brilliant *Tearoom trade* (1970), a study of sexual behavior in public men's rooms, was condemned in many quarters for the deception that was necessarily involved at different stages of his project. Humphreys was fortunately able to deal with the ethical problems to his own satisfaction so that the work was not sabotaged.

Long-term confinement with members of the same sex, as in a prison, may lead to "deprivation homosexuality" among heterosexuals.

There are, however, many studies short of full-length Kinsey-type projects that could be done. The work of the several anthropologists mentioned throughout this book is evidence of that. Even in the course of nonsexological studies, significant information could be gathered. For example, linguists would do well to study sexual terms as a semantic field. Physical anthropologists could finally get basic data about genital size to the relation to overall body size and structure. An exceedingly easy and basic task would be to collect photographs of people regarded as physically attractive and unattractive.

Paul Gebhard, writing up his own proposals for future research, has put forward suggestions that are relatively straightforward and of considerable theoretical interest. For example, he notes that our knowledge of fetishes would be deepened if we would isolate variables as much as possible, such as dimensions (e.g., must a boot be of a particular size to be a turn-on?). Gebhard proposes that fetish objects be varied by small degrees to determine precisely such information. Another of his proposals: since it is known to be the case that heterosexuals develop "deprivation homosexuality" when confined with members of the same sex for a long period of time — in prisons or on boats — it would be interesting to see if "deprivation heterosexuality" should appear if say a man, hitherto exclusively homosexual, were placed in a closed institution with only women.

It is unlikely that any of these studies will be made in the near future.

But some other studies are likely. For one thing, as more and more of the primitive world becomes literate and as more and more anthropologists study nonprimitives, new strategies in massive sex research open up. Informants could be urged to keep sex diaries. At a minimum, questionnaires could more readily be distributed and filled out. Furthermore, with the greater knowledge of both anthropology and sexology, members of cultures or subcultures could undertake their own studies. One that comes to mind is the subculture of the European aristocracy and in particular of royal families. At least some of the members of this subculture are known to have studied anthropology on the university level. And this subculture would be interesting because in societies where we have some information, there seems to be noticeable differences between the sexual lives of commoners and aristocrats. Apart from rumors and scandals we know little about sexual practices and norms in these circles. It has been asserted that in England, circumcision and sodomy are U (upper class, aristocratic) but birth control is non-U. These assertions warrant being checked up and we probably need a U anthropologist–sexologist to do so.

Women's groups oppose pornography as generally degrading, with specific reference to sadomasochistic materials.

The very great freedom that exists nowadays in publishing and film (in comparison with former times) generates considerable controversy. When attacks are made on these freedoms by otherwise liberal people, the situation gets complicated and sometimes very specific indeed. For example, women's groups have recently been launching a crusade against pornography. But a moment's reflection reveals that it is not the traditional definition of pornography that is used here but something very much more specific: sadomasochistic pornography in which women are depicted as tortured and abused, even killed. Attempts to rescue pornography as a legal category after much legal obfuscation had led to curious results. A United States Supreme Court ruling that local judgments can be made as to what is objectionable in light of community standards about prurience brought an acquittal in the case of a man who had produced films showing sexual acts between two men and a dog. A jury in Manhattan ruled that these films starring a German shepherd were too disgusting and repulsive to appeal to the average person's sense of prurience (the guidepost of the law). The judge agreed, saying "If you're not aroused, it's not obscene." The film maker was let off.

What we have seen developing is a kind of legal schizophrenia because of attempts to uphold traditional morality through the laws. It seems likely, however, that the laws will be changed if social trends in the western world continue.

These trends are, however, difficult to assess. The apparently greater tolerance of nudity and premarital sex experimentation, described for the 1960s and 1970s in the United States, seem to have persisted. On the other hand, various studies suggest that sexual fulfillment is not universally considered one of the highest priorities in life. A 1979 survey of 1,990 American men between the ages of 18 and 49 (given in *The Playboy report on American men*) placed sex as ninth in a list of values most likely to contribute to a life of satisfaction. The list read, in order of preference: health, love, peace of mind, family life, work, friends, respect from others, education, sex, religion, and money. (I wonder if it might not be argued that sex was taken for granted as a necessity — after all, food, shelter, and clothing are not on this list at all.) Eighty-four percent of the men interviewed considered family life very important, but only 25 percent thought so because it was important to have a stable sex life.

Some scholars maintain that the sexual revolution is a revolution in name only. The culture of sexuality is perhaps more stable than had been supposed.

An even more striking phenomenon — given the sexual revolution — is the emergence of what has been called "the chastity underground": people who are sexually bored or who have sought refuge in asexuality (at most solitary masturbation). The number of people involved is not known. The scanty information available about them suggests that they are not generally subject to sexual dysfunction, but reveal an often astonishing unenthusiasm for orgasm.

It is also difficult to be clear about the behavioral side of the sexual revolution. The studies of American behavior since Kinsey's work simply do not approach the massiveness of his sample (although they attempt to avoid the errors his sampling has been charged with), so the picture is even more sketchy than the one he presented. On the basis of these more recent studies, it seems reasonably clear that more college women engage in premarital intercourse than was true in Kinsey's study, and that young people are beginning their sexual careers even earlier. Not all scholars agree however, and some maintain that the sexual revolution is a revolution in name only.

Even today, basic information about sexual behavior in most cultures is largely nonexistent, apart from one or two pioneering studies.

Other differences between present trends and the patterns described by Kinsey include the following. Fewer men experience their first intercourse with a prostitute, 20 per-

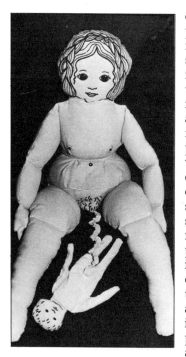

A doll with foetus and umbilical cord testifies to a growing concern with sex education in recent decades.

cent in Kinsey's findings. Present estimates range from 2 percent to 11 percent. This change would seem to follow from the greater availability of ordinary women. Fellation seems to be the sexual service most frequently requested from prostitutes; in Kinsey's findings it was intercourse. At the present time, oral–genital acts seem to be more commonly practiced by the general public or are more readily admitted. They do not carry the very great stigma that was fairly general in Kinsey's day. If true, what may have happened is that "upper level" practices have spread to working-class people. It has been said that the increased sale of vaginal deodorants in the past few decades has accompanied the spread of cunnilingus. The correlation sounds plausible but remains speculation. Pomeroy has suggested that homosexual experiences may be more common than in the 1940s. Other scholars see evidence that the percentage of exclusive homosexuals has gone down. The incidence of sexual intercourse within marriage, on the other hand, seems to have gone up. The incidence of adultery may also have gone up, in part because of the spread of a philosophy of "open marriage," which in some versions includes "swinging" and consensual adultery. All of these practices were known in the United States in Kinsey's time and before. What seems to be different is percentages. And these differences may not be great.

From a cross-cultural perspective, none of these things verge on the extraordinary. Even the divorce rate, which has clearly gone up, is unexceptional cross-culturally. A study by G. P. Murdock of 40 societies led him to conclude that American society was nowhere near levels of family disorganization that would be truly disruptive socially. Furthermore an emotional ideological commitment to family exists in spite of the absolute (but not relative) increase in the number of unmarried adults in the society.

Human sexuality has a variety of cultural components superimposed on a biological structure. The basic biological adaptations and constraints do not change. No sexual revolution is going to permit human males to experience 100 orgasms a day no matter what ideology is involved. The relation of sexuality to culture is more complicated. Clearly the cultural aspects can change dramatically, but the culture of sexuality is perhaps more stable than has been supposed. The much discussed recent changes may prove to be less of a revolution than has been proclaimed.

Part Two

THE GEOGRAPHY OF SEXUAL PRACTICES

Sexual customs and ideologies
differ enormously from culture
to culture throughout the world.
This diversity often challenges
accepted western notions of
sexuality, society
and the individual.

Tutelary deities with prominent sex organs guard against evil and ensure fertility in a Chad (Central Africa) village.

Twelve ❦ AFRICA

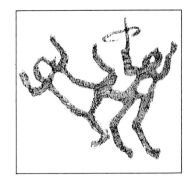

A footprint nearly four million years old from Africa may provide a clue about the earliest sexual preferences of humanity. Modern African sexuality too may have lessons for the West.

Sex in its distinctively human forms must have started out in Africa. For one thing, the earliest fossil evidence for humanlike forms is found there, going back nearly four million years. More specifically, the earliest clear indications that humanlike beings walked erect on two feet come from Africa; this human peculiarity led to major changes in primate sexuality.

The most dramatic evidence for erect posture and walking on two feet is surely human footprints 3,600,000 to 3,800,000 years old discovered in 1979 by Mary Leakey in Laetolil, Tanzania. The prints, preserved in volcanic ash, have even led Leakey to believe that they indicate the first traces of a nuclear family. There are three sets of prints, apparently of two adults walking side by side leading a child: if these represent a man, a woman and their single offspring, we have at once the modern western ideal and the dream of zero-population proponents; but we cannot know for sure.

But something else is suggested by these footprints; the distinctively human big toe revealed by the prints is good evidence not only for upright posture but probably also for preferential frontal entry intercourse (and possibly a whole range of other distinctively human sexual practices).

There are at present no unambiguous Palaeolithic representations of sexual intercourse, whether human or otherwise. In Africa, the earliest so far is believed to be a sandstone engraving found at Tel Issaghen

in Libya; it dates from 7000 BC (an even earlier representation comes from the Middle East). Although this engraving almost certainly shows sexual intercourse, it is not clear what it means, because one of the figures has a wand or implement of some sort in one hand. It is even hard to see what coital position is shown.

In southern Africa, rock paintings are also to be found,

but of a considerably more recent date (as late as AD 1800). The people shown in these drawings resemble modernday Bushmen and Bantu-speaking peoples. Occasionally female figures seem to be shown with long labia, the so-called "Hóttentot apron." What is strange, however, is that male figures, usually shown naked and with erections, have some sort of decoration on their penes. Some have suggested that this is a kind of *ampalang* (penis bar), found nowadays among groups in Borneo and the Philippines.

Earliest known depiction of intercourse from Africa. A sandstone engraving from Tel Issaghen, 8th millennium BC.

Petroglyphs found at Ti-N-Lalan, Fezzan, dating to 3rd or 4th millennia BC.

Rear entry is suggested in a rock painting (above) *by hunter-gathering Bushmen.*

Bushman rock painting from South Africa (below) *showing the mysterious "crossed penis."*

The odd thing is that nothing in presentday cultures in southern Africa — or anywhere else in Africa — helps explain the "crossed penis."

Hunters and gatherers

For about 99 percent of all of man's existence, hunting and gathering have been the predominant ways of getting food. The raising of crops and the herding of animals developed only about 10,000 years ago and brought about a dramatic change in human lifestyles, referred to as the Neolithic Revolution.

Today, very few peoples in Africa live as hunters and gatherers: fewer than 200,000 out of a total population for the continent of over 350,000,000. Even at the beginning of European exploration in the fifteenth century, most groups were already agricultural and only a few were herders. But African hunters and gatherers probably represent an unbroken line from the earliest kind of economy.

Generally, African hunter-gathering groups appear to begin an active sexual life early in childhood. According to Marjorie Shostak, all the !Kung Bushman women she interviewed had experienced sexual intercourse as children. Even though adults say they do not approve of this and maintain that it should wait until the children get older, they do nothing to prevent such sexual experimentation unless it occurs near them.

The same general lack of concern about childhood sexuality has been reported for the neighboring Hóttentots, who are related to Bushmen hunters and gatherers linguistically, culturally and physically. But Hóttentots have taken up herding.

All hunting and gathering groups permit a man to have more than one wife. In actual fact, however, few have more than one at a time and the greatest number is seldom more than three or four. Although there are sporadic instances where a woman might have more than one husband, these are highly irregular.

Little is known about the sexual repertoire of hunters and gatherers, but for the !Kung we have more information than for most. Most striking is the rear entry coital position: both the man and woman lie on their sides, the man at the back. Lee maintains that this position is assumed at night, around communal fires under a shared blanket and is prompted by a desire to be inconspicuous. It may be that rear entry is the most common position, but it is not necessarily the preferred one. In sexual encounters during daytime away from camp, the most common is the missionary position. Frontal entry is a distinctively human copulating manner, so these Bushman data are important.

What seems to be the most reasonable explanation for the development of the Bushman position is not the continuation of a basic mammalian pattern, in spite of walking on two legs, but another human peculiarity that no baboon or chimpanzee can ever understand: a sense of modesty. Bushmen cannot escape into a hut or a room because they have none.

The ancient Egyptians

The earliest documented commentaries about the sex life of any group living on the African continent exists for the ancient Egyptians. This is no earlier than 5,000 years ago. Although they may have influenced other cultures in Africa, it is not clear that they did so directly. But the sexual life of the ancient Egyptians is interesting in its own right and will be considered here in some detail.

In the ancient world, the Egyptians enjoyed a reputation

for being, in a word, sexy. Their erotic freedom and skill seem to have been as proverbial to their contemporaries as that of the French in modern times.

Kambyses, king of Persia, started a war with Egypt in the sixth century BC because the pharaoh would not let him marry one of his daughters. According to a Greek commentator, he had heard that "Egyptian women excel all others in passionate embraces." The Hebrew prophet Ezekiel spoke

with disgust of the "whoredom brought from the land of Egypt." According to Suetonius, the Roman emperor Tiberius kept, in his villa on Capri, a sexual manual, possibly illustrated, by an Egyptian courtesan named Elephantis. Egyptian dancing girls were particularly popular in Rome because of their erotic dances and songs.

In light of such a reputation, it is perhaps surprising that little direct information has survived about ancient Egyptian sexual behavior. This has been compounded by the prudery of modern Egyptologists. Representations of the god Min, for example, have embarrassed many Egyptologists because he is usually represented with an erection. One young museum curator told me of having found a box of over a dozen wooden phalli removed from statues of Min by previous curators and then merely hidden away. The great Egyptologist Flinders Petrie found publishing illustrations of the god so awkward that he placed the label of the illustration over the phallus to block it out.

In the absence of a codified law dealing with ancient Egyptian sex and marriage, it is not clear what their conceptions of incest might have been. Incest within the royal family was permitted: pharaohs regularly married their sisters or half-sisters, possibly because succession to the throne went in the female line. King Akhenaten is known to have married several of his own daughters. But the problem is compounded because their use of the words "brother" and "sister" is generally extended to sweethearts without apparently implying incestuous attachments.

The king married several

Egyptian dancing girls (above) and a figurine of a man with enormous penis (left). The ancient Egyptians enjoyed a great reputation for sexual freedom and skill.

Ancient Egyptian sexual gymnastics are seen in the Turin papyrus (above), including a man trying to copulate with a dancing woman, and copulation with a woman from the rear in a chariot drawn by two girls.

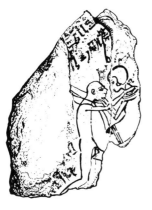

Erotic graffitti (above), scratched on ancient Egyptian shards (ostraka). The goddess Isis as sparrowhawk (right) hovers above the living phallus of her dead consort Osiris

wives and both he and the rich frequently had harems, but monogamy predominated among people at large.

There is some evidence that marriage was arranged by parents, perhaps even in childhood. Adultery was condemned, and an adulterous wife could be killed (death by burning is mentioned in at least two stories). Adulterous husbands were not similarly punished, but men were admonished against adultery and frequenting of prostitutes. In the late period, the position of women seems to have improved, and divorce was substituted for death. Also, there was the development of a form of temporary marriage in addition to the traditional permanent kind. Marriage contracts often mention a period of five months. Love magic from this period reflects this contractual possibility. One inscription from the first century AD reads, "Make Niké, daughter of Apollomes, be stricken with love for Pantus, son of Tmesis, for five months."

Premarital chastity was not stressed, although a word for "virgin" (referring to a sexually mature female) existed. Lifelong celibacy seems to have

been discouraged, but at least some priestesses were virgins. Sexual acts were apparently forbidden in temples. But the evidence is not altogether conclusive, and at least in Ptolemaic times sexual acts may have been performed as part of a religious role in the so-called "Bes chambers" in Saqqara (Bes was a god of sexual love). According to some authorities the worship of the god of virility and generation, Min ("the bull who covers females"), was accompanied by orgies. The general feeling, however, was that sexual acts in holy places were unseemly or at best inappropriate. In various texts of the *Book of the dead*, the negative confession (which the dead man recites to justify his life after death) includes statements such as "I did not fornicate in the sacred places of the god of my town" and "I have not masturbated [in the sanctuaries of the god of my city."

Prostitutes other than sacred prostitutes did exist and were quite common. Coital positions are shown in drawings made by the ancient Egyptians and described in their literature, usually religious, in which sexual acts of various gods are discussed in some detail. There seems to be only one clear

illustration of the missionary position in all of Egyptian art; a petroglyph at Beni Hasan from the XIth dynasty. Nevertheless, it was probably the most common position used and thought of as normal. This is clear from a story about the goddess Isis, who has to copulate with her husband Osiris by sitting upon his prostrate body. In the story Isis says, "I have played the part of a man though I am a woman" — which makes sense only if the missionary position was taken for granted. In the Turin erotic papyrus a number of acrobatic and whimsical positions are illustrated: one scene shows the woman standing above the man, suggesting the woman-on-top position highly reminiscent of common representations of the earth god Geb, often shown with an erection, and the sky goddess Nut, who hovers above him.

Almost no information about homosexuality survives in the literature. But there are said to be illustrations showing homosexual anal penetration. For a man not to play the "man's role" in a sexual encounter or for a man to be emasculated in certain ways was degrading. Penes were collected as war trophies. A text from the Middle Kingdom suggests that a dead man can render the gods powerless by foration ("Atum has no power over me, because I copulate between his buttocks").

Masturbation and fellation are rarely if ever shown and yet both had religious significance. The world was believed to have been created through an act of divine masturbation by the god Atum, whose hand was his celestial spouse. The earth god Geb is sometimes depicted as performing autofellation. Of the god Re, it was said that "he copulated with himself."

Nekrophilia was known and disapproved of at the time of Herodotus. He specifically says that the corpses of noble and beautiful women were protected from embalmers. It may have been different with the corpses of men because some sort of ritual pseudocopulation with the actual mummy was performed to restore the dead man's virility.

Herodotus also reported bestiality. He was shocked by seeing a woman having public intercourse with a he-goat. This act may well have had religious significance, since the province in which the incident occurred held "all goats in veneration, but the male more than the female." There was a single, especially sacred, he-goat before whom women traditionally exposed themselves in order to strengthen his generative power and possibly to guarantee their own fertility.

Egyptian erotica is scanty, mostly in the form of figurines. One common theme is musical, such as a man with a gigantic penis having intercourse with a woman playing a harp.

Erotic figurine from 650 BC shows a man with a woman playing the harp. This frequent theme may reflect a similarity in the Egyptian words for "harp" and for "to have an erection."

Marriage in Africa as a whole

Returning to the "ethnographic present" (the time when westerners first came in contact with a group), I shall deal with Africa as a whole, emphasizing black Africa south of the Sahara.

The general, ideal marriage pattern throughout all traditional African cultures is for a

Among the Zande, harems for a few men mean scarcity for the majority.

man to have more than one wife. In some groups, such as the hunting and gathering societies already mentioned, this is permitted but rarely achieved. In other societies, notably the Zande and the Nupe, a few men control great numbers of women, leaving many men without any legitimate mates.

The only traditional societies on the whole continent for whom the ideal is monogamy are the Ethiopian Christians, the Berbers of North Africa (even though they are Muslim), the Mbugwe (a Bantu-speaking group in mainland Tanzania) and the Nigerian Daka and Jibu.

For a woman to have more than one husband has been described as almost nonexistent throughout Africa. But there are instances where a woman may have several recognized mates.

What is clear is that in many societies — whatever the label

The ancient Egyptian god Min, shown in characteristic pose (opposite top right), shares features with a black African statuette (opposite below right) from the Congo.

given by the particular society itself to the arrangement — women are allowed to have many sexual partners. This fact is a serious problem for exponents of sociobiological theories of differing male and female reproductive strategies. And this does not even consider the illegitimate affairs of women. These may be extensive, even in societies that trace descent through males, which sociobiologists believe have a lower rate of female promiscuity than those that trace descent through females. An extraordinary counterexample is that of the patrilineal Muslim Nupe, where married women are so free with their sexual favors that it has been described as bordering on prostitution.

A husband may share his wife with other men, at least occasionally, and for various other reasons as well. In some instances he is supposed to make her sexually available to a close relative. Among the Mongo-Nkundu, for example, his brothers have the right of copulating with her; if she refuses, her husband may scold or even beat her.

Sex hospitality, in which a wife is offered to a guest, is reported from a number of societies, mostly Bantu or East African. Among the Maasai, etiquette specifically requires that a man leave his own hut so that his wife can entertain their guest alone. A married woman may have sexual intercourse with any man belonging to her husband's age group.

Tabus

Sexual intercourse performed out of doors is condemned in a considerable number of societies, including the West

African Dogon, Mossí, Edo, Edda, Ibibio, Twi and Tallensi, the Nilotic Lango and also some Bantu groups such as the Mongo-Nkundu, who think it is inappropriate even for illicit affairs. Among the Tallensi and the Lango, who came from otherwise very different cultural traditions, if it is discovered that copulation has occurred out of doors, the very spot must be covered and everyone who passes by must throw leaves, grass or branches on it. Bowdich, an authority on the Twi, says that formerly the custom was that if a couple were discovered copulating in the open, they became the slaves of the first person to discover them (they could, however, be bought back by their families). Among the Bini, a man guilty of copulating in the bush was charged with manslaughter and chained for up to three months.

This tabu is not held by all African groups, for example the Bushmen, who lack houses in the first place, and the Pigmies, who prefer sexual encounters in the forest. If we consider the practices and tabus of people from other areas of the world, this tabu on sex *outside* a house contrasts strikingly with the rules of New Guinea tribes where sex *inside* a house is forbidden.

A similar, fairly commonly reported tabu is on intercourse during daylight hours. The Zulu feel that this rule is merely part of common decency — otherwise people would be like dogs. The Bambara believe that doing so would produce albino offspring. The Kikuyu prohibit daytime copulation except in certain ritual situations; breaking this tabu would cause sickness among the people and their cattle. Others with the same tabu are the Mongo-Nkundu, Fang, Ganda and Maasai.

Tabus on sexual intercourse during menstruation, pregnancy and nursing are common throughout the world and are not unusual (though by no means universal) in African societies. Among the Kikuyu and Maasai it is believed that sexual intercourse during pregnancy causes a miscarriage. The Kikuyu permit the practice of a restricted kind of intercourse, in which the husband may insert his penis up to a certain point (said to be about 2 inches/5 cm); full penetration would destroy the womb and the foetus. The limit for penetration is actually gauged on the penis itself because of a peculiarity of the Kikuyu circumcision operation; the foreskin is not totally removed but is arranged to hang at the appropriate distance below the glans in a kind of tassel called *ngwati*. This practice is explained both in terms of its use for determining the proper depth of insertion in restricted intercourse, and also because in unrestricted intercourse it serves to increase sexual excitement — presumably like a French tickler. Peoples who lack such a tabu generally believe that more than one ejaculation is necessary to produce a child, or that in some other way copulation during pregnancy helps the foetus. The majority of Kgatla–Tswana believe that conception requires at least three or four nights of successive copulation; people who want to avoid pregnancy consequently take precautions on the third or fourth nights only — with sometimes unexpected results.

Tabus on copulation during menstruation are the rule; I know of no exception for the whole of Africa. To break the tabu leads to ritual contamination, and it may also be injurious to the man's health.

Punishment for adultery is shown on a wooden seat from the West African Chokwe.

A tabu on sex during breast-feeding is not universal in Africa; it is absent, for example, among the Rundi. The duration of such tabus when found is quite variable: from four months to two years for the Yao, from six to eight months for the Twi, for three years for the Tallensi. The usual justification for the tabu is that if the mother gets pregnant before a child is weaned, the child will suffer.

Another widely held rule requires abstinence from all sexual behavior before warfare. Similarly a tabu exists in many societies before and during a hunt or a fishing expedition. The Hóttentot observe such a tabu only before an elephant hunt. The Ila do so before fishing, but some believe it is good luck to have sex before hunting. The Zande believe that a wife's adultery during a husband's hunting trip may result in an accident to him.

The Mongo-Nkundu believe that adultery during the period of ritual seclusion on the part of a man will hurt his newly born child, but after that period it will not — provided the father does not take the child on his knees the very day he commits adultery. A wife can easily guess at her husband's infidelity through his refusal to take the child on his knee. The Nkundu use the expression *ba ngó b'âbé*, "a father's bad knees," when talking about this adultery.

Adultery during pregnancy by either husband or wife is considered exceedingly serious by many groups. The Bemba, for example, hold to the common

Bantu belief that if a man commits adultery when his wife is pregnant, the baby will be born dead. The Ganda, Ngoni and Yao require even the husband to confess publicly during a difficult labor, but usually only the wife is forced to do so.

As a matter of fact, some groups define adultery more strictly than mere sexual intercourse. The Lozi, for example, count that a man has committed adultery with a married woman he is not related to if he walks along a path with her or gives her snuff or a drink of beer.

Stepping or jumping over people, or sitting in certain positions may be treated as the equivalent of sexual intercourse or at least as fraught with sexual overtones. For a man to sit on his daughter-in-law's mat is a sin of the first magnitude among the Tallensi. Among the Ganda, on certain ritual occasions a man and a woman must have sexual intercourse even if they are divorced or separated, and this may happen on the night of the wedding of their daughter. If the girl's parents do not actually copulate, the woman must jump over the man, which is taken as the symbolic equivalent of sexual intercourse. In the same vein, the Zulu forbid a person to step over someone else of the opposite sex.

The Zulu have a number of very specific prohibitions. For example, a woman should not have sexual intercourse with her husband after he has killed — or even touched — a python, hyaena or crocodile. A man involved in a law suit may lose it if he sleeps with his wife. Copulation should be avoided after a bad dream and during a storm (because thunder and lightning can interfere with sex).

Among the Twi, if a man or woman should be overheard

bragging or even talking about a dream in which the dreamer has sex with another person, a charge of adultery may be brought against the dreamer by the husband or wife of the dream partner.

The sex life of royalty

One characteristic of several African kingdoms was brother–sister unions in the royal family. The practice of such first-degree royal marriages very likely spread from Egypt to various kingdoms in black Africa and in some instances were purely symbolic. In some Lunda kingdoms in Zaire, the king at his enthronement goes through a ritual in which he lifts his sister's skirt and looks at her genitals. The Luba of Zaire actually require incestuous consummation, but only once — as part, again, of the ritual of enthronement. In at least six eastern or central African kingdoms — Ankole, Buganda, Bunyoro, Zande, Shilluk and possibly also Rwanda and Burundi — the royal brother–sister unions were supposed to be sterile; from a practical point of view this means that abortion or secret adoption was probably practiced. In the Fon kingdom of Benin, children produced by incestuous marriages could not be heirs to the throne.

Societies in which first-degree marriages were customary or permitted among royal (and sometimes noble, less frequently other) families with no restrictions on offspring include not only the ancient Egyptians but also the former Monomotapa Empire of Zimbabwe, and the Nyanga. Sociobiologists point out that in such a setting, brother–sister marriage could

well hit a genetic jackpot if it produced a fit offspring with unimpeachably high status, carrying on the royal genes to an unprecedented extent.

In some societies there was another aspect to royal sexual life. If a king proved to be sterile or impotent, it was a matter of grave concern for the whole kingdom, for he embodied the health of all the people. The ancient Hausa kept an official (the *Kàryà-gíiwáa*, the breaker of elephants), who was supposed to strangle an infirm king.

Sex rituals

There are a few instances in which sexual acts have to be performed for ritual purposes. For example, the Ila force boys during their initiation training to imitate sexual intercourse with one another after they have been given the traditional sex education, and they are also ordered to masturbate.

In at least three societies a widow must perform sexual intercourse ritually to remove her polluting status as a widow. The Twi of Ghana require that the widow (before she remarries) has sex with a stranger who does not know she is a widow. By doing so, she is cleansed of the spirit of her dead husband. The Thonga and neighboring Yao have similar customs, and believe that the widow actually transmits her contamination to the man she copulates with.

There is a variety of other forms of required, ritual sexual acts restricted to Bantu-speaking groups.

With regard to ritual copulation, consider the custom of "ceremonial rape" formerly found among the Kikuyu, Rundi, and possibly also Chaga. Among the Kikuyu, boys who

Yoruba royal stool. *As with many other societies, West African sexual customs are different for the high-born.*

An African royal chair details many of the area's sexual practices.

had been circumcized had to find a married woman who was a stranger to them and have sex with her. The rape became rape in name only because most of the boys simply masturbated in her presence, although some also ejaculated on her body. As soon as this ritual act was accomplished, each boy threw away a ceremonial bundle of sticks and the wooden plugs that had been stuck in his ear lobes as a sign that he was now a man. Until his ceremony was completed, no boy or man could lawfully copulate with or marry a Kikuyu woman.

Initiated girls have to undergo a similar experience, the descriptions of which are not clear.

Many African societies practice widow-inheritance: a man inherits all his dead father's wives except his own mother. No matter how unusual this may sound to Westerners, the custom makes sense if marriage is thought of as an alliance between families. Although the custom is fairly common, there is a detail in the transfer of wives that is quite remarkable and found to my knowledge only among Bantu groups — it is reported only from two (but probably has occurred in more): the Chaga and the Nyakyusa. In both these groups the heir must have intercourse with each one of the wives in a single night. Among the Chaga, this is done the day when the widows' heads are shaved as a sign of mourning. Only pregnant and nursing wives are excepted. If the man does not go through with this ceremony, it is taken as proof that he has renounced his claim on his father's property. Among the Nyakyusa, a man must sleep with all the wives no matter how old or unattractive, or else the women's legs will

swell and their minds and bodies grow weak.

Semen has a certain ritual importance among the Bantu — particularly the eastern Bantu — which is not reported from other groups in Africa. For example, the Bemba, Nyika and Yao perform semen testing. Among the Yao, the first intercourse after menstruation must take place on the veranda of a girl's home (one of the few instances in which out-of-door copulation is permitted in Africa) and her husband should withdraw before he ejaculates so that his semen falls upon a cloth. The cloth is then taken by the girl to some old women in the village who will evaluate its qualities.

The Bemba and Thonga require ritual sexual acts in founding a new village. The Bemba custom is for the village headman to "warm the bush" by copulating ritually with his wife before the huts of a new village are occupied. The Thonga have a more elaborate set-up. First, the headman and his principal wife must go through with the ritual copulation at the spot chosen for the new village. From that point on all the people in the community must observe a tabu on sexual relations until all the huts have been built and the fence surrounding the whole village has been completed. Then, after a purification ceremony, each couple in the village copulates in a fixed order of precedence, one every night. The principal wife of every man is the last to do so.

The Zande share a custom found in several Bantu groups: a belief in the magical detection and punishment of adultery. The Zande version of this is for a man to smear a special poison on his own penis before having intercourse with his wife. The poison enters the woman but does not harm her since it affects only men (the husband has taken an antidote beforehand). Any man who copulates with her will be affected by the poison: his penis will rot and he will develop a skin disease that will eventually kill him.

The Ngoni and Zulu similarly use medicines to cause their wives' lovers to die. The Zulu also have an adultery punishment magic that causes the adulterous lover's muscles to shrivel up and become stiff, his veins to become full of blood clots, his testes to swell up and throb painfully. In addition to the pain, he becomes impotent.

A custom that may have been developed by Nilotic-speaking groups (or by some Kushitic group) and then borrowed by the Bantu is a sexual act without actual penetration, such as copulating between the thighs or against the belly. Among a great many traditional Africans, young unmarried people are permitted to do so quite freely. From a cross-cultural point of view, this practice of external intercourse is almost entirely restricted to black Africa.

I suspect that the institutionalization of such a prac-tice probably started in a society that insisted on late marriage, as do the Maasai. Maasai society is broken up into a number of age grades so that males are classified as uncircumcized boys, circumcized boys, junior warriors, senior warriors and elders. Only senior warriors may marry, although juniors are expected to sleep around.

A right–left symbolism among Bantu and other African groups may point to wider cultural ties. For example, a common position for sexual intercourse involves both the man and woman lying on their sides, facing each other. The custom is that the man should lie on his right side, so that his left hand is free for sexual play. The woman lies on her left side. In many African languages the right hand is said to be the male hand, the left the female hand.

Homosexuality

References to homosexual behavior among African peoples are often confusing. Western travelers, themselves sometimes homosexual, who recount their own experiences have suggested a fairly high

André Gide and friend during *African journey. He reported a high tolerance of homosexuality.*

Transvestite African shaaman. *A culturally recognized role.*

tolerance in some areas for homosexual acts. Perhaps the best known of such travelers is André Gide, the Nobel prize-winning novelist and self-proclaimed pederast. In his last book, *Ainsi soit-il (So be it)*, 1952, he describes how a young boy called Mala was given to him, along with another boy, by the Sultan of Rey Bouba in Cameroon in 1926. Gide's affair with him, hidden from public view only by a mosquito net when they were on safari, occasioned the lines, "Gentle Mala! It is your elfin laugh, it is your joy, that I should like to see again on my death bed."

Observers from other areas seldom leave such personal accounts and what they say may be contradictory. For example, Wandres and Fritsch writing about the Nama Hóttentot deny the occurrence of any kinds of homosexuality, but Falk maintains it is fairly common and regarded as a matter of custom. A special, intense, institutionalized friendship called *soregus* is often (according to Falk) a homosexual relationship, especially between boys, who are described as watching over each other jealously.

Because the strong feeling against homosexuality in the West may tip the scales against getting or giving adequate information about the subject, I shall assume that disagreement about its presence or absence should be resolved in terms of the positive description.

With regard to the Zulu, the only unambiguous reference to homosexual acts to be found in the records involves purification, when a warrior has contracted a ritual disease known as *izembe* after killing an enemy. The warrior cannot go to live in his own home until he has had sexual intercourse with any woman not of his own tribe, thus removing the *izembe* disease. But if the warrior cannot find an appropriate woman, he may substitute a boy. This indicates little except that ritual pederasty is at least known and sometimes tolerated.

Western notions of homosexuality often raise problems when used cross-culturally.

J. H. Driberg, for example, writes that the Lango of Uganda punish "sexual aberrations contrary to the order of nature" by death. In his own official government capacity he was occasionally called in to decide such cases, which usually involved involuntary nocturnal emissions by boys sleeping near each other in a communal hut. Now if these had been deliberate acts, the situation would have been very serious. In a footnote, however, Driberg mentions that a number of Lango men have opted to live as women, wear women's clothes, simulate menstruation — and marry other men. They are not killed but fill a culturally recognized role. Driberg notes that in the related Iteso and Karimoja tribes, "such people of hermaphroditic instincts are very numerous."

Clearly in the Lango instance we are dealing with one style of homosexuality not usually distinguished by Westerners. The laws relating to homosexual acts apply in the West whether the participants are transvestite or not. Without Driberg's footnote, a most misleading notion of Lango life would have developed: it is not homosexual acts in themselves that are crimes (since some are in fact institutionalized), but only such acts when they occur in noninstitutionalized contexts. The Nyakyusa reverse the Lango pattern: male adolescent homosexual acts are not punishable with death but are accepted as a natural part of development. Other kinds would be regarded as witchcraft and the perpetrators punished.

Among the Mbundu and the Fang, one or another kind of homosexuality is known but is condemned. The Fang are said to treat homosexuals with public contempt, and to believe that they are punished supernaturally with leprosy. But it is not clear whether the people reporting this found out about all the possible variants — which, as we have seen, makes a difference. In spite of the contempt the Fang are reported to show, they consider homosexual intercourse as one of the ways of acquiring wealth — not through prostitution but through the "medicine" (or spiritual power) that rich men have and which is believed to be transmitted by sexual contact.

Male homosexual techniques are rarely mentioned, although there seems to be a convention among ethnographers that anal foration is to be understood unless otherwise noted.

Information about female homosexuality is even more skimpy. Turnbull says lesbians are unknown among the Pigmies, but gives an expression for "lesbian" in their language (*dora bopa*). Lesbianism is said to be completely unknown among the Bala and Kikuyu as well. Mongo-Nkundo girls and women engage in homosexual acts, and co-wives reportedly do so. The Kgatla–Tswana women may also do so when their husbands or lovers are away.

The Zande

In the western world, male homosexual acts have been far more intensely condemned than female ones. The situation is dramatically reversed among the Zande, whose sexual customs have been particularly well described by E. E. Evans-Pritchard, and whose treatment of homosexuality is closely interwoven with the rest of their sexual practices.

Zande practices include a marked difference between the sexual behavior of noblemen and commoners; institutionalized incestuous marriages between noblemen and their daughters and paternal half-sisters; betrothal and, in some legal sense, marriage of very young girls, often at birth or a few hours after; the keeping of large harems by royalty, the nobility and rich commoners; and a resultant scarcity of women for younger men, who had, therefore, to marry fairly late in life (well into their 20s and 30s). This large-scale monopoly of women by a few men encouraged the widespread practice of homosexual acts by both men and women. Such acts were institutionalized for men but condemned for women.

The wives in a harem might be sexually deprived, but because adultery was severely punished, young unmarried men were loath even to attempt it. Death for an adulterous wife and her lover was a possibility. The minimum punishment for the lover was a very stiff fine. Some irate husbands were not satisfied with this, but demanded that the offender be mutilated. Jan Czekanowski, in his expedition to Central Africa in 1907–08, met a man who had been found guilty of adultery and had had both his hands as well as his penis cut off. He was married and his wife was sufficiently fond of him to stay with him after his adultery was

The Zande believe that it is injurious or unlucky for a man if a woman exposes her vagina to him provokingly. It is even more serious if she exposes her anus.

discovered and the mutilations inflicted. He satisfied her sexually by gantizing her with the stump of his arm.

Adultery, clearly, is a very serious offense. But unless a couple are caught in the act, the only proof is provided by the poison oracle. The poison used is a red powder made from a forest creeper mixed with water so that it forms a paste. Some small domestic fowl are forced to eat it. The fowl generally experience violent spasms and may even die. Their behavior forms the basis of the judgment.

Institutionalized male homosexual acts were associated with the military organization of the various Zande kingdoms. Before the coming of the Europeans, large numbers of adult men were organized into military units of either married men or bachelors. It was the custom for the men of the bachelor companies to take boy-wives, who could be as young as 12 or as old as 20. The relationship between the two was regarded as a legal union as long as it lasted. The older man had to pay a bride-price of five or more spears to the parents and performed services for them as he would if he had married a woman. If he proved to be a good son-in-law, he might later get one of their daughters as a wife to replace their son, who would in turn become a bachelor soldier and take a boy-wife. If another man had relations with the boy-wife, the husband could go to court with a charge of adultery.

The Zande thought the sole reason for such marriages was the shortage of women, not the lure of boys, but the custom was never spoken of as disgusting or abnormal. In post-European times it entirely disappeared, most probably because of a

breakdown of the traditional morality, the suppression of the traditional punishment for adultery, and because it was easier for young men to marry women.

Lesbians are regarded as especially dangerous, being associated with the most feared of all evil creatures, the *adandara*, fantastic wild cats that live in the bush, and utter shrill cries in the night. It is unlucky even to hear their cries and Zande carry whistles round their necks to help ward them off. The male cats copulate with women, who give birth to kittens and breast feed them as though they were human babies. It is fatal for a man to see one of these women suckling her kittens. It is said that the great king Bazinbi died precisely in this way. He opened the door of a hut belonging to one of his wives, Nanduru — who was also his daughter — and saw a cat run out of it. She was executed along with her two cat children.

In the past, if a prince discovered that any of his wives were involved in homosexual activities, he would not hesitate to execute them. At present, such women are merely expelled from princely households in disgrace.

However, it was precisely in large polygamous households that lesbianism was practiced — in large part, because of sexual deprivation. Men may, in a sense, initiate such relationships. A prince might actually give a slave girl to one of his daughters (simultaneously his wife) and the two would be likely to have an affair.

Sexual techniques and statistics

Very little evidence of a statistical nature is found for any

Basically just head, legs and penis: *an anthropomorphic goblet from Kinshasa, Zaire.*

African group for any kind of sexual act. Among the Zande, Kgatla-Tswana and Nyika two or three coital acts are said to be normal every night for a married man, and one of these occurs early in the morning upon rising. Chaga men have been reported as copulating as often as 10 times in a night, and it is claimed that this is not unusual. Among the Kgatla-Tswana, the maximum reported for a man is six or seven times in succession, but this would occur only after a period of ritual abstinence or a long absence without sexual contacts. Thonga men may copulate with three or four of their wives in a single night. This is unusual: elsewhere a man rotates among his wives and copulates with only one of them a day or a week. The most complete data on coital frequencies come from the Bala: 10 men kept sex records for 20 days. The rate of intercourse varied from once a day to 1.9 times.

With regard to sex technique, the African position (side by side) and external intercourse have already been mentioned. The missionary position is reported from the Kanuri, Zande, Chaga and Nyika; rear entry from the Bushmen and Hóttentot. Other forms are rare or not reported.

Very little mention is made of any kind of oral sex in African societies. Kissing is specifically mentioned as either unknown or not practiced in sex play among the Kikuyu, Rundi, Thonga, Mongo-Nkundo and Somali. Bala and Kgatla-Tswana men suck on the breasts of their wives as foreplay, but the Nyika find this disgusting and would use it as grounds for divorce. The Fang consider fellation by a wife or her husband as grounds for divorce. The Ila regard all oral–genital contacts as crimes.

Information about anal foration is very scanty. It is reported from Arabicized groups, but little is known about it in heterosexual contexts. Foration is said cross-culturally to be the most common homosexual practice, but it is specifically denied for the Zande, for example. Orgasm is achieved in homosexual contacts for the older partner by rubbing his penis between the boy's thighs (interfemoral foration) — the younger partner has to be satisfied as best he can with the friction of his penis on his husband's belly or groin.

Unique customs

Certain African sexual customs or beliefs are nonexistent or rare cross-culturally.

The Cewa believe that if a girl does not copulate before she starts to menstruate she will die. Cewa parents specifically encourage childhood copulation when children are playing house. If by misfortune a girl had not been deflowered by puberty, her hymen was forcibly ruptured in a prescribed way. This idea that death is the consequence of virginity is apparently unique in Africa. The neighboring Ngoni, for example, expect girls to be chaste (although Cewa views seem to be spreading).

Among the Ngoni, if a girl has no lover after puberty, her grandmother will call a young man to her house to copulate with the girl. This is done to see if everything is all right and, more particularly, to find out if the girl is proficient. The boy is rewarded for his "investigation" by the grandmother.

The Ganda have a custom somewhat reminiscent of this. A bride's aunt (more specifically,

Erotic dance with dildoes from Central Africa.

her father's sister) is actually present in the bridal chamber during the first week or so of the honeymoon.

The Yao have special regulations about sex and salt. A boy may not eat food containing salt until he has had sexual intercourse. Furthermore, if a woman who has committed adultery puts salt into the food while cooking, it is believed that her husband will die if he eats it.

The Nyakyusa have a rule that a woman must avoid drinking for a day the milk of a cow that has copulated with a bull.

There are many other sex-related customs on the African continent, and elaborate sexual symbols that permeate the thinking of various societies, such as the Bemba identification of sexuality and fire. An elaborate variation of views on sexuality also occurs, from the notion that sex is debilitating (as found among the Bushmen and the Kikuyu) to the ideal that sex should be performed as often as possible (Ila) and that its major purpose is pleasure (Ngoni and Kgatla-Tswana).

Recent developments

Many traditional African views are changing because of contact with the West and the breakdown of long-established cultures. We have little precise information about how this influences sexuality, although we can see implications of it in statements about what people look for in a partner. In several societies, lighter skin color has become more highly thought of. In at least one instance, the Fang, the ideal for breasts has changed because of European (movie) influence: girls no longer bind their breasts with strips of bark or cloth to make them fall

Erotic art for tourists: *today African gold-weights are manufactured for sale at airports.*

and hang — the older ideal. Among Ngoni women, a man is considered attractive if he has a part in his hair (following European fashions).

There is only one study, for any African groups, that has attempted acquiring statistics about sexual behavior among modern-day, westernized Africans: Pierre Henry's 1970 book on the sexual behavior of Guinean adolescents. There were 720 boys and 80 girls (high-school students), who filled out questionnaires. The striking thing is that only one student in the whole sample belonged to a traditional African religion; the rest were atheists, Christians or (the great majority) Muslims. Even so, at least 84 percent of the girls had undergone clitoridectomy, and of the Christian group 9 percent had fathers who still had more than one wife (70 percent of the families in Guinea are polygamous).

From this study, two interesting patterns emerged, which differ from western, specifically European patterns. One is that boys were never sexually initiated by an "older woman." The female partners of teenage males were generally between 17 and 20.

The second difference is much more striking. Sex is seen simply as a need, not a symbol of being a man or an adult. Boys who had had sexual intercourse did not get any particular prestige from their fellow students because of their conquests. Henry suggests that for a Guinean, the first sexual intercourse does not count as an initiation rite as it seems to for many Westerners. Consequently sexual behavior does not play the same role in the total personality of an individual. If true, this could have implications for psychology, psychiatry and social engineering.

Thirteen
THE MIDDLE EAST
and neighboring societies
influenced by Islam

Middle Eastern sexuality is commemorated in art 10,000 years old. Contemporary Islamic societies celebrate sex as a foretaste of Paradise – at least for men.

Earliest known representation of copulating couple. A stone sculpture, Natufian, dated c. 8000 BC.

The earliest evidence of sex techniques, sex tabus, sexual dysfunctions, marriage laws, prostitution, love magic and other aspects of human sexuality comes from the area around the Tigris and Euphrates rivers and extending west to the Nile river.

A limited amount of information on prehistoric sexual practices can be culled from ancient works of art. A small Natufian stone sculpture showing a couple copulating is the earliest known representation of a sexual act; it may date from as early as 8000 BC. The stone seals from Ur, made a few thousand years later, show a variety of coital positions. But our main source of knowledge about ancient sexual beliefs and practices is written records. This is, after all, where writing began.

The society in which the written word evolved was that of the Sumerians in about 3000 BC. The symbols used for male and female in their writing system were stylized representations of the sex organs. Juxtaposing these representations created a new symbol designed to mean a married person.

Not much is known of Sumerian sexual customs, but it seems that ritual sexual intercourse was practiced by a priest and priestess in the New Year festival to ensure fertility for the coming year. The goddess Inanna personified sexual love. In later times and among succeeding cultures in the area she was known as Astarte or Ishtar, the patron of prostitutes. Some scholars hold her to be the precursor of the biblical Esther,

since there is no evidence that she was a historical person. In fact, her other name, Hadassah, meaning bride, is known to have been used of Inanna-Ishtar as well. If true, then in a sense the cult of Inanna still lives!

The Assyrians and Babylonians carried on much of the Sumerian way of life and probably perpetuated many of their sexual customs. Ritual sex acts, for example, are known to have been practiced. Certain acts — including premature ejaculation — were taken as omens, and nocturnal emissions counted as a sign of good luck.

There seems to have been more than one kind of temple prostitution: either priestesses were sexually available to devotees or to the priests of the temple, or ordinary women were called upon to perform an act of ritual intercourse once (or at least once) in their lives. Male temple prostitution, transvestism and the making of eunuchs were also a traditional part of these early religious customs.

Precisely how much sexuality and what kinds of sexual acts entered into Sumerian, Assyrian and Babylonian religious observances is unclear. Clearly some did, including heterosexual vaginal and anal intercourse. But it has been suggested that some more elaborated sexual and specifically phallic cults were known in this area.

There are even some tantalizing references in Hebrew writings to what may have been masturbatory rites, as in the biblical tabu: "And thou shalt not let any of thy seed pass

Ancient Mesopotamia. Ritual copulation while woman drinks through a tube. From Uruk, fifth millennium BC.

through the fire to Molech''
(Leviticus 18:21).

The oasis of Siwa

In the oasis of Siwa in Egypt
there were believed to be
ancient phallic cults dedicated
to the god Amun, which
required nocturnal orgies of
ritual masturbation, sodomy
and promiscuous copulation.
This particular detail is based on
certain statements about
modern Siwans together with a
few ancient sources.

The people who lived in the
oasis of Siwa in the Libyan
desert are an important group
because it is possible that they
have maintained earlier Near
Eastern customs intact. They are
still considered so notoriously
''loose'' in their sexual behavior
that some of the Egyptian
officials stationed there refuse to
give out their real address and
tell friends they are posted
several hundred miles away at
Marsaa Matruuh, a port on the
Mediterranean coast.

By AD 1100 the Siwans had
converted to Islam. Apparently
the Siwans are now fairly good
Muslims in everything but sex,
and the fact that they eat dog
meat (which they consider a
cure for syphilis).

The Islamic laws about sex are
flagrantly disregarded. This
disregard is found primarily in
three areas: the widespread
practice of prostitution,
indulged in even by respectable married women; the
prostitution or lending out of
adolescent boys to older men by
their parents — usually their
mothers (formerly there was
also institutionalized homosexual marriage); and public
orgies allegedly held in honor of
certain local saints.

A girl marries for the first time

Considered exceedingly licentious in their sexual habits, the people of Siwa, Egypt, may still practice pre-Islamic customs including, it is claimed, public orgies.

An elaborate Siwan wedding celebration scandalized a visiting Egyptian official in 1926 when he discovered that the marriage was between a man and a boy.

at such an early age that she is
probably a virgin. After that she
may live quite a promiscuous
life. Although a married woman
must observe a certain decorum
— for example, she must turn
her face to the wall or cover her
eyes with her veil when a man
passes her on the street — it is
said she would prostitute
herself for less than five dollars.
Husbands sometimes condone
this behavior; a few even share
their wives' earnings.

Although Siwans are allowed
to have four wives at a time, for
a man to have more than one
wife is rare. Divorce, however,
is exceedingly common — more
so than elsewhere in Egypt.

Belgrave met a man at a
wedding who was at least 85,
looked about 90, and was said to
be 102 years old. It turned out
that he was the bridegroom and
that this was his thirty-sixth
wedding. The bride was 14. The
groom died eight months later,
''a victim of connubiality.''
Serial monogamy is by no
means rare and it is quite usual
to find women in their 40s who
have been married 10 times or
more. The novelist Robin
Maugham, who visited Siwa in
1947, mentions a girl of 25 who
had been divorced 19 times.

The practice of pederasty —
including pederastic marriages
and pederastic prostitution —
has been reported from a
number of sources. Some of the
descriptions were reported by
travelers who were not
professional anthropologists
and might therefore have
inflated the facts. But even so,
we may assume homosexual
behavior was and is very
common and accepted socially.

According to Robin
Maugham, the passion of men
for boys is greater than for
women and fatal triangles are
almost invariably homosexual:

"They will kill each other for a boy. Never for a woman."

Boy marriage was practiced until at least 1926, when a high Egyptian official escorting an English tourist was scandalized to find that an elaborate wedding celebration was in honor of a man and a boy. An imaam (a Muslim holy man) was sent to help the Siwans mend their ways, but according to Robin Maugham, two years later this same imaam married a boy.

The boys are between the ages of 12 and 18 (they start to marry heterosexually at about 17). The dominant sexual practice seems to be anal foration (intercourse). In many instances it is the boy who is the active partner, which goes against the practice in other societies where pederasty is institutionalized.

Boys are rented out for the night for 5 or 10 piasters (less than 35 cents or 20p). Prominent men lend their sons to each other, and these love affairs are common knowledge among all local Siwans.

The last distinctively Siwan aspect of sexuality that is strikingly at variance with Islamic rules is the public orgy that functions at least partially as a religious rite. These orgies are said to involve both heterosexual and homosexual acts. Their history is not clear, but they may go back to rituals performed at the oracular temple. The historian Quintus Curtius Rufus says in his Life of Alexander the Great that a statue of the god Amun was carried in procession by 80 priests "behind which followed a train of matrons and virgins singing certain uncouth hymns after the manner of their country."

Remnants of the sex cults persisted for a long time in various cultures. Among the Israelites, for example, sacred prostitutes probably existed as late as 608 BC and in pre-Muslim communities much later. The ancient Near East tolerated or even enjoined a variety of sexual practices.

Out of this setting arose several important religious traditions, which have survived to this day. One of these, Zoroastrianism, developed among the Persians about 600 BC. Without going into the details of the religion — which posits a battle between the forces of light and darkness — we can characterize the sexual code associated with it as apparently something new: a restricted sexual life was regarded as one aspect of the good life and a necessity for salvation. Marriage was for reproduction only, sexual acts that did not lead to procreation were condemned and homosexual acts were considered more serious than homicide. Nocturnal emissions were also regarded as offenses (not good luck, as earlier).

Sacred prostitute from the ancient Mesopotamian temple at Assur of the love goddess Ishtar. While reclining she copulates with one man and stimulates the penis of the other.

Some Zoroastrians had many wives and even practiced wife-sharing, but generally polygamy was condemned, as were

Priestess of Anahita, goddess of fertility, depicted on a 6th-century Sassanian (Persian) silver vase. High-ranking women served as sacred prostitutes before marriage.

adultery and the frequenting of prostitutes. But prostitutes had a kind of patron: Jeh, the demonness of menstruation and the primal whore.

An extraordinary social feature associated with Zoroastrianism is marriage with close relatives. The Parsis (modern Zoroastrians) take this to mean marriage between first cousins, but scholars tend to accept the interpretation that such marriages were between brother and sister, father and daughter, and even mother and son. The Greek writer Philo maintained that the children of a mother–son marriage were considered particularly well born. A number of other authors (including Strabo and Plutarch) wrote that the Persians married their mothers, daughters and sisters. The custom continued as late as the Sassanian dynasty, but was extinct by the fifteenth century AD.

Certain elements of Zoroastrianism may have influenced the Judaeo-Christian-Islamic continuum that eventually came to dominate the Middle East.

Sexual customs

In some instances, the Hebrew tradition is known to have turned away from an earlier pattern reminiscent of either ancient sex-cult religions or of Zoroastrianism. Of these elements we can include half-brother–half-sister marriage. Evidence suggests that marriage between paternal half-siblings was legal in ancient Israel at least until the tenth century BC.

This type of marriage seems to have been a general Near Eastern custom, found among the ancient Egyptians and Phoenicians as well as the Per-

sians. Among pre-Islamic Arabs, it was legal for a man to marry his half-sister, and even his daughter or daughter-in-law. The Bible itself does not explicitly forbid father–daughter marriage though it does forbid mother–son marriage.

Quite possibly the ancient Hebrews practiced another custom they later dropped — sex hospitality. The story of Lot before the fall of Sodom offering the men of the town his virgin daughter is paralleled in the tale of the town of Gibeah (Judges 19:21), where a virtually identical incident takes place. Raphael Patai has suggested that only a tradition of sex hospitality could make sense of these incidents. The custom has had wide distribution in the Middle East, ranging from the Berbers in northwest Africa to the people of Baluchistan.

Both of these customs have been condemned in general by the Orthodox Judaic and Islamic teachings.

The only vestige of the ancient Near Eastern sex cult that has possibly survived in the later monotheistic religions is the *metsitsah*. This is part of the Jewish circumcision ritual which refers to the sucking of a drop of blood from the penis of a newly circumcized infant. The usual explanation for it is hygiene. The Talmud, for example, says: "If a surgeon does not suck the wound caused by circumcision, it is dangerous and he is dismissed" (Gemara 133d). The custom, however, may date from the Middle Ages and not be truly ancient.

If we look at the history of traditional Jews and Muslims, as well as of the Samaritans (who broke off from the Jews about the fourth century BC and who preserve many ancient customs long since abandoned by the Jews), several themes can be seen to pervade their approaches to sexuality. On the whole, I shall not discuss Christian groups here because they depart most from these shared themes and I will deal with them in a later chapter. Furthermore, I am not now talking about highly urbanized, westernized, secularized groups such as the élite of Cairo, Tehran, Istanbul or Tel-Aviv.

One of the general themes of the Middle Eastern morality is modesty. This includes a prohibition on the public display of affection between men and women, even when married. On the other hand, it does not prohibit men from holding hands in public — actually quite a common sight, not fraught with homosexual overtones. Covering the body is another aspect of modesty. Some Muslim commentators

insist that even in a medical examination, neither a man nor a woman should look directly at the genitals of a patient but must use a mirror, except in cases of

absolute necessity. According to the Talmud, a female nurse may tend a man even if she might have to see his genitals, but a male nurse may not tend a woman in the same circumstances. In everyday life, Muslim women must cover their whole bodies and often even their faces in public. Although hiding the face was never adopted by Samaritans or Jews, there is nevertheless great concern about covering the head and hiding the hair — which among some European Jews evolved into the custom of married women wearing wigs (often shaving off their own hair as well). Nudity in all groups is suspect and public nudity almost always forbidden, although there have been exceptions. For example, the Haqqa, a radically deviant Islamic sect in Kurdistan, is said to have required that men and women (along with dogs!) bathe together naked in the basin of a mosque.

Another characteristic of Samaritans, Jews and Muslims is the general opposition to celibacy: it has been tolerated by only a very few groups, such as the Jewish Essenes and some of the Sufi sects of Islam (particularly the Bektaashiiyah of Turkey). On the other hand, sects that have played up sexual license are also few and far between; they include the Jewish Shabbetaians, who believed in the "sacredness of sin" and thought sexual excesses would hasten the coming of the Messiah.

All the groups (including Koptic and Ethiopian Christians) practice male circumcision. Some Muslims, the Falashas (the black Jews of Ethiopia) and Ethiopian Christians practice various forms of female circumcision. A few

Arab men embracing. *The Islamic code of modesty does not preclude public displays of affection between men.*

A woman bathing (top): 18th-century Ottoman miniature from Istanbul. A women's communal bathhouse (above). The Islamic marriage rite requires a man to "marry the bride and make her wash."

Muslim groups also practice infibulation.

Sexual secretions are considered unclean among all the groups. A ritual washing is required after menstruation and nocturnal emissions. It is also required after sexual intercourse: in one part of the Muslim marriage rite the bridegroom is told to "marry the bride and make her wash."

The control by men of the sexuality of women is an overriding theme that shows up in various ways.

One of these ways is stress on the virginity of brides. Tokens of virginity are frequently required and some groups insist on public or near-public deflowering. In the Orthodox Jewish wedding ceremony a time is allotted for consummation, but it is not actually used for this purpose today — the bride and groom simply withdraw from their guests for a few minutes. Although the consequences of the test for virginity can be a

calamity for the bride — death in some instances — the whole consummation business can be traumatic for the bridegroom as well: impotence is always disturbing but here becomes a public disgrace. Among the Fellahin of Egypt a religious man is called in to read to an impotent groom or to write out a charm that the unfortunate man must wear under his clothes.

Stressing the fidelity of wives is another important way of realizing the theme of male control of female sexuality in the Middle East. In all groups, adultery committed by a woman is a grave offense. Although the Koran says that the punishment for adultery, by a woman or a man, is public flogging of up to 100 strokes, in practice it is the woman who suffers most. In Saudi Arabia she is liable to be buried up to her waist in a pit and then stoned to death. Among Afghans both may be bound in sacks and carried out into a field to be stoned to death by outraged neighbors. Men, however, are allowed several wives and concubines.

Prostitution is native to the Middle East and of long standing. Although it is not forbidden, it is considered shameful. Muslim prostitutes sometimes wear conspicuous crosses and pretend to be Christian so that they will not be punished for fornication or adultery under Muslim law.

The Middle Eastern treatment of women can be related to a topic played up by sociobiologists: the concern for ensuring physical paternity. Bukhaarii, writing in the ninth century, mentions various kinds of marriages practiced in pre-Islamic Arabia in which women were able to have several husbands; at least concern for physical paternity seemed not to play a role in them and a social father was designated either arbitrarily by the mother or by some specialist who was called in to decide which man the child most resembled. But this is very foreign to the mainstream of Near Eastern and modern Middle Eastern society: practically all the societies in the Middle East, whether Muslim or not, trace descent through men.

The Muslim veil has come to symbolize male dominance in the area (left), implying the disruptive sexuality of women. But on the fringe of Islamic cultures, as in African Chad (above), some women wear veils but go bare-breasted.

Male dominance in the Middle East has become associated with the public separation of men and women, symbolized in the custom of veiling. The rationale for this separation is the belief that women are a threat to men through their disruptive sexuality. The custom varies considerably throughout the Muslim world, however. Tuareg women go unveiled but the men are veiled. Sometimes it is a matter of social standing, as among the Kanuri and Hausa of West Africa, where only upper-class women observe purdah. Elsewhere, it may be part of urban as opposed to rural custom. The Dard of Afghanistan do not practice the usual seclusion of women, but in more remote areas, where Islam has not penetrated so deeply, a different kind of seclusion is the rule: the sexes are kept strictly apart from May until September. Reports seem to suggest that sexual intercourse is forbidden at this time even between husband and wife. Any detected attempt to break this tabu is punished with a fine.

It seems clear that the practice of monogamy among European Jews (which has become part of Israeli law) was influenced by the large Christian society in which these Jews found themselves. The Torah specifies no limitation on the number of wives a man may have, and the Talmud admits the legitimacy of four wives at one time — the orthodox Muslim practice. Furthermore, Jews living in Muslim countries sometimes have more than one wife.

But it is not so easy to trace the general development of all such customs. Consider, for example, the rules concerning incest.

Milk incest

The Koran forbids marriage not only between blood relatives but also milk relatives: a man and his wet-nurse, or a man and woman who have been breast-fed by the same woman. In some interpretations this tabu is extended to mean that a man may not marry the wet-nurse who breast-fed his present wife.

Among the Dard of Afghanistan, milk regulations have proliferated. If a man drinks milk with a woman it means that she has become a milk relative and that they cannot marry. In some instances milk adoption is practiced: a man places his lips upon a woman's breast in the presence of the ruler or vizier, and from that time on the woman is regarded as the man's foster-mother. Such adoption takes place when a woman dreams she has adopted the man, or when the man dreams he has been adopted by the woman. A jealous husband may also force adoption on his wife of any man suspected of being her lover.

Milk incest (a sexual union between those who have in some way shared the same breast) is forbidden in the Koran.

The distribution of these milk-incest rules throughout the world is not clear at present. Among the non-Muslim Mende of West Africa, a man may not marry any woman who has suckled him. This may be Muslim influence, however, since a number of Mende are now Muslim or have come into contact with Muslims. The prohibition on marriage between two people who have been breast-fed by the same woman is found also among the Samaritans and in some Christian groups, notably the Kopts of Egypt and Ethiopia, Eastern Orthodox groups and Italian Roman Catholics. A Muslim influence cannot be ruled out for at least some of these groups. What seems most likely is that it is an ancient Near Eastern trait. It is true that Jews do not recognize the tabu — but I suggest that they have lost the custom. Raphael Patai is undoubtedly right when he suggests that a milk-incest tabu existed among the ancient Hebrews, though there is no biblical reference to it. Even among Samaritans it is regarded as an ancient custom, not a biblical injunction.

Temporary marriage

A temporary marriage involves a contract for a specific time — sometimes only a night, three days or some other very short period of time. The contract may even specify the kinds of sexual acts that may be performed. Although there is some Koranic justification of this custom, today most Muslims reject it as a kind of prostitution, but it is recognized by Shi'as (who live predominantly in Iran and parts of Iraq). Temporary marriage has never been recognized for married women whose husbands are away.

Although most scholars do not agree, some have suggested that temporary marriage is recognized in the Torah and that the Hebrew term *shipxaah* refers to a temporary wife.

To my knowledge the Amhara of Ethiopia, a Christian group, is the only other society since ancient Egypt to institutionalize temporary marriage. It is highly improbable that the Ethiopian Christian and the (Iranian) Muslim customs are unrelated, but both probably represent a continuation of pre-Muslim Semitic customs. Bukhaarii mentions that temporary marriage was known in pre-Islamic Arabia.

So far I have discussed what has or has not been permitted by moral codes. When the evidence for actual behavior is examined it becomes clear that people often disregard and depart from these regulations.

Orthodox Jews and religious Muslims believe that the only truly legitimate sexual acts are between married couples; but a questionnaire answered by 269 rural Moroccan youths in 1969 showed that 14 percent practiced masturbation or bestiality; 20 percent practiced homosexual acts; and 34 percent went to a brothel as often as they could afford.

A Muslim is encouraged to combat all desire for illicit intercourse, and one of the ways is to have sex with his wife as often as necessary. Similarly, Jews believe that to prevent sexual fantasies from distracting him, a young religious scholar should marry early. In Islam, the need to protect a man from adultery is so great that even if his wife is menstruating (a time of pollution during which intercourse is discouraged) a man may nevertheless approach her. Al-Ghazaalii, an important Muslim divine of the early Middle Ages, maintains that the menstruating wife can be asked to cover her body between the naval and the knee with a cloth and to masturbate her husband with her hands. Jews forbid contact altogether during the menstrual period.

Samaritans, Jews and Muslims are all opposed to celibacy — the former two on the grounds of the biblical commandment "be fruitful and multiply," the latter partly because the prophet Mohammed was married and partly because of a fear that a sexually frustrated person is dangerous to the community. There are religious–legal requirements for the frequency of sexual relations. When a man has more than one wife, he is supposed to distribute his favors equally among his wives. According to the Talmud, each wife should have sexual intercourse with her husband at least once a month.

Jewish tradition even developed minimal frequency obligations associated with occupation. The Talmud (Ketubbot 5:6) lists the following frequencies: gentlemen of leisure, every night; sailors, once in six months; laborers working in their home town, twice a week, but once a week if they are working elsewhere; donkey drivers, once a week, but camel drivers, once a month; scholars, once a week, customarily on Friday night (unlike Samaritans, who forbid sex on the Sabbath).

But again, these are the religious–legal requirements; we have no definite information about actual frequencies.

The stereotype of Middle Eastern sexuality is extreme licentiousness, but this is probably a consequence of being written up by monogamous and sexually repressed Westerners, who seldom provide any statistics. Harrison, for example, says that Arabs show an unusually high level of sexuality and that their emotional lives evolve around gratifying their sexual appetites.

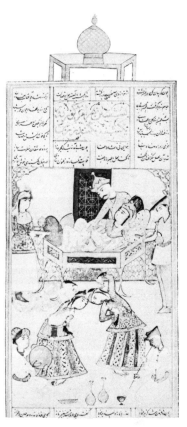

A Persian miniature shows *Middle Eastern sexuality in terms of uninhibited gratification of sexual and other appetites.*

Coital frequency

Philby (1951) has reported stories told in the presence of the King of Saudi Arabia in the 1930s. A man called Sayyid Hamza was said to cap all the stories that had been told one evening by claiming that he regularly copulated at least once a night and not infrequently in

Illustration from a Persian erotic book:
"A Jug of Wine, a Loaf of Bread — and Thou/Beside me singing in the Wilderness . . ."

Fragment of early Islamic sex manual, Egypt, 11th century AD.

of Mecca, any child that is produced will be blessed and have a face "shining like the sun and moon." (Al-Ghazaalii says, however, that one should not copulate facing Mecca, out of respect.)

There are, it is true, several handbooks of eroticism, the most famous being *The perfumed garden*, written in the sixteenth century by Shaykh al-Nafzaawii of Tunisia, but in spite of this we have little information as to what is actually done.

Samaritans, Jews and Muslims in particular tend to have a certain latitude about sex techniques. For example, although masturbation is discouraged by all of them, some Muslims feel it is permitted in times of sexual deprivation. It is never so regarded by Orthodox Jews, however, some of whom think it is the worst of all sexual offenses. For most Muslim married couples, fellation and anal intercourse are permitted — provided that the wife agrees. The same attitude is acceptable to those Jews who follow the authority Maimonides' (1135–1204) views on the subject —

the morning as well. At that time he had three wives (none of whom had ever met either of the others) and probable access to several slave girls in his three households. This hardly approaches satyriasis.

It is somewhat astonishing in the light of relatively detailed discussion of such matters in Jewish and Islamic treatises on religion, that there is such scarcity of information about sex techniques. The Human Relations Area Files produce almost no evidence for the whole of the Middle East. The Kanuri are said to find any intercourse position where the woman is above the man undesirable for social reasons. By the same logic — that social inferiors should not be physically higher than their superiors — they object to western-style buildings with many stories, unless an emir is in possession of the top floor while the lower floors house people of successively lower social positions.

Intercourse between the thighs (interfemoral foration) is reported for the Tuareg, apparently as a contraceptive technique. The Rif believe that if a man copulates in the direction

views probably influenced by Islamic thought. Other Jews (a minority at present within the Orthodox tradition) believe that only vaginal intercourse is acceptable. Even Maimonides forbids a man from trying to derive sexual satisfaction from an act that is not gratifying to his wife.

Ritual abstinence

Samaritans tabu sex on every Friday night and Saturday of the year and also on seven other holidays. Jews do not require Sabbath abstinence and tabu sex on only two days of the year: Yom Kippur (the Day of Atonement) and Tisha-be-Av (the commemoration of the destruction of the Temple). Muslims forbid sexual intercourse during the daylight hours of the whole month of Ramadaan. For ritual and legal purposes, sexual intercourse has been strictly defined by Muslims and Jews: the glans of the penis must penetrate the vaginal opening. Among Muslims, to determine whether the fast has been broken, it is necessary to know how far the penis has entered: if it goes in only as far as the "circumcision ring" (the point at which the foreskin has been cut off), the fast has been broken even if ejaculation does not occur; if it goes in less deeply (and no ejaculation occurs) or if the man cannot determine for sure how deeply his penis has entered, the fast has not been broken.

During the American conflict with Iran after the overthrow of the Shah in 1978, a book purporting to be extracts from the writings of Ayatollah Khomeini was published. It caused some amusement and virtual disbelief because it dealt with such matters as what to do with a sodomized camel. Although only part of the book can be attributed to the Ayatollah, *The little green book* does, in fact, present traditional ritualistically correct views on this matter and similar issues. Westerners, however, should not find the work so bizarre, since the law relating to sodomized camels follows the biblical ruling but is actually less strict. According to both Jewish and Muslim regulations, sodomized animals must be killed and cannot be eaten, but the biblical ruling also states that "whosoever lieth with a beast shall surely be put to death" (Exodus 22:19).

Earlier Near Eastern laws were not so strict or so apparently consistent about bestiality as the Torah or Muslim codes. In the Hittite code (probably from the thirteenth century) a man must be killed if he sins sexually with a cow, sheep, pig or dog. There is no punishment if he sins with a horse or a mule,

Man sodomizing camel.
Ayatollah Khomeini reiterated the Islamic condemnation of this practice in 1978.

though he may not appear in the king's presence and is not allowed to become a priest. In the Talmud, the nonoccurrence of bestiality seems to be proclaimed in the assertion that "a Jew is not to be suspected of pederasty or bestiality" (Qiddushin 82a); on the other hand, a widow is forbidden to keep a pet dog on the principle that "Caesar's wife must be above suspicion."

Among the Muslim Rwala, bestiality is said never to occur because it is punishable by death, but in fact the threat of a death penalty has never eradicated forbidden sexual acts from any society. Rif boys are known to sodomize she-asses in the belief that it will enlarge their penes (some also dip their penes into a heap of fresh donkey dung for the same purpose).

In spite of the Muslim rule against all bestiality, an interesting distinction has been reported from Turkey, where some people regard it as sinful only when it involves animals that are eaten, such as cattle or sheep (a rule reminiscent of the Hittite code). Like the Rif, Turks believe that sex with donkeys makes the penis grow large.

Homosexuality

The Zoroastrians, Samaritans, Jews and Muslims specifically condemn homosexual and other nonprocreative acts. With regard to Islam, it should be noted that no punishment for homosexual acts is contained in the Koran. Some commentators have therefore assumed that homosexuality is only a minor infraction. What seems to be the case is that there is a very complicated interplay of Islamic views and folk notions, which blend but sometimes also contrast with actual practice.

One of the problems is that Middle East folk notions about homosexuality distinguish sharply between active and passive roles. For a male to play the active, inserting role with another male is generally not thought of as homosexuality at all, yet it is shameful for a male to play the passive role as a vagina substitute. Throughout the Middle East, words for a passive homosexual are serious insults. Studies of psychological problems among males in Turkey and Algeria disclosed a great fear of retreating into passive homosexuality. The process of becoming an adult male is seen as putting aside the boy's female passive role — whether sexual or social.

In Turkey, teenage boys engage in verbal duels to trick opponents into acknowledging that they play a passive homosexual role.

There is very little evidence with regard to actual practice, in spite of literary references to Arab homosexual proclivities or the accounts of travelers from Richard Burton to André Gide, who described the accessibility of North African boys as astonishing. But when he writes of naked boys among the sand dunes, he is really depicting a kind of outdoor brothel. Pederastic prostitution has probably been cultivated in that area for centuries, mainly for European tourists; it cannot really count as evidence for the toleration of homosexual acts.

A certain amount of institutionalized homosexuality involving transvestism and prostitution can be found in many Muslim areas, including Oman and other countries on the east coast of Africa. Such transvestites are socially recognized and regularly entertain at weddings and on other social occasions.

The Mossí of Upper Volta used to observe a rule of not having sex with their wives on Fridays (the Muslim holy day),

Middle Eastern homosexuality. A Persian miniature of the Safavid period, end of 16th century.

but the chiefs got around the prohibition by sleeping with their boy pages, who were dressed like women. These pages were between the ages of seven and 15 (or 10 and 20 according to another account).

Reports on homosexual activity elsewhere are often contradictory. For example Lhote, writing in 1944 about the Iklan Tuareg of the Sahara, says they practice pederasty and other vices; Blanguernon (1955) insists that among the Tuareg, both male and female homosexuality is unknown. Concerning the Rif of Morocco, Coon (1931) discusses markets where boys who had been kidnapped were sold either to become apprentice musicians or sex slaves used for foration, but Blanco Izaga (1975) says that homosexuality is nonexistent among the Rif.

Other comments found in the Human Relations Area Files are fairly brief. Of the Dard, it is said that Muslim influence stopped the tradition of men and women dancing together and introduced dancing boys, which according to a commentator writing in the 1890s brought "a worse evil."

Information about female homosexuality is even less extensive. Lesbian activity is assumed to exist in the harem and, according to Oskar Baumann, among the heavily Arabicized peoples of East Africa involves the use of ebony dildoes.

The most vivid description comes from Kuwait, where Dickson (1951) says that a sex-starved Arab woman will take a black woman as her lover. The black woman inevitably takes the male role and gets the Arab girl completely under her power. Whereas the Arab develops "a depraved and absorbing affection for the negress, [the negress] becomes an overbearing, jealous tyrant." This is not the level of description expected of a Kinsey-trained investigator — which Dickson decidedly is not.

Distinctive customs

The Islamic religion is widespread and many local customs have been maintained that are sometimes at variance with orthodox teaching or not associated with Arab culture. For example, in a number of groups a man will sometimes keep more than four wives. Among the Kazakh of Central Asia, it seems that a man can have as many wives as he wants, given certain conditions.

Sex hospitality, though originally found throughout the Middle East, is against Islamic precepts. Nevertheless, it is still found, or was until fairly recently, in a number of areas. Among the Dard and Burusho, in Hunza and in Hazara, a man is expected to place his wife at the disposal of a male guest. In Nager, a man considers himself honored if his wife attracts the attention of the *thum* (the local ruler). In the Caucasus, a kind of sex hospitality exists among the Akhvakh (Daghestanians): a guest might do anything he wants with a young girl, provided her hymen remains intact. (The same rule also applies to an unmarried girl's lovers.) In some groups, sex hospitality involved only slave girls.

The orthodox Islamic tabus concerning menstruating women occasionally seem to be ignored. Although Caucasian groups observe these tabus and even require that menstruating women go to live in special menstral huts, the Burusho add a

Nineteenth-century Persian playing card.

The uninhibited pursuit of sex
— *A Persian painting illustrates a theme stressed by Christian travelers in the Middle East.*

decidedly un-Islamic touch: at the end of her menstrual seclusion the woman, instead of performing the required ritual washing in water, washes in cow's urine (urine is by definition impure and polluting in Islam and so is totally inappropriate). A Zoroastrian origin for this custom has been suggested.

The Caucasus has a number of distinctive customs. Among the Abkhazians, Cherkess and Ossetes, for example, a girl must wear a chastity corset, which is not to be removed by anyone except her husband on their wedding night.

An extraordinary report by Interiano maintains that at the funeral of a prominent person in the Caucasus, a girl of about 13 is placed on the skin of an ox that has just been killed. A robust young man must attempt to deflower her publicly. After several failures, the young man promises to marry her (or makes some other promises) and the girl usually consents to the deflowering.

Another peculiarity restricted to the Caucasus is the custom — still practiced — of marrying a little boy to an adult woman.

The boy's father is allowed to have intercourse with his son's wife until his son comes of age. Any children produced by the father belong to his son (or sometimes belong to both of them): the father is simply "raising seed" for his son, or helping to build up his son's house, just like the seed raiser found in many societies who helps impotent and elderly men. Seed raising is not permitted by Islam but is known to occur in Islamic groups, for example among Libyan Beduins. It is related to the custom of ghost marriage: the wife of a man who dies leaving no children will sleep with or marry another man, but the first child of this second union counts as the child of the dead man. This custom is sanctioned in the Bible.

An exceedingly rare if not unique custom is reported for the Burusho. The bridegroom's mother shares the bridal couple's bed, and actually sleeps between them until they feel ready to consummate the marriage. Apparently she is there to guide them through the difficulties of marital and sexual adjustment. It is possible that she may create more difficulties than she solves.

Whereas the Christian West tends to see civilization as a struggle against sexuality, the Middle East leans to the view that civilization is the product of satisfied sexuality. Muslims in particular believe that sexual delights on earth are a foretaste of the pleasures of Paradise. In this vein — at least for men — the Koran promises ". . . those who served Allah with sincerity . . . For them awaits a bountiful repast . . .
Beside them large-eyed women, modest, chaste
Like pearls inset in jewelry."
(Suuraah 15:40–49.)

Fourteen ❦ INDIA AND SOUTHERN ASIA

Sexuality has been regarded as divine in the high cultures of India and southeastern Asia. Yet nowhere has chastity been more honored than in India. Today, the paradox continues.

A Kaama suutra position that *"requires practice."*

*I*n one Hindu tradition, sexuality began when the god Shiva fell in love with the female aspect of himself. To celebrate his discovery, he composed 10,000 books on the subject. Shiva's servant Nandin reduced these to 1,000. Later scholars continued the condensation until we get to the distillation by Vaatsyaayana, which is the *Kaama suutra*.

At one point, a scholar from Paañcaala called Baabhravya is described as editing this divine manuscript into a manageable sex encyclopedia. He delegated the various chapters to a number of scholars, the most notable of whom was Dattaka, entrusted with the section on prostitutes. It is said that Dattaka lived among the prostitutes of Paataliputra and they commissioned him to write a textbook for novice whores.

The *Kaama suutra* is supposed to be a distillation of Baabhravya's compilation. It has, in any event, the cool, unromantic air of an academic treatise reminiscent of an encyclopedia.

It is not surprising that in an area where such erotic manuals developed, in part sanctioned by religion, sects arose that taught that sexual intercourse (and sometimes even adultery — or especially adultery) is an act of the utmost piety leading to a mystical experience. But what may be surprising is the fact that this is also the area where celibacy was first considered a virtue — a doctrine refined by Buddhists and Jains in the fifth century BC. Furthermore, Hindus place great value on chastity — in men — for two basic reasons: the fear of ritual contamination and the certainty that semen is the basis of strength, health and long life. Letting semen leave the body is always detrimental, although justified for the production of children.

Notions of ritual pollution and purity permeate everyday behavior in many south Asian countries. For example, many orthodox Hindus do not touch their mouth to a cup they are drinking from but will pour the water in so that the lips will not be defiled by contact with the drinker's own saliva.

The semen ejaculated in sexual intercourse pollutes both the man and the woman — but the woman more. The man's contamination is merely external: he can wash his genitals with water. But the woman cannot: her contamination is internal. This difference in pollution justifies a social practice: men may have sexual relations with women from a lower caste, but for a woman to have sex with a

Shiva, the Great God, is worshiped throughout India in the form of the lingga (phallus), set in the female emblem of the yoni.

lower-caste man is a crime since she cannot remove the added contamination. Thus a woman of higher caste would be expelled from her own caste for such an act.

Semen power

The second reason justifying abstinence is the superpower believed to be found in retained semen. It is widely believed that semen is stored in a special organ in the head. The person who does not lose his semen will become a superman. For this reason, medicines to prevent nocturnal emissions are common, and masturbation is frowned on — not so much as a sin but because it will sap the body of strength. This belief that semen is vital in maintaining and regaining bodily strength

Ascetics in India and elsewhere have practiced sexual abstinence, through which great physical and psychic powers may be developed. A 17th-century South Indian woodcarving shows asceticism and arousal combined.

and prolonging life is an essentially Hindu doctrine but is also found among the Muslims of

India and neighboring areas, as well as Buddhists (at least of Sri Lanka).

The practice of celibacy is really abstinence to develop "semen power." Ascetics are believed to develop great powers both physical and psychic. These ideas have wide currency even among western-educated peoples. A notable example is Mahatma Gandhi, who is said to have gone to extraordinary extremes to develop semen power.

In later years, he would share his bed chastely with young girls. He did so with his 19-year-old grandniece because he believed that by doing so he could gain control over political events, including the riots brought on by the partition of Bengal. It is known too that Gandhi became very much upset because he spilt his semen in a train compartment when the train stopped at a railway station.

This great concern about semen among Hindus is reflected in the fact that some men do not use soap while bathing because it would rob the skin of oil necessary for the production of semen. Instead, oil is used. It is rubbed all over the body in the belief that it will eventually seep down to the sexual glands and nourish the semen.

In part, these notions about semen power come from the idea that semen is somehow a distillation of blood. The Sinhalese and other groups throughout the area believe that one drop of semen is produced from 80 drops of blood. This is, of course, not true: semen is not derived from blood at all. But similar ideas have been held even by western scientists in the nineteenth century.

Among some sects of Hindus, Jains and Buddhists, sexual

intercourse may be considered a significant spiritual rite, which permits in some sense a mystical union with a god. But often the male worshiper is cautioned not to ejaculate. Instead, he should draw the semen up the spinal column by a technique of "nonspilling" (Sanskrit *askanda*), represented in Hindu and Jain art by the *nicha medhra* "down penis" (shown for example on the famous statue of the Jain saint Baahubali, the Gommateshvara, at Sravana-Belgola in the Karnataka province in India). In short, the worshiper is exhorted to develop what in the West would be regarded as a sexual dysfunction: ejaculatory incompetence (or, more euphemistically, retarded ejaculation). In part, the importance of preserving or developing semen power explains this.

The Hindu, Buddhist and Jain traditions are exceedingly complicated and constitute enormously varied approaches to sexuality. Certain archaeological finds in Harappaa, in Pakistan, a third millennium BC civilization, suggest an early and probably pre-Hindu origin of present-day Hindu phallic worship. At Harappaa were found various objects resembling the modern *lingga* (or *linggam*), which modern Hindus revere as a symbol of the god Shiva.

Phallic worship may not have been approved in early Hinduism but was probably borrowed from the non-Hindu native peoples by the Aryan invaders. *Linggas* of various sizes are used in Hindu worship, and some function specifically as dildoes used in religious sex rites. The real penis itself is sometimes the object of veneration. In some contexts, the penis of a particular guru or saintly ascetic may be touched and even kissed by his followers, especially by women who want children.

Phallic worship is found in some Buddhist groups as well, as is attested by the veneration of *lingga* in Sri Lanka. The *lingga* as a religious motif has been reinterpreted by Nepalese Buddhists as the lotus in which a certain Buddha (Aadi-Buddha) revealed himself. The mystical phrase *om mani padme hum* ("hail the jewel in the lotus") is probably a reference to the divine copulation of the soul with the godhead. A specific phallic cult is reported from Thailand, where the phallus is worshiped and known under the name *phra sephaling*.

By about 2000 BC the historical form of Hinduism known as Vedism developed, associated with the scriptures known as the *Rig veda*. At that time monogamy seems to have been the only recognized form of marriage, although a younger brother may have had rights of access to his elder brother's wife and some scholars suggest that brothers might even have been able to marry the same woman. Moreover, women seem very much to have been in charge of their own sexuality: they were allowed to carry on love affairs before marriage, could choose their own husband, and were not forced to marry. By 1000 BC, the time of the scriptures known as the *Atharvaveda*, men were allowed several wives, and widow immolation was practiced, although widows had the option to remarry.

From the *Mahaabhaarata*, one of the major Indian epics equivalent in some ways to the *Odyssey* and the *Iliad*, a number of other points can be inferred. It may have been compiled about 400 BC or as late as AD 200, but basically refers to events that occurred around 1000 BC.

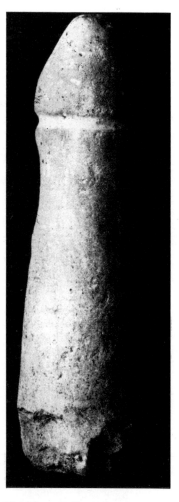

Five thousand years ago **phallic** *objects similar to the modern* lingga, *principal ikon of the god Shiva, were made and worshiped in the ancient city of Harappaa.*

Lingga from Madras, 1st century BC, shows the god emerging from his emblem.

Part of the epic deals with the life of five heroes, the Paandava brothers, who jointly married the same woman, Draupadii. This would seem to indicate that women were generally allowed to marry many men, although it may have counted as something special. Such a custom certainly did not exist in the later Hindu system. Furthermore, premarital sex is reported for women. Sex hospitality (with the host's wife) is also mentioned. A. K. Sur, maintaining that sex hospitality is nowhere practiced in India today (not quite accurate), mentions two references to it in the *Mahaabhaarata*, including an incident involving the mother of one of the more important figures, Shvetaketu.

By 500 BC, two "purifications" of Hinduism developed, Buddhism and Jainism. Both kept such fundamental Hindu doctrines as reincarnation. But originally both sects emphasized an austere life-style and apparently encouraged celibacy. They were the first large-scale cultural movements that played up celibacy as a virtue. Quite possibly, this (in addition to a general tendency toward vegetarianism) was a response to food shortages and population pressures. In later times both relaxed their sexual rules, for lay people at any rate, and even monks and nuns were associated with rumors — and facts — of quite liberal sex behavior. When asked why the Buddhist nuns in the Lepcha area did not shave their heads, one woman laughed and laughed and eventually gave the reason: "Once a woman's head is shaved, it is no longer possible to sleep with a man." Nuns in other parts of the Buddhist world have sometimes even been characterized as plying prostitution.

Buddhist monks have often fared no better, although some areas are reputedly stricter than others. Their social reputations are similar to that of Christian monks during the Middle Ages. Abel Rémusat, writing in 1875, maintained that in thirteenth-century Cambodia Buddhist priests were obliged to deflower young girls before they married. In Bhutan, new monks and nuns are recruited either from the sons of a family who cannot share the same wife (traditionally only three brothers were allowed to share a wife) or from the illegitimate children of monks and nuns.

Incest and ritual laws

Buddhism has been fairly tolerant of a variety of sexual customs and has accommodated a number of marriage forms. It has also sanctioned royal incest, found among the Burmese, Cambodians and Thai. Among the Burmese, the king could marry his (presumably paternal) half-sister, although this was forbidden to all other people in the country, including royal princes.

Among the Cambodians, the king was placed above ordinary laws and could also marry his paternal half-sisters (and possibly also his maternal half-sisters, although this is not entirely clear). Other members of the royal family could do the same. The only marriage between siblings that was absolutely forbidden was with full sisters. On accession, a new king inherited the entire harem of his predecessor.

The Thai do not seem to have any clearly stated laws forbidding incest at all for any class of people, but only in the royal family was uncle–niece marriage practiced, as well as marriage between paternal half-siblings. At the beginning of the twentieth century, King Paramindr Maha Culalongkorn married two of his half-sisters (his father had had 35 wives and sired at least 84 children).

By AD 100 the Hindu *Code of Manu* appeared, the first systematization of ritual laws. Some of these laws include the following punishments for sexual crimes: " A man who has committed a bestial crime, or a crime with a female, or has intercourse in water, or with a menstruating woman, shall subsist on cow urine, cow dung, milk, sour milk, clarified butter and a decoction of kusa grass, and fast for one day and one night.

"He who has had sexual intercourse with sisters by the same mother, with the wives of a friend, or of a son, with unmarried girls, and with females of the lowest caste shall perform the penance prescribed for the violation of a guru's bed."

Now adultery with the wife of your spiritual teacher, or guru, turns out to merit uniquely dreadful punishments. One punishment requires the evildoer to sit down on an iron plate that is glowing hot and cut off his own penis. Another is similar: he is to clasp a metal statue of a woman that has been heated until it is red hot so that he dies in simulated lovemaking. Yet a third punishment: the culprit must cut off his own penis and testicles and walk holding them in his hands until he literally drops dead. The least gory of the options is that he give up his life on behalf of a Braahman.

In the same vein, among Buddhist Vietnamese it is specifically forbidden for a student to marry the widow of his professor.

Erotic sculptures
*of the temple of
the Sun, Konaarak,
13th century AD.
Some scholars suggest
that these sculptures may
link up with the practice
of sacred prostitution,
formerly widespread.*

Erotic sculptures from 13th-century
Konaarak (below right), and from
11th-century Khajuraaho (below).
Vishnu and Sri Lakshmi (right), from
the Paarshvanaatha temple,
Khajuraaho.

A panel from the 13th-century Sun
temple at Konaarak (right).

Other legal codes spelling out Hindu sexual behavior were drawn up later. For example, fellation, according to the law commentator Mahaanirvaan-gat, is to be punished with death. Other authorities talk of forbidden forms of sexual inter-course as the moral equivalent of murdering a Braahman, an exceedingly heinous crime.

There is so much variety within Hinduism, however, that no one code reflects some universally approved standard. Sexual acts such as fellation, that were condemned in the legal writings, actually appear in sculptures on the outside and inside of various Hindu tem-ples. The most famous of these erotic sculptures are found in the surviving temples of Khajuraaho (built AD 950 to 1050), and in particular the Sun temple of Konaarak from the thirteenth century. The tradition of erotic temple sculp-ture survives in Nepal, and there couples in various coital positions are regularly used as ornaments for carved gable brackets. In India the tradition has ended. Indeed, for many In-dians the preservation of such sexual scenes in a sacred spot has been an embarrassment, perhaps as a legacy of Victorian English domination.

It should be noted that some of the sexual scenes represented in Indian temples (though not in Nepalese ones) seem dictated by aesthetic considerations rather than the actual sexual behavior of the people. For example, couples are most frequently shown standing, even when copulating. Such a posture is rarely practiced by ordinary people (although standing positions are recog-nized in erotic handbooks).

The religious aspects of sexuality can be found in a num-

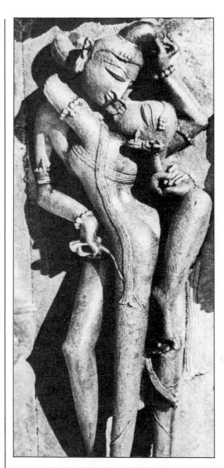

ber of areas, including the belief that intercourse with temple prostitutes is an act of devotion. At least one modern scholar, Michael Edwardes, has pointed out the economics involved in such devotional acts as well, and has suggested that erotic sculp-ture found on temples was done not exclusively out of piety but, in a word, to entice to a business proposition. The Raajaraajesh-vara temple in Thanjaavuur (Tanjore) employed some 400 sacred prostitutes (*devadaasiis*) in the eleventh century and their earnings probably constituted an important source of income.

Temple priests themselves are involved in sexual acts with the laity because of the belief

Standing copulation depicted on the Devi Dagadamba temple, Khajuraaho, may reflect aesthetic considerations rather than everyday sexual practice.

An 18th-century carving from Katmandu, Nepal. The "Rati Lila".

that they can cure barrenness in women. Some temples — Triupati in the Karnataka, for example — have priests particularly renowned for this. Childless women copulate with the priests believing them in some sense to be gods.

Yet another element is an approach that cuts through theology and across religious boundaries: Tantrism. One of the doctrines of the Tantrik approach is that every act of sexual intercourse is a repetition of the primal sexual act, and is a mystical way of transcending material barriers of all kinds, including one's own sex. In one of the Tantras (Tantrik scriptures), called the *Niruttara-tantra*, even adultery is regarded as a necessary religious act: the worshiper will not gain merit in this life unless he unites sexually with a married woman. A doctrine of primal androgyny also pervades the Tantrik approach: a male seeks out a female, and the female a male, because they do not know that the opposite sex is lodged within their own being. To realize this fully is important for the future life. In some ways this doctrine resembles that attributed to Aristophanes in Plato's *Symposium*, where the first beings were imagined to be double-sexed and then split apart, but are for ever seeking to reunite with their other selves.

The south Asian religious traditions are extremely varied in their approaches to sex and in some instances seem to reverse western morality and belief altogether. In particular, virginity for women is not approved and girls traditionally in Hindu society were to be married as early as possible, since each menstrual flow was thought of as an act of murder.

The traditions considered are associated with high cultures that have themselves evolved in historic times. Throughout the area there are various groups who have not capitulated to these high cultures, and at least some of them may have continued sexual practices and ideologies even more ancient.

<hr/>

Hunting and gathering societies

A few hunting and gathering cultures continue to exist, such as the Cencu (Chenchu), Andamanese, Vedda and Semang, but descriptions of them are sadly lacking in information about sex.

Some authorities have said that both the Andamanese and Semang employ no marriage ceremony. But a Semang couple will eat together as a kind of ritual. When this act has taken place it is forbidden for them to consummate their marriage on the same day. According to one informant it is always forbidden to have sex in the camp, and couples must go off to the jungle to copulate. Related groups such as the Negritoes of Grik do not observe this prohibition. All the Semang prohibit sexual intercourse during the daytime, which is regarded as a great sin that has to be expiated with blood sacrifice.

As for the Andamanese, there is a kind of minimum marriage ritual: the husband takes "possession" of his wife in the presence of the rest of the group, but this is unlikely to mean public copulation.

As to tabus on sexual intercourse, the information available is minimal. The Andamanese forbid sex during menstruation. The Semang regard obscene talk as on a level with adultery: both may be punished by death caused by lightning or by falling trees brought down in a storm or by a flood. The expiation for these offenses is a blood sacrifice.

According to early accounts, Vedda men were allowed to marry their younger sisters, but this is untrue. There is an aphrodisiac made from a ground-up orchid, the very name of which suggests disapproval of brother–sister incest: *nagamarualla* "you who killed a sister." This name derives from a story told about a girl who tasted this aphrodisiac by accident and became sexually attracted to her brother, who killed her when she made amorous advances toward him.

Various assertions have been made about the Andamanese that are fairly idiosyncratic. Some British colonists believed that they practiced rear-entry intercourse, a belief based on the assumption that women refuse to remove or even lift their pubic apron. While it is true that the women are very modest and will not renew these leaf aprons, even in the presence of another woman, the assertion about rear entry appears to be false. A custom that is fairly rare cross-culturally had to do with the apron worn during a girl's first menstruation. Menstrual blood is, exceptionally (from a world-wide perspective), thought of as an especially good thing, and the aprons of the first menstrual periods are worn later on by relatives of the girls because they are thought to ensure good health. Only a few other societies in the world have similar customs.

Menstruation is believed by the Andamanese to be the result of previous sexual contacts. The same belief has been attributed to the Lepcha of Sikkim; possibly early marriage and sexual

intercourse were quite general throughout the whole of this area. Sexual intercourse during menstruation is forbidden by the Andamanese: if the tabu is not observed the girl's arms or legs will swell.

The most striking thing about Andamanese sexual behavior is the claim, by a fairly recent writer, Cipriani (1961 and 1966), that homosexuality is rife among the men. He maintains that all the Andamanese have homosexual tendencies, and believes this is biologically rather than psychologically motivated.

This view is made less plausible with the sentence that follows his exposition ". . . kissing is unknown; sexual excitement is aroused instead by nose-rubbing."

To my knowledge, no other theory relating to nose-rubbing, homosexuality and absence of kissing has ever been proposed.

Andamanese males embracing. Homosexuality is believed to be very widespread among the groups inhabiting these Indian Ocean islands.

Sex without feelings?

The societies that have been considered can perhaps be seen as representing ancient patterns, in a journalistic sense "living anachronisms." Living virtually side by side with these groups are others that exhibit the kind of sexuality described in such futuristic scenarios as, for instance, Aldous Huxley's *Brave new world*, where sexual fidelity is a sin, jealousy is a joke, and children are considered disturbed if they do not take part in school-run sex play.

No society on earth has all the characteristics of Huxley's vision, but two societies from this part of the world, the Múria of Madhya Pradesh, in India, and the Lepcha of Sikkim, have played up sex without emotional entanglements and fidelity.

The Múria are a subdivision of the Gond in central India. Like many neighboring groups they have what are known as dormitories or communal houses. But the Múria maintain a co-ed youth dormitory system in which premarital sex is actively encouraged.

There are two kinds of dormitories, or *ghotul*. One kind is called the *jodidaar*, or "yoking," ghotul, in which every boy and girl is paired off and required to be sexually faithful to each other. This may be the earlier of the two kinds. In the second, called the *mundi-badalna ghotul*, any lasting connection between a boy and girl is strictly forbidden. If a boy is discovered as having slept with the same girl for more than three days in a row, he is punished.

Not only is fidelity not rewarded, extraordinary improprieties can occur even from the Múria point of view. The basic problem comes from the lack of privacy.

For most of the year in the smaller *ghotuls*, boys and girls must sleep together in a small, smoky room. And this means that relatives may often perform sexually in front of each other — at least in each other's presence if the dark can count as a way of maintaining privacy. It is not merely embarrassing but morally wrong for a boy to copulate in his sister's presence, and the other way round. Although this is avoided as much as possible, it nevertheless occurs. What is surprising is that incest does not occur by accident in such situations.

In the *mundi-badalna ghotul*, lovers try to preserve decorum by waiting until the others are asleep, but often the place is so crowded that it is hard not to wake the others up. Although the Múria are acquainted with several positions for intercourse, the normal position practiced in the *ghotul* appears to be merely a variant of the missionary position.

Few rules exist in the *ghotul* with regard to sexual behavior. In most *ghotuls*, no permission is needed from *ghotul* leaders to start a love affair or to engage in sexual intercourse at a particular time. No ceremony of sexual initiation is performed, and no formal act of defloration is practiced. Boys wait until a girl starts menstruating before they approach her sexually and during her menstrual periods she is avoided as dangerous. With regard to sexual acts, there seem to be few restrictions, but rear-entry intercourse is generally regarded as improper. Homosexual acts do not occur in the *ghotul* and the Múria seem to lack homosexual interests. In the stricter *ghotuls*, the frequency of intercourse is regulated, so that a couple are not allowed to copulate more than two or three times a week.

In Binjhli, a couple is allowed to sleep together only on Fridays, but they may copulate every day outside the *ghotul*, and three times on Fridays. In most *ghotuls* copulation is allowed every day. Sometimes when a pregnancy occurs the rules become stricter, and *ghotul* leaders demand that couples ask and receive permission for intercourse.

In part, fears about pregnancy and illegitimacy are alleviated by a belief that having sex within the *ghotul* lessens the likelihood of conception. Perhaps this reflects an earlier view that sexual intercourse should not be performed in a house at all but in the jungle. The Múria do not believe this at present (if they ever did), but their close Gond cousins, the Hill Mariaa, traditionally consider it indecent to have intercourse in a house. They feel that a man and his wife should go into the jungle to make love. This view is dying out even among the Hill Mariaa. This rule of outdoor copulation is strikingly at variance with the widespread African tabu. A number of other south Asian societies share the Mariaa notion, such as the Kadar of Cochin and the Semang, as well as various New Guinea societies. The Santal of India copulate indoors as a rule, but sex in the jungle is a popular theme in folk songs.

That the Múria at one time observed the custom of outdoor copulation is suggested by a certain saying relating to impotence. It is taken as a matter of course that a woman will want to divorce an impotent husband, and this is tersely expressed in the phrase: "As soon as the penis weakens, the

Múria (southwestern India) girl *who sleeps in the traditional* ghotul *dormitory with her lover.*

vagina runs to the forest."

The institution of the dormitory, particularly the men's house, is found in a number of other south Asian societies such as the Naaga, Mikir, Munda and Juaang. In New Guinea it is usually forbidden to bring women into the men's houses, but elsewhere similar dormitories seem to be associated with some degree of sexual license. Among the Kachin of Burma, the co-ed youth dormitory (called *blaw*) fits this pattern, as it does among the neighboring Brec. But another neighboring group, the Sgaw Karen, have only bachelor dormitories — the girls staying with their mothers. They follow the New Guinea pattern and are not associated with sexual freedom.

The Múria justification for the *ghotul* system is simply that sex is something good. One Múria stated it succinctly: "The penis and vagina are in a joking relationship to each other."

But there is further incentive to Múria sexual behavior, similar to but very different from Hindu beliefs. Both orthodox Hindus and the Múria believe that celibacy creates and stores up power. Whereas the Hindus see this as a virtue, the Múria fear it. Too much power may be built up; when released, it may turn out to be *too* powerful.

The Lepcha

The Lepcha, according to Geoffrey Gorer, seem to be almost cut off from passion. Sexual gratification is compared to food and drink; it does not matter who you get it from just as long as you get it. And once the day's work is done, the only things left to do are drinking and sex.

This down-playing of personal involvement also leads to a down-playing of physical attractiveness. There are features considered beautiful about individuals. Both women and men are considered good-looking if they have long hair, a straight nose, flat face and a straight body (ugly features include eyes too big or too small, pop eyes, dimples, buttocks that stick out and — on women — big breasts). But these criteria are said to play no role in deciding on a temporary partner. Gorer found that most of the men with young and pretty wives would also sleep on occasion with promiscuous, haggard old women. The invitations of these women were never, as far as Gorer could make out, refused. (It should be noted, however, that youth is not a criterion of attractiveness among the Lepcha; many young men — in spite of the predictions of sociobiologists — find older women more attractive,

and no one found it strange that a man would go to bed with a woman twice his age.)

There is little romance among the Lepcha. Courtship barely exists. Techniques of seduction are minimal. Lovers neither kiss nor embrace and the only kind of foreplay is for the man to fondle the woman's breasts, but this occurs immediately before intercourse. Occasionally a man may fondle a woman's breasts in public as a direct invitation to sex. This is considered more funny than shameful. Morris (1938) tells about a boy who actually did so. The woman's reaction was simply to aim her breast at him and squirt milk all over the boy.

Nakedness is not considered exciting or enticing. One or two men admitted that looking at a woman's naked thighs turned them on, but the great majority are not sexually stimulated by anything but immediate anticipation of sex.

Lepcha men of the Himalayas (above and right). Sex without emotional entanglement or fidelity is the rule in this society.

The Lepcha think it absurd to pay for sex. Native prostitution does not exist, but some Tibetan prostitutes live in the neighborhood and of the two Lepcha men who made use of these services, at least one preferred them to Lepcha women. The Tibetan whores were at least lively; Lepcha women lie completely motionless and relaxed during coitus. This would suggest that they do not experience orgasms, but the Lepcha believe, however, that men and women enjoy sex equally and there are some who say that women enjoy it more.

Marriage patterns of the area in general

The marriage patterns of the area tend toward de facto monogamy, even in those groups where the religion is not theoretically opposed to a man having many wives, as among Hindus and Muslims. The Hindu Marriage Act of 1955, undoubtedly influenced by British law, prohibited polygamy among Hindus and also child marriage: girls had to be at least 15 (later, the age was raised to 16). In Pakistan and Bangladesh, Muslim men seldom have more than one wife and the governments have fostered the idea that Islam forbids polygamy in normal circumstances. Among Muslim Malays and neighboring Muslim groups, such as the Minangkabau of Sumatra, monogamy is preferred.

The *Ethnographic atlas* lists only two societies for this general area that permit a woman several husbands: the Sherpa and Toda, but a number of others are known, including the Sabubn Semang, Lanoh, Kandyan Sinhalese, Pahaarii,

Lepcha and Bhot (Bhutiya). Most groups permit only brothers to share the same wife. Among the Sherpa, normally only two brothers may marry the same woman; in the other groups more than two may do so. In Bhutan, formerly the custom was for not more than three brothers to share a wife, but in the 1960s, having more than one husband was banned altogether.

A fairly unusual marriage custom is reported from several south Indian groups in Kerala. There, a small boy may be married to a mature woman, and the bride's father-in-law functions as a "seed raiser," having regular sexual relations with his daughter-in-law. Any children produced in this way belong to the son. Among one of these groups, the Reddi, the boy-husband may never actually consummate the marriage, even when he grows up, but instead have an affair with the wife of some boy kinsman of his own.

Among the Toda in the southern part of India, a woman may not only have several husbands (usually brothers) but she may also have several officially recognized lovers, just as a man may have several concubines.

Toda woman of Tamil Nadu, south India. In this society women are allowed more than one husband.

The great majority of societies in this area mentioned permit premarital sex without any restrictions. Only nine insist on virginity of the bride at marriage. Some Hindus believe that intercourse with a bride whose hymen is unbroken is dangerous for the groom. Consequently, some mothers practice "deep cleansing" on their very young daughters which tears the girls' hymen.

Erotic handbooks and art

Erotic manuals are part of the cultural heritage of south Asia. Sometimes the sexual techniques indicated in them are creative and highly gymnastic, with little likelihood of being performed by any significant number of people.

The *Kaama suutra* is, of course, the starting point of this handbook tradition. Many derivatives and offshoots appeared in subsequent centuries.

An important work from the twelfth century is now widely known as the *Koka shastra*, by Kokkoka. It differs in part from the *Kaama suutra* because it reflects the stricter social norms of medieval as opposed to ancient India. Whereas the *Kaama suutra* distinguishes a code for marriage and a code for sex outside marriage, and is geared for the Don Juan working within the second, the *Koka shastra* is geared for the husband. Its purpose is to preserve marriage by reducing sexual boredom: "The husband, by varying the enjoyment of his wife, may live with her as with thirty-two different women, ever varying the enjoyment of her and rendering satiety impossible."

The *Anangga rangga*, a similar work, became important because its author, Kalyaanamalla, was employed by a Muslim nobleman. Through this connection the information in the book spread throughout the Islamic world, and the book itself was translated into Arabic and other languages spoken in countries under Muslim control.

In addition to this written tradition there is also that of the sculptured figures performing sexual acts on the walls of temples. The two traditions coincide, so that an enormously rich repertoire of sexual acts has been known for some time.

Sexual behavior and statistics

It should come as no particular surprise, however, that in spite of this potential variety the information we have about actual sexual activity suggests a very limited repertoire on the part of ordinary people. Part of the reason for this is that, unlike the women of the handbooks or the

An 18th-century Mughal depiction of "Lovers on a Terrace." The Hindu tradition of erotic manuals spread through the Islamic world, but was given a different emphasis.

divine maidens of the temple sculptures, real women throughout the area are traditionally passive. Múria women, however, are described as aggressors and unique in India because they actually undo their own pubic cloth before coitus. Otherwise, although women may be highly interested in sex and find sexual pleasure an absolute necessity in marriage, they are very unlikely even to move about much while copulating.

Kissing in the western sense is denied for the Andamanese, Santal, Thai and Vietnamese. Nose sniffing or rubbing is said to be practiced instead. Kissing, however, is the rule in m st of the area, even though for Hindus contact with saliva renders the act ritually contaminating.

With regard to coital positions, the little information available can be summarized as follows. Neither the Santal nor the Balinese use the missionary position; the Balinese consider it impractical and clumsy. Both use a variant of the Oceanic position. The only description of Balinese coitus says that the man kneels, the woman reclines. Santal copulation has been described more vividly: the man takes the lead by suggesting intercourse and he removes the woman's clothing. The man penetrates the woman immediately. The woman lies on her back with her thighs raised. The man squats on his toes between her thighs. Her legs are sometimes entwined on his back, and his hands might be placed on her shoulders or breasts. She raises her thighs even higher during the act and shakes her hips when experiencing orgasm.

According to Prince Peter, some of his Toda and Thandan (Kerala) informants said that other groups performed intercourse with the woman on top. There is no direct confirmation of this, however, and it was specifically denied by the Toda and Thandan themselves. The Thandan accused members of higher castes of doing so, but felt it undesirable because it "was not favorable to the procreation of warriors."

The most varied copulatory repertoire comes from the Múria. In a *ghotul*, they usually copulate using some form of the missionary position. But elsewhere more choices are possible, including the Oceanic position; both sitting and facing each other; and a variant of the missionary position in which the woman either raises or extends her legs.

Kissing in the western sense (below) is found on temple sculpture of the Chitragupta temple, Khajuraaho.

Detail from the Temple of Konaarak shows fellation.

One of the aggressive traits attributed to Múria girls is that sometimes a girl will actually catch hold of a boy's penis, play with it, and put it between her thighs. This is not done as a substitute for real intercourse, but simply to entice the boy into real honest-to-goodness copulation.

Cunnilingus and fellation are shown on temple sculptures. The *Kaama suutra* devotes a whole chapter to fellation, called *auparishtaka* or *maukhyaa*. Vaatsyaayana says that in his time fellation was prevalent among the people of the eastern provinces of India. Richard Burton, in a footnote to his translation of the *Kaama suutra*, notes that an ancient Indian medical text, the *Shushrutaa* (perhaps 2,000 years old), describes as a cause of a particular disease the biting of the penis — not recommended in the sex manuals but suggestive of the likelihood that mouth–penis contacts were practiced.

Information about frequency of sexual intercourse is available for only two societies in the area other than the Múria. Some Santals copulate in the early part of their marriage as often as five times a day every day. After children appear on the scene, copulation goes down to a maximum of once or twice a day, with days missed.

The other society we have information about is that of the Lepcha. Gorer has suggested that because the Lepcha seem to be emotionally uninvolved with sex they can be quite prodigious in their potency. Men boast that when first married they copulated five or six times and even sometimes eight or nine times in a single night. But Gorer's 1938 assertions (and comparable statements made by Morris) were seriously questioned by Hermanns in 1954.

Hermanns says in effect that Gorer's whole picture of Lepcha sexuality involves unwarranted generalizations from a few oversexed men.

Sex tabus and rituals

Tabus on sexual intercourse are generally similar to those found elsewhere. A unique tabu is found among some Hindu groups who forbid copulation during certain phases of the moon: for example, the first night of the new moon and the night of the full moon. These days (as well as the fourteenth night and eighth night of each half of the month) are considered especially unlucky: evil spirits are about, particularly near trees and pools of water, as well as in graveyards and deserted houses. All these places are considered especially dangerous for sexual intercourse.

Sexual intercourse is forbidden to Hindus during a woman's menstrual period. Women take a ritual bath at the end of four days and are then sexually available. The Naayar specifically believe that a man who copulates with a menstruating woman is likely to become impotent.

To my knowledge there is no group in south Asia that does not tabu intercourse with a menstruating woman.

Although sexual acts are performed in many parts of the area as an aspect of religious devotion, ritual intercourse in the sense we have seen it for many African societies is rarely mentioned. The Lepcha practice a ritual intercourse that is very similar to some of the African customs. Three, seven or twenty-one days after the birth of a baby the father must copulate with his wife in a special way: rear entry, with the couple lying on their sides. The movements are to be slow and gentle; the purpose is that lubrication from the ejaculated semen should get rid of the pains of childbirth.

Homosexuality

Homosexuality is said to be unknown to the Múria, even in prisons. It is also denied for the Santal and there is no clear evidence that Toda practice it.

Homosexuality is a "meaningless concept" for the Lepcha, according to Gorer (1938), although he does note that boys attempt a certain amount of mutual masturbation. Morris, writing in the same year, corroborates Gorer to a certain extent by saying that homosexuality is practically unknown. Morris adds that homosexuality is considered disgusting. Furthermore, although no specific word exists corresponding to "homosexual," the idea can be expressed with the astonishing phrase, "one who has eaten uncastrated pig." For a Lepcha man to eat such a pig would induce homosexuality.

From this end of the spectrum we can go to the other: Andamanese men, as we have seen, are described as being almost universally homosexual.

Generally in Hindu Indian culture, homosexual acts are usually considered defiling, but male transvestite sacred prostitutes have been reported from certain temples in the Bombay area. These men tend to be associated with the worship of particular goddesses, such as Ambabai and Yallamma, and are forbidden to marry. As early as 1792 to 1823 Dubois writes about men found in larger towns who wear their hair like women, pluck out their beards and affect the mannerisms of female prostitutes. Eunuch transvestite (transsexual?) prostitutes called *hijra* still exist.

Pederasty was outlawed in an act passed in 1871, in which possession of little boys for sexual purposes was condemned. All homosexual acts are now illegal in both India and Pakistan. But transvestism is not, as far as I know, similarly outlawed. These laws, even to the extent that they go, seem to be the result of British influence.

Burmese and Karen homosexuality would seem to center on transvestism and effeminacy — the general pathic type. Marshall, writing in 1922, said that he had known of some instances among the Karen where two men lived together as husband and wife, but adds that transvestite homosexuals seem to be less common among them than among the Burmese. Among the Burmese such men are called *mein ma sha* "women half." They wear face powder and jewelry like women, among other things. Although tolerated, they are said to be scorned. Rare in villages, they have tended to congregate in Rangoon, where they form a subculture. Folk belief explains their existence as punishment for having committed sexual sins in a previous life. The Burmese believe that there is a similar kind of person who had committed even more serious sexual sins. Such a person is said to undergo a complete physical sex transformation from month to month, so that he is alternately a man, then a woman, then a man again, and so on — a built-in switchable transsexual.

Homosexual guidebooks describe Malaysia as having fairly bisexual traditions and Thailand is highly recommen-

A transvestite prostitute from Bombay. Homosexuality and transvestism are more closely connected in southern Asia than in the West.

ded for its beautiful and accommodating young men. But a closer reading of the text suggests that these guides are dealing with prostitution geared to foreigners.

The general characteristics of male homosexuality in south Asia (female homosexuality is almost never mentioned in the literature) is that it usually involves transvestism to some degree, or less commonly pederasty, or a combination of the two. It is rarely described as being seriously condemned, although it may be regarded as undesirable. True homosexual marriages are not reported from any group in the area.

Paraphilias and other sexual interests

Native handbooks on sex technique suggest considerable interest in various degrees of sadomasochism. It is possible, according to the suggestion of Dr Alex Comfort, that the longest word ever created to describe a sexual talent may have reference to sadomasochism. This is the Sanskrit *premanibandhanaikanipunaa*, used to describe women of Andhra in the *Koka shastra*. Dr Comfort suggests it might conceivably be translated as "skilled in sexual bondage." But bondage is not known as an erotic theme in this area, as it is in Japan or the West.

The *Kaama suutra* has separate chapters on scratching, biting and hitting. It specifically says that the women of both Balhika and Malwa "are gained over by striking." In the Burton-Arbuthnot translation, a section is devoted to south Indian customs of "striking with instruments," but according to Alex Comfort the "instruments" refer not to real tools but to

The yoni mudra *(hand position) symbolizes the union of male* lingga *and female* yoni.

positions of the hand known technically as *mudras*. But even so, the consequences of their use can be lethal, as stories about ardent southern Indians attest. For example, the king of Cola embraced the fragile courtesan Citrasenaa so violently that he crushed her; in his passion he was unable to control himself and hit her on her chest with the "wedge" and killed her.

Information about bestiality and masturbation is also rare. The Múria consider bestiality ludicrous, not repulsive, and label it a "crime of civilization." The Santal find animal contacts abhorrent, requiring a ceremonial purification.

Perhaps the most extensive information about masturbation is from the Telugu. Both boys and girls start masturbating at about six. The practice is condemned by adults.

Lepcha boys practice a certain amount of mutual masturbation, but this ceases at adolescence.

This chapter started out with a paradox, by referring to the area as the homeland of chastity as a virtue even though sexuality itself was seen as divine. We may close by pointing out that at the present time India has been the country in the forefront of advocating population control — surely one of the consequences of the ancient virtue of chastity. Furthermore, even though the great masses of people in south Asia may be totally ignorant of the *Kaama suutra* and the erotic tradition of their own high culture, this tradition has spread to the West, where it flourishes on many levels. The paradox continues.

Fifteen 🐚
THE FAR EAST

The Far East has a very ancient and sophisticated tradition of erotic culture. But the modern threat of overpopulation is perhaps the most potent factor affecting sexual customs and ideologies.

At least eight Chinese sex manuals are known from the early Han dynasty (206 BC to AD 220). But they have not survived intact. It is possible that Indian manuals of even greater antiquity existed, but apart from a mythologized history of the *Kaama suutra* we have no knowledge of them. The Chinese books — known generally as *Fáng-zhōng* (*Inside the bedchamber*) or *Fáng-zhōng-shū* (*Art of the bedchamber*) — were closely associated with the second Far Eastern theme, which was stressed in Daoist (Taoist) philosophy: the need for the conservation of semen, *especially* during sexual intercourse. Like their south Asian neighbors, the Chinese believed in a version of semen power.

Yīn and yáng

The Chinese view builds on the doctrine of the opposition of cosmic forces: *yīn* and *yáng*. This opposition was accepted in several schools of thought. The opposition *yīn*/*yáng* permeates the universe and is realized in a number of ways: dark/bright, female/male, heart/stomach, outer body/inner body, moon/sun, earth/heaven. At birth, the body is filled with both principles. But *yīn* tends to increase at the expense of *yáng*. Death is caused by a serious imbalance between them. In both sexes, long life is achievable by retaining as much *yáng* as possible.

In specifically sexual terms, *yáng* can be identified with semen or seminal essence (*jīng*). In sexual intercourse, if a man

ejaculates, he would of course lose his *jīng*, thereby diminishing his *yáng*. If he could prevent ejaculation, he would not only build up *jīng* but retain *yáng*. The best thing for a man would be not to ejaculate but to enable the woman to reach orgasm and give off her *yīn* essence, which would strengthen the man. Conversely, the best thing for a woman would be not to reach orgasm (and so lose her *yīn* essence) but to gain the man's *yáng*. Abstinence is no good because it does nothing to increase *yáng*

Anatomical chart of the body, *from a Daoist Handbook of Internal Alchemy.*

Sex manuals and "pillow *books" are an ancient theme in Chinese sexuality, often associated with the conservation of semen. A 17th-century painting (below) on silk.*

and so leads to death.

Traditional Chinese stories about the success of Daoist sex control stress the great age attained by practitioners. The mythical Yellow Emperor, Huang-di, became immortal by having had Daoistically correct sex relations with 1,200 women. A woman, the Queen Mother of the West, was said to have duplicated the immortality of the Yellow Emperor by having gained the *yīn* essence of more than 1,000 women in homosexual unions, and by taking the semen of numberless men who did not know the arts of the bedchamber, and therefore were not able to prevent the loss of their *yáng*.

Female yīn and male yáng (below) conjoined in the enclosed world of paradise, the hu-lu.

Early Daoism encouraged wife exchange and created liturgies of sexual rites organized down to the minutest detail. The Daoist Canon of the Ming includes the only record of these pre-Buddhist rituals, which took place in a special closed cell. After several mental exercises and prayers, couples would stand up face to face and intertwine fingers. At a certain point the officiating Dao master ordered the couples to undress and undo their hair after which the couples performed a great many complicated movements, involving genital touching. But penetration with ejaculation was legitimately not practiced at all in this setting.

A number of heterodox schools of Daoism existed that took even more literally the need to conserve seminal essences. One practice of the School of the Master of the Three Peeks was to get young men and women together and gather up their sexual secretions, which were to be swallowed by the faithful.

Confucian and Buddhist approaches to sex

These Daoist practices came under attack from Confucian and Buddhist groups. Eventually the Daoists themselves chose reforms, and some sought to join together Confucian and Daoist principles into a single system. The ancient sex feasts, however, ended after the fifth and sixth centuries and more and more Daoists saw sexual control in figurative rather than in real terms. Daoism virtually retreated to monasteries organized along Buddhist principles. But Daoist teachings on sex have lingered, although virtually ignored by all except a few of the scholarly elite.

Much more important in shaping the practical approach to sex in the high cultures of the Far East was Confucianism. It was not only dominant in Chinese life for over 2,000 years, becoming the state orthodoxy as early as the emperor Wu (140–87 BC) in the Han dynasty, but it also spread to Korea, Vietnam and Japan.

Although much of Daoist thought was eventually incorporated into Confucianism, many Confucianists were opposed to Daoist sexual ideas. Confucianists generally held that love was a sentiment unworthy of a perfect gentleman, and that no decent man would show public affection for his wife. As for women, it was held by some at least that for a woman to make herself sexually attractive, even to her own husband, was a crime of the worst order. Sex itself was all right, but love and tenderness were suspect and physical displays of them were forbidden.

These are not just philosophical precepts observed largely in the breach, but they have had a deep-rooted standing in traditional Chinese society. Francis L. K. Hsu reports that in 1943 a young man, returning to his native Chinese village from westernized Hong Kong with his bride, was punished for walking hand in hand with his wife by furious villagers, who drenched them with human excrement.

Furthermore, with the tremendous emphasis on an orderly family life associated with Confucianist teachings, a strict segregation of the sexes was demanded throughout Chinese history. This was to ensure that women would enter marriage as virgins and remain faithful to their husbands. Sex segregation even came to include a tabu on hanging a husband's and a wife's clothing on the same clothes rack.

Such segregation of the sexes and concomitant prudishness increased during the period of the Mongol invasions and the establishment of the Yuan dynasty (1279–1368). Thus, the making of an erotic book was deemed to deserve 1,000 demerits. Nevertheless, one of the characteristics of the area is the development of erotic literature and art.

Buddhism first entered China about 2,000 years ago and did not originally require sex segregation, but in its Chinese form it blended with Confucianist customs and the social position of women was not high. Women, however, could enter Buddhist nunneries, permitting them a degree of independence not usual for respectable women elsewhere in China. Perhaps because of this departure from the general Chinese pattern of female subservience, nuns were often disapproved of and distrusted. It was common to accuse them of lesbian activities.

Chinese Buddhism codified a hierarchy of punishments for sexual sins in various hells in the hereafter. The worst sexual sin was raping a Buddhist saint.

Buddhism as well as Confucianism spread to Japan, where they contended with native Japanese religious beliefs ancestral to modern-day Shintoism. But Japanese society made profound compromises, so that we find most of the country following both Buddhist and Shinto practices. For example, nearly everyone gets married according to Shinto rituals and customs, but at funerals Buddhist ceremony wins out. Per-

***Phallic shrines associated with** Shintoism dot the Japanese countryside.*

Japanese Shinto phallic procession *(above) with priests carrying gigantic penis.*

A sexual interest in stones is alleged for the Siberian hunter-gathering Koryak peoples. In some cases men are believed to have "married" stones instead of women.

haps the predominance of Shinto marriage has something to do with the more obvious concern of Shintoism with fertility.

The native religions of the high cultures of the Far East are generally quite sex positive. Sex in itself is seen as good. There is nothing like the Christian idea of original sin.

Hunters and gatherers

There are hunters in the Far East, but only in extremely out-of-the-way areas — notably in parts of Siberia. Their life-style may represent a peculiar adaptation to a fairly harsh environment rather than a continuation of earlier customs possibly ancestral to those found in China, Japan or Korea.

The few hunters that exist are referred to by anthropologists as Paleosiberians and include the Ainu of northern Japan, and the Koryak, Kamchadál, Gilyak (or Nivkh), Chukchi and Yúkaghir of eastern Siberia. Some groups include both hunters and herders, such as the Chukchi and Koryak. Explicit information about these groups is practically

nonexistent. Seeland (1822) writes that Gilyak men and women seldom kiss, but they eat each other's lice, and "wash each other's faces with saliva."

One oddity is surely unique: the maritime Koryak custom whereby men "marry" stones instead of women. It is true that in many societies pseudo-marriages are contracted with trees (or belts), but there is no evidence of any sexual interest in the tree. But the Koryak situation is somewhat different. The Koryak "husband" will put clothes on his stone, put it in his bed, and sometimes caress it as though it were a person. The Russian traveler Krasheninnikov was given two such stones by a man called Okerach; one of these stones Okerach referred to as his wife, and the other as his son.

Among the Chukchi, as many as 10 couples may participate in a kind of group marriage, and the men are called *newtumgit* "partners in wives." They share sexual rights to all the women. A special ritual is performed in making couples members of the group: as in an ordinary Chukchi marriage, this involves anointing each other with blood.

All the Paleosiberian groups permit a man more than one wife and so do most of the other peripheral groups.

Sex hospitality is widely practiced. The Koryak are particularly incensed about having their hospitality refused. A man would be mortally offended if a guest turned down his wife or daughter and might even kill for such an insult.

Premarital virginity in girls is seldom valued. The Gilyak, on the contrary, value the pregnant bride, who has proved her fertility. Information about the Ainu is conflicting: one source denies it for girls, another affirms it; in the *Ethnographic atlas*, however, they are listed as permitting premarital sex quite freely, as are also the Chukchi and Yakút. But the Yakút have at least some interest in a girl's virginity; girls are required to wear what has been called a "chastity girdle." It is actually a kind of leather trousers tied securely round the girl with many leather straps. The girdle is supposed to be worn constantly — presumably until marriage. Possibly the use of such an article is related to similar chastity devices found in the Caucasus; but it is unique in the Far East.

Marriage and adultery

Kamchadál marriage ceremonies seem to consist of a sort of ritual copulation: all that must be done for the marriage to be legal is that the groom touch the girl's naked vulva with his hands (in one account he actually has to stick his fingers into her vulva). This is not as simple as it may sound because even though parents may give a man permission to marry their daughter, he must "capture" her, which often turns out to be more than a mere formality. All the women of the village protect the girl from him and she is specially dressed in several layers of clothing. The groom must find her when she is alone or else fight off other women at the same time that he tries to tear off the girl's clothes. If the girl wants him there are few problems. But one case has been reported of a man who tried to touch his promised wife's genitals for 10 years and was much the worse for wear, since she fought him off vigorously and left his head and body covered with bruises.

Many of these groups are much concerned about a wife's adultery, even though sexual arrangements seem fairly loose in general. Although some Koryak practice sex hospitality, the nomadic Koryak do not, and a man will sometimes even kill his wife if she is suspected of adultery. To avoid any such lethal suspicions, women go to pains to look unattractive. Whereas sedentary Koryak women decorate their faces and wear fine clothing, their nomadic sisters never wash their faces or hands, and do not even comb their hair. They wear dirty, ragged, torn clothes when they go out (hidden underneath, is their good clothing).

Sex-change shaamans

One last trait that is found in these Siberian cultures but absent in the high cultures of the Far East is the presence of transvestite medicine-men (or shaamans). Writers often refer to some of them as sex-change or transformed shaamans, but they do not really undergo any kind of transsexual operation. They are often thought of by natives as a third sex.

Some of these transvestite shaamans marry other men, who are not themselves transvestites. Such sexual marriages are reportedly as durable as any other. The shaaman plays the passive role, but he may also have mistresses in secret and father children by them.

Transvestite, "sex-change" female shaamans are also known among the Chukchi.

Among other Siberian peoples, homosexual marriage is not reported, but their shaamans are nevertheless associated with various degrees of transvestism.

During a difficult labor, the custom of the Samoyéd is for both the men and the women to confess sexual acts. In the man's case, this confession may uniquely include all the times he has had sex with female dogs and reindeer.

Tibetan sexual life was unique
in the number of men and
women who became monks
and nuns, after which they
theoretically lived chaste lives.
At the time of Chinese
annexation one quarter of the
entire population belonged to
monastic orders.

The yab-yum *of Tibetan
Tantrik Buddhism celebrates
sexual ecstacy as a metaphor for
religious transcendence.*

Marriage patterns in general

Most of the societies in the Far East permit a man to have more than one wife. The high cultures of traditional China also permitted concubinage. Monogamy is found only among the Japanese, Koreans, Okinawans, Shantung and Ket.

Only one large group in the area permits a woman to have more than one husband: the Tibetans. Until the Chinese Communist takeover in 1959, the custom of having more than one husband was more prevalent here than in any other country in the world, and existed in a number of varieties. The most common is for brothers to share one wife. It is seen as a way of keeping land within a family and not breaking it up into portions that would ultimately force males to leave home en masse.

The problems derived from having one woman shared by several men have been discussed by commentators. According to Prince Peter, in one marriage, where five brothers were married to two women, the four older brothers became impotent because they were put off by the need to share wives. The younger brother was not, however, and he boasted that he was the one who had sired all the children of the family.

Another, very practical, problem is that of privacy. Unlike most societies where men have many wives, and the wives normally have their hut or at least a separate room, the co-husbands in a Tibetan family usually do not have separate accommodation.

Another aspect of Tibetan sexual life is the extraordinary number of men and women who have become monks and nuns, and are theoretically supposed to live chaste lives. The estimate is that one-quarter of the entire population were members of monastic orders at the time of the Chinese annexation of the country.

Buddhism began as a monk-oriented religion. But the appeal of monasticism in Tibet probably comes not only from piety but out of economic necessity. Monks and nuns have had a very mixed reputation not only in Tibet but throughout the Far East. It is said that a Buddhist monk first brought a rubber dildoe from India via Tibet in the seventeenth century. Even earlier, in the thirteenth century, Tibetan monks were said to have introduced to Mongol emperors a kind of genital device referred to as a "goat's eyelid" or "happy ring." The device made use of goat's eyelashes, which were tied round the penis and served to stimulate the woman during coitus.

Tibetan monks have developed a very lively reputation for homosexuality. Homosexual acts are theoretically condemned, even in — if not especially in — monasteries, but jokes about master–novice affairs are common.

In addition to this side of the monk's reputation there is also a heterosexual one. References to women who had straying lovers almost inevitably invoke images of the promiscuous monk; such a woman would be referred to as a la-dud "dragger away of a lama [monk]."

Tibetan Buddhism shows a variety of influences, including Tantrism, which began in India and spread to China. In China it declined, but revived under the Mongols (1280–1367) in a basically Tibetan form. The decline of the Mongols brought a similar

decline in Tantrism.

Tibetan Tantrism sees sexual ecstasy as a metaphor for religious transcendence. Sexual union with another person is a way of lighting the spark of an individual's Buddha-nature. Such a union is usually but not always thought of in literal physical terms. In intercourse of a transcendent sort, a male will realize his femaleness, a female her maleness. In an inauthentic sexual experience, this realization does not occur but merely the temporary quenching of a biological hunger. In Tantrik terms, "Buddhahood abides in the female organ": that is, in a male's experience of his own female nature (and vice versa).

Religious art in the Tantrik tradition often depicts sexual acts in many positions, but in Tibetan tradition these portrayals seem more symbolic than realistic.

In spite of the considerable interest that Tantrism and Tantrik approaches to sex have generated in the West, ordinary Tibetan sexuality seems to be little affected by it. With regard to the variety of positions for intercourse that Tantrik doctrine encourages, the everyday Tibetan seems to want none of it. Informants are reported to state with some feeling that the only appropriate position is with the man on top.

Erotic handbooks and art

The very first sex manual books from China have virtually disappeared, but the Japanese carried on the tradition and their versions have survived. *Ishinhoo* or *Ishimpoo* (*The essence of the medical prescription*), by Tamba Yasuyori (912–995), a Chinese doctor living in Japan, lists about 30 coital positions. At least one,

Unusual themes occur in *Chinese erotic manuals, including the use of a swing (right), threesomes (below), and the lifting of the woman by female attendants (bottom).*

labeled the "dog of early autumn," seems to be utterly impossible: the lovers have to copulate back to back. Other positions were frequently named after animals, suggesting their movements, such as flying or swimming or running.

Because of Confucian prudery, however, the ancient tradition of erotic handbooks was not kept up to the same extent as in India.

A characteristic of both China and Japan is the development of an elaborate tradition of erotic art, even though this was against Confucian principles as well. This art was secular, unlike the temple erotica of India, and in the form of "pillow books" was in part used for the sex education of a newly married bride and groom. That these books were a source of titillation and not merely instruction seems clear.

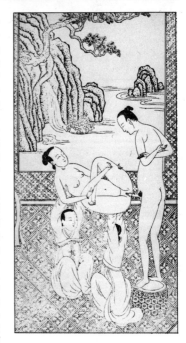

Chinese foot fetishism (below), a 19th-century painting. The earliest Chinese erotic art (bottom) may date from the 10th century.

According to Chinese tradition, erotic art was invented by Xiao-jing (Hsiao-ching) in the second century BC. He is credited with painting erotic murals on the walls of private houses. Certain themes of a fairly unusual sort appear in Far Eastern erotic art. One picture shows a woman hanging from a bamboo tree and sitting upon the erection of a naked reclining man; the woman apparently moves up and down with the swaying branch. Other pictures show the woman lifted above the ground and held by female attendants.

Sex in some sort of seated position is fairly common in Chinese erotica. According to Wu-shan Sheng, the earliest known Chinese erotic painting shows a naked man seated with his legs outstretched and his female partner sitting on top of his penis while she is embracing him.

Threesomes are common in these pictures. It is interesting to note that in the *Ishinpoo* coital positions, there are three that require a third person.

Chinese erotica — quite unlike comparable Japanese materials — has the peculiarity of showing women (otherwise frequently naked) with some sort of socks or slippers over their tiny, deformed feet. This of course played up the national fetish for bound feet that was never borrowed by the Japanese or Mongolians or Tibetans.

The women of Yangzhou (Yangchow) were particularly famous for the beauty of their bound feet. The Chinese custom of foot binding was started at least as early as the seventh century AD and spread from aristocratic families quite far down in the social hierarchy. Even prostitutes who had not had their feet bound were at a disadvantage.

Japanese erotica emphasizes other physical details, more specifically pubic hair on both sexes and gigantic penes on men. The only other Far Eastern group that has been reported as having comparable interest is the Chukchi, where abundant pubic hair is regarded as a mark of beauty in a woman.

The other physical characteristic stressed in Japanese erotica, gigantic male genitals, is reflected not only in the actual sizes shown in the pictures but also in the content of scenes, which frequently depict penis contests of one sort or another.

Further peculiarities of Japanese erotica include very great interest in sexual gymnastics (almost but not quite as extreme as in Hindu representations) and human–animal contacts, often with very unlikely animals such as octopuses.

"The dream of the fisherman's wife," by Hokusai (1760–1849).

Sexual behavior, statistics, tabus and rituals

The actual sexual repertoire of Far Easterners seems to have little to do with either the handbook recommendations or the pictorial representations. But in some sense the high cultures of China, Japan and Korea were at least familiar with the possibility of several positions for intercourse, as well as cunnilingus, fellation, soixante-neuf and other sexual acts.

Except among Muslims, very long tabus on sexual intercourse between husband and wife after the birth of the child are not found. Generally speaking, long tabus (of at least one year and sometimes longer) are absent throughout Asia and found mostly in the disease-ridden tropics of Africa, New Guinea and South America, or in hunting and gathering societies (although not among Siberian sea-mammal hunters). Some anthropologists have seen such a tabu as a very significant birth-control method to ensure individual and group survival in hard situations.

More frequently mentioned are tabus on sex during menstruation, found among the Chinese, Manchurians, Japanese, Chukchi and Gilyak. Sources for Okinawans both affirm and deny such a tabu. The Chukchi (and Asiatic Eskimo)

believe that menstruating women are so dangerous that even their breath is contaminating and may cause a man to drown at sea. The Gilyak have similar fears (apparently not found in the high cultures): a female shaaman can kill her shaaman competitor by rubbing menstrual blood on her eyes.

The exceptional nature of Ainu beliefs can well be appreciated because of the striking contrast to Chukchi and Gilyak views. Among the Ainu, menstrual blood is good luck. There is no mention of a tabu on sexual intercourse during a woman's period. Furthermore, menstrual blood is believed to be a very powerful medicine to relieve pains, bring success in the hunt and ensure wealth. If someone sees a drop of menstrual blood on the floor, he should dip a finger in the blood and smear the chest with it.

Sex tabus in association with death are reported from a few groups. The Gilyak are said to tabu intercourse after the death of a man. The Miao require the husband of a dead woman and her children to observe sexual abstinence for a year after her death; but if a man dies, the widow has to observe only a week's abstinence. Koreans, following Confucian rules, are supposed to abstain from sexual intercourse for three years after the death of a relative.

Among the Taiwan Hokkien,

Sexual gymnastics feature in Japanese erotica, as well as emphasis on genitals. A composite of illustrations attributed to Hokusai.

when people become grandparents they are supposed to give up sex entirely. Other societies sometimes feel that sex for the old is inappropriate, as traditionally in the West — hence such expressions as "dirty old man." But the Hokkien specifically relate a tabu on sex to a change in social status.

Traditional Chinese have very elaborate sexual tabus, in association with the birthdays of gods or days on which the gods are believed to be more active than otherwise. The list of tabu days varies. One Daoist book gives 24 as the maximum number of tabu days, the minimum being 21. Nearly all Chinese who were interviewed about the matter (by Francis Hsu) agreed that it was absolutely necessary to observe sexual abstinence during any epidemic or when prayer meetings were being held.

Insistence on virginity for unmarried women is found only among the Chinese, Japanese, Minchia and Koryak. The Koreans, Okinawans and Gilyak also prohibit premarital sex, but the rules are not strongly enforced. Most of the other groups permit premarital sexual freedom. The only group in the whole area (as listed in the *Ethnographic atlas*) tracing descent through women is the Ainu, but it does not seem to be any more free in the sexual relations of its women than the other groups.

There is almost no information about ritual occasions that require sexual acts to be performed. It must be said, however, that the rules for copulation that were imposed on the Chinese emperor, with regard to his various grades of wives and concubines, approach ritual. Each one of these women had specific calendar days allotted to her for intercourse. The lower ranking women would have sex with the emperor more frequently than those of higher rank. The queen was to have intercourse with him only once a month at the time he was regarded as most potent (he was required also not to have squandered that potency by having had intercourse to orgasm with other women).

Other sexual interests

The nineteenth-century traveler Richard Burton described the Chinese as *omnifutuentes* ("all copulating"), that is, willing to copulate with anything, including not only little boys but ducks, goats and any other animals available. Very few paraphilias have been recorded for the area, although Japanese erotic pictures suggest at least the presence of voyeurism and interest in erotic bondage (other forms of sadomasochism are not common).

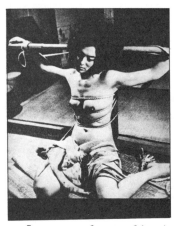

Japanese sadomasochism is seen in 19th- and 20th-century versions (above). Voyeurism (above right) is also a theme in Japanese erotic paintings.

Specific information about foreplay is also not usual. Okinawan men are said to enjoy caressing breasts, but there is a generational difference with regard to kissing: older people do not like kissing, but some younger couples include it in their foreplay. Kissing is specifically denied for the Ainu and Miao. Kissing of a sexual nature is reported for Manchurians, Tibetans, Chinese and Japanese. But except for Tibetans, kissing is avoided in public. Georges Valensin (1977) considers the Communist Chinese rule of "oral chastity" (at least in public) as a continuation of an earlier tradition.

Landor, writing in 1893, says that kissing was apparently unknown to the Ainu — at least to a woman who was virtually throwing herself at him — but biting was not: "Loving and biting went together with her. She could not do the one without doing the other . . . when she had worked herself up into a passion she put her arms round my neck and bit my cheeks."

Nose rubbing is mentioned only for the Formosans. In traditional Chinese society, masturbation leading to ejaculation was discouraged for males because it would deprive them of *yáng* without any *yīn* compensation. Nocturnal emissions were similarly a matter of concern; they were thought to be caused by evil fox spirits, who changed into beautiful women to rob men of their vital fluids. After the Communist takeover, male masturbation continued to be discouraged: Mao Zedong (Mao Tse-tung) publicly condemned masturbation and suggested vigorous exercise as a preventive measure.

Foreplay really does not seem to have played a great part in actual Far Eastern sexual behavior. Valensin believes that traditionally Chinese sex play was minimal. Descriptions of marital sexuality in several Far Eastern societies (at least on the peasant level) seems to point to a general poverty of affection and sensual enjoyment. Cornelius Osgood, writing in 1951, surmises that marital sex among Koreans is not even adequate "relative to any standard except that of conceiving children."

Descriptions of Japanese marital sexuality are more or less the same.

Homosexuality and paraphilias

Homosexual acts and paraphilias are for the most part ignored in anthropological accounts for the area. The last Han emperor, Ai-di (6 BC–AD 2), was involved with a boy, Dung Xien (Tung Hsian), and the story goes that the two were in bed and the boy fell asleep on the emperor's sleeve. Rather than disturb the boy, Ai-di cut off the sleeve with his sword. The expression *dànxiù*, "cut sleeve," is used for "homosexuality" in recollection of that occurrence.

Throughout Chinese history, pederasty was associated not only with the court but also with actors. Female roles were traditionally played by effeminate young men, so possibly pathicism or transvestite pederasty was involved.

In any event, exclusive homosexual interests are rarely discussed in the Chinese literature. Instead we find bisexuality within the Confucian tradition of the obligation of producing children — with the exception of Buddhist monks and nuns (and possibly also of actors).

Valensin maintains that under the present Communist regime there is almost a total absence of homosexual acts — as well as of prostitution and of extramarital heterosexual acts in general. But evidence one way or the other is lacking.

Among contemporary Japanese, according to John Beatty, the concepts of "homosexuality," "masculinity" and "virility" are perceived in a manner profoundly different from usual American or British attitudes. If a man visits a married couple, a normal Japanese sleeping arrangement would have the host sleeping in the same room as his guest, and his wife in another room or sent off to her mother. The western pattern of married couples sleeping in the same room would not occur to the Japanese, whose solution is perfectly in accord with their notions of "masculinity," defined in terms of social relations with other men. Japanese are concerned that exclusive homosexuals will have no children to care for them. But homosexual acts in a bisexual

life-style are socially irrelevant.

No doubt conceptualizations of this sort vary from culture to culture and profoundly influence personality adjustments.

The Japanese

Data based on Kinsey-type interviews exist for the urban Japanese, the only non-western culture about which this can be said. The data deal, however, almost exclusively with the sexual behavior of students after World War II.

An attempt to do an investigation into sexual behavior as early as 1922 was made by Senji Yamamoto, a zoologist, in association with Tokutaro Yasuda, a medical student. Yamamoto, however, was assassinated in 1929 by ultra-rightists opposed both to his socialist politics and to his sexological studies.

Since World War II, Shin'ichi Asayama did a number of surveys on the sexual development of university and high-school students. In 1949 only three percent of the males (21 out of 693) and four percent of the females (12 of 283) admitted to having had any homosexual contacts such as kissing, petting and mutual masturbation (oral and anal contacts are not mentioned at all). By 1974, the figures were about seven percent of males (184 out of 2,674) and four percent of females (84 of 2,101). These percentages are much lower than comparable Kinsey figures for the United States but approach the incidence of exclusive American homosexuals. Very striking differences in heterosexual behavior can also be found. For example, in the 1974 survey, only 15.1 percent of Japanese males admitted to having had sexual intercourse (and this spans an age group of

Chinese pederasty illustrated in an 18th-century painting, "Two Actors."

The Ainu girl described by Landor in Alone with the hairy Ainu *(1893) showed affection by biting rather than kissing.*

16 to 21), whereas in the Kinsey sample, 85 percent of males who did not go beyond eighth grade in elementary school and 42 percent of males who went on to college experienced premarital intercourse by the time they were 20 years of age.

The Japanese studies show an increasing similarity over the years between the sexual behavior and sexual desires of Japanese men and women, with women more and more approaching the male levels.

With regard to extramarital intercourse, it is believed that all Japanese married men before World War II had some sort of sexual contact outside of marriage and this was sanctioned by the prevailing mores. Since the war, in spite of profound social changes, the majority of married men (60 percent in a survey of Tokyo; 75 percent in the Kansai area) have extramarital intercourse; rich men show much higher figures (90 percent). For women, the figure was about five percent between the ages of 30 and 40. American women show a range five times greater than that. As for husbands, Japanese men exceed Americans by 20 percent.

Unique customs

Certain customs that have been reported from this area are unique, or nearly so, even cross-culturally. Korean women traditionally wear a small rod-like silver pin, which is stuck in the bun of hair at the back of the head. Its use is primarily decorative, but it can also, as was stated in all seriousness, be used by the woman to jab her husband's testicles during intercourse and prod him on when his passion lags.

In Mongolia and among the Monguor, certain pseudo-marriages occur where the daughter is offered to a guest. If she should get pregnant, she gets married to a belt, which must be left behind by the guest. The belt is simply symbolic of the man, who may never return. Similarly in Mongolia, if a girl gets pregnant outside of a situation of sex hospitality, she is formally married to a prayer rug.

Finally, an unverified custom is the ceremony reportedly initiated by the Tang Dynasty empress Wu Hou (AD 625–705). She is said to have required that all government officials and visiting dignitaries should, by royal decree, perform cunnilingus on her in public. I have been unable to corroborate this account but it is included in *Simon's book of world sexual records* (1975) as "world record No. 348: cunnilingus — only royal example."

The future of sexual customs and ideology in the Far East promises to be complicated and invariably interesting. The overriding reality is the huge population in the main centers: China and Japan. Policies of massive contraception and abortion have been adapted to counteract the disastrous consequences of sexual activity. The present Communist government in China has been fostering an antisexual ethic that goes beyond Confucian prudery. A country which once produced philosophers who maintained that "the more women a man has intercourse with, the greater will be the benefit he derives from the act," now has generated slogans like: "Making love is a mental illness that squanders time and energy." It remains to be seen how the people themselves will deal with the situation.

Sixteen & OCEANIA

The South Seas have stirred the sexual imagination of the West ever since the earliest reports of a paradise of the flesh inhabited by beautiful people uncontaminated by civilization.

The spirit of sex.
Aboriginal Australian rock carving.

This fantasy distorts the real world in several ways. But it is true that many of the sexual customs found in the Pacific differed considerably from Judaeo-Christian morality.

The general tolerance of premarital promiscuity is a case in point. But it is one thing to tolerate promiscuity, another to practice it. You cannot do so unless you find willing partners. A very important restraint on sexual life on small islands is found in incest tabus. For example, on Raroia, an atoll in Tuamotu, there were only 109 people in all in 1951.

The incest rules on Raroia prohibited any unions at all — whether marriages or love affairs — for seven of the nine women of marriageable age. In the neighboring atoll of Tepuka in the 1930s, some young people were so related to all otherwise potential partners, that they had to journey to other islands or wait for the arrival of visitors.

Early explorers were amazed and usually delighted by native women who, according to some reports, would swim out to the boats naked and climb aboard in the same condition. Further study suggests that this sort of uninhibited sexuality was part of a conscious strategy to keep foreigners peaceful. Only women who had a reputation for looseness were allowed to participate in this form of sexual diplomacy; high-ranking women were kept well out of sight. The *ariori* society of Tahiti was made up of men and women who traveled about the Society Islands as singers, dancers, athletes and sexual exhibitionists. They were permitted promiscuous relationships wherever they went. Early travelers did not realize that they represented a religious organization and that much of their sexual behavior had a religious justification: after all, the society had been founded by a god of fertility.

Greater knowledge of Pacific cultures has considerably modified the simple-minded notion of sexual paradise. In the first place, there is too much variation to set up a single pattern for this gigantic geographical area. In the second, certain ritual considerations must surely put a damper on the joys of sex in many cultures. In some parts of New Guinea, for example, beliefs about pollution from menstrual blood may do just that. All sorts of dreaded diseases and disorders are said to come from contact with a menstruating woman. Premarital sex is said to be rare because the men are simply too frightened. Before his wedding, a man is given magic charms that will help to protect him from menstrual contamination. But he still has a problem about *where* he will copulate. Because of extensive tabus, couples are left with few options and usually have sex in the bush, often even in mud.

Australian hunters and gatherers

The aboriginal Australians were once taken to be the most primitive peoples on earth. Hence, they were thought to be

Paul Gauguin's illustration from the MS Noa-Noa. *Westerners saw Oceania as a sexual paradise, but the truth was often rather different.*

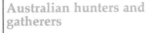

A girl of the Áranda tribe, central Australia.

Carved phalli in wood and stone show subincision (slitting) of the penis as practiced by Australian aboriginals.

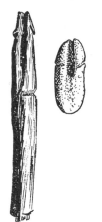

living examples of what the earliest human beings were like.

But it is clear that the aborigines had developed their own regional differences not shared by other hunting and gathering groups such as the Bushmen in Africa. So we cannot legitimately assume that their sexual and marital customs are truly representative of the earliest human culture.

Spencer and Gillen (nineteenth-century anthropologists) asserted that the Áranda and presumably Australian aborigines in general did not understand that men were necessary for the procreation of children. Malinowski claimed the same thing for the Trobriand islanders of Papua New Guinea, and a few other Pacific cultures have also been characterized in this way. This assertion at first went along with the idea of a kind of superprimitiveness. But later evidence suggests that the anthropologists did not get the story quite straight. Lloyd Warner reported that he originally got the same story from the Murngin, another Australian aboriginal group. But when Warner finally changed the wording of his question and asked what semen did when it entered the womb of a woman, several old men expressed contempt for his ignorance and replied: "That's what makes babies."

Of the Tasmanians we know next to nothing except that they practiced rear-entry intercourse (although even this is uncertain), that kissing in the European sense and even embracing was possibly unknown to them, and that men had the habit of holding on to their foreskin with the left hand — which also means that they were not circumcized.

A great deal more is known about several Australian groups. The Áranda have a ritual dance called the *wuljankura*, the purpose of which is said by Strehlow to arouse the sexual interest of women for strange men. At the end of the dance, a woman tells her husband which man she is attracted to, and the husband arranges a rendezvous between them.

Among the Murngin, a special ceremony involving a ritual exchange of wives is performed called the *gunabibi*. Not to participate causes sickness — both in oneself and in one's potential partner. The ritual intercourse is thought to be purifying and it is said that "it makes everyone's body good until the next dry season."

Before the *gunabibi*, a girl participating in it must be ritually deflowered. In many Australian groups — Spencer and Gillen say this is true of all the desert tribes — defloration is done by the girl's husband, after she has begun to menstruate, by inserting his index finger into her vagina. But defloration can also be done as a part of the *gunabibi* ritual with a special boomerang.

In Australia, such acts of defloration generally go together with two other customs: subincision (a slitting of the penis) and introcision (an operation to enlarge the vaginal opening to make – it is said – childbirth easier). The Matuntara require that the girl's husband must have intercourse with her immediately after introcision while the vagina is still bleeding, because the wound will heal more quickly that way.

The ritual exchange of wives in the *gunabibi* serves as a kind of grand finale to the entire ceremony. A person may copulate more than once during the ceremony, either with the same or with a different partner. A woman is said to be especially proud of the number of men she copulates with.

The other main variant involves mass simultaneous copulation. After the ceremonial dancing is finished, all the women lie down on the ground in two rows depending on their kinship group. They assume the position for sexual intercourse. The men dance into place in front of their female partners and are so positioned that they have their back to one another so that husbands cannot see what their wives are doing. The men then copulate with their partners. When they are finished the men get up and go to the side.

Rear-entry intercourse is sometimes reported as the usual nonritual form used by married people at night in a camp. They do so out of modesty, so that no one else will know what is going on between them.

The Áranda also practice side-by-side copulation. Intercourse with the woman on top also occurs, although some male informants vehemently deny it, insisting that "the penis might break."

Quite generally, then, Australian aborigines seem to regard sex not only as pleasurable but also as sacred, conveying health and vigor. The Áranda, and presumably other groups, believe in a spirit of sex, called Knaninja, who is worshiped with special ceremonies.

Homosexual relations are also recognized. Among the Áranda, homosexual acts are said to play a "conspicuous part" in the life of a young girl.

Male homosexuality has also been reported from other Australian groups. Strehlow, writing in 1913, says that

Arnhem Land boys decorated *"to be like women" as a prelude to a coming of age ceremony.*

pederasty was institutionalized among the Námbutji. Various authors talk of boy-wives, as though a homosexual marriage were implied.

Marriage rules throughout Oceania

Among the Námbutji, every young man becomes the boy-wife of the man who has performed circumcision and subincision on him during initiation. They live together for a while and the boy plays the passive role. Eventually when the boy is considered fully adult he will marry his "husband's daughter."

Mervyn Meggitt, from his work among the Walbiri, believes that these descriptions are highly unrealistic. He thinks that although homosexual acts during puberty rites occur widely and are expected, they are not approved of.

All Australian groups permit a man to have more than one wife. In this respect, they resemble the majority of peoples in the Pacific. Although a classic description of Marquesans says that they permitted a woman more than one husband, more recent work suggests that this

Anthropologists have asserted that some Australian societies did not realize men were necessary for procreation. But it now seems that it was the anthropologists who got it wrong.

Detail of a gable,
men's clubhouse, Palau Islands (opposite page, top). The preferred sexual outlet for many Oceanic societies is not necessarily marriage.

was not so. The Lesu and Trukese, however, are Oceanic examples of societies that permit women to have more than one husband. Few women, however, avail themselves of the possibility.

Another group where women have been described as having multiple husbands is the Marshallese. Closer examination of the description shows that the natives themselves do not regard the unions as marriages. A striking aspect of the sexual situation, however is the fact that the chief's wife among the Marshall islanders had the power to force every one of her male subjects to have intercourse with her. This was somewhat awkward for the men because the chief in turn had the right to kill any man — and his family — who committed adultery with his wife. Even though she undertook her intrigues with great secrecy, handsome young men tried to avoid possible calamity by staying out of her sight. It is reported that, formerly, such men would even disfigure themselves to avoid attention.

In a few groups, all the women are married to a very few, usually fairly old, men. A case in point is the Tiwi, a northwest Australian group. In one study, all the men under 28 had no wives and few men under 40 had any either — when they had, the women tended to be very unattractive or old widows. But the sexual reality was that all the women had young lovers. This seems to be true no matter how fond they were of their own husbands.

The Tikopia

With regard to modes of marriage, the Tikopia (a Polynesian group) are of special interest because of their tradition of marriage by capture. Early anthropologists sometimes speculated that bride capture had been a characteristic of primitive society in general and that various mock abductions found as part of the ritual of marriage in a number of societies represent survivals of an earlier reality. Theorists nowadays reject this reconstruction.

Tikopia represents a society in which bride capture (fairly common until the 1920s) actually formed an integrated structural part of the culture.

Of course, marriage sometimes took place between sweethearts, and elopement of varying degrees of secrecy constituted the most frequent prelude to marriage. But capture occurred in a significant number of instances, although it was characteristic mainly of the families of chiefs.

The capture itself was real and sometimes involved true violence. Nevertheless, it was surrounded by various considerations of etiquette. It was not good form, for example, to abduct a girl when she was working in the fields or walking along a path. The correct thing was to take her from her father's house. If an improper way was followed, sometimes the struggles over the girl became so severe that deaths occurred — virtually never the case when decorous abduction took place.

The morning after the kidnaping the woman was taken to her future husband's house and a ritual feast was held constituting the formal proclamation of the marriage. It was also the prelude to the public sexual consummation of the union, which occurred that night. This public consummation was really ritual rape, with the bride held down. The remarkable thing from native accounts is that once she had been penetrated, she gave up resistance immediately and accepted her status as wife from that moment on.

Sexual outlets outside of marriage

For many Oceanic cultures, one often has the feeling that marriage is not the preferred outlet. Even incest seems to have its charms — especially with forbidden relatives not in the immediate family.

In some societies among the families of chiefs, father-daughter incest was permitted. On Truk, at least one chief was known to have married his own daughter. Among the Marshallese, a chief deflowered his own daughter. On Hawaii and Rarotonga brother-sister marriage was permitted in the royal family.

One source of legitimate sexual outlet outside of marriage was sex hospitality, probably common throughout Polynesia, but specifically reported from the Samoans, Marquesans and Maori. The Maori did not use the custom to any great extent, however, because women frequently accompanied men on their travels. Nevertheless, it *was* a possibility, as even an Anglican bishop was to learn. The bishop's companion cried out in horror when the suggestion was made: "What? A wife for the bishop!" The chief who made the offer reconsidered and grudgingly obliged: "Oh well, give him two!"

Oceania is the area par excellence where public copulation, erotic festivals, ceremonial orgies and sex expeditions have

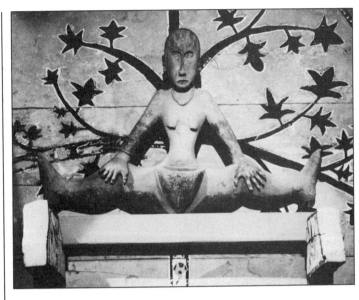

been reported. For the most part they have disappeared with European colonization and Christian missionaries. The Kwoma, for example, have two ceremonies involving sexual license — something like the Australian *gunabibi*. Similar erotic festivals have been reported from the Orokaiva, Trobrianders, Yapese and Normanby islanders.

Naked dances occurred formerly on Easter island and the Marquesas. According to Linton, at the close of feasts, Marquesans would hold public group copulation displays. The women taking part would take pride in the number of men they serviced. Linton recalls one nice old woman who boasted about having made the entire crew of a whaling boat happy.

Both the Trukese and Trobrianders had the custom of sex expeditions. A group of young men (also young women among the Trobrianders) would get together to seek out sex partners. Trukese sex parties who

Erotic festivals
with public copulation may occur among the Yapese (above) and in many Oceanic groups.

251

met with refusal would sprinkle "magic oil" on uncooperative women to make their hair fall out and ulcers and boils appear on their bodies.

The Pukapukans have developed a sex institution to rival any American swingers' club. They set aside places called *ati* where men and women go to form sex parties. They chant and dance and have sex under the watchful eye of a general organizer and guard who keeps out jilted lovers and irate husbands.

Clearly, over much of Oceania a pro-sex attitude prevails. Concern for sex technique and even aspirations to sex virtuosity exist. Sex education is known in some instances to involve a practical as well as a theoretical side. Among the Mangaians a boy is sexually trained by an older experienced woman some two weeks after he has had his penis superincised. The old custom was for this instruction to take place on the beach where the water comes up to the sand.

In Polynesian societies, there is little concern for virginity except for the daughters of chiefs. Such girls may have to prove their virginity in a public defloration. On Tonga, a girl of high rank slept with her legs tied together so that her virginity might not be lost to some night-crawler. General insistence on a girl's virginity in marriage is found among only a few peoples.

If we look at Oceania as a whole, we can see considerable diversity in spite of the general pro-sex orientation. In some instances the variation reflects obvious social factors, but in many cases no clear-cut reason is readily apparent. The Wógeo, for example, think masturbation is all right for children (because they are just "trying out their

A Mangaian necklace (far right) decorated with replicas of sexual organs.

Spring dance of Solomon Island maidens.

organs") but bad for adults. The Trukese believe children will get sick from masturbation, but not adults; in fact there is said to be a god of masturbation, Olefat, who taught it to the Trukese.

So, similarly, knowledge about sexual anatomy also varies widely. The Trobrianders are described by Malinowski as

having only a rudimentary knowledge; they lack words for such parts of the female anatomy as mons veneris, labia minora and majora and hymen. A Mangaian youth in Marshall's account, on the other hand, has a sexual vocabulary rivaling that of a western doctor. Certain Mangaian words have no common or even scientific English counterpart, for example *tipipaa* "ridge of the glans of the penis."

Sexual practices and statistics

A majority of the societies we have such information about use the missionary position as the main or very frequent position. The Oceanic position is a close second.

The Trukese and Yapese

practice a variation of this that is apparently unique. The Trukese themselves seem to be aware of this uniqueness since they call their coital technique *wechewechen chuuk* "Trukese striking." The man sits on the ground with his legs wide open and stretched out in front of him. The woman faces him, kneeling. The man places the head of his penis just inside the opening of her vagina. He does not really insert it but moves his penis up and down with his hand in order to stimulate her clitoris. As the couple approach climax, the man draws the woman towards him and finally completes the insertion of his penis. Before climax, as the partners become more and more excited, the woman may poke a finger into the man's ear.

A Yapese variant, called *gichigich*, is not used by a man with his wife because she would insist on it all the time and this would wear him out, making it impossible for him to work like other men. Nor could the woman work as she should. Consequently, as soon as a couple marries — even though they may have practiced *gichigich* before as lovers — the man substitutes the standard marital form: none other than the missionary position.

The description of the Yapese *gichigich* is one of the most graphic in the anthropological literature, written up by Salesius in a report from about 1906. The man just barely inserts his penis between the woman's outer sexual lips as she sits on his lap. The head of the penis is moved up, down and sideways for a period of time, which can be quite long. The rate of this movement varies, and can become quite intricately contrapuntal. All this is said to make the woman frenzied,

weak and helpless. She experiences one orgasm after another and involuntarily urinates a little after each orgasm (the sensation for the man is that he is on fire).

Coincidence, I think, accounts for the fact that the Yapese with this rather strenuous frenetic sexual technique have one of the lowest rates of frequency for

intercourse found in the world. A number of other coital positions are reported from Oceania as a whole. Having the woman on top as a common option seems to be more frequently admitted here than elsewhere. Possibly this is related to a greater concern for the sexuality of women than is shown elsewhere. A sitting position (with the woman astride the man's lap) somewhat like the Yapese custom but without the *gichigich* addition, is mentioned for the Wógeo and Marquesans. A side-by-side facing position

Before marriage the Yapese *practice a coital technique, the* gichigich, *said to make the women "frenzied, weak and helpless." Once married, therefore, it is discontinued and the missionary position becomes standard.*

(without any symbolism attached to which side the male or female lies on, as in Africa) has been reported as very common among the Marquesans, Mangaians, Tikopia and Alorese.

Although some societies have a fairly limited traditional sexual repertoire, others have a quite large one. The Trobrianders, for example, recognize only two acceptable, "natural" coital positions: the Oceanic and side-by-side facing. The Mangaians include in their repertoire all the basic coital positions and several other techniques.

Interestingly, what may have been the traditional coital position, the Oceanic, is becoming rarer today, although it is admitted that "older people believe that this is best." The most common coital position at present is the missionary position, probably as a result of western influence.

The use of foreplay even in societies with great emphasis on technique is often minimal. What is desirable in much of Polynesia is delayed ejaculation so that the man can bring his partner to orgasm. The adept lover will not only be concerned about satisfying his partner but he will want to have multiple orgasm himself in any one session. Unlike the Yapese, who consider a tight, nearly impenetrable vagina a sexual ideal, Mangaians want a well-lubricated path: saliva or a concoction from the hibiscus or even soap may be used.

Oral sex has been characterized as well established in parts of Oceania, but specific information turns out to be really quite scanty. Marquesans and Mangaians seem to be completely permissive about cunnilingus and fellation. The Woleaians also practice both.

Coitus interruptus is reported from the Maori, Marquesans, Tikopia and Yapese. The Tikopia clearly do it for birth control.

With regard to frequencies of sexual acts, we have only cultural expectations (or fantasies) and an occasional anecdote to go by. One Marquesan man claimed to have set an island record and possibly a world record by copulating 31 times in a single night. He later became "alcoholic, psychotic and impotent." Frequencies for Marquesan adolescents are sometimes said to be more than 10 times in a single night, whereas older married couples may copulate from five times a night to two or three times a week.

The Yapese, at the other extreme, apparently copulate about once or twice a month. Alorese informants said the custom was to have sex every night, but DuBois, the anthropologist studying them, thinks every other night is more likely.

A study approaching the Kinsey method, that of Marshall for the Mangaians, suggests that for males nightly orgasm varies considerably for different groups, the average being three for 18-year-olds, seven nights a week (perhaps somewhat less frequently); two for 28-year-olds, five to six nights a week; one for 38-year-olds, three to four times a week; and one for 48-year-olds, two to three times a week (perhaps somewhat more frequently). Marshall concludes that Mangaians copulate more frequently than Europeans and Americans but probably pay a price in a higher rate of impotence and sterility in later life. Considerably more information is needed, however, before such a correlation can be accepted.

Copulating ancestors from a Maori doorpost. The traditional Oceanic coital position is apparently on the decrease.

Sex tabus

Sexual frequencies are in part modified by various tabus. The kinds of tabus found in the area are fairly usual, involving such occurrences as menstruation, pregnancy, ceremonies and warfare. A tabu on sexual intercourse during menstruation is specifically mentioned for the Aranda, Kwoma, Lesu, Toraja, Trukese, Wógeo and Yapese; for only one group, the Tongans, is it specifically denied. The Lesu insist that only the mother observe the tabu during pregnancy. Interestingly, they extend the tabus to the time pigs are giving birth — apparently a man must observe continence for his piglets but not for his own offspring.

Tabus for a period after the birth of a child are mentioned only occasionally; and the length of time varies considerably, from two to five months among the Apayo to five to six years among the Yapese and the Dani. The Yapese spacing of children indicates that this tabu is almost always observed in the breach.

Heider says that Dani spacing of children fits the tabu and that he believes their testimony about having no other outlets. He concludes that they have a low level of sexuality that simply does not tie in with Freudian or other universalist notions of human sexuality. His assertion is so at variance with human behavior elsewhere that he must expect skepticism.

Tabus in association with going to war are fairly common. The Trobrianders believe that if a man should break this tabu a spear would pierce his penis and testicles. The Yapese have what seems to be a unique tabu: never go into the water the same day that you have sexual intercourse (elsewhere on the islands in Oceania, bathing in the sea after intercourse is almost de rigueur).

These tabus no doubt affect sexual behavior to a certain extent but occasionally one finds counter-tabu techniques to offset the harm that breaking them may cause. The Buka, for example, have "medicines" to neutralize the tabu before fishing.

In the same vein, rules against adultery are often simply ignored. A Wógeo man admitted adultery was wrong but when asked what he would do about his unfaithful wife said: "I can't keep my fingers in her vagina from sunrise till dark and on till sunrise again so I keep quiet."

Among the Lesu, actually committing adultery is the "correct" thing to do (even though forbidden).

Nevertheless, in many societies the breaking of tabus and the committing of adultery in particular is believed to cause sickness or other disorders — particularly in a child of the wrongdoer.

In a few instances, confessions of sexual misconduct are required — but this custom is not reported as widely here as for African or Siberian groups. The Pukapukans and Wógeo require detailed confessions of adulterous acts by a woman who has a delayed delivery. The Trukese extend the need for a parent's confession beyond delivery to cure a child's sickness. The Tongans do not limit confessions to mothers in labor. They believe that any member of a family can get sick because another member has broken a sexual rule. A man might get sick because his son committed adultery — and it is the son who would have to confess.

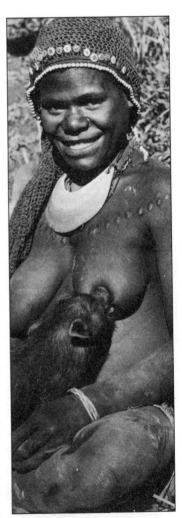

Huli woman from the New Guinea Highlands suckling a pig – a fairly common custom throughout the area, where pigs are highly regarded and women's breasts are not considered particularly erotic.

Woodcarving frieze
(above) in a Micronesian clubhouse
tells the Oceanic story of a man
with a penis so long that he and
his wife made love from separate
islands.

Male image
from the Cook Islands, with three
secondary images sprouting from
the god's body.

Homosexuality

According to Malinowski, the Trobrianders admit that homosexuality, though contemptible, was formerly practiced — but only by mentally deficient people. Male homosexuality is denied for Easter islanders, but female homosexuality occurs and is both tolerated and accepted.

Adolescent homosexual acts are said to be nearly universal for Makassarese boys and Lau girls before marriage. In Samoa such acts are regarded simply as play and not given much thought.

The general pattern of adult male homosexual acts has a striking distribution according to "culture area" in Oceania: pederasty in Australia and Melanesia (where it is often ritualized as well as institutionalized); but pathicism (which involves transvestism) in Polynesia, Indonesia and the Philippines.

The Polynesians share a number of traits both because of a common ancestry as well as trade connections. From a sexual point of view a number of traits are sufficiently common to be significant: the practice of superincision in males and an intense interest in genital cleanliness; a preference for broad-hipped fairly stocky women with light skin coloring who have mastered a considerable amount of sexual technique; the practice of night-crawling by young men, whether considered admirable or not; premarital sexual freedom except for high-born girls; and, formerly, public copulation as part of religious ceremonies.

To this add the component of institutionalized transvestites, *mahu*, who frequently enter into homosexual relations with nontransvestite men. This pattern is found among the Marquesans, Tongans, Tahitians and Samoans. In old Hawaii, this was also the case, and homosexual practices were reportedly common, especially among aristocrats.

The Melanesian and New Guinea pattern of pederasty involves quite a different setup. It is usually associated with a puberty cult. Melanesian and New Guinea pederasty is often but not invariably associated with a belief that menstrual blood is extremely dangerous. Sometimes extensive tabus on heterosexual coitus exist but none on homosexual contacts. This is true of the Étoro, who tabu heterosexual contacts for between 205 and 260 days a year (an earlier account suggested as many as 295 days). Although hard and fast statistics are lacking about the degree to which these tabus are observed, the seasonal clustering of births suggests general compliance with the rules.

None of these tabus holds for homosexual acts. In fact they are positively encouraged because semen is seen as a life force, of which men have only a finite amount. Boys are believed to have no semen at all at birth. It is through oral insemination by older men that they acquire the necessary semen to become men and to provide life for their offspring. Consequently, boys between the ages of 10 and the mid-twenties are continually inseminated by older men. Among the neighboring Marind-anim the cultural preference for homosexuality has allegedly helped produce so

low a birth rate that to sustain the tribe, large numbers of children must be kidnaped from other groups and raised to become Marind-anim.

Among the Malekula, the institution of pederasty is closely associated with circumcision. Both circumcision and ritualized pederasty are symbolic expressions of the holiness of men (as compared with women). Layard suggests that just as in some societies tracing descent through women the female line of descent is conceived of as "an umbilical cord joining all generations to the first ancestress, so here the continuous penis unites all those belonging to the male line of descent."

In all these pederastic societies, the sexual role played depends on age. The initiate into sexual behavior with a partner starts as passive homosexual and then shifts to active.

The reasons for the development of such elaborate homosexual setups, seldom paralleled elsewhere in the world, remain obscure.

In another Melanesian society fictitiously called East Bay, neither transvestism nor ritualized pederasty exists, but almost every male has extensive homosexual contacts during his lifetime. Furthermore, there are no fears of ritual contamination through contacts with women or very strict tabus about associating with women. Although a few men may be exclusively heterosexual, and no men are reportedly exclusively homosexual, the great majority are openly bisexual.

There is no report of cult lesbianism corresponding to the male cults described. This may be simply because of the anthropologist's ignorance of the subject rather than a clear-cut absence of the practice.

Paraphilias and other sexual interests

Information about paraphilias and miscellaneous other sexual interests is few and far between. The paraphilia level for Oceania — in spite of fairly extensive reporting of sexual behavior in general — seems to be fairly low.

The only two Oceanic societies for which there is any evidence at all of nekrophilia are the Pukapukans and Kainantu. Although reports on the Pukapukans deny the existence of paraphilias in general, reference to nekrophilia occurs. At the outset it must be said that sexual contacts with corpses are strictly forbidden; it is tabu for a relative or friend even to take a last look at the deceased's body. Nevertheless, there is a cultural twist that makes sex with a corpse excusable and that is the belief that the grief of a cousin will be naturally so intense that the tabus will be broken — not only by looking at the corpse, but even embracing it and sometimes having intercourse with it. Sex in this setting even has a special word: *wakaavanga*. Reactions to such behavior reveal no horror; other mourners find it unseemly and extreme but almost expected. (The practice has disappeared in modern times.)

Animal contacts are reported from a few peoples: Buka, Trukese, Marquesans and Toraja. Such contacts are denied, condemned, or apparently unknown among the Wógeo and Trobrianders.

Oceanic ancestor staff god from *Rarotonga, Cook Islands. The middle is wrapped in barkcloth and the ends terminate in a head and a penis.*

The Marquesans — both men and women — make use of animal contacts as an "emergency practice." Women sometimes induce dogs to perform cunnilingus on them. Men commonly copulate with chickens. Larger animals such as dogs and horses are also sometimes used, for foration (sodomy).

Although there seems to be no reality in the belief, a few societies think of eels as particularly lecherous as well as phallic. Marquesans have legends in which sexual relations occur between women and eels, and the Maori have a myth of a phallic eel tickling a woman with its tail as she bathes.

Reports about rape span a remarkable spectrum. The Yapese have no concept of rape at all and reportedly find the idea that a woman would have to be physically overwhelmed to submit to sex amusing. Among the Trukese, rape is unknown, whereas on Tonga it is reported to be the most frequent criminal offense.

Rape is here distinguished from night-crawling, which is a common Polynesian practice also found in the Philippines. It is generally accompanied by the idea that a man can copulate with a sleeping woman without waking her.

Maori box lid
with copulating ancestors, used to store precious sacred feathers.

The Trukese

The Trukese are especially famous in anthropological literature for their sado-masochistic practices (which a western SM adept might not find particularly impressive). Women often like to leave a minor mutilation on their partner's body. Today, this mutilation is usually a series of cigarette burns arranged in two parallel rows down the upper arm on both sides; four, six or eight burns in each row are normal. In the past, powder from dead breadfruit stumps was ignited on the man's skin, but it left a less neat scar. Women are not mutilated except for a scratch on the cheek from the man's thumbnail (men used to grow long thumbnails specifically for this purpose).

The Trukese have a variety of sexual preferences. Men appreciate women who urinate when they climax, and women also like it when a man urinates inside them after orgasm (this is reminiscent of the Yapese). What is valued in a woman is prominent labia minora and a prominent clitoris; girls often pull at their labia minora whenever they bathe — and they do so at their mother's request. Formerly small tinkling objects were inserted into the pierced labia minora and they sounded as the woman walked. These objects were matters of honor. If women got into a fight, one of them might get completely undressed and dare her opponent to compete in a kind of "vulva contest." They did so even in the presence of men.

The Trukese look with tolerance and good-natured amusement on the sexual activities of the old. Older women often entice dogs to lick their vaginas by putting fresh coconut meat in them; older men often perform cunnilingus on pre-adolescent girls. Both practices are viewed with acceptance and humor.

Unique customs

Among the Tikopia it is tabu for a man to touch his own genitals or the genitals of his female partner. During intercourse the woman may have to guide his penis into her vagina herself. Among the Wógeo, it is tabu for a man to touch a woman's genitals.

Ponape is, as far as I know, the only Micronesian island to have hit *Playboy* magazine (1976 December). The *Playboy* article referred to the sexual use of a certain large stinging ant native to the island. The ant is placed on the clitoris because its sting produces a brief but acute tinglingly erotic sensation.

The most extraordinary example of erotic ingeniousness developed by the Ponapeans involves the placing of a small fish into the woman's vagina, which is gradually licked out by a man before they attempt intercourse. A fuller account is simply not available. And we may be dealing with folklore rather than actual practice.

Of the many interesting aspects of Marquesan sexual culture, two are perhaps most

unusual. One of these is a husband's obligation to have sex with his wife almost immediately after she has given birth: as soon as she has expelled the afterbirth and has bathed in a stream. According to one informant, the husband should copulate with her in the stream itself. Doing so is believed to stop the flow of blood.

Another unusual feature involved the etiquette surrounding a chief: it was considered good form to talk about his genitals and this was done constantly. They were given names indicating their vigor and size.

The western impact

The West had profound significance for Oceania: a mixed blessing at best and often painful to the natives of the area.

In many instances, traditional sexual morality was undermined. The result was the very opposite of what Christian missionaries and white colonialists were officially sponsoring. Sexual license often increased rather than decreased. This is said to be true in relation to the Murngin *gunabibi*, described earlier. The missionaries attempted to abolish the ceremony altogether, which encouraged the Murngin to play up the sexual aspects of the *gunabibi* even more, so that the sacred character of the whole proceeding was lost.

An even more striking account of missionary influence comes from Tonga, reported by Thompson in 1894. They apparently succeeded in breaking down the traditional social structure and morality but were unable to build up a Christian counterpart.

Reactions to the whites set in throughout the Pacific and

Prominent labia minora, *as shown in a Rapanui carving (above), are still valued in a woman in Oceanic societies. A carved figurine from the Tubuai Islands (left) emphasizes the vagina.*

anticolonial movements proliferated. These were aimed at getting rid of whites but keeping their possessions. Although political, these movements often had religious overtones and are generally referred to as "cargo cults." In some instances, the sexual mores of a group were deliberately violated in the practice of the cult, or else some new notion about sexuality was taken up. The Tuka movement of Fiji in the 1880s is an example. It was founded by a prophet called Ndugumoi, who surrounded himself with a special group of female attendants. It was rumored that he had sex with these women but promised that they would remain perpetual virgins nonetheless as long as they drank a special holy water.

Another cult, which was quite radical in breaking old tabus, was the Naked Cult on the island of Espiritu Santo of Vanuatu (the New Hebrides). European contact had created virtual anarchy. The cult employed drastic measures to restore some semblance of order, including an overhaul of laws on marriage and sex. For example, marriage within a clan was now permitted although formerly regarded as incestuous. The cult got its name because of a ban on clothing and body ornaments.

Christian missionaries convinced the European administration to take action against the cult, which was eventually driven underground.

The western and Christian influence on these movements was sometimes quite obvious even though they were antiwestern and anti-Christian. For example, the Mambu Movement of the Madang district of Papua New Guinea, which occurred in 1937 to 1938. Part of the initiation into this cult involved a "baptism" of the sex organs: women had their grass skirts cut away, and men their pubic coverings. Their genitals were then washed or sprinkled with holy water. After that, the initiates had to wear European-style clothes.

The initial western fantasy of Oceania as a sexual paradise lingers in Hollywood movies and elsewhere. But despite considerably more freedom than in the West, sex was never devoid of problems even here and could occasion considerable anxiety. The western presence did not alleviate these problems and sometimes added to them. Even language shows this: the Marshallese word for "venereal disease" is *merika* (from *America*).

Fertility symbol from the Torres Straits shows the traditional Oceanic position.

Seventeen ❧ THE AMERICAS

They were not supposed to exist at all. St Augustine had argued learnedly that people on the other side of the earth were an impossibility. And there was certainly no biblical reference to them.

For the most part anthropologists are now agreed that the aboriginal American peoples came from Asia across the Bering Straits at least 25,000 years ago. All these Siberian immigrants had to pass through Alaska and must have had skills and technology similar to those of more recent Alaskan peoples merely to survive. Possibly they also had similar social and sexual customs.

A base line or comparison with other New World cultures may perhaps be built up from descriptions of Athapaskan Indian groups as well as those of the Eskimo and their close kinsmen, the Aleút. The Eskimo are probably the most recent immigrants and are unusual in several ways, so that by including them we are probably making our base broader or at least more generous than it really was.

The Eskimo and others

Marriage options seem to have been quite fluid among the Eskimo and especially the Aleút. The Aleút had neither marriage nor divorce ceremonies, they permitted a man to have many wives, and a woman to have more than one husband, and also allowed group marriages. A wife could be sold, loaned and exchanged. A man could legitimately have sex with his wives, his brothers' wives, his wives' sisters, as well as concubines. The only tabus involved parents and children, and brothers and sisters related through their mother.

The various Eskimo groups had almost equally fluid arrangements. It is generally said that men could have many wives, and women many husbands, but having more than one husband was normal only among the Netsilik Eskimo.

People with the same name could not marry (some Eskimo groups did not distinguish be-

tween men's and women's names) nor could people in some groups who shared the same "amulet" (or magic charm). Mother–son marriage has been reported from the Kóniag Eskimo (although a later source says mating between known relatives was discouraged by them). Formerly the Ingalik, a neighboring Athapaskan group, may have permitted brother–sister marriage. The Hare, another Athapaskan group, seem to have tolerated

Tlazoltéotl,
Aztec goddess of sexuality.

Caribou Eskimo family
of northern Canada.
The marriage arrangements can be very flexible.

brother–sister incest but forbade brother–sister marriage.

The great flexibility of these basic marriage rules makes it unlikely that any form of marriage would have to have been reinvented in the New World.

Sex hospitality and wife exchange are reported from both the Eskimo and Aleút. In anticipation of a catastrophe, Eskimo men would exchange wives, presumably because doing so changed the individuals' identity and therefore confused evil spirits. The Eskimo also practiced "seed-raising." This suggests (but does not prove) that Indians entered the New World knowing about the relationship between sex and procreation. If this is true and an assertion that the Pomo of California at one time denied this relationship is also true, then a curious loss of knowledge must have occurred.

Institutionalized homosexuality occurred among the Kóniag Eskimo and among the Aleút, and involved some degree of transvestism.

These facts suggest that customs involving transvestism and homosexuality could have been part of the original New World immigrant pattern. However, neighboring Athapaskan groups show very little of either.

Paddle of the Western Eskimo (above) shows sexual stimulation to promote fertility.
Blood from the penis (far right) is offered by a Totonác priest, c. 12th century.

The Old and New Worlds

These northern cultures showed much tolerance and fluidity but they clearly lacked certain customs. The presence of such customs in the New World means that they must have been invented independently of the Old World, e.g.:

A very high status given to virgins is found especially among the Plains Indians and among the Inca of Peru, where women who broke their vow of chastity were burned alive.

In the Old World, Europe developed chastity belts, and the Caucasus developed chastity corsets. Among some Plains Indians and others, as part of their interest in female virginity, a rope was bound around the loins of women as a symbolic "chastity belt."

At least at some levels the Aztec priesthood were required to be chaste. Apparently, certain classes of priests had to have their sex organs totally cut off.

No contemporary American Indian group practices male genital mutilations. Palerm states that boys were aboriginally circumcised among the Totonác of Mexico. Voget notes that circumcision has been reported for the prehistoric Mochica.

Early explorers among the Maya of Mexico sometimes said they practiced circumcision, but

a more detailed account by Diego de Landa, written about 1566, shows that this was not the case. Rather, the penis was cut in a variety of ways to draw blood for use in religious ceremonies. Landa also describes a ritual in which a number of men had holes punched through their penes on the sides and then a long thread was passed through the hole. The same thread was passed through all the penes of all the men, binding them together. Blood from the wounds was smeared on idols. Landa adds "and it is a horrible thing to see how inclined they were to this practice."

Only two societies are reported as practicing any female mutilations: the Pano of Ecuador, who are reported as having developed clitoridectomy, and the Conibo of Peru, who seem to have developed a kind of infibulation.

Several Old World societies, including cultures in China and India (as well as the contemporary West), have been concerned about size of penis, and developed a number of techniques to enlarge it. This is seldom reported from anywhere in North or South America, but the Tupinambá of Brazil shared this concern. A report from the sixteenth century by Soares de Souza says that men let poisonous animals bite their penes, which causes the men to suffer for six months, during which time their members become so monstrously big that women can hardly stand them.

Australian aborigines, Hindu groups from India and some Indonesian groups deflower girls when infants by inserting a finger into the vagina. Finger defloration in the New World is reported from a few South American groups such as the Yãnomamö, Bororó, and Tukano, as well as the Totonác of Mexico. Among the Totonác, the deflowering is done by a priest 28 or 29 days after birth: he inserts his fingers into the vagina to destroy the hymen and orders the girl's mother to repeat the defloration six years later. To my knowledge, no aboriginal groups north of Mexico appear to have a comparable custom.

The belief that menstruation is caused by intercourse is found in a number of New World groups: Tepoztecans, Apinayé, Timbira, Bororó. There are no reports of this belief north of Mexico.

Sheath covers for the penis are worn by certain South American groups such as the Kashuiana, Parantintin, Tupinambá and Tupi.

The practice of various kinds of foreskin tying has much the same distribution as that of penis sheaths, but was sometimes found in North America as well. The northernmost group that practiced it was the Mandan, who lived along the Missouri River. They tied the foreskin with deer sinew during certain rituals. Navaho men did so before going into a sweat-house, otherwise (they believed) they would go blind.

The penis bar of the Araucanian Indians is like the penis bar of Borneo; and the *guesquel*, used among certain Patagonian tribes. The *guesquel* was made of hairs from a mule's mane and was comparable to the "happy ring" used in China made from a goat's eyelashes. The *guesquel* may not be aboriginally American since mules were introduced into the New World after Columbus. Possibly the llama or some other animal source was used more anciently.

Sex rites

Because agriculture developed independently in the New World, sex rules associated with it must have done so, too. Among the Maya Kekchi, Mam and various other groups, married couples had to abstain from sex before the planting of maize. But some Indian groups required that sexual acts take place before the planting.

Girl from the Amazonian Conibo tribe, which alone in South America practices infibulation.

Erotic ceramics from the Mochica culture (above and below) of Peru (200 BC to AD 600). Today potters still make erotic drinking vessels for wedding presents. Sex with a skeleton (right) is a frequent theme in Mochica ware.

Public copulation is reported from contemporary Aymara during the carnival. Since this is hardly a Catholic custom, it may represent a vestige of pre-Christian rituals. Among the Inca, who lived in the same general vicinity of the Peruvian highlands, massive public copulation sometimes took place. The historian Pachacuti states that the Inca ruler Huascar ordered 100 male dancers to copulate in public with special women.

Cieza de León, 1553, suggests that ritual homosexual acts took place on feast days between (transvestite?) priests and noblemen in certain areas of the Inca empire. Details are not clear. The Spanish invaders tried to stamp out all such practices, which they regarded as abominable. It is known that at least one Peruvian gold statue showing a homosexual act was destroyed by the Spanish.

There are Indians whose sensibilities approach those of the primmest Victorians. The Kuna of South America, for example, go out of their way to keep children totally ignorant of sexuality and refuse to permit children to look at animals mating or giving birth. The Kuna are modest about exposing their genitals even in the presence of the same sex, and use euphemisms in talking about sex.

A number of other apparent parallel developments could be cited. But I think the point has been made that many exist.

Sex in the high cultures of Mexico and Peru

Many of the sexual customs that developed independently in the New World are associated with the high cultures of Mexico and Peru. This is no surprise since this was the area where agriculture was developed independently and profound changes in society, such as the emergence of social classes, took place which paralleled developments in the Near East and elsewhere.

An extraordinary source of information is the erotic ceramics from Peru, associated with the Mochica culture from about 200 BC to AD 600. They are also found at about 850 BC in cultures of northern Peru known as Vicús and Salinar, and continued down to about AD 1400 in the kingdom of Chimú. The tradition ended with the arrival of the Inca empire.

Precisely what the purpose of the ancient Peruvian pots was is not certain. Paul Gebhard has suggested that the sexual acts shown probably reflect actual sexual practices and tabus. At least they show that a particular sexual technique was fantasized about. There are some interesting gaps. Male, but never female, masturbation is shown. Fellation by a female is shown but never cunnilingus by a male. Male homosexual acts are shown on only two pots, but no instance of female homosexual acts is shown at all. Heterosexual intercourse in nine positions has been noted, including the missionary, Oceanic, woman-on-top and side-by-side rear entry positions. Since in Mochica ceramics a woman is often represented having sex with a skeleton or corpse, these representations are hardly to be taken as clinically accurate. Rafael Larco Hoyle suggests that this motif indicates that the acts are disapproved and the pots are, in a sense, three-dimensional morality lessons.

From Spanish accounts, the Maya, Aztecs and Inca seemed to be quite intolerant about sexual deviations. Both the Inca and earlier Maya were monogamous, except that men in the highest social class may have had many wives or concubines. The Aztecs allowed men to have many wives and also permitted the keeping of concubines. Spanish chroniclers denied that the Maya practiced homosexual acts, although there may have been considerable local variation. The Aztecs and Inca were decidedly anti-homosexual and punished such acts severely, but in some areas of the Inca empire, notably in the district of Pueblo Viejo, it was quite common. The Aztecs were very severe in their punishments of homosexual acts, transvestism, and father–daughter and brother–sister incest: death was by strangulation or stoning. Only in the Inca royal family was brother–sister marriage required.

The Aztecs also severely punished adultery and even fornication. If a man had a reputation as a womanizer he was strangled, shot with arrows or cast into a fire alive — if he survived the fire, he was beaten with maguey spines or with sharpened bone.

In at least one religious context, sexual license was permitted, but the result was death: the Aztecs practiced human sacrifice as part of their religion. For 20 days before a victim was sacrificed he was given four beautiful, specially trained young women, apparently as a kind of earthly reward for his impending fate.

Marriage

The New World followed the basic trend in human marriage patterns in permitting a man to have more than one wife. The Kaingáng of Brazil are considered to be the only legitimate New World example of group marriage. The Aleút, with their extremely fluid arrangements, are possibly another. The Kaingáng are also unique for allowing father and son to share the same wife (this is very rare cross-culturally and is reported elsewhere only from a few areas in Tibet).

Permitting a woman to have more than one husband was sometimes allowed in societies that permitted a man more than one wife. In North America the groups that permitted multiple husbands include the Aleút, Bellacoola, Comanche, Tlingit, Eskimo, Pawnee and various subdivisions of the Klamath.

An example of brother–sister marriage comes from the Aymará of Bolivia and Peru, who, like the Balinese, permitted twins to marry. The Araucanians also permitted father–daughter marriage, to my knowledge the only group in either North or South America that did so. Marriage between grandfather and granddaughter was fairly frequent among the Tlingit.

In addition to marriage, several other options were

Maya carving of a captive with erect penis stripped for sacrifice. Among the Aztecs, a sacrificial victim was rewarded (or consoled) by four beautiful women.

War god of the Zuni (New Mexico) Indians. Warriors who had taken a scalp were required to refrain from intercourse for one year.

frequently available by way of sex partners. Sex hospitality or wife lending is mentioned for a number of groups, but such customs seem to have been more common in North than in South America.

Wives were exchanged in a number of social contexts. Among the Tarahumara, wives were exchanged as part of social drinking customs. Timbira men were expected to exchange wives after hunting special animals, such as the anteater, armadillo and peccary.

In a few societies a special class of promiscuous women was recognized who made themselves available without charging a fee. This was true among the Pápago and Pima, who called them by a name that meant "playful." The traditional Pápago myth of origin for such "wanton women" (as they were usually called in the American Indian literature) is that long ago a young man charmed them out by playing the flute and drove them mad. They always wore festive clothes. The relatives of such women did not punish them but allowed them simply to do what they wanted. The Omaha, Osage and other Dhegiha groups also had such wanton women, as did the southeast Salish — but among them a promiscuous girl was sometimes killed by her father and left unburied.

Another approach to sex partners outside of marriage is night-crawling, found in both North and South American groups. A peculiarity of the North American version is that men sometimes crept into houses or slid their hands under tents merely to touch the genitals of a sleeping woman.

In spite of these possibilities for sex outside of marriage, many societies nevertheless held female chastity and fidelity in high repute — particularly the Plains Indians.

Sex beliefs, tabus and rituals

The belief that sexual misdeeds can harm others — usually the perpetrator's own children — is reported for a few groups. The obligation of confessing misdeeds to avoid causing this harm is reported from the Aleút, Ojibwa, Yurok, Timbira and Kágaba. The Crow once required a warrior to announce publicly before a war that he had slept with a married woman even in front of the woman's husband. The cuckolded husband could do nothing against the warrior, although he might leave his unfaithful wife.

Generally, people were quite free in their talk. For example, several groups gave sexual or other obscene names to places and people that would be the height of bad taste in English. Hopi place names, for example, include: Horse Cunt, Clitoris-Spring, Shit Kiva. Examples of Crow nicknames are In-the-corner-of-his-balls and Shit-in-his-face.

Tabus in association with religious ceremonies and important or dangerous events appear to be the most common. The Mundurucú forbade a headhunter who had taken a head from having sex for a certain length of time, and both he and his wife were forbidden to look at someone who had had sex recently. The Zuni required warriors who had taken a scalp to abstain from intercourse for a year.

More commonly, it was the shaamans who had to abstain from sexual activity — among the Nambikwara a shaaman (to ensure his powers) should not even see others engaged in

Hopi fertility rite from a 17th-century bowl shows dancers filing past a female figure, probably the Corn Maiden. But actual intercourse in a cornfield was tabu.

intercourse. Sexual abstinence for several months was frequently the rule for people training to be shaamans.

Although no society in the New World formulated a doctrine quite like the "semen power" found in India and elsewhere, the Bellacoola of the northwest coast have a notion that is similar but unique: *sxetsta* "ceremonial chastity." What is peculiar about the Bellacoola version is that even though abstinence alone conveys power, abstinence coupled with intercourse (not necessarily with one's own wife) at ritually proper moments enormously increases that power. There is a special term for such intercourse: *xoldujut*. Even women (apparently lesbians) who live like men will hire men to sleep with them when they embark on a *sxetsta* cycle. Once begun, not to follow the rules of *sxetsta* leads to death.

In some societies, men were expected to go out on a vision quest to acquire supernatural power. Among the Crow and Klamath sexual abstinence was seen as a necessary preparation for that quest.

A few groups forbid having sex outdoors (Tzeltál, Yucatec Maya). The Hopi specifically forbade having intercourse in a cornfield because it would offend the Corn Maiden spirits who protect the maize crop. The opposite view was held by the Navaho and Mandan, who thought it a good thing to have sex in cornfields. A very few groups insisted that intercourse should be performed outdoors.

A tabu on intercourse during menstruation is reported from a few societies; probably many more have the same tabu. In some North American groups, breaking the tabu is believed to lead to immediate pregnancy.

Some groups in both Americas say it causes sickness of one sort or another. Tabus during some part of pregnancy are recorded from even fewer societies. In a few Central and South American groups, it is obligatory to copulate during pregnancy, sometimes right up to delivery, because semen is thought of a food for the foetus.

The most consistently reported tabus on sexual intercourse were those after birth. Long tabus of one year or more (up to three years) were found among Central and South American groups — often from tropical areas. Short tabus of a few days to a few months were found in North America, but not in South America except for nontropical groups.

The Jvaro forbid sex after planting narcotic plants (as well as while preparing poison for arrows). Few groups have extensive tabus in association with mourning, although formerly the Hare required a widow to abstain for one year, and the Tlingit for seven months.

The Hopi used a lot of simulated sex in their rituals. For example, at a shrine dedicated to a supernatural being called the Salt Woman a man would insert his penis into a small black stone shaped like a vagina. He did this four times (a magic number).

The most dramatic instances of sex ceremonies in North America come from the Great

Plains. The Mandan and Hidatsa believed that power could be passed from one man to another by having sexual intercourse with the wife of the man seeking power. This idea spread from the Mandan and Hidatsa to neighboring but unrelated groups such as the Arápaho, Gros Ventre and Blackfoot. The Cheyenne modified the notion that a woman could be the channel for the transfer of power and stopped short at real sexual intercourse: during the Sun Dance, the chief priest and the wife of the sponsor of the dance simply stayed under a bison robe for part of the ceremony.

In one Mandan ritual, the Buffalo Dance, the wife's intercourse was seen as a religious act of copulating with the bison, and thereby drawing power from the primal bison. The Buffalo Dance was performed to ensure abundant bison herds and prosperity to the Mandan.

The Gros Ventre changed this in their own ritual of power transfer by making it into a kind of sex test. This occurred in a ceremony known as the Crazy Dance, as well as in the Kit-Fox Dance. Again, it was the wife of a man who was the channel of the power transfer. The women assembled for the test were all naked and were handed over to ceremonial "grandfathers," who were also naked. A "grandfather" would lie on top of a woman, put his lips against hers, and pass a chewed up sacred root or powdered "medicine" from his mouth to hers. But he was not to have sexual intercourse with her, nor was her husband to show any jealousy — that was the test.

Among South American Indians the Kágaba require ritual coitus interruptus in some instances, religious offers of semen and sometimes of pubic hair and ritual copulation in association with mourning.

Among the Kubeo (a subdivision of the Tukano), at the end of a boy's coming of age ritual he has to have sexual intercourse with his own mother in the presence of his father. That marks the start of the boy's public sex life. If this report is true, it is — to my knowledge — the only instance in the entire anthropological literature to record compulsory mother–son incest.

The Tukano in general apparently permitted public incestuous acts at a lunar eclipse and even on the occasion of a new moon. Non-incestuous public sexual acts are, if the reports are accurate, not considered shocking among the Tukano-Kubeo. The remarkable aspect of these rituals is the incest.

In spite of great sexual laxity among the Tukano-Kubeo, some things were forbidden. For example, real sexual intercourse between a brother and a sister was thought abominable.

A Kubeo girl was deflowered at the age of eight by an impotent old man with his fingers. He kept stretching at the vaginal opening until he could insert three fingers. When he could do that, he proclaimed "You are a woman." If this was not done before her first menstruation, it was believed that sex would always be painful and childbirth difficult. Although much of Tukano-Kubeo sexual life was performed in public this finger defloration was done in secret. The view was that a girl does not lose her virginity to the fingers of an old man, but through copulation with the moon.

Another interesting feature of the Tukano-Kubeo is that women were sexually aggressive (a trait commonly mentioned for Indians of the

Rawhide cutouts hung from the "World Tree" of an Oglala Sioux Sun Dance ceremonial lodge.

Amazon Basin). Rather than forgo sexual intercourse during nursing (which custom required), many women would rather not have children at all, and practiced abortion or infanticide. The sexual passion of women was so great that many men sought relief by giving their wives anaphrodisiacs (medicines to cool ardor). Adultery in a woman was considered natural. In a man, it was a sign of hostility, not machismo. When adultery occurred, it was assumed that the woman seduced the man, not the other way around.

Other South American societies where women were said to be the aggressors include the Cayapa, Choroti, Kallinago and the perennially interesting Kágaba, where groups of women have been known to rape men on occasion. In North America, such levels of aggression were seldom reported but in some groups nightcrawling took place not only by men but by women, too.

Sexual statistics and techniques

The Yurok believed a man who could copulate 10 times in a single night would become rich. This number was apparently considered so unlikely that something extraordinary would have to be associated with it. The Polynesian mentioned in the previous chapter who copulated 31 times in one night would surely have become the Yurok equivalent of a multimillionaire.

But we cannot really know anything definite because of a lack of reporting and the fact that many of the societies described no longer function in a traditional way.

Information about sexual technique is equally sporadic and unsatisfactory, but perhaps somewhat fuller. Few societies are reported as using more than one coital position.

Rear entry was reported from a number of South American societies: the Ona, Chiriguano, Nambikwara, Timbira, Apinayé, Sherente and Guayaki. From a world-wide perspective this is high.

The missionary position was reported as the most common position in North America for the Hopi, Navaho, Nahane, Crow and Penobscot (the last two according to Ford and Beach); and in South America, for the Araucanians, Carib, Kágaba, Kaingáng, Chamacoco, Kaskihá, Tapirapé, as well as the Rãmkokamekra (a subdivision of the Timbira), Barama, Colorado and Rucuyén (the last four according to Ford and Beach).

In addition to rear entry, the Nambikwara used a variant of the missionary position not recorded elsewhere as a standard form of intercourse. The woman lay on her back, with the man on top facing her, his right leg between her legs and his left leg outside them.

A peculiarly South American penchant for copulating in a hammock has its risks. The Sirionó often joked about the awkwardness of the whole business. Sometimes — virtually at the moment of orgasm — a man's knees would slip through the holes of the hammock and he would get an unpleasant emotional jolt.

Fellation was used by the Ojibwa and Pomo in both heterosexual and homosexual encounters. The Nahane denied practicing fellation and also rejected cunnilingus as poisonous. The Ojibwa thought that it was disgusting, the Hopi

The South American Tukano–Kubeo give anaphrodisiacs (medicines to cool ardor) to the women because their sexual passion is thought to be so great.

that it caused sickness, the Yurok that it would keep the salmon from running. Aboriginal Americans were not noticeably oral in their sexuality.

Foreplay is seldom reported, and kissing in the European sense seems not to have been aboriginal, although it is reported for the Hopi. No society is reported where men are interested in delaying ejaculation to

Cherokee stone pipe showing fellation. However, oral sex is not generally stressed among aboriginal Americans.

help their partners achieve orgasm. In general, quick ejaculation seems to be the ideal.

Homosexuality and transvestism

Two patterns for homosexuality predominate in the Americas: pathicism, in which one of the partners is a transvestite (almost always referred to as a *berdache*), found primarily in North America; and adolescent experimentation or deprivation, in which young men who have little or no access to women have sex with each other — the most usual South American pattern. Information about female homosexuality is scanty.

The Tukano generally regard homosexual acts outside of puberty rites as something reprehensible, whether male or female, and such acts had to be performed secretly (if at all) to escape punishment. But the Kubeo reverse these exceedingly uncommon rites: heterosexual acts are done secretly but

homosexual ones apparently occur quite openly.

Several societies are mentioned as having *berdaches*, but whether they were homosexual or not is not discussed. I suspect that in some of these cultures at least a few of the *berdaches* engaged in homosexual acts.

In one North American group, the Nahane, there were remarkably enough no male transvestites at all, only females. Cross-culturally, this is almost unique as far as I know (the closest parallel, which shows many striking similarities, is found among the Albanians of Europe). If a married couple felt they had too many daughters and wanted a son to hunt for them when they got old, they picked one of their daughters to live like a man. When the girl was about five, the dried ovaries of a bear were tied to her belt (the reason for which is not clear) and she was henceforth raised as a boy. Later on, such a girl would very likely have lesbian relations.

Several societies permitted homosexual marriage. Male homosexual marriages were reported from the Arápaho, Navaho, Klamath and Achómawi. The Achómawi and Sawa'waktödö recognized female homosexual marriages.

These customs are in marked contrast to American cultures from Mexico and farther south. Although homosexuality seems to be quite common in a great many societies there, transvestism is much less commonly reported. Among the Warao, the only male transvestite seen was said to be married to three men younger than himself. The other society, the Tupinambá, recognized pathic homosexual marriage as well, but only involving women.

The Yãnomamö, written up in

famous studies by Napoleon Chagnon, are particularly interesting in terms of a causal model that links welfare and homosexuality to the widespread practice of killing off girl babies and of developing an extremely brutal version of male chauvinism. One view of this whole complex offered by Marvin Harris suggests that the Yãnomamö had experienced a population explosion possibly because of the acquisition of steel axes and machetes, originally of white origin, and also because they had begun to grow bananas and plantains introduced into South America (where they are not native) after Columbus. The growth in population led to a need to expand into other areas already settled by Indians, and also to cut down on the population. The consequence: warfare and female infanticide. But the killing of girls led to the need for even more warfare to raid neighboring groups for their women. Even so there was a tremendous sex imbalance, with the result that almost all bachelors had sex with each other.

Schneebaum discusses a Peruvian group, the Amarakaire, where the young men also seem to be universally involved in homosexual acts. According to Schneebaum, most tribes in that general area show the same general homosexuality; if so, it may be independent of a population explosion model.

Information about female homosexuality in South America is scanty and minimal, as elsewhere. An almost lyrical note is recorded for the Araucanians. It is said that lesbian acts are common among young girls in the spring, but such activities are generally regarded as a sign that the girls are now ready to marry — boys.

Other forms of sexual behavior

Information about masturbation, bestiality and paraphilias is uneven but suggests a wide variety of attitudes and behaviors throughout the Americas. Bestiality is said to have been unknown among the Chiriguano, but common among the Crow, who apparently had no scruples in having sex with mares and wild animals that had just been killed in the hunt. Ojibwa women also made use of dogs, but Ojibwa men had a more varied cast: not only dog, but also moose, bear, beaver, caribou and porcupine! Despite this apparent freedom, all forms of animal contacts are tabu among the Ojibwa. The Hopi regard sex with animals unemotionally, with neither guilt nor affection.

In South America, several

Sioux Dance to the berdache *(transvestite), recorded by George Catlin, 1876: "The* berdache . . . *is looked upon as* medicine *and sacred, and a feast is given to him annually."*

groups have made use of the llama or related alpaca for sexual outlets. Under the Inca, laws were enacted against this and llama drivers were not permitted to make journeys

Intercourse with porcupines has been reported among the North American Ojibwa, who are also said to have had animal contacts with moose, bear, beaver and caribou. All forms of animal contact are, however, officially tabu among the Ojibwa.

unchaperoned but had to be accompanied by their wives. An interesting aspect of llama/alpaca–human contacts is that syphilis may thus have been transferred to human beings.

Biting and scratching in a sexual encounter are sometimes reported, for example from the Mataco, Ojibwa and Nahane. Hints of sadomasochistic tendencies in a few particular people have been noted for the southeast Salish. Sirionó lovers seem not to have been particularly gentle: poking a finger in the eye counted as affection, and couples emerged with scars after passionate encounters in which head, neck and chest had been bitten and scratched — the scars being something of an embarrassment in the case of an illicit interlude.

Rape has been reported primarily as gang rape, often as a form of punishment. This was true, for example, for the Cheyenne and some other

*A **Mimbres lottery bowl** from southwestern USA, c. AD 1200, shows intercourse with a deer.*

Plains Indians. In South America, among the Bororó any girl not married by puberty was fair game for gang rapes. Gang rapes by women of a man is reported only for the Kágaba.

The Navaho believe that a woman is able to defend herself against rape. Her strategy: grab the man's penis and threaten to drag him home. He would, it is believed, almost certainly give in because of the pain and fear of scandal.

Some groups, such as the Tepoztecans and eastern Apache, discouraged childhood sexuality as much as possible and punished masturbation quite severely. But in other societies, even adults openly played with the sex organs of children. Babies have their genitals stroked by their mothers among the Hopi, Navaho, Sirionó, Kaingáng and Kubeo. In a few instances, such contacts decidedly approach paedophilia. Among the Yãnomamö, for example, fathers would often put their mouth on the vulva of their little daughters and suck on it.

A more unambiguous case of cultural paedophilia comes from the Sirionó. Not only did a nursing mother fondle her infant son's penis until he got an erection, she then rubbed his erect penis over her vulva — which was not necessarily to soothe the child. Similarly, men have been observed getting partial erections (men wear no clothes at all among the Sirionó) when playing with the sex organs of infants. The Sirionó approach to adult–infant sexual relations was exceedingly casual and open — and probably quite shocking — to western sensibilities. In the light of psychoanalytic theories about the effects of childhood seduction, it is important to know what, if any, the effect of such treatment had on adult sexual adjustment. As far as the Sirionó go, sex did not seem to present an area with many adult problems. But this may just possibly be because they were so preoccupied with food shortages.

Among the Trumai, little boys would often initiate sex play with men (seldom did men start it) and sometimes even with their own fathers. The boys would pull at the man's penis.

The Kágaba

The only society in all of North and South America — indeed in the world — where adults generally admit that masturbation is their preferred form of sexual release is the Kágaba. Furthermore, only among the Kágaba — again, from a worldwide perspective — are sexual contacts with animals said to play an important part in the sex life of almost everyone in the society. Children of about five or six are frequently subjected to sexual advances by adults, so there seems to have been an exceptionally high incidence of paedophilia. The Kágaba are one of two societies in the world about whom it is reported that women commit rape. And in the introductory chapter they were singled out as possibly the only society in the world where, in order to expiate for the sin of incest, incest has to be repeated.

Information on the Kágaba comes from the work of Bolinder (1925), Preuss (1926) and especially Gerardo Reichel-Dolmatoff (1951), the last a renowned anthropologist. There seems to be enough consistency in the accounts to take them quite seriously.

The Kágaba are an agricultural people of northern Colom-

bia. They developed an elaborate cosmic theory of sexuality, referred to in Chapter One, that ideally should have suppressed all masturbation and incest but which in fact was accompanied by a reality where both seemed to have occurred to a remarkably high degree — along with what might have been the highest rate of sexual dysfunction for men anywhere in the world.

Their general attitude to sex is that it is dangerous and bad. The Kágaba ideal is to abstain totally from sex and to become asexual. This is a view held most often by men. Women seem to be much more positive about sex but unsatisfied. Perhaps the occasional instances of rape by women relate to this.

Men have an extraordinarily high rate of impotence, which several openly admit. These sexual dysfunctions may have come about because of bad diet, ritual fasts, alcoholism, the consumption of coca (thought by the men to lessen sexual interests) and religious beliefs. But there is an additional factor that they recall with dread: as soon as a boy was thought old enough to copulate, he was put in charge of an old woman with whom he had to have intercourse. The woman was a widow, usually between 50 and 60 — which probably means quite wizened and toothless in that society. As in other ritual copulations, the sexual secretions were collected and offered up to the god of sexuality. Men remember this experience with horror. When they talked about their own impotence (which occurred just before ejaculation), men tended to relate it to their first experience of copulation with the widow, and said that they "remembered the old woman."

Kágaba men regard sex as dangerous and bad, and have a high rate of impotence. This may at least in part be due to the practice of putting young Kágaba boys in charge of wizened, toothless old women, with whom they must have intercourse.

Unique customs

Certain customs or beliefs associated with sex reported from the Americas are unique, or nearly so, even cross-culturally. Some of these have already been mentioned; others include the following.

The Kabedile Pomo did not practice vaginal intercourse on the wedding night because the bride was likely to be a virgin and vaginal penetration was believed to hurt too much. Instead, the bridegroom penetrated her anally (which does not sound like much of an improvement).

Nootka brides were sometimes very hesitant about consummating the marriage at all; some were known to delay for several months. If the groom found his wife totally unresponsive to his advances, he would cut off (or bite off) the end of her nose. The bride's family sided with the husband if they wanted the match to continue. This act of the husband's was said to be 100 percent effective.

Among the Pawnee, a woman could have sex with one man only, in any given menstrual period. This was to make sure that she would know who the father of any resulting child might be. As soon as she knew she was pregnant, she told the man, who was then obliged to be concerned with the child's welfare and had to supply it with fresh meat until it reached maturity. In other societies such rigor in establishing paternity was associated with marriage rules only. The Pawnee rule is apparently the only one to occur outside of the framework of marriage. It would be interesting to know how scrupulously it was observed.

Puna Indians of La Paz, an Aymará group, had a belief that clearly developed after contact with Europeans, but possibly reflected some older notion that had been transformed to fit a Christian setting. According to Forbes (writing in 1870), the Puna believed that on Good Friday any crime could be committed without fear of punishment, and sexual sins would not count as sins. It was said that on that day, fathers had been known to rape their own daughters in the presence of their mothers. The folk explanation for this extraordinary license was that on Good Friday, God is dead and for that reason could not remember anything the next day.

This chapter started out by citing speculations denying that the American Indians could exist. Not only do they exist: they provide incredibly rich data for anyone mapping the sexual variations of mankind.

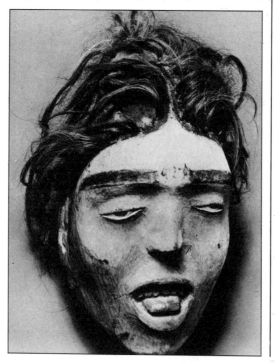

Portrait carving of Nootka woman from northwestern America. Brides reluctant to consummate marriages could be penalized by losing their noses.

Eighteen ✤ EUROPE AND EUROPEAN OUTPOSTS

A contraceptive culture. A people addicted to masturbation and pornography. The only civilization to develop a scientia sexualis (science of sex) but lacking an ars erotica (art of love).

Version of an erotic illustration *by Giulio Romano, 1527.*

These labels, and many others like them, are attempts to characterize in part or in whole the vast culture complex developed by Europeans and their cultural kinsmen outside of Europe. Michel Foucault, the modern French philosopher, relates these attempts to what he thinks is really a European cultural rule: translate sex into talk. Although first crystallized in the seventeenth century, this "rule" goes back to the medieval penitentials and the church requirement of confessing all sexual sins. It stays with us in the form of seemingly interminable pornography and of psychoanalytic sessions — or the writings of certain anthropologists, alas!

Many aspects of western sexuality have been discussed throughout this book. This chapter will deal primarily with prehistoric and folk perspectives.

Some of the folk cultures have preserved customs that city people from industrialized centers would find remote and exotic. This is particularly true of certain areas in the Balkans where ancient kinship structures have survived into the twentieth century.

In rural Balkan communities there seems to be a very lively sense of the difference between "sacred" and "profane" women. Sacred women include one's mother, sister and wife. Sex with a wife is not regarded as fun (although it might be pleasurable): after all, a sacred woman cannot be expected to be a whore in bed. Sex as fun can be found only with profane women: gipsies, singing girls

from cafes, widows who have become prostitutes, foreigners — and particularly Scandinavian tourists.

There is the expectation that men are intensely interested in sex, but women are sometimes said to dislike intercourse. Among the Sarakatsani shepherds of Greece, women often deny that they find any physical pleasure in sex at all. During intercourse, a decent woman should not move and should not make noises. A Sarakatsani bride sometimes threatens before her wedding to hide a knife under her clothes so that when the bridegroom comes to claim her virginity, she will be ready to castrate him.

Sexual intercourse is thought to have its dangers. Shepherds throughout the Balkans tend to avoid intercourse in certain critical situations. In Rumania, they avoid women altogether from the time they arrive at the spring pasture lands until July 20 (the Feast of St Eloi). The Sarakatsani feel that the shepherds who milk ewes should be unmarried. In any case, a man must wash his hands before milking if he has slept with his wife.

Similarly, Bulgarian peasants believe that soldiers in active service would be quite vulnerable if they engaged in intercourse. These notions are clearly associated with ideas of ritual pollution rather than anything else. The Sarakatsani regard male virginity much as Hindus do: as a source of power and invulnerability: a virgin soldier, for example, is thought to be invulnerable to bullets. Sex, sin and death are all related in the

Penitentials and the confession of sins *form part of the European tradition of "translating sex into talk." Woodcut by Albrecht Dürer (1471–1528).*

Sarakatsani world view; virginity and continence are life-giving and life-preserving.

Throughout the area, male dominance (at least publicly) is the order of the day. In Montenegro, Serbian women may not eat at the same table with men and are expected to kiss men's hands as a sign of greeting, to rise when they enter the room, and to step aside to let them pass on the road. Public affection between husband and wife is forbidden.

Hammel (1967) writes that among Serbians sexual intercourse may be fairly infrequent for a married couple. One time, when he was asking some working men about the monthly frequency of intercourse between husband and wife, he received the answer, "Better to ask about *yearly* frequency."

Sex hospitality was formerly practiced in Yugoslavia and some historians think it was widespread. "Seed raising" was found in some areas; among Serbians a priest or monk could serve as the vicarious husband.

A Balkan married couple. Sex with one's wife may be pleasurable, but it is not regarded as fun.

There was also the custom of marrying young boys to much older girls (the boy's father very likely having sexual relations with his daughter-in-law).

Faithfulness in a wife is expected. There are cases reported where husbands have been away from home for five and six years on end and even so their wives are (believed to be) faithful. Nevertheless, some evidence suggests that at least among Serbs the brother of the woman's husband may take some sort of sexual liberties with her. One man who was teased about fondling his sister-in-law's breasts said: "She's mine down to her belt; below that she's his." Another Serbian custom permits the best man (usually the groom's brother or another male relative) to sleep with the bride on the day of the wedding and for the first two or three days after she has gone to her new home. They are not to have sex but only to *sleep* together fully dressed.

Trial marriage is reported in some areas of Yugoslavia and also among the Albanians where a couple could cohabit once they were betrothed but no marriage ceremony would take place until the birth of a son. The birth of a son was so stressed that even though a woman might have borne several daughters and in spite of church pressures, a marriage might never take place. A woman who never gave birth to a son would be regarded as worthless and treated like a widow (although she might stay in the family house).

Among the Dinaric Serbs, a simple thing like a wedding party could end in a tragedy. Marriages traditionally take place only in certain months of the year, and a potential calamity could occur if two wedding parties were going in opposite directions and met each other on the same road. For one party to step aside and let the other pass would be an intolerable admission of inferiority, a serious blow to one's honor. Unfortunately, these wedding parties went about armed. Sometimes fights would break out so serious that the result was almost the complete annihilation of both parties.

The same kind of sense of honor obtained when a girl was kidnaped from a village, to be married by capture (this sort of thing still occurs occasionally but seems to be rigged with the girl's permission). In such an instance the honor of the girl's whole village was at stake, but it was an even greater question of honor for the kidnapers, who were prepared to die rather than give her up.

One of the customs reported from Albania is to my knowledge unique in Europe. A girl could escape from an arranged marriage in only one way: she must find 12 elders of her tribe and in their presence swear that she will remain a virgin for the rest of her life. Once she had done so, she was allowed to dress and behave as a man, carry arms, eat and smoke with men (otherwise forbidden), and work as a herdsman. If the woman eventually broke her vow, the honor of the 12 elders who vouched for her would be blackened and a blood-feud could ensue.

Although trial marriages are reported from some areas, ideally a bride should be a virgin. Proofs of the bride's virginity in the form of her bloodstained nightgown or sheet were publicly displayed after the wedding night. Among Greeks, the custom usually took the following form: the bride's mother-in-law

Balkan female partisan. Under certain circumstances women of the region may dress and behave as men.

was the one to do the testing by sticking a finger into the girl's vagina. Without this proof, the bride's family was disgraced.

Among Catholic Albanians, the marriage bed was prepared at midnight on the wedding day by two female attendants who undressed the bride, put her into a long silk shirt and laid her forcibly on the bed. The groom was brought in by two male attendants. The wedding guests waited outside the bridal chamber and sang traditional marriage songs and shouted advice through the keyhole until the consummation had taken place and the bridal couple emerged completely re-dressed as befitted their new status. Only then were they left alone.

Among Slavic groups even outside the Balkans, a married couple had to be seen in the marriage bed together by a number of witnesses. In Pojko, Czechoslovakia, the bride and bridegroom had to lie down on a blanket spread out before the wedding guests. Another blanket was spread out over the couple; after a few minutes, the couple got up, clasped hands, and wine was poured over their hands. No copulation actually took place. Among Russian peasants, copulation on the wedding day has been described as so important that if for some reason the groom could not actually perform, he would have to call in a friend to take his place.

The Irish

At almost the opposite end of both the geographical boundaries of Europe as well as of the sexual spectrum are the Irish. According to a controversial study by John Messenger, who studied the rural Irish of Innis Beag (a fictitious name for a community in the most conservative part of the country), they may be among the most sexually naive people in the world.

Sex is never discussed in the home and there is no formal sex education because "after marriage nature takes its course."

Marriage is late. The average age for men is 36; for women, 25. A high percentage of the adults are single (29 percent). Premarital sex is said to be limited to masturbation. Marital sex is always in the missionary position with little foreplay. Women seem not to know about or experience orgasm. Nudity is intensely disapproved of: intercourse takes place between husband and wife with at least some clothes on.

According to Messenger, the Irish have produced a culture that has traditionally been fearful of overt sexuality. He cites sources to show that St Patrick himself was surprised to observe how Irish converts to Christianity flocked to monas-

Irish woman from Aran. *Sexual behavior is said to be infrequent, and finding out about it enormously difficult.*

teries and nunneries with a zeal unknown in other parts of Christendom.

Messenger's picture has been severely attacked by informal Irish critics. An earlier study of rural Irish society by Arensberg and Kimball, *The Irish countryman*, goes along with the strictness of sexual morality but adds that "the country-bred boy and girl grow up in an atmosphere of constant reference to sex and breeding." It must be added that other commentators on the Irish scene have reported that some married couples were childless because they did not know the basic facts of procreation.

The industrialized urban West

The West has indeed become a contraceptive culture tolerating more and more premarital sex for both men and women. The double standard has given way to one in which women have equal rights to sexual outlets.

This modern culture is virtually unique in the world's traditions in making sex almost totally profane: there are no fertility ceremonies or phallic cults, and even tabus on sexual intercourse (such as before an athletic event) are justified for health or hygiene rather than ritual pollution or sin.

Specific sexual interests that have developed in or are practically restricted to the area include the enormous interest in written and especially photographic pornography. The very category of pornography is probably missing in most societies. The "pillow books" of Japan — illustrated sex manuals given to married couples at their wedding — are not thought of as pornographic in traditional

Japanese society but would be in a traditional European context.

Even drawings and sculptures that are specifically made to be sexually titillating are seldom if ever found in primitive societies, although outrageously "sexual" representations occur in fertility cults of some religions. At present, pornography of all kinds is a major multimillion dollar business in America and Europe, with millions of people actively involved — either in its production or in its enjoyment. One of the extraordinary signs of the increased respectability of pornography is the film *Caligula*, ostensibly a serious historical study of sexual depravity in the Roman Empire, showing not only men and women copulating but also fellation and cunnilingus (both heterosexual and homosexual) as well as simulated gantizing. Its cast included very well-known and respected actors (Malcolm McDowell, Peter O'Toole, and Sir John Gielgud).

Another development of cultural interest is homophilia, a kind of homosexuality in which the partners are both adult and neither tries to change his sex role (say, by becoming a transvestite). This is rarely found outside the western world. For the most part, true homophilia is essentially a northern European, especially English- and German-speaking phenomenon; elsewhere pederasty or pathicism (which involves transvestism or extreme effeminacy) is still a common and perhaps predominant form of homosexual interest.

A last striking aspect of western sexuality is the development of a number of paraphilias virtually absent from other cultural areas. Sadomasochism in particular seems to be a

northern and eastern European phenomenon (found also in people of such ethnic background outside of Europe). Fetishism is also more frequently reported from here than in other areas. A very general explanation is that western societies are perhaps more

Sexual equality for women is emphasized in graffiti appearing in a "sexist" advertisement, London.

Flagellation in an 18th-century London brothel. Sadomasochism of an extreme kind appears to be characteristic of Protestant European countries.

Ritual pollution may still be associated with menstruation in some parts of Eastern Europe, including Poland.

"Venus" figure *from Vestonice, Yugoslavia, c. 30,000 BC.*

repressive of both sexuality and aggression in general than most other cultures and that these interests are realized in more indirect ways than elsewhere. Also, it may simply be a matter of reporting.

Sexual customs and religious boundaries

In general, features of sexuality and sexual customs seem to follow the division of Europe along historic religious boundaries. Thus, the extreme development of sadomasochism and other paraphilias as well as homophilia come from historic Protestant territories. Protestant areas sometimes also developed various kinds of trial marriages or permitted some sort of premarital sexuality for both boys and girls, whereas the Roman Catholic areas were more usually involved with an honor and shame complex where the bride's premarital virginity was highly stressed.

Such customs as "handfasting" in Scotland or "ring engagement" (*ring-forlovelse*) in Scandinavia (which tacitly permits intercourse before the actual marriage ceremony) do not have counterparts in southern Europe.

Eastern Europe, associated primarily with Eastern Orthodoxy, has been characterized by a more lively sense of ritual pollution and still observes tabus that were discouraged in western Europe at least as early as Pope Gregory about AD 600. In Eastern Orthodoxy, for example, menstruating women are not allowed to make their communion, nor may they kiss holy pictures. Women cannot even serve as cleaners behind the holy doors of the church (the ikonostasis) for fear that men-

strual blood might possibly contaminate the altar. There is some evidence that even in Roman Catholic Poland, which borders on the strongholds of Orthodoxy, this notion of ritual uncleanliness survives. It is no wonder that with such beliefs, the Eastern Orthodox churches broke off talks with the Anglican Communion when American Episcopal churches ordained women as priests. It is interesting to note that Pope John Paul II, who has come out against women as priests, is Polish.

In Greek Orthodox households, holy pictures and crosses are not allowed in the bedrooms of married couples: copulating in their presence would be an act of sacrilege. (Peasants who live in one-room houses do not observe these niceties.) This is very different from Roman Catholic practice, where crucifixes are regularly found prominently displayed over the beds of married people. (In some parts of Spain — and possibly elsewhere — holy pictures are turned to face the wall during copulation.)

The Orthodox churches maintain a tabu on milk incest: a person may not marry the child of his wet-nurse. The feeling that this is incestuous is widely found among older people in the Soviet Union, even among atheists and Jews (elsewhere Jews do not observe such a rule). In other parts of Europe, for example Italy and Majorca, I have found milk-incest sometime observed not so much as a religious rule but simply as a folk custom.

Eastern Orthodox groups also require atonement for nocturnal emissions.

In many ways, then, the Eastern Orthodox groups preserve an ancient tradition that was given up several centuries ago in Catholic and Protestant Europe.

Ancient and prehistoric Europe

Prehistoric cave art gives a very flimsy picture of sexuality. What exists is subject to very differing interpretations. In any event it can be said that in the cave art of the Paleolithic (the Old Stone Age, lasting in Europe until about 10,000 BC) — stretching from France and Spain to Siberia — no representations of either human or even animal copulation exist. There is one dubious exception: an unfinished double sculpture from Laussel from about 23,000 years ago, accepted by a few archaeologists as a genuine scene of human sexual intercourse (in a flattened-out, stylized Oceanic position). Others think that it shows a woman giving birth or some sort of hermaphrodite or possibly an unfinished representation of a woman.

Statuettes of women (Venus figurines) of very large proportions are fairly common, as are drawings that seem to be kusthic symbols (symbolic vulvas). Very few unambiguous phallic symbols are found and representations of men (as opposed to women) are fairly rare. Elizabeth Fisher thinks that this probably means that people then did not connect fertility, their prime concern, with sexual intercourse. Phallic symbols, she believes, became important only when the male role in procreation was realized, which she assumes began with the Neolithic, the great cultural revolution that involved the cultivation of plants and domestication of animals. However, hunting and gathering societies are known to have a knowledge of the importance of sexual intercourse. Even Australian aborigines, who have been cut off from Neolithic insights — and have often been described as ignorant of paternity — have proved in at least some instances to have had a perfectly practical knowledge of the "facts of life" — as Lloyd Warner has shown for the Murngin.

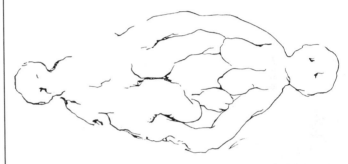

Some scholars are willing to see phallic representations in Paleolithic art. A number of pierced staffs from France have been interpreted as phallic objects and possibly even used for ritual defloration. From La Madeleine, a "double phallic" staff has been found as well as a bone incised with a picture of a bear possibly licking the end of a penis.

It seems very unlikely, however, that we shall ever be able to find out the symbolic value of cave art in any convincing detail because to do so would mean somehow getting into the minds of the long dead artists.

To return once again to phallic symbols. The ancient Romans used them in a variety of situations, often highly decorated, to ward off evil. Phallic breads and cakes persisted in many parts of Christian Europe in spite of their pagan background. Statues and drawings of gods with erections also figured in Old Norse religions. The god Freyr was depicted with an enormous penis and it may be

Human sexual intercourse (top left) was possibly first depicted in a carving from Laussel, Dordogne, France, more than 20,000 years ago.

Branching antlers engraved with phalli (above) from Dordogne, France, c. 15,000 BC.

Wooden figure with erect penis, found in a bog, North Jutland, c. 4th century BC.

Shelah-na-gig figure (right) from the church of St Mary and St David Kilpeck, England. 11th century.

The Flagellation of Christ *(far right) by Luis Borassá, 1396–1424, founder of the Catalan School.*

that he was worshiped with ritual copulation. The penes of stallions were used in magic. Such practices seem now to have almost entirely disappeared from the European scene except among the Lapps of northern Scandinavia where reindeer penes as well as reindeer uteri are sacrificed to the family gods. The Lapps are not necessarily representative of an earlier form of European culture, however, but are more closely tied to Siberian cultures discussed in the chapter on the Far East.

European art in later times can be used to show that there was a kind of counter-Christian cultural base. Some representations often include crude and sometimes even scatological carvings on the outside of churches including the so-called shelah-na-gig figures of women exposing their vaginas. Horse-shoes still hung over doors are supposedly a vestige of these figures once meant to frighten off the devil and other evil spirits. But more subtle touches are also found: unmistakable phallic carvings in otherwise innocent contexts, or the visual double entendres of scenes as sacred as the Flagellation.

It is possible that a later sensibility makes us read in some unwarranted sexual touch, but

the reverse may also be true, in the case of, say, much of Michelangelo's religious work, now taken to be entirely appropriate from a religious point of view but denounced when first exhibited. The nudity of Christ and the saints in his *Last judgment* was condemned as fit for a brothel and forced the painting of pubic coverings by another artist, Daniele da Volterra (called, contemptuously, *Il Braghettone* "the trouser-maker.")

Even statues that did not show total nudity were described as "figures that undermine faith and devotion" carved by "that inventor of obscenities, Michelangelo Buonarroti." One of these is the *Pietà* now in St Peter's. Leo Steinberg in a fascinating analysis of the statue points out that it is almost identical in composition and treatment with pagan depictions of Venus lamenting the death of her lover Adonis.

More surprising is Steinberg's analysis of another *Pietà*, now in Florence, which originally made use of a pagan symbol of sexual union or sexual aggression revived in the Renaissance: the slung leg motif. Christ's left leg was originally slung over the Virgin's thigh, as indicated by a drawing from the original. Steinberg points out that this use of the slung leg motif was "a direct sexual metaphor" employed "on a scale unprecedented in Christian devotional art." But Michelangelo himself smashed the statue and when it was restored, refused to have the left leg replaced. Could it be that even for him the sexual imagery in dealing with the Virgin as the Bride of Christ was too much?

Some art from important European masters was not veiled sexual symbolism but straightforwardly erotic, and almost always remained — until recently — private or secret. One of the most famous of these is the erotic frescoes painted by Raphael for Cardinal Bibbiena's bathroom in the Vatican. Several of these were subsequently whitewashed. The Vatican seldom allows even scholars to visit what remains.

Even more famous are the drawings by Giulio Romano for a book of obscene sonnets by Pietro Aretino published in 1527 (the engravings were done by Marcantonio Raimondi). These constituted a kind of visual *Kaama suutra.*

The study of pornography could be pursued in some detail with reference to a variety of cultural implications. But what must be conceded is that

pornography has played an enormous role in the sexuality of the West.

Marriage

Marriage in Europe from ancient times has been overwhelmingly monogamous. The Greeks and Romans were solidly monogamous. Bigamy was declared a civil offense under the pagan emperor Diocletian. Christians, who had no biblical sanction for monogamy, departed from Jewish custom by following pagan monogamy. The Germanic tribes to the north of the classic Mediterranean area were also basically monogamous. With the coming of Christianity as the state religion throughout Europe, monogamy became the official church statement adopted even by Jews.

In the sixteenth century the Anabaptists preached and practiced polygamy. But the most important break with established Christian tradition was that of the American Mormons,

A detail from The Last Judgment, *by Michelangelo, Sistine Chapel, Rome, 1541. A demon appears to be thrusting his hand up the anus of one of the damned in what may be the earliest representation of "gantizing." Michelangelo's religious work was sometimes described as "fit for a brothel."*

two divisions of whom encouraged the practice of taking many wives in what was called "celestial marriage." They believe that polygamy was divinely sanctioned. Their justification for it was not only taken from the example of Old Testament heroes but remarkably enough from the life of Jesus himself. Whereas all other Christian groups (to my knowledge) maintain that Jesus did not marry and lived a chaste life — the very basis for the Catholic insistence on priestly celibacy — Mormons believe that Jesus did marry. The wedding at Canaan is believed to be Jesus' own wedding. They also believe he had several wives. How else explain why he appeared to Mary, Martha and Mary Magdalene first after his resurrection rather than to his male disciples?

The practice of polygamy flourished for 50 years and then was given up in order for Mormon groups in Utah to become part of the United States. But sporadically polygamy still occurs.

The Mormons also have a dogma quite at variance with the rest of Christendom — that marriage continues after death, and so does sexuality and procreation. Sex goes on in all of eternity: if an individual can create enough descendants he will become a god himself.

The Mormons with their ideal of polygamy are perhaps the best known deviants from the western heterosexual monogamous ideal. But occasionally others have appeared on the scene. Epiphanius, a fifth-century cataloger of heresies, mentions a libertine sect where the communion banquet became an orgy and the rule was that semen was not to be ejaculated into a woman's body but caught in the hand, offered up to God and eaten. He mentions sects that played up masturbation and others such as the Levites who restricted themselves to homosexual relations, as the Albigensians of the later Middle Ages were sometimes alleged to do. Some of these heretical groups believed that with Christ, sin could no longer exist; therefore, any behavior was acceptable. A number of such groups, usually called Adamites, have existed from time to time in Christianity.

A number of recent utopian communities have tried to change western sexual mores. In 1851, a community called Modern Times was founded on Long Island, New York, that was accused of promoting free love. It apparently did not disown monogamy but made wife-swapping acts perfectly legitimate. The community was shut down in 1857. The most revolutionary of all the utopian arrangements with regard to marriage was probably that of the Oneida Community in New York, with its "complex marriage": every man in the community being married to every woman simultaneously.

Russia after the Revolution

With the Russian Revolution another attack on monogamy was briefly launched. Marx and Engels took a position on sex relations that can be summed up in the notion that sex was a private matter for the individual and not for the state.

The laws on marriage and sex were changed dramatically right after the Russian revolution. Laws against bigamy, as well as adultery, incest and homosexuality were

Nudist Christian Adamites seized by guards in Amsterdam.

dropped. Abortion was available on request. The early Soviet Union supported the League for Sexual Freedom. But Lenin seems to have had misgivings.

Local developments were sometimes found, such as the "nationalization of the women act" passed by the City Soviet of Vladimir in 1918. According to this act, any unmarried women 18 years of age or older had to register at the Free Love Office of the Commissariat of Welfare. Men between the ages of 19 and 50 would be permitted to choose any woman they wanted as a wife — the woman's consent not being necessary. Children of such unions became the property of the state.

Under Stalin, in the 1930s, most of these rules were revoked. In 1934, homosexual acts were reinstated as serious crimes. During 1935 and 1936, a campaign began against promiscuity, bigamy and divorce.

Trotskyists, who have kept to the earlier position that sex is no matter for the state, accuse Stalin of trying to entice powerful conservative peasants to cooperate with his regime by making concessions to their moral code. Others have argued that society simply cannot tolerate sexual anarchy. No doubt other reasons existed as well, including psychological motivations on the part of the political leaders.

Today, the Soviet Union is sexually one of the most repressive societies in the world. Pornography is not tolerated. Sex education for children is frowned on and interest in sexual matters receives a puritanical response. Divorce is possible and birth control available; but in the USSR today western traditions find their most rigid fossilization.

Sexual behavior

Actual sexual practices from folk societies in Europe and the rest of the West are seldom reported. We have information about the sexual behavior of certain groups, generally of the educated elite, but they may not be indicative of folk practices at all.

The most extensive national study on sexual behavior outside of the Kinsey report comes from France, the *Rapport Simon* based on work done in 1970 involving 2,625 interviews.

Interviews were done partially face-to-face by 173 interviewers and partially in a written questionnaire. The oral part was largely geared to determine attitudes about such subjects as adultery, prostitution and birth control. The written part dealt with actual sexual behavior. The procedure was clearly very different from that of the Kinsey team. There was, for example, no attempt to establish an independent grid of events in the life of the person being interviewed so that an internal check could be made about dating first occurrence of masturbation, intercourse or other sexual acts. The statistical rigor of the procedure was offset by problems in getting answers.

According to the *Rapport Simon*, the coital position used overwhelmingly by the French was the missionary position. For the rest, 80 percent of the men and 75 percent of the women had experienced intercourse with the woman on top (more than half had done so frequently.) A number of other positions were reported, more often by men than women, but they were infrequent. Cunnilingus and fellation were reported as practiced by 60 percent of the

"Ulla,", a prostitute of Lyon, France. French sexual behavior has been well documented in the Rapport Simon, 1970.

men and 55 per cent of the women. Here there was a significant difference according to generation, which suggests that there has been a major increase in oral–genital contacts since World War II — is this because of American influence? Abstinence during menstruation is the general rule, but intercourse at that time is somewhat more common among people younger than 30 and among non-churchgoers. Anal intercourse is fairly uncommon among heterosexuals, over 81 percent of the men and 86 percent of the women denying that they had ever experienced it.

These findings are interesting in light of certain stereotypes associated with different cultures. Fellation is sometimes referred to in the United States by expressions that suggest it is partially associated with the French — an association that is unsupported by the facts. (In the personal advertisements of sex magazines, "French culture" is a code expression for oral sex, whereas "Greek culture" is used for anal contacts. Sadomasochism is referred to as "English culture.")

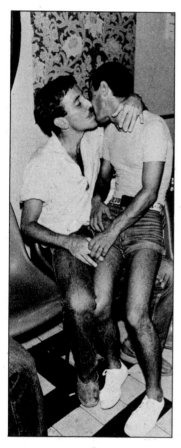

Homosexual reunion in Marseille, 1979. *The modern "gay sensibility" apparently was not present in earlier European cultures.*

Homosexuality

Information about homosexuality and homosexual acts is not extensive, at least when it comes to peasant societies. For example, John Messenger writing about the rural Irish says he was unable to discover any information about overt homosexuality although it was his assumption that latent homosexuality was very common. Concerning the Sarakatsani, the only information in the Human Relations Area Files is a casual reference to the word *pustis,* "passive homosexual." The use of this

word suggests that among the Sarakatsani as elsewhere in Greece, the notion about homosexuality is the same as in the Middle East: the "insertee" (or vagina substitute) role — called *pustis* — is shameful.

Institutionalized homosexual relationships might possibly exist among the Dinaric Serbs of Yugoslavia. Among them, two men from different clans may enter into a special sworn "brotherhood" relationship. In Montenegro, this sometimes involves a church ceremony. Church officials occasionally came out against it because — as Pope Gjuro of Njegushi is quoted as saying — it was "the marriage of two men and against all nature." Sworn sisterhood relationships also exist, although a homosexual connotation here is apparently not so clear.

The recent statement made by John Boswell that in AD 342 "gay marriages" (his term) were outlawed in the Roman Empire although they "had hitherto been legal (at least de facto) and well-known" is difficult to understand. There is no hard and fast evidence from the Greeks and the Romans that they conceptualized homosexual unions as marriages and there was no recognition of legal claims of any kind between homosexual couples because of their union. Boswell seems to project a modern notion of "gay culture" and "gay sensibility" into antiquity quite unwarrantedly, since modern homosexuality is of a different variety: homophilia rather than the older style of pederasty.

A related issue concerns transferring stereotypes from one culture to another with regard to jobs. In the English-speaking world, male hairdressers and ballet dancers are generally thought of as being homosexual. In Russia, although ballet dancers may be suspect, hairdressers are not: on the contrary, they have the reputation of being womanizers. In Denmark, hairdressers are thought of as homosexual, but not ballet dancers.

These findings show that such stereotypes vary tremendously even within the same culture — not to speak of cross-culturally. What is probable is that a tradition of stigmatizing a profession may deter heterosexuals who might be interested. Hence the tradition tends to be self-perpetuating.

Something that is much more perplexing is that certain professions that have no traditional stigma attached to them attract homosexuals, but closely related professions do not. Ned Rorem, the distinguished American composer, says in his *The final diary 1961-1972* that he suggested to Alfred Kinsey in the 1940s certain percentages of male homosexuals in the arts. Thus, in the 1940s, Rorem's observations led him to believe that 75 percent of serious western composers were homosexual, but in 1966, only 50 percent. He believes that no more than 10 percent of solo violinists are homosexual (because they are predominantly Jewish and "the solid Jewish family" produces heterosexuals), but 50 percent of pianists are and 95 percent of harpsichordists. In a telephone conversation, Rorem told me that in the United States over 90 percent of organists are homosexual, but in Europe they number only one percent.

Alfred Kinsey had planned a thoroughgoing study of the sexuality of artists. His death unfortunately precluded writing it and the Kinsey Institute

seems unlikely to finish the job.

Some evidence links male homosexuality with ritual specialists (priests, ministers and cult leaders) in the western world. This is reminiscent of shaamans who in some cultures are transvestite and enter into pathic marriages. Allegations about prominent members of various hierarchies of several denominations are sometimes made. Obviously no study is going to settle the question of percentages in religious professions because no such study will be tolerated.

Although institutionalized male pederastic relationships were part of ancient Greek culture, nothing comparable has survived anywhere in Europe.

The *Rapport Simon* gives a very low figure for the incidence of homosexuality in France. The figure for people who have had any homosexual experience at all is about five percent, almost the percentage Kinsey gives for exclusive homosexuals in the United States (those who had had any homosexual experience numbered 37 percent). Possibly the low French figure is correct but it is more likely that it reflects the fact that written questionnaires were used that devoted many pages to heterosexual behavior and only near the end asked a few questions about other activity.

Male hairdressers may be thought of as homosexuals in the English-speaking world; in Russia they have the reputation of being womanizers.

"Hamboning," an unusual sexual practice from Australia, involves a kind of male striptease in a party of men.

Unique sexual customs

The Files reveal very few sexual customs for European groups, and few that can readily be considered unique cross-culturally. Nevertheless, there are some and I have come across other instances from informal sources that may be of interest.

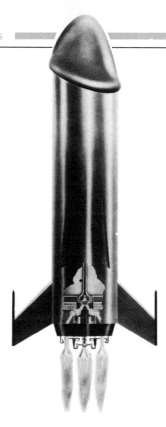

A contemporary western view of sex: phallic rocket by Alfred Beloch, Germany.

Genital contests among males are sometimes reported, especially from teenagers. Usually the reports are simply of comparing size. A fairly unusual one comes from Norway, where males in the country occasionally take part in informal penis-weight-lifting contests.

Although not a contest, Australian "hamboning" suggests a similar motivation, and sheer exhibitionism may be involved. What is involved is a kind of male strip-tease: exposing oneself in a party of men. The name perhaps comes from identifying the penis with the bone in a cut of pork. No doubt hamboning occurs occasionally in other societies as well, but I suspect it is not culturally recognized, as is the case in Australia.

The most exacting goals for male masturbation contests in the world, to my knowledge, come from the English and United States private-school systems. The function of these games is not only sexual gratification but also the maintenance of a kind of age-based power hierarchy, since some of the participants are unable (because of age) to ejaculate at all.

Unique customs involving women are nearly always related to prostitutes or women in sex shows: women, for example, who can pick up coins in their vagina or who can twist their labia into a knot.

Sexual customs and ideology differ considerably throughout Europe and its outposts. It is not possible to assume a constancy merely because of the influence of Christianity. However, there are customs (such as hand tickling to initiate a sexual contact) that may be found over an enormous area and cut across national boundaries, the distribution of which we do not really know. There are sophisticated practitioners of contraception as well as their rural relatives, like the Dukagini Albanians, who keep a pair of goats or sheep in their living-room to guarantee fertility even when that room has to be shared with 20 people. There are urban people who are perfectly happy to stay single (if not chaste) all their lives, as opposed to the Sarakatsani who feel it is a disgrace to die unmarried and bury such a person in wedding clothes, the funeral in effect being a marriage to the earth.

This diversity is more and more being homogenized to a general international sexual culture, with less symbolism perhaps but a greater variety in technique.

Nineteen & CROSS-CULTURAL SURVEY

This chapter is arranged alphabetically. It provides a summary of topics not dealt with in a unified way elsewhere in this book, but it is by no means exhaustive.

Abstinence, celibacy and chastity

"What would you call a woman who has grown up without knowing a man?"

"Well, I should call her a fool."

This is a fragment of an actual conversation between an anthropologist and a member of the Ila of southeastern Africa. The anthropologist was trying to learn an Ila equivalent for "virgin" (which turned out not to exist).

The Ila reply was not unusual from a cross-cultural perspective (and similarly a word for "virgin" or "virginity" does not exist natively in several languages, including the Ila of southeastern Africa, the Tukano of South America and Pukapukan and Trukese of the Pacific).

Among most human societies, chastity (a life without sexual intercourse) is considered abnormal, intolerable or dangerous. On the other hand, abstinence (not having sexual intercourse on certain days or during certain periods) is almost universal.

Sexual abstinence, even chastity, is sometimes given specifically religious sanction. In the Muslim world, abstinence from sexual intercourse and even passionate kissing is obligatory for all believers during the daylight hours of the month of fasting, Ramadaan.

Priests and other religious specialists are sometimes required to live chaste lives. This was true of the vestal virgins and some of the Aztec priesthood. Buddhism started out as a celibate order. Although celibacy for priests was encouraged rather early in the western Christian church, it did not become general until the tenth century.

Chastity is not prized among hunting and gathering groups, pastoralists or among people who practice rudimentary agriculture. As a culturally defined virtue it does not appear in human history until about the fifth century BC with the development of Buddhist and Jain monasticism in India. This was a time when India was experiencing problems with regard to food resources and overpopulation.

Anaphrodisiacs

Anaphrodisiacs are drugs or substances used to diminish or eradicate sexual excitement.

Pliny the Elder says that the vestal virgins of Rome helped maintain their virginity (and their lives — the punishment for violating their vow of chastity was being buried alive) by the use of anaphrodisiac drinks. Buddhist monks in Cambodia allegedly make use of a substance known as *bhesajja*. The Kubeo of South America consider their women to be so passionate that a worn-out husband may resort to plying his wife with anaphrodisiacs.

The best known anaphrodisiac in western folklore is saltpetre, often rumored to be mixed in with the food served to boys in boarding school and to men in prison. It is a diuretic lacking all anaphrodisiac properties.

Aphrodisiacs

Aphrodisiacs are drugs and other substances used to produce, heighten or sustain sexual excitement. Perhaps the earliest known was a drug made up of powdered dried crocodile penis recommended by the ancient Egyptians.

More common is the use of penis-like objects such as stag's horn (in Europe), birds' beaks such as the billknob of the king eider (by Eskimo groups in Greenland) and most notably the horn of the white rhino, especially highly prized in Southeast Asia and China.

The root of the mandrake or man-

Human alphabet from Germany, 16th-century woodcut.

dragora has been said to have all sorts of powers as well as aphrodisiac. In spite of its remarkable history, and the fact that in appearance it resembles both the male and female genitals, the mandrake has no aphrodisiac effects at all.

Another category of aphrodisiac includes spices and spicy foods, presumably in the hope that the heat of the dish will inspire the heat of passion. A wild variety of ginger found on the Solomon Islands is believed locally to be quite effective. One aphrodisiac mentioned by the Romans involved rubbing the soles of the feet with pepper and the penis with the urine of a bull that had just copulated.

Cantharides, a fine powder made from the dried bodies of Spanish Fly (a beetle found in southern Europe) may actually produce prolonged erections; it can also produce an exciting sensation in the genitals of both sexes (and may even bring about premature menstruation in women). It is, however, exceedingly dangerous and deaths have been reported after its use. The Bush Negroes of the Guianas make use of mashed seeds of the mucca-mucca plant, which produces a similar kind of irritation. The seeds are actually inserted into the urethra and may cause urethritis.

Muriacithin, produced from a root grown in the tropical forests of Brazil, was used aboriginally as an aphrodisiac and may actually have some effect.

The most generally acknowledged likely candidate for a full-fledged aphrodisiac is yohimbine, derived from the bark of a tree native to Africa. Its aphrodisiac properties were discovered by natives in Cameroon.

From this same general area of Cameroon and Gabon came perhaps the most elaborate collection of aphrodisiacs as well as the greatest cultural appreciation of them. The Fang make use of about 100 different plants as aphrodisiacs and a large number of other items such as the bones of albinos, the teeth of chiefs, and even the sex organs of women who have been mothers-in-law. Parents who are afraid their sons are not sexually active enough give them aphrodisiacs to spur them on. Sometimes aphrodisiac or love medicine festivals are held to help renew the sexual life of the young people of a whole village.

Taking all the evidence into account one cannot say there are any known genuine, safe aphrodisiacs. Helen Singer Kaplan in her book on sex therapy, in which all these things are investigated in some detail, puts it this way: "No chemical substance has as yet been discovered which can rival the aphrodisiac power of being in love."

Astringents

Chemicals used to shrink the mucus membranes of the vaginal wall. In the western world, the use of alum has been reported from brothels where prostitutes must pretend to be virgins to satisfy the taste of clients who are into deflowering.

The most detailed account of the use of astringents is given for the Marquesans of the Pacific. For them, the use of astringents is an important and probably ancient tradition. Treatment usually begins in infancy and continues until the onset of menstruation. In the opinion of Marquesan men this treatment renders Marquesan women greatly superior to European or even to Tahitian women.

Bestiality

Bestiality refers to any kind of sexual contacts with animals. Formerly, among the Ijǫ, animal contacts were part of the male coming of age ritual. Every boy had to copulate successfully with a specially selected sheep to the satisfaction of a circle of elders who witnessed his performance.

Among the Yoruba there was the

Bestiality. *Iron Age cave painting, Val Camonica, Italy, 7th century* BC.

custom (now long discontinued) that a young hunter had to copulate with the first antelope he ever killed — while it was still warm.

The only society where animal contacts are said to be an important part of most people's sexual experience is that of the Kágaba of South America. Bestiality seems also to be fairly common among the Hopi. Hopi boys are apparently sometimes directed to animal contacts so that they will leave girls alone.

A few societies are known in which bestiality occurs and is not condemned, but for the most part it is both condemned and occasionally severely punished. Hanging was the appropriate punishment among the Inca.

The most common animals used for bestiality are domesticated mammals: dogs, cattle, sheep, goats, pigs, horses and burros.

Occasionally other animals such as snakes, turtles, eels, octopuses and frogs are mentioned or depicted in art, but they are for the most part either mythical or whimsical. The explorer Richard Burton described some Middle Eastern natives copulating with female crocodiles. It

was considered a magical act that would make the man rich and important. Burton said that a crocodile on her back was almost helpless, so the story might just be less apocryphal than it sounds.

The only data about the frequency of bestiality are found in the Kinsey volumes for the United States. In Kinsey's overall sample, bestiality is rare. But it is fairly common among boys raised on farms: about 17 percent had at least one orgasm through animal contacts.

Birth control and related topics

Societies throughout the world have developed a number of ways for regulating the size of their population. In some, the Lepcha and the Trobrianders, for example, no contraceptive methods are even attempted.

Coitus interruptus is supposed to be the most widely used contraception method cross-culturally. On the small Pacific island of Tikopia, it was part of a conscious population control policy and was used by the married and unmarried alike.

Attempts to remove the semen

from the vagina are reported from a few societies. Kavirondo women stand up after coitus and shake their bodies in a quick jerky rhythm. Zande women try to get rid of the semen by slapping their backs.

Hunting and gathering groups have no chemical or mechanical contraceptives that work. Other societies outside of the influence of modern western technology also tend to lack any truly useful contraceptives.

The Navaho believe that some drugs will render even men sterile, but for the most part all drugs are taken by women. Certain Indian tribes in Nevada make use of a plant *Lithospermum ruderale*, which has been subject to scientific investigation and found to inhibit the functioning of rats' ovaries.

Contraceptive charms are not rare. A "snake girdle," made of beaded leather and worn over the navel, was used by certain Plains Indians. Ancient Roman charms included the liver of a cat placed in a tube and worn on the left foot, or a part of a lioness's womb kept in an ivory tube.

Considerably more effective than these devices is abortion, which is tolerated and even institutionalized in a great many societies, and practiced in a great many others. Hunting and gathering groups know numerous plant and animal poisons that are effective in inducing miscarriages. Other means include the tying of tight bands round the stomach, beating the stomach or inserting sharp sticks into the vagina.

Infanticide would seem to be of considerably greater effectiveness in primitive population control than the other techniques. Nevertheless, Moni Nag has concluded that infant mortality due to infanticide is far lower than mortality due to natural causes.

Bisexuality

Bisexuality is an expression that has been used in two basically different ways. In the one sense, a bisexual individual is a hermaphrodite. In another sense, a bisexual individual is anyone who is attracted and can respond sexually to members of both sexes. Although this sense is fairly common and is used by many psychologists, anthropologists have for the most part ignored it.

William Davenport's study of East Bay (the fictional name of a society in the Pacific) is an exception. He points out that in that society, and a great many others, homosexual acts are tolerated and sometimes encouraged — but within the context of a general bisexuality. In such societies, the exclusive homosexual might well be considered deviant. On the other hand, where ritual homosexual acts are considered necessary to insure the growth of children (as in New Guinea societies), the exclusive heterosexual would be deviant.

Bundling, night courting and related customs

Bundling is a custom in which two people of opposite sex share the same bed while remaining fully clothed. Bundling has popularly been identified as a colonial American practice suitable in a country without hotels, where cold nights were unalleviated by central heating. The custom, however, is a continuation of what is sometimes referred to as night courting, reported from various northern European areas such as England, Scotland and Scandinavia.

In the United States, bundling was abandoned by 1800, although sporadic instances of it occurred as late as 1845. It seems to have been most prevalent in Connecticut.

Comparable customs are sometimes reported from outside of Europe. The Kikuyu of Kenya have a similar custom, called *nguiko* "fondling." In this society it is the girls who visit their boyfriends in a special hut where they eat and sleep together (without full intercourse).

The Blackfoot and Dakota Indians allowed a girl to sit with her suitor in the daytime under the same blanket in full view of her whole family.

Chastity belts

Chastity belts, devices attached to the bodies of women to prevent sexual intercourse, were in Europe usually made partly of metal. Some had barbed openings to permit urination but not copulation.

Making and using chastity belts in Europe began during the later Middle Ages. The common belief that the crusaders attached chastity belts to their wives as they went forth to fight for the Holy Land seems to be pure myth. One of the earliest representations of such a device is a drawing from 1405, representing a chastity belt known as the "Bellifortis."

Chastity belts are manufactured commercially today by at least one firm. Every once in a while, in letters to various newspaper columns, people admit to using them. Among some Plains Indians such as the Cheyenne, an easily removable non-metallic chastity belt was worn by all girls until marriage and thereafter when their husbands were away. In the Caucasus, chastity corsets were used. All these traditions apparently developed independently.

Child marriage and infant betrothal

Among the Australian Aborigines and the Yãnomamö of South America, men may promise the daughters of their female relatives to other young men even before the daughters are born. The reason is that marriage is thought of primarily in terms of alliances between groups and the romantic inclinations of the individuals involved are generally ignored.

There is no evidence in societies such as that of the Zande that men actually copulated with their infant brides (a girl could technically be married shortly after birth).

Among the Kadar of Northern Nigeria, most marriages are arranged by a girl's father when she is between three and six years old. She may not go to live with her husband until 10 years later and may actually conceive another man's child during that time. The Kadar do not value premarital chastity. On the contrary, her pregnancy is taken as welcome proof of fertility.

In northern India, however, where traditionally infant betrothal or marriage before menstruation was the rule, great emphasis was placed on a girl's virginity. To ensure virginity, a girl was married off before puberty and sent to live in her husband's household.

Child marriage in India has been severely attacked by Christian missionaries and Indian reformers. The Hindu Marriage Act of 1955 set the minimum age for girls at 15; this was later raised to 16.

Cisvestism

This is a term coined by Magnus Hirschfeld that refers to a sexual interest in dressing in a style that would usually indicate an inappropriate age or social role but is otherwise appropriate.

Unlike transvestism, which occurs in the great majority of cultures and is often institutionalized, cisvestism seems to be restricted to highly advanced societies, particularly in the West.

One variety of cisvestism is the wearing of diapers or other infantile clothes by adults in sexual scenes. Another, possibly more common, involves wearing uniforms. An accountant or business executive might, for example, choose to dress up as a construction worker, cowboy, policeman, sailor, marine or Nazi officer. Most of these are fairly common in the contemporary sadomasochistic world. In former decades, for women to dress up as a riding mistress had a certain vogue. The social inappropriateness of the styles is seen in the fact that many men who wear motorcyclist garb — almost totally a homosexual sadomasochistic style — do not own and cannot even ride a motorcycle.

The origin of the motorcyclist fashion is usually believed to be the Marlon Brando film *The wild ones* (released in 1953), which was about a motorcycle gang. An even earlier possible influence was Jean Cocteau's *Orphée*, made in 1949 but released in the United States in 1950. In the film two police motorcyclists figure prominently.

Leather bars, now commonplace in large metropolitan centers in the United States, England and Germany, were unknown before the 1950s. Such bars are the meeting places for male homosexual sadomasochists, leather fetishists, and men generally attracted by supermasculinity.

Condom

A condom is a sheath worn over the penis during intercourse. The earliest evidence of such a device comes from the sixteenth century. Its invention is debatably attributed to the Italian anatomist Gabriel Fallopus (1523 to 1562), known for his description of the fallopian tubes. He described (and claimed to have invented) a linen sheath to fit over the glans to prevent the spread of syphilis. Since then, the condom has developed to become the most widely used mechanical method of contraception.

The only nonwestern society that developed a condom-like contraceptive is that of the Dyuka Bush Negroes of Surinam, who were reported in the 1930s to be using a seed pod as a contraceptive device. The pod was about five inches long (c.12 cm), with one end snipped off. The man inserted his penis into the pod when it was already in the woman's vagina.

Dildoe. Also spelled Dildo.

A dildoe is an erotic device usually in the shape of a penis, occasionally of exaggerated size. Dildoes were known in the ancient world, and were clearly familiar to the ancient Babylonians, Greeks, Indians and Chinese.

Dildoes have been produced in a variety of sizes and from different materials. Chukchi women in Siberia are said to use the calf muscle of a reindeer, Tikopian and Zande women are both known to use bananas as well as appropriately shaped roots.

France was reputed the master of dildoe manufacture in the eighteenth century. In the early twentieth century that distinction was associated with Japan, and after World War II American soldiers bought elaborately decorated Japanese dildoes back as souvenirs and started a western popularization that has resulted in widely displayed sales of "vibrators."

Droit du seigneur

The droit du seigneur refers to the right of a feudal lord in Europe to deflower or at least have sexual intercourse with any bride on his estate on the first night of her marriage. Scholars disagree as to whether such a right actually ever existed in Europe.

Those who believe it did differ among themselves as to the extent to which it was practiced. One conservative reconstruction limits it to some parts of Scotland in early times. A more expansive view maintains that not only feudal lords but even some monks held this right.

Customs similar to the droit du seigneur have been reported from a few nonwestern cultures: the Dard of Asia, the Zande of Africa and the Tonga of the Pacific.

Some groups believe that the first act of sexual intercourse with a virgin is dangerous. A shaaman has to do the deflowering among the Kágaba of South America. Among the Seri of Mexico, a chief must do it. If the droit du seigneur actually existed in Europe, it may have had a similar justification.

Fetishism and partialism

Both of these represent the most common of the paraphilias. They are almost entirely restricted to males and seem to be unknown in other animals.

Technically, fetishism refers to a sexual interest in some inanimate object, generally some article of clothing; partialism refers to an intense sexual interest in some particular part of the body, usually not the genitals.

At one time the term fetishism was regularly used for both notions and frequently still is. But if a distinction is made, we can generalize that fetishism seems to be absent or at least highly uncommon in primitive societies, whereas some partialisms occur at all levels of societal evolution. More specifically, the great interest in elongated labia among the Hóttentot and other groups is an example of a partialism. Intense sexual interest in feet or breasts is almost always restricted to highly developed civilizations. The Chinese passion for bound feet is an example of this and could be considered a national partialism.

Fetishes have been classified as to whether they involve media or form. A media fetish is one where the material or substance rather than the form is a crucial aspect. Leather fetishism is a common example of this. It does not matter for the leather fetishist what article of clothing is made of leather: it is the material that counts. Form fetishism reverses this: lingerie or shoe fetishes are common examples.

Some forms of fetishism frequently accompany sadomasochism, for example those involving high-heeled shoes and boots. Fetish objects that are fluffy, furry and frilly, such as lingerie, are less often associated with sadomasochism in spite of Sacher-Masoch's famous fantasy of being beaten by a woman in a fur coat.

Some articles of clothing are seldom fetish objects. Hats are an example. Although underpants are quite popular among fetishists, brassieres seldom are, and a true stocking fetishist is rare.

Frigidity and other female sexual dysfunctions

The main types of sexual dysfunction found among women are frigidity (inability to experience either orgasm or more generally any sexual pleasure), vaginismus (uncontrolled spasmodic contraction of the vagina) and dyspareunia (pain during coitus). It seems clear from therapeutic work done in the United States that culture plays a significant role in bringing these about. For example, Masters and Johnson, as well as other sex therapists such as Kaplan, agree that "religious orthodoxy" (by which they mean strict conservative Judaism and Christianity) is of major importance in almost every form of sexual dysfunction for women.

Sexual dysfunctions in a nonwestern culture (the Ganda of Uganda) include *ewuzza* (frigidity), *matabo* (a condition in which a woman could have sex only after an attempt was made to strangle her by the neck) and *olwazi* (a woman with a tight vagina, the traditional cure for which is to pour grain into the vagina itself and let a rooster peck the grain out). Among the Ganda, a woman's sexual satisfaction in marriage is regarded as vital.

Frigidity is often considered a serious disorder in western society at present. But Helen Singer Kaplan suggests that women who do not get orgasms but are not otherwise frigid are not dysfunctional at all. Their response may simply represent a normal variant of female sexuality.

Gadgets

Gadgets are a variety of devices used to produce, heighten or even prevent sexual response. Basically, three kinds of sex gadgets have been produced: genital substitutes used mostly in masturbation; genital modifiers used to facilitate or enhance pleasurable sensations during copulation; and devices like chastity belts to make intercourse difficult or impossible.

Genital substitutes include the *rin-no-tama*, a device generally believed to have been invented by the Japanese. It was known at least as early as the eighteenth century in France, where it was sometimes referred to as *pommes d'amour* "apples of love." The *rin-no-tama* consists of two small metal balls, which are inserted into the vaginal canal. The erotic effect of the *rin-no-tama* comes from the movements of the balls and their delicate vibrations when the pelvis changes position — no matter how slightly.

Vagina substitutes are less common. Among Hindus a device known as a *viyoni* has been employed by men in fertility rites. It was made in the shape of a woman out of wood and cloth, with a vagina (*yoni*)-like opening of fruit, vegetables and leaves.

The second kind of sex gadget includes all sorts of genital modifiers. With few exceptions, such modifiers are attached to the penis and are described as aids to inducing orgasms in women.

One kind of a device is called a tickler or French tickler. One of the earliest known examples, called the happy ring or goat's eyelid, was reportedly introduced into China by Tibetan lamas in the thirteenth century. A similar device was used by some American Indians in Patagonia.

In the contemporary West, comparable ticklers are usually made of rubber or plastic and in some instances are built into the design of a condom.

What are known as tickling stones are reported from Southeast Asia. Little stones or sometimes pellets made of metal (occasionally even gold or silver) are inserted into cuts made into the skin of the penis. The motivation for doing so is that the resulting lumpy surface of the penis is reportedly arousing to women.

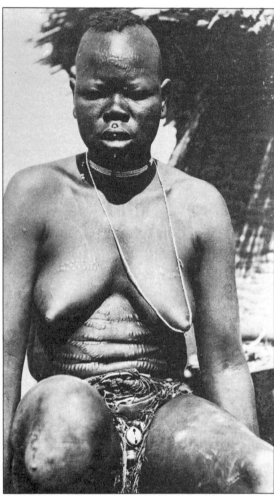

Genital adornment on an African woman

Genital jewelry

In the overwhelming majority of human societies, the genitals are hidden and unadorned. Very rarely in some societies what might be called genital jewelry is used.

Formerly on the island of Truk, some women would perforate their labia and insert objects that tinkled when they walked in a certain way. A number of sadomasochists in the western world have taken to piercing nipples, foreskins (or remnants of foreskins), labia and, more rarely, other parts of the sexual anatomy.

In the cross-cultural literature, the best known example is the penis bar, reported as early as AD 1590 in the *Boxer Codex* from the Philippines. In that description the penis bar is mentioned primarily as a way of securing a ring to the penis — worn, it is said, in the same way that a ring is put on the finger. The custom has survived, and penis bars of one sort or another are still used in the Philippines and in Borneo.

The device is seldom thought of as an adornment but rather as a means of increasing the sexual pleasure of women. It is said that women readily become addicted to its presence, although it does not add much to the pleasure of the male.

In Europe and America various kinds of ring have been used around the male genitals, for the most part to help the wearer keep an erection but possibly also for decoration. Such penis rings may have been derived from the erotic devices developed by the Japanese, where so-called "pleasure rings" have long been in use. These proliferated in the West after World War II, probably because of extensive American contact with the Japanese.

Genital preservation

In several societies, genitals — almost always male genitals — have been preserved for one reason or another. In various East African societies, ancient Egypt and some Ethiopian groups such as the Sidamo, male genitals have been taken as war trophies, much like scalps among American Indians.

Among the ancient Egyptians, at least two pharaohs, Seti I and Ramesses II, had their penis and testicles removed in the process of mummification. Their genitals were mummified separately and placed in a kind of penis coffin.

In Imperial China, eunuchs preserved their amputated genitals in a container. The penis and testicles were put through a kind of pickling process right after they were severed from the man's body. The pickled genitals had to be presented as proof of his eunuchoid state as he proceeded up the civil service or palace servant hierarchy — staffed largely by eunuchs. These pickled genitals were traditionally buried with the man in expectation that he would become whole again in the next life.

Genital tatoos

Tatooing of the genitals as an established custom is generally restricted to various Oceanic cultures and seems to be predominantly a fashion for women. Occasionally it is reported from other parts of the world, e.g. the Mongo of Africa.

Genital tatooing seems to be done for aesthetic or erotic reasons as well as to mark the adult status of the person. On Nukuoro it has been reported that tatooing marked a girl as a woman. Children born to those who had not been tatooed were put to death.

Vulva tatooing on Easter Island had the unusual implication that the woman had been seen by a man while she was copulating with another man.

Penis tatooing is extremely rare cross-culturally. Successful Don Juans on Mangaia often get a vulva tatooed on their penis. At least one king of Tonga is known to have had the glans of his penis completely covered with tatoos to show his disregard for pain. Penis tatooing is an idiosyncracy occasionally found among western men, notably sailors and male prostitutes.

Homosexuality

Homosexuality refers in one sense to a sexual orientation to members of one's own sex. In another sense it includes the practice of any homosexual acts no matter how they are thought of by the people performing them or what their motivation is, for example lack of a partner of the opposite sex (as in prisons or aboard ships) or for ritual purposes (as in various puberty rites). The work of Kinsey and his associates in the United States has shown that the life histories of a great many people who consider themselves to be heterosexual include some homosexual experiences. Most anthropologists talk about homosexual acts as though they implied a homosexual orientation, even though these acts may be performed in a bisexual context.

Of all aspects of human sexuality, western anthropologists have probably dealt least objectively with homosexuality. Even Malinowski's account of the Trobrianders turns out to be suspect.

A further problem is that female homosexuality is hardly ever mentioned — which of course does not mean it does not exist. We just do not know.

Consequently, it is difficult to answer questions frequently asked of anthropologists: how common is homosexuality throughout the world and what are the attitudes about it?

In an earlier classic cross-cultural study by Clellan S. Ford and Frank A. Beach (1951) 49 groups (64 percent) considered at least some homosexual acts "normal and socially acceptable for certain members of the community."

For the present book, I have made use of a much greater range of societies: the 274 (as of 1980) plus 8 others mentioned in Human Relations Area File sources but not given a separate treatment, as well as 12 others not in the Files at all.

Of the 294 societies considered in all, 142 had no information at all about male homosexuality, and a larger number (178) none about female homosexuality. I was able to find only 59 that made any clear-cut judgments on the topic of male homosexuality: 18 condemned (31 percent), 41 (69 percent) approved. These are virtually the same percentages as those given by Ford and Beach, though the later figures suggest somewhat greater approval. I found 25 societies for which it was denied; societies that both condemned and denied totalled 36 — which swings the percentages in the other direction.

Ford and Beach sometimes list a society as disapproving if one kind of homosexual relationship is condemned though others seem not to be. A case in point is the Chiricahua (not considered by me). As Randolf Trumbach has pointed out, they apparently condemn homosexual acts between two men only if one of them is not a transvestite. The same thing is true of the Lango, listed by Ford and Beach as approving. The same label should apply to both.

If we combine Ford and Beach's sample with mine, then at least 63 societies in the world are tolerant of homosexual acts in some instances and for some purposes. This is a very rough estimate. But my guess is that given the general bias of western reporters, whether anthropologists or not, this figure is low.

Societies said to be lacking homosexuality altogether, or where homosexual acts are exceedingly rare, include the Kwoma, Lepcha, Wógeo, Nuer, Timbira, Lesu, Kikuyu, Ulithi, Truk, Pukapukans, Kaingáng and Sirionó. At the other extreme are societies in which there is virtually total participation (by males) in homosexual acts, within a larger bisexual context. One of the important lessons from such societies is that although the first sexual experiences of boys are frequently if not always homosexual, the boys themselves do not grow up to be exclusively homosexual. Surely this fact alone undermines all theories that directly derive homosexuality from early adolescent sexual experiences, especially seduction by older

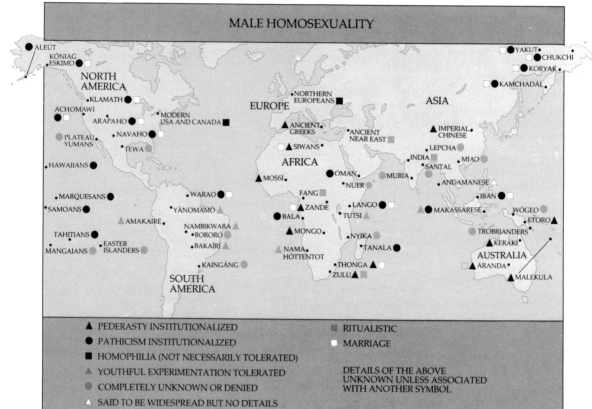

MALE HOMOSEXUALITY

NORTH
AMERICA

ALEÚT
KÓNIAG
ESKIMO
KLAMATH
ACHOMAWI
ARAPAHO
P'LATEAU
YUMANS
NAVAHO
TEWA
HAWAIIANS
MARQUESANS
SAMOANS
AMAKAIRE
TAHITIANS
MANGAIANS
EASTER
ISLANDERS

MODERN
USA AND CANADA

WARAO
YÁNOMAMO
NAMBIKWARA
BORORO
BAKAIRÍ
KAINGÁNG

SOUTH
AMERICA

EUROPE

NORTHERN
EUROPEANS

ANCIENT
GREEKS

SIWANS

AFRICA

MOSSÍ

FANG
ZANDE
BALA
MONGO
NAMA
HÓTTENTOT
ZULU
THONGA
NYIKA
TANALA
TUTSI
LANGO
NUER
OMAN
MURIA
ANCIENT
NEAR EAST

ASIA

YAKUT
CHUKCHI
KORYAK
KAMCHADÁL

IMPERIAL
CHINESE
LEPCHA
INDIA
SANTAL
MIAO
ANDAMANESE
IBAN
MAKASSARESE
WÓGEO
ETORO
TROBRIANDERS
KERAKI
AUSTRALIA
ARANDA
MALEKULA

▲ PEDERASTY INSTITUTIONALIZED
● PATHICISM INSTITUTIONALIZED
■ HOMOPHILIA (NOT NECESSARILY TOLERATED)
▲ YOUTHFUL EXPERIMENTATION TOLERATED
● COMPLETELY UNKNOWN OR DENIED
△ SAID TO BE WIDESPREAD BUT NO DETAILS

■ RITUALISTIC
□ MARRIAGE

DETAILS OF THE ABOVE
UNKNOWN UNLESS ASSOCIATED
WITH ANOTHER SYMBOL

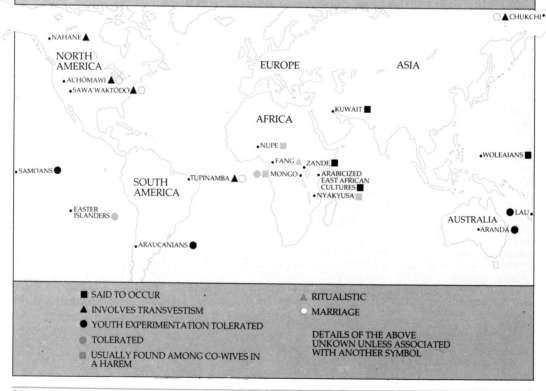

FEMALE HOMOSEXUALITY

NORTH
AMERICA

NAHANE
ACHÓMAWI
SAWA'WAKTÓDO
SAMOANS
EASTER
ISLANDERS
TUPINAMBA
ARAUCANIANS

SOUTH
AMERICA

EUROPE

AFRICA

NUPE
FANG
MONGO
ZANDE
ARABICIZED
EAST AFRICAN
CULTURES
NYAKYUSA
KUWAIT

ASIA

CHUKCHI

WOLEAIANS

LAU
AUSTRALIA
ARANDA

■ SAID TO OCCUR
▲ INVOLVES TRANSVESTISM
● YOUTH EXPERIMENTATION TOLERATED
● TOLERATED
■ USUALLY FOUND AMONG CO-WIVES IN
A HAREM

▲ RITUALISTIC
○ MARRIAGE

DETAILS OF THE ABOVE
UNKOWN UNLESS ASSOCIATED
WITH ANOTHER SYMBOL

homosexuals. The majority of reports from these societies also tends to rule out genetic explanations for homosexuality.

Several different styles of homosexuality exist. Geoffrey Gorer distinguished three: *pederasty*, which involves a considerable age difference between the partners, with the younger partner in his teens or very early twenties; *pathicism*, which involves a role change on the part of the passive (pathic) partner, who is often a transvestite or in some other way does not play a masculine role sexually or socially; *homophilia*, in which both partners are adults and there is no interest in changing sex roles.

These styles tend to cluster geographically. Adolescent experimentation is the type most commonly reported from South America; pathicism from Siberia, North America and Polynesia; pederasty from New Guinea and Australia. It may be, however, that once one kind was recognized by a field anthropologist, the other kinds were not looked for and so not reported.

From the scanty information about female homosexuality cross-culturally, it nearly always seems to occur in the third style, homophilia — although counterexamples can be found in western societies.

Among homosexual men in the western world, the predominant homosexual style is homophilia — but this is quite exceptional from a cross-cultural point of view and seems to be a fairly recent phenomenon. Homophilia is virtually unknown in primitive or peasant societies and very little evidence for it appears before the nineteenth century. Words denoting homophilia are recent. Even the word homosexuality itself is quite recent, dating first in print (in German, as *Homosexualität*) in 1869, coined by a Dr Károly Benkert.

Why homophilia should have appeared within the past two centuries and not before remains unclear. Gorer thinks it has to do with the fact that modern families are small and isolated and that boys are not exposed to enough male models. I think this is unlikely. Also, it does not explain the homo-

philic style of lesbian relationships.

Until very recently in traditional societies, men were in dominant power positions in families, as fathers and as husbands. The pederastic and pathic styles simply reflect these traditional power relationships in a homosexual context. Even the homophilic relations sometimes reported between kings and mature men preserve an unequal power relationship: king to subject. By the eighteenth century in England, there was a change in the structure of the upper-class family, which has spread through the social classes and to other countries so that it has become the general family structure in Europe and America. This new structure was the egalitarian family, where husbands and wives counted as equals. It developed as women became more independent financially; and as romantic love became a justification for marriage. This model of equality between spouses who are romantically attached to each other is precisely the homophilic model — and it developed for men only after the heterosexual model changed.

Pathicism is institutionalized in a great many societies, but it normally involves no more than a handful of members in any given community. In societies where pederasty is institutionalized, all the males in the society may participate. Pederasty — as in ancient Greece and among the Zande — seems to appear particularly often when the women are secluded and unavailable to young men. With both pederasty and pathicism, homosexual marriages are occasionally socially recognized and include a bride-price. In my own sample, 19 societies are said to permit such homosexual marriages. To my knowledge, there are no societies as yet that recognize marriage in a homophilic context. Western homosexuals sometimes celebrate their own informal and not legally binding marriage ceremonies. A recent study of such "marriages" shows that they tend to be less stable than simple cohabitation without a ritual.

Generally speaking, anal foration (anal intercourse) seems to be the

most common male homosexual act in primitive societies. Also fairly frequent is interfemoral foration (rubbing the penis between the thighs of the passive partner).

Among homosexuals in the United States, fellation is the most common act: European homosexuals sometimes refer to fellation as the "American vice." A kind of psychoanalytic interpretation is tempting if only because American heterosexual men have developed an intense interest in female breasts. Now the penis may, psychoanalytically, symbolize a breast (compare the udder of a cow). Add the fact that many middle-class American infants are orally deprived and you have the beginnings of a fairly tidy — if involved — theory.

One of the consequences of the various factors that characterize western homosexuality — exclusivity, homophilia, together with the generally despised status of homosexuals necessitating a quasi-secret organization — is the development of a "gay" subculture, characterized by fashions in clothing and the development of ghetto-like communities.

Not all homosexuals are members of this subculture. In fact, it is sometimes useful to restrict the word gay to people in it, and not use the word as totally synonymous with homosexual. Some observers do not agree with this statement, however. For example, Esther Newton says "Gay life is rather like the early Christian church: it exists wherever and whenever gay people are gathered together."

Very little is known about female homosexuality cross-culturally. I found only 5 societies in the world that specifically approve of lesbianism for at least some people. But usually it is not discussed at all. It is reported most often in societies where men have many wives, especially when the co-wives live a secluded harem-type of life.

Impotence and other male sexual dysfunctions

The main types of sexual dysfunction found among men are various degrees of impotence (inability to achieve or sustain an erection), premature ejaculation, retarded ejaculation (or ejaculatory incompetence), and several conditions that Masters and Johnson have called dyspareunia (pain during coitus).

Sex therapists suggest that religious orthodoxy (strict conservative Judaism and Christianity) is of major importance in almost every form of sexual dysfunction among men, with the possible exception of premature ejaculation. Furthermore, the incidence of such dysfunctions seems to vary considerably in different cultures. Impotence is said to be relatively infrequent among, for example, the Mangaians and extremely common among the Kágaba.

Nonwestern cultures have produced a variety of folk explanations for impotence, including witchcraft. The Dogon, Hausa and Fang say that if milk from a woman's breast drips onto her baby son's penis while nursing, he may grow up impotent. The Wolof tabu sex on Wednesdays and believe that if a boy should be conceived on that day, his impotence will result from breaking the tabu. Both the Fang and the Bemba associate impotence with elephant tusks. For the Fang a man need only step over a tusk to become impotent. The Bemba say it will occur if he sees the nerve inside. None of these beliefs has any scientific validity.

Among the ancient Mesopotamians incantations existed to prevent impotence, as well as ointments for its cure. The potency incantations were recited by women to their lovers.

Impotence almost universally produces shame in the afflicted individual. In some cultures, it is considered symbolic of even wider social repercussions. For example, in a number of African societies where the king was regarded as a god or very closely linked to a god, the king's physical health and in particular his sexual potency were regarded as barometers of the kingdom's health and vigor. Among the Shilluk, a king who became sick or senile or was unable to satisfy his wives sexually was strangled or walled up in a house and left to die.

A strict puritanical background is one of the scientifically accepted causes of impotence. Donald S. Marshall in his discussion of impotence among the Mangaians, suggests almost the opposite. He says the Mangaians suffer from impotence and sterility as a biological penalty they must pay for very frequent copulation — and very vigorous copulation at that.

The Mangaians themselves recognized several degrees of impotence, the most serious being *tiranaro* "lost (or hidden) penis," in which the penis withdraws into the body and will kill the afflicted person unless he abstains from sexual intercourse for some months and is treated with smoke therapy, which involves squatting over smoldering herbs, the smoke seeping through punctured coconut shells.

This condition — retracting of the penis into the belly — is also believed to exist by some Chinese and other Southeast Asian groups. The condition is known as *koro* and is said to be caused by sexual excess.

Kissing

Kissing as an erotic act is almost universal in the western, Arab and Hindu worlds. In a few societies, it is totally unknown, for example the Somali, Cewa, Lepcha and Sirionó. In other societies, kissing is regarded as disgusting. The Thonga of South Africa find all mouth-to-mouth contacts revolting because of the possibility of getting the other person's saliva into one's own mouth.

Although in the West kissing is considered so innocuous or commonplace that it is regularly performed in public, in other cultures such open expressions of affection are forbidden. As late as 1978, the Hindi motion picture *Satyam Shivam sundaram* (called *Love sublime* in English) occasioned a scandal in India and created a national debate over censorship because it depicts several (to Westerners, rather chaste) kisses between a man and his wife.

According to the Persian erotic manual *The perfumed garden*, the only kiss that can appropriately accompany copulation is the one variously known in English as a deep kiss, soul kiss, tongue kiss or French kiss. One of the earliest representations of deep kissing is found on the erotic Mochica pottery in Peru, dated about 200 BC.

Another kind of erotic kiss has been called the "smell kiss" or "olfactory kiss"; the nose is placed near or against the partner's face and one inhales. The ancient Egyptians probably used this; their words for "kiss" and "smell" are the same.

Nose rubbing may be a variant of the smell kiss or simply an inaccurate label. But rubbing has been specifically reported for the Eskimo, Tamil, Ulithi and Trobrianders.

Love magic

The majority of societies in the world for which we have reasonably adequate information have developed love potions, or created magical spells to entice a particular person to become a lover, or a spouse to be faithful, or some related desire. Among the Trobrianders, virtually all success in love is believed to result from magic.

Love magic has a considerable antiquity. Possibly the oldest example known is a Sumerian charm, which dates from several thousand years before Christ.

Although love magic is very common there are a few exceptions. The Tewa of North America and the Sirionó and the Kaingáng, both of South America, are reported to have no love magic at all, and the Kaingáng assume that all people except little children are "spontaneously, vigorously and indiscriminately sexual, and act accordingly."

Ford and Beach suggest that the use of love magic is least developed or nonexistent among people who are direct about their sexual advances. They cite the Lepcha, who have a little love magic but rarely use it because requests for sexual favors are usually met.

Some cultures have a reputation for the efficacy of their love magic. In Europe, Gipsies traditionally have been the dispensers of the best magic. In aboriginal North America, the Cree Indians were among the most illustrious in this field.

One technique to make someone fall in love is either by gaining control over the person through something intimately connected with him or her, such as a lock of hair, nail clippings or a piece of cloth, or by bringing the person into contact with some intimate physical part, particularly some body excretion such as sweat, semen or menstrual blood. Both these ways are varieties of what is known as contagious magic.

Love magic with a modern touch comes from African-derived Latin American possession cults sometimes called Santería. Because of the migration of many Cubans and other peoples from the Caribbean to the United States, these cults are found in many cities such as New York and Miami. One of these recipes is peculiarly American: "Prepare a hamburger patty. Steep it in your own sweat. Cook. Serve to the person desired."

Various other kinds of love magic exist, sometimes less easy to categorize. They may even involve human corpses or parts of corpses. One ancient Irish love recipe begins by advising: "Find a corpse nine days old."

The Hausa of West Africa have a number of different kinds of love magic, not only to attract a partner but also to blind your spouse to the fact you have a lover.

In spite of the wide variety of Hausa love magic and the belief in its efficacy, the practical nature of the Hausa appears in a proverb, which refers to a well-known love magic involving dried-up bats: "Forget the bat magic, the real charm for getting a woman is money."

Male pregnancy

The Ila of Zambia tabu male homosexual acts because they believe pregnancy would be the outcome.

Among a number of black homosexuals in America, it is also believed that a man can get pregnant as a result of anal foration. If the semen comes in contact with a certain organ (invariably unspecified), the semen itself develops into a "blood baby." The "pregnant" man's belly begins to swell after about the third week. Labor pains accompany actual delivery of the blood baby, which comes out of the rectum along with some faeces.

This belief in blood babies may represent a continuation of African beliefs such as those found among the Ila. But such a belief has not, to my knowledge, been recorded for West African groups, who were ancestral to most contemporary blacks in the United States. At least one American Indian group shares a similar notion, but they are even less likely to be the source: some Navaho state that a man will get pregnant if he copulates with the woman on top. Also, that male pregnancy can occur if a menstruating woman steps over a man.

The belief in the possibility that male pregnancy may result from anal insemination is also reported from New Guinea. Among the Kéraki, boys go through a period associated with their puberty rites in which they are regularly forated by older men; the belief is that otherwise they would not grow. It is further believed that the boys can become pregnant, and to prevent this, a lime-eating ceremony is performed. After the period of passive homosexuality, boys graduate to playing the active role both homosexually and heterosexually.

Masturbation.

Generally, masturbation is considered as normal adolescent behavior and not taken seriously unless practiced by adults, when it is almost universally frowned on. Although male masturbation is condemned by the Kágaba of South America as an exceedingly serious offense, married men tend to concede that it is their preferred form of sexual activity — an admission unique in the world's cultures. In many nonwestern societies, the actual rate of masturbation is low — as it is known to be in working-class groups in the United States, as opposed to upper-level groups.

Masturbation with the aid of a device like a dildoe is widely reported cross-culturally for women. Anal and urethral masturbation, which also require the insertion of some foreign object, have not been discussed in primitive cultures; in the western world, an amazing number of items have been used — from hair-pins to Coca-cola bottles.

Not much information about group masturbation (or circle jerk, as it is informally known in English) is available, even for western society. College fraternity initiations are frequently rumored to involve various relatively uncommon sexual acts like group masturbation, but no statistical information exists about these practices.

Masturbation contests have also been reported — among certain American Indian groups, in Polynesia and West Africa, as well as among Europeans and Americans. To my knowledge, masturbation contests are everywhere restricted to males.

Masturbation has sometimes held religious significance. The ancient Egyptians believed that the creation of the universe occurred through an act of masturbation by the god Atum, whose hand was his divine partner. The existence of such a myth suggests that possibly masturbation was used in some sort of Egyptian religious rite.

Nekrophilia

Sexual attraction to and sexual acts with dead bodies are both subsumed under the term nekrophilia, a kind of paraphilia.

According to his biographer Wardell Pomeroy, Kinsey — in spite of his massive survey of sexual behavior — never met anyone he could regard as a real nekrophile. Anthropologists have seldom mentioned the topic for any society, even as a personal quirk. But when nekrophilia has been reported, it has nearly always been confined to men.

The earliest reference to nekrophilia occurs in Herodotus's account of ancient Egyptian mummification. He noted that the bodies of beautiful or illustrious women were not handed over to embalmers immediately after death because of fear that they might be defiled.

Embalmers and morticians have been occasionally thought of as pimps of the dead, even outside of Egypt. Patricia Bosworth's biography of the movie star Montgomery Clift asserts that he knew a plastic surgeon and illegal abortionist who in the early 1960s occasionally "supplied dead bodies to a notorious homosexual 'funeral parlor' on Sixth Avenue. For fifty dollars one could go in and have sex with a corpse."

In at least one society, that of the Luo of East Africa, a kind of ritualized obligatory nekrophilia is said to be practiced. The ghost of a young girl who died as a virgin is regarded as extremely dangerous: to pacify this ghost a stranger is called in to deflower her corpse. No comparable nekrophiliac act for males is performed; instead a woman would be "married" to a dead man who had no children in order to bear a child that could then count as his offspring.

The Bellacoola of British Columbia formerly considered it appropriate for a man to copulate with his wife's corpse as a sign of profound grief (this is now totally tabu). Similarly, among the Pukapukans of Polynesia — who forbid even looking at a dead body — it is considered understandable if not desirable, if a sorrowing *cousin* should be driven by despair to have intercourse with the dead person.

The most extensive anecdotal accounts of nekrophilia are found in reports by Ronald M. Berndt for the Káinantu of New Guinea. Among these people nekrophilia is seen both as an aggressive act (it is usually performed on the bodies of enemy women killed in warfare) and as a source of pleasure.

Night-crawling.

Night-crawling is the practice whereby a young man steals into a room (or tent, etc.) to have intercourse with an unmarried girl without her prior consent, even though her whole family may be sleeping in the same room. In Polynesia and the Philippines, this practice may be accompanied by the fantasy that a man can copulate with a woman without waking her.

North American night-crawling lacks this peculiarity but has two others of its own: the night-crawler simply tries to touch the girl's genitals and does not even attempt intercourse; and women are sometimes reported as the night-crawlers — at least among the Comanche, Hopi and Navaho. (The Lau of Fiji in the Pacific share the latter practice.)

According to Margaret Mead, on Samoa only young men who are unpopular would resort to such a practice and they did so out of desperation because no one would accept them otherwise. She calls the practice "surreptitious rape." Once a boy is caught as a night-crawler, no girl will ever pay attention to him again and he can marry only when older, when he may have a position and title to offer.

The practice seems to be considered in a different light on Mangaia, where it is quite widespread and highly praised if successful.

For two such different reports of virtually an identical practice to exist may simply reflect actual cultural differences. Since one account was written by a woman (Mead), the other by a man (Donald Marshall), these differences perhaps only reflect varying attitudes about rape found in western culture among men and women.

Paraphilia

Paraphilia refers to specialized sexual interests that are relatively infrequent. They do not include the sex of the persons preferred as partners, however (the sexual orientation). Thus, there is no question of paraphilia if a man is sexually attracted to women as such, but it is quite a different matter if the only women he is attracted to are redheads, over six feet (183 cm) tall, and wearing black leather boots.

The term paraphilia was historically coined to replace another term, perversion, which suggests either condemnation or perhaps a (faulty?) diagnosis in terms of pathology.

It is mostly in large, complex societies that such interests are developed or cultivated. Another striking characteristic of paraphilia practices is that they are overwhelmingly male interests.

Members of primitive societies seldom develop or practice an interest in paraphilia except partialism (intense sexual interest in some body part) and transvestism. Sexual contacts between adults and children or between fairly old men and girls who have not yet begun to menstruate are reported from several societies, where such practices may even be institutionalized. But true sexual preference for children (paedophilia) or for the elderly (gerontophilia) is rarely described.

An interest in enemas (klismaphilia) occurs among Westerners. It may also have occurred among the ancient Egyptians, who believed that the enema had been invented by the god Thoth. The Mayans of Mexico even included hallucinogens in their enemas. In neither instance is it clear that klismaphilia was involved.

Biting and scratching, sometimes even mild burning, have been reported as part of the sexual behavior found in many societies. But an intense interest in pain or humiliation, which accompanies sadomasochism in advanced societies, seems to be generally absent. Sexual behavior involving corpses (nekrophilia) is occasionally found in nonwestern as well as western cultures. There is no mention at all for primitive societies of a sexual interest in amputees (apotemnophilia) or in filth (mysophilia) — in particular excrement (koprophilia or koprolagnia — even koprophagy "eating of excrement"). An intense interest in urine (urolagnia) has been reported for the Trukese: men like women who urinate when reaching a climax and women want men to urinate inside them after ejaculation. The same thing may be true in part for the Yapese, another Pacific culture.

The geography of paraphilia (opposite, above).

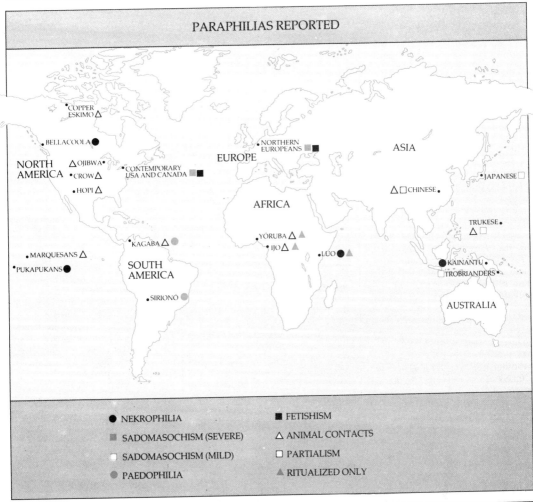

PARAPHILIAS REPORTED

COPPER ESKIMO △

BELLACOOLA ●

NORTH AMERICA

△ OJIBWA •

• CROW △

• HOPI △

CONTEMPORARY USA AND CANADA ■ ■

EUROPE

• NORTHERN EUROPEANS ■ ■

ASIA

• JAPANESE □

△ □ CHINESE •

AFRICA

• YORUBA △ ▲

• IJO △ ▲

• LUO ● ▲

TRUKESE •
△ □

KAGABA △ ●

• MARQUESANS △

• PUKAPUKANS ●

SOUTH AMERICA

• SIRIONÓ ●

KAINANTU •
TROBRIANDERS • □

AUSTRALIA

- ● NEKROPHILIA
- ■ SADOMASOCHISM (SEVERE)
- □ SADOMASOCHISM (MILD)
- ● PAEDOPHILIA
- ■ FETISHISM
- △ ANIMAL CONTACTS
- □ PARTIALISM
- ▲ RITUALIZED ONLY

Penis holding

The custom of holding another person's penis is occasionally reported from different parts of the world as a nonerotic ritual.

Among the ancient Hebrews, men swore an oath while holding the penis of the man the oath was made to, the biblical euphemism being "Put your hand under my thigh" (no direct expression for "penis" is found in the Bible).

Among the Wálbiri of Central Australia, a man accused of a serious offense may try to place his penis in the hand of a close male kinsman. If the kinsman permits this, he has symbolically sworn to plead for the accused and even to fight for him. Similarly, when men from another tribe arrive for certain ceremonies, they usually first offer their penes to their hosts (much as Westerners shake hands).

In certain rituals found among the Nuer of East Africa, women have to grab the penes of men and even tie a cord to the penes and pull on them.

According to John Disney, writing in 1729, a "phallic oath" was recognized at one point in Welsh law. A woman accusing a man of rape could convict him if she held in her right hand the relic of some saint, and took hold of the accused man's penis with her left hand while swearing that he had violated her chastity with "that member."

I know of no customs where touching the vulva had quite a comparable significance, but among the Fang of West Africa, girls initiated into a secret women's ritual were required to touch the vulva of the presiding woman.

Phallicism and kusthicism

These terms refer to the worship of sexuality or fertility, especially in the form of the male and female sex organs. No traditional word exists to

Phallicism. Ancient Egyptian figurine from the Middle Kingdom.

denote the feminine counterpart of phallicism. I have, therefore, coined the term "kusthic" from the Greek word for vagina (*kusthos*). Examples of kusthic symbols include cowrie shells, triangles and, for the Freudian-oriented, any tunnel or room.

One of the noticeable cultural universals is that phallic representations are more frequent than kusthic ones. In some societies breast representations more commonly indicate aspects of femaleness rather than kusthic symbols (e.g., Artemis with many breasts).

The two most famous examples of phallic cults are the Dionysiac rites of the ancient Greeks and the *lingga-yoni* worship of modern Hindus. For Hindus the *lingga* or *linggam* (phallus) is a representation of the god Shiva; the *yoni* (kusthos), which the *lingga* may be set in, is frequently taken as a representation of the goddess Shakti — the two together representing the sacredness of sexual intercourse, and the totality of existence.

In Japan, phallic cults as part of Shintoism have been quite widespread and phallic representations are found throughout the countryside. In 1972, the Japanese government tried to suppress phallic ceremonies, but ceremonies and the shrines still persist.

Some commentators have been prone to see phallic representations wherever stone columns exist, or wherever anything remotely penile comes into view. Others have tried to interpret the Bible to show that the ancient Hebrew religion involved phallic cults. Most Biblical scholars disagree. We can call them literalists: they tend to call a stone a stone. But which of these two camps is right is not immediately obvious.

Proofs of virginity

The virginity of a bride (but not of a groom) plays an important role in many societies of the world, and "proof" of this virginity is sometimes demanded.

The most widespread culturally accepted proof is a piece of cloth (less commonly some other material) that has been stained with the blood shed because the bride's hymen has been broken in the first intercourse she has with her husband. This is the usual test in the Old World.

In the Americas, the only society I know of where an intact hymen is taken as proof of virginity is the eastern Apache. Among the eastern Achómawi of California, if either girls or boys got tired during a ritual puberty dance it was taken as a sign that they were not virgins; spectators were on the lookout for this.

The "tokens of virginity" mentioned in the Bible most probably refer to bloodstained garments from the bride's first intercourse with her husband. The parents of the bride are advised to keep them if ever her husband should accuse her of not having been a virgin at her wedding. If her husband makes such an accusation falsely, he will be forced to pay a stiff fine of 100 shekels of silver to her father and will not be able to divorce her ever (which was otherwise not the case). If bloodstained garments cannot be produced, the bride is to be stoned to death (Deuteronomy 22:13-19).

Similar practices have been reported from other Arab and Islamic societies, the Kopts in Egypt and various other Mediterranean groups such as the Greeks and Sicilians. Moreover, similar customs have been found in eastern Europe (among Russian and Estonian peasants), in many parts of Africa, the Far East, and a number of Oceanic societies. Eastern European immigrants to the United States have been known to send blood-stained sheets back to their families in "the old country" to legitimize their marriages traditionally.

For modern Egyptian peasants, the test does not come with the first marital intercourse, but before that: the bridegroom wraps a piece of cloth round his index finger, which he inserts into the bride's vagina. The tremendous interest that such rituals show in the state of the hymen is remarkable, since bleeding does not invariably accompany first intercourse. The hymen itself varies greatly with regard to size, thickness, flexibility and sturdiness.

Cases have been reported of women with repeated sexual experiences whose hymens are so elastic that they remain unbroken.

Public copulation

In most societies, sexual behavior takes place in private, or at least what passes for private by convention. The word might merely mean in the dark — while surrounded by dozens of other people, sleeping, or pretending to sleep, in the same room, as in some Polynesian or European peasant households.

A few instances of public copulation as a custom have been recorded, as in Captain Cook's account of such a scene on Tahiti, but the accounts are frequently inadequate.

Public ritual copulation has been reported from certain Polynesian groups such as the aboriginal Mangaians, where married couples had sexual intercourse in sacred enclosures before battles.

Public outdoor nonritual copulation has been reported from contemporary Aleúts, Tukano, Yapese and Formosan aborigines.

Romantic love

The notion of romantic love is rare in all cultures except that of Europe and America. The literary notion of romantic love is usually associated with the medieval constellation of knighthood, chivalry and feudalism. In theory, such romantic love was unrequited since it necessarily involved the near adoration of a sexually unobtainable, virtuous married woman. The reality was no doubt sometimes different. Even the ideal changed, as the poetry of the troubadours shows.

The idealization of this strictly defined kind of romantic love began in eleventh-century France, but soon became part of general European culture. Coinciding with this development was the spread and intensification of the cult of the Virgin Mary, but a connection between the two phenomena can be disputed. Curiously enough, neither the cult of the Virgin nor romantic love actually elevated the status of women in the real world.

Romantic love can be less strictly defined as involving some degree of idealization, attraction and willing loyalty between lovers or spouses. Since such a conception is lacking in some societies, at least as a basis for marriage, a basic question is why should romantic love develop in a society and what rôle does it play.

Two interesting correlations have been made between the degree of importance of romantic love and other aspects of society. It has been found that romantic love is unimportant in societies where husband and wife are held together because of their dependence upon each other for an adequate food supply. But in societies without such dependence, the motivation for staying in a stable marriage is less secure. Romantic love may function as a substitute for dependence based on food sharing.

Secondly, when a married couple lives on their own away from the relatives of either husband or wife, romantic love tends to be unimportant cross-culturally. On the other hand, when the couple following cultural rules has to live near kinsmen of one or the other spouse, romantic love tends to be stressed. What may be going on is that such love helps protect the marriage from the pressures that relatives may impose on it: the couple in a sense can cut themselves off from the rest of the world.

The major exception to these generalizations is obviously western industrialized societies, where food dependence need not exist and married couples normally do not live near relatives. One suggestion to account for this glaring discrepancy is that these societies have developed a highly sophisticated technology of communication, which really does not shut off kin pressure. In a word, the telephone may make romantic love a necessity to help a marriage withstand the onslaught of in-laws.

Western sadomasochism (right). *Illustration by Aubrey Beardsley, 1896.*

Sadomasochism

(Also referred to in terms of its components **Sadism** and **Masochism**.)

The term masochism was coined by Richard von Krafft-Ebing, with reference to the Austrian novelist Leopold von Sacher-Masoch, whose most famous book *Venus in Pelz* (*Venus in furs*; 1870) has the hero tortured by an icy domineering woman dressed in furs.

The term sadism was coined with reference to Donatien Alphonse Francois, Comte de Sade — usually called the Marquis de Sade. The term was popularized by Krafft-Ebing, but seems to have been in use before his time.

Sadomasochism involves sexual pleasure associated with the giving or receiving of pain and humiliation. In this sexual sense it is rare in primitive societies, or else it is restricted to such activities as biting and scratching.

The western world has had a long tradition of flagellation and similar acts associated with Christian penance. The West today has seen the secularization of sadomasochism, once looked upon as an exemplary religious experience.

In the West, very few women are involved in a conscious sadomasochistic life style. (Psychoanalysts generally believe that masochism is a component of femininity, but here we are speaking of a more specific and deliberate kind of sadomasochism). Masochistic heterosexual men usually must rely on the services of prostitutes who specialize in sadism.

Northern and eastern European societies have produced the greatest number of sadomasochists — this, in spite of Japanese bondage pornography and the works of the Marquis de Sade as well as the confessions of Rousseau. The most frequent ethnic backgrounds of sadomasochists found in one study undertaken in New York were British, German and Dutch, and eastern European Jews. Latin-Americans, Orientals and to a lesser extent Mediterraneans and blacks were seldom involved in the sadomasochistic subculture.

Although the reasons why people become sadomasochists are obscure, it seems likely that a major component has to do with restrictions on expressions of aggressiveness. In societies where fairly high levels of overt aggression are tolerated, people tend not to become sadomasochists. Compare Italians with the English. Italian culture tends to tolerate an openness about anger that would shock the average Englishman. At present, in England, practically every overt expression of aggression is accompanied by guilt. It is considered not only morally wrong but bad form.

If these characteristics are true — and they seem to be — one might think of sadomasochism as an eroticization of anger and aggression that cannot generally find other outlets. Since other northern European societies tend to play down overt aggression as well, it is likely that this cultural factor is important in the development of sadomasochism.

The most public and obvious sadomasochistic subculture in the western world is associated with homosexual men who meet in leather bars and motorcycle clubs. It might be useful to distinguish between sadomasochistic and S/M (the in-group term) in the same way that homosexual and gay have occasionally been distinguished. The first term would refer, for example, to the practice of sadomasochistic acts whether the person performing them labels them as sadomasochistic or not. The second would refer to the subculture.

Sex shows

In 1964-65, a man's buttocks were glimpsed for a moment on the London and Broadway stage in Peter Weiss's play *The persecution and assassination of Marat as performed by the inmates of the asylum of Charenton under the direction of the Marquis de Sade.* This daring display has since been followed by various other "respectable" productions, including the rock-opera *Hair,* and in 1968-69 a more elaborate production played almost totally in the nude, and dealing with subjects such as wife swapping, group masturbation and rape: *Oh! Calcutta!*

These productions in the 1960s were dramatic changes in recent western theatrical tradition. But, in a few nonwestern societies sex shows are known to have been performed for audiences.

The most famous example of institutionalized sex shows outside the high cultures of the East and West was associated with the *arioi* society in Tahiti. Owing to the strenuous efforts of Christian missionaries and other Westerners, the society was abandoned shortly after French colonization.

In India at various times (but apparently no longer) groups of traveling entertainers would sometimes perform public sex acts of incredible gymnastic virtuosity. It should be noted that such virtuosity is required for many of the coital positions advocated in the *Kaama suutra* and other sex manuals.

In the West, sex performances have historically been associated with various royal courts. Erotic displays are said to have been sponsored by the Roman emperors Tiberius and Caligula.

A particularly American variety of

sex show is the striptease, which has been said to have developed in frontier towns in the West. In a classic striptease, however, no actual sex acts are performed.

The ascendancy of Christianity as the official religion of the Roman Empire gave even nonerotic theater an ambiguous and often condemned status. Nevertheless, specifically erotic private theaters have existed in Christian countries from time to time.

In the nineteenth century, sex shows became increasingly democratized and were included in brothel entertainments, which might include scenes of copulation, lesbian acts and bestiality — some places becoming known for shows in which women would have sex with dogs or horses. At present, topless and bottomless bars continue to exist in the United States, and sex shows are publicly advertised in many larger western cities such as Amsterdam and New York.

Transvestism

The term transvestism was coined by Magnus Hirschfeld to cover a variety of phenomena perhaps better called cross-dressing.

In the contemporary western world, cross-dressing involves a whole complex of different behaviors, which range from temporary theatrical roles to lifelong fetishistic obsessions. Generally, people within the culture assume that transvestism is a homosexual matter. Although some forms of transvestism are, the great majority of transvestites turn out to be heterosexual men.

Very few women are involved in transvestism. One psychiatrist, Robert Stoller, denies that female transvestites even exist. But he defines transvestism very strictly as having "erotic value" for the wearer and he believes that women who dress up as men do not feel erotic about doing so. He calls such women "female transsexuals."

Transsexuals believe they are one sex but trapped in the body of the other, unless surgery mercifully removes the impediment. This

desire to escape from one's genitals is not true of transvestites. Very frequently, transvestites will do something to give away their biological identity. It is interesting that a transvestite is usually despised or subject to ridicule and contempt in western society, but transsexuals — at least those who have actually undergone surgery — are granted greater tolerance.

Heterosexual and homosexual transvestism are associated with totally different life-styles. Male homosexual transvestism is usually drag: a satire that makes fun of women and indulges in an obvious, camp misogyny. The heterosexual transvestite, on the other hand, tends to wear drab, old-fashioned clothes. Occasionally, he may even dress up like a pregnant woman. The heterosexual transvestite usually dresses up only in private; the homosexual seldom does so and is sometimes drawn toward female impersonation as a career.

In nonwestern societies, transvestism is frequently institutionalized. Among the Navaho, who lump both transvestites and hermaphrodites together under the same term, *nadle*, a family that had a *nadle* among its members was traditionally considered to be very fortunate. Because Navaho mythology describes them as having been given charge of all wealth in the beginning of time, families into which they are born are believed to be assured of wealth.

Not all societies that have institutionalized transvestism have been so kind as the Navaho, but it must be added that it is sometimes difficult to find out what the traditional attitudes were because of the intense hostility to the phenomenon by Westerners.

Although, in the western world, transvestism is predominantly heterosexual, outside the West it seems generally to be associated with homosexuality. Transvestite men will frequently be allowed to marry nontransvestite men. Nevertheless, there are a few examples recorded in the anthropological literature of transvestites who apparently were not homosexual.

The term *berdache* is generally

used of institutionalized transvestites (or hermaphrodites), particularly those found among North American Indian and Siberian groups. In accounts of Polynesia, the native term *mahu* (or some variant) is used.

In Tahiti, *mahu* were kept by the principal chiefs and functioned as servants in the chief's households. (The custom of dressing the male servants of a chief as women also occurs among the Moss of West Africa, but transvestism there is otherwise not reported.)

There was once a wide distribution of institutionalized male transvestism throughout the Pacific, Asia and Africa. In general, in societies that have institutionalized pederasty, there is little evidence of transvestism as well. Perhaps the most famous examples of institutionalized transvestism come from the Plains Indians of North America.

Among the Sioux, the *berdaches* were merely tolerated, but among the Cheyenne (as among the Navaho) they were treated with great esteem. They were considered powerful and important to bring along on war parties (all scalps collected were placed in their custody). They were believed to have the most powerful love magic as well as to be skilled doctors.

Becoming a *berdache* seems sometimes to have been compulsory. Among the Dakota and the Omaha, for example, young men had to become *berdaches* if they dreamt a certain kind of dream or vision.

Perhaps because of the notoriety of the Plains Indian *berdaches*, a very common theory accounting for why transvestism came to be institutionalized has been developed. The sex roles of the Plains Indians seem to have been extremely differentiated, and in particular being a man in the traditional sense was so demanding and difficult that some men would probably either be unwilling or even unable to make it as a man. Institutionalized transvestism, then, has been interpreted as cultural recognition of the hardship of meeting intolerable sex stereotypes set up by the culture. When we realize that the Mandan Indians

required men to validate their social positions sometimes by grueling self-torture (such as being suspended by thongs inserted under chest muscles) this explanation appears to be quite attractive.

However, more recent studies seem to show that institutionalized male transvestism does not generally occur in societies that emphasize sex difference. On the contrary, it tends to appear in societies that verge toward a unisex style. The Plains Indians are an exception to this generalization.

Transvestites are frequently — particularly in their North American and Siberian settings — thought to have supernatural powers of various sorts and become healers and ritual specialists, more technically shaamans. Among the Zulu of South Africa, divination (fortune-telling) can be done only by transvestites. The fact that in some societies transvestites are despised and considered disgusting but in others are highly esteemed tends to support a theory by Mary Douglas that things that do not fit into the native categories or are somehow outside of what is felt to be "natural" (such as twins, or men dressing up as women) are perceived in different cultures in terms of the extremes of contamination versus supernatural power.

Vaginal teeth and similar folkloristic themes

A great number of cultures throughout the world have folklore about a woman whose vagina has teeth and who kills men she has intercourse with. The best known examples of such *vagina dentata* myths come from American Indian groups north of Mexico. The same motif is also found in South America, India, Siberia, Greenland among the Eskimo, and in the Pacific on the Marquesas and Tuamotu.

Folklore about men includes the motifs of the penis that can cut down trees (found among the Klkitat American Indians), the extendable penis that can perform long-distance sexual intercourse and, from India, the *penis dentatus*

(the penis with teeth), not to mention the penis that eats and drinks.

Venereal diseases and diseases of the sex organs

The expression venereal disease was first used by Jacques de Bethercourt in 1527, and is today a legal term referring only to gonorrhoea, syphilis and chancroid. Several other diseases, however, can be spread during sexual intercourse and other sexual acts.

In some societies, various diseases have been thought to be venereal that actually are not. Among the Apache Indians, for example, tuberculosis was at one time thought to be venereal and shameful, which made treatment of it very difficult.

Gonorrhoea has definitely been known from ancient times. The term was invented by Galen in the second century AD. But it was very likely known long before that. For the most part, however, among the Greeks and the Romans there is no mention of venereal diseases at all. In the Middle Ages, various references are clearly made to gonorrhoea. In 1161 a law was enacted in London prohibiting brothel keepers from hiring women suffering from "burning," probably a term derived from an old French expression for gonorrhoea.

The history of syphilis is a matter of great debate. No genuine instances of syphilis in Europe are known to have existed before the winter of 1494–1495, when French soldiers in Naples reported tumors on their genitals. One very widely held theory is that syphilis did not exist in Europe, Asia or Africa until Columbus and his men brought it with them after the discovery of America in March 1493. Several lines of evidence support an American origin for syphilis — a position known as the Columbian theory. Ancient syphilitic bones have been reported, but perhaps incorrectly, from the Americas.

European and Asian commentators from Columbus's time said that it was a disease that was not known before. In China, no early references to syphilis occur. The first reference is not found earlier than the Ming Dynasty — at a time that agrees with the Columbian theory. Li Shi-chen, writing in that dynasty, specifically denies that syphilis had occurred in ancient times. No ancient European descriptions of syphilis are known to exist. But according to Ferdinand Columbus (Christopher's son), a friar Ramón, who had accompanied Columbus, observed syphilis among the Arawak Indians and even found that there was mention of it in Indian folklore.

Even names for the disease suggest that it was unknown and brought in by travelers. The first clinical description of it, by a Portuguese physician, Ruy Diaz de Isla, in 1497, says that Columbus's men referred to it as "Indian measles." Terms used in other languages spell out the spread of the disease and support the Columbian theory. Syphilis was spread to the Orient by the crews of Vasco da Gama and other Portuguese navigators: in both Chinese and Japanese it is called "the Portuguese disease." The Turks called it "the Christian disease." And so on. In the languages of American Indians, on the other hand, there are no words for the sickness implying a foreign origin. The Aymará word, for example, is *cchaca-usu* (literally "bone disease").

According to another theory, for which there is some evidence, the development of syphilis in Europe was basically an alteration in some already existing disease, such as yaws. This does not rule out yet another possibility: Europe was hit almost at the same time by two waves of disease, one from Africa, the other from America.

The history of the other diseases mentioned earlier is even less clear. Chancroid was confused with syphilis and leprosy, and then only with syphilis until 1889, when the distinction was firmly established.

Folk treatment and beliefs about venereal diseases vary considerably. The Mangaians believe that not ejaculating into the vagina of a girl with gonorrhoea is a sufficient prophylactic, so coitus interruptus

Copulating elephants: *sexually attractive to Hóttentots?*

is frequently practiced. On the other hand it is believed that copulating with a menstruating woman causes venereal disease in a man. In Europe at various times it was believed that copulation with a virgin was a cure for syphilis. This belief is apparently still held by rural Serbians and Jamaicans. What may be an ancient remedy against syphilis among the Aymará of South America is mercury mixed with animal fat. In some Cuban cultures, syphilis is held to be a scourge visited upon a person by the god of syphilis, Shango. Its cure involves exorcising his spirit.

A number of nonvenereal diseases specifically involve the sex organs. Women sometimes develop inflammations of the vagina and vulva. These sometimes occur as the result of intercourse in very young girls who do not produce sufficient vaginal lubrication — as well as among rape victims. In men, inflammation of the glans and infection of the foreskin are comparable disorders.

Venereal diseases have represented one of the major calamities of mankind. Unfortunately, as Havelock Ellis pointed out, western civilization and syphilization have gone round the world almost inseparably. In some societies the effect of conversion to Christianity has been to break down the traditional sexual code without successful replacement by the Christian code, so that syphilis and other venereal diseases have spread excessively. It

has been asserted that at the turn of the century in some parts of Uganda as many as 90 percent of the people suffered from syphilis and half or more of the cases of infant mortality were caused by it.

More recently, venereal diseases have been brought under more effective control, although outbreaks occur at various intervals and new strains generally resistant to established medical treatment appear on the scene. One aftermath of the Vietnamese war was that the American soldiers brought back with them particularly virulent strains of venereal diseases.

Zoöphilia

Zoöphilia refers to sexual attraction to animals. It should be differentiated from bestiality, which is the more general term for human-animal sexual contacts whatever the motivation. The only instance I have come across is from the Nama Hóttentot. Schultze, writing in 1907, says that Nama Hóttentot men found the sight of animals' sex organs sexually arousing. The sex of the animals is curiously enough never mentioned. One man went up to an elephant that had been killed in the hunt and was so aroused by looking at its genitals from the rear that he developed "an uncontrollable erection which made him walk lame."

BIBLIOGRAPHY

AUTHOR'S ACKNOWLEDGMENTS

ILLUSTRATION ACKNOWLEDGMENTS
AND SOURCES

INDEX

BIBLIOGRAPHY

Because of problems of space, only a few references that
are especially important can be included here.
Information on specific cultures was often
drawn from materials included in the Human Relations Area Files:
these items alone would add 1,000 or more titles to the present list.
As it is, an original bibliography of well over 500 titles
(not including HRAF materials) has been condensed
to about 50. Readers requiring more precise references
are requested to write directly to me.

Barash, David P., 1979. *The whisperings within.* New York: Harper & Row.

Beach, Frank A., ed., 1976. *Human sexuality in four perspectives.* Baltimore & London: Johns Hopkins University Press.

Boswell, John, 1980. *Christianity, social tolerance and homosexuality: gay people in western Europe from the beginning of the Christian era to the fourteenth century.* Chicago & London: University of Chicago Press.

Broude, Gwen J., 1975. "Norms of premarital sexual behavior: a cross-cultural study." *Ethos* 3:381-402.

Broude, G. J., and S. J. Greene, 1976. "Cross-cultural codes on twenty sexual attitudes and practices." *Ethnology* 15:409-429.

Bullough, Vern L., 1976. *Sexual variance in society and history.* New York: John Wiley and Sons.

Daly, Martin and Margo Wilson, 1978. *Sex, evolution, and behavior: adaptations for reproduction.* North Scituate, Mass.: Duxbury Press.

Ellis, Albert, and Albert Abarbanel, 1967. *The encyclopedia of sexual behavior.* New York: Hawthorn Books.

Epstein, Louis M., 1948. *Sex laws and customs in Judaism.* New York: Bloch.

Evans-Pritchard, E. E., 1973. "Some notes on Zande sex habits." *American anthropologist* 75.1:171-175.

Ford, Clellan S., and Frank A. Beach, 1951. *Patterns of sexual behavior.* New York: Harper.

Foucault, Michel, 1978. *The history of sexuality.* Vol. 1: An Introduction. New York: Pantheon Books.

Fox, Robin, 1980. *The red lamp of incest: what the taboo can tell us about who we are and how we got that way.* New York: Dutton.

Gebhard, Paul H., 1968. "Human sex behavior research." In M. Diamond *et al, Reproduction and sexual behavior,* pp. 391-410. Bloomington & London: Indiana University Press.

—— 1969. "Fetishism and sadomasochism." *Science and Psychoanalysis* 15:71-80.

Gorer, Geoffrey, 1966. *The danger of equality.* London: Cresset Press.

Guthrie, Dale, 1976. *Body hot spots: the anatomy of human sexual organs and behavior.* New York: Van Nostrand Reinhold.

Harris, Marvin, 1977. *Cannibals and kings: the origins of cultures.* New York: Random House.

Kaplan, Helen Singer, 1974. *The new sex therapy: active treatment of sexual dysfunctions.* New York: Brunner/Mazel.

Katchadourian, Herant A., and Donald T. Lunde, 1975. *Fundamentals of human sexuality.* New York: Holt, Rinehart and Winston.

Kinsey, Alfred C., Wardell B. Pomeroy, and Clyde E. Martin, 1948. *Sexual behavior in the human male.* Philadelphia & London: W. B. Saunders.

Kinsey, Alfred C., Wardell B. Pomeroy, Clyde E. Martin, and Paul H. Gebhard, 1949. "Concepts of normality and abnormality in sexual behavior." In P. H. Hoch and J. Zubin, eds. *Psychosexual development in health and disease.* New York: Grune and Stratton.

—— 1953. *Sexual behavior in the human female.* Philadelphia & London: W. B. Saunders.

Malinowski, Bronislaw, 1932. *The sexual life of savages in northwestern Melanesia.* London: George Routledge and Sons.

Marshall, Donald S., and Robert C. Suggs, eds., 1971. *Human sexual behavior: variations in the ethnographic spectrum.* New York & London: Basic Books.

Masters, William H., and Virginia E. Johnson, 1966. *Human sexual response.* Boston: Little, Brown.

—— 1970. *Human sexual inadequacy.* Boston: Little, Brown.

—— 1979. *Homosexuality in perspective.* Boston: Little, Brown.

Minturn, Leigh, Martin Grosse, and Santoah Haider, 1969. "Cultural patterning of sexual beliefs and behavior." *Ethnology* 8:301-318.

Money, John, 1966. "The strange case of the pregnant hermaphrodite." *Sexology,* August 7-9.

Money, John, and Geoffrey Hosta, 1968. "Negro folklore of male pregnancy." *The journal of sex research* 4:34-50.

Montagu, Ashley, 1969. *Sex, man, and society.* New York: G. P. Putnam's Sons.

Morris, Desmond, 1969. *The naked ape: a zoologist's study of the human animal.* New York: McGraw-Hill.

Murdock, George Peter, 1964. "Cultural correlates of the regulation of premarital sex behavior." In Robert A. Manners, ed., *Process and pattern in culture: essays in honor of Julian H. Steward.* Chicago: Aldine.

Nag, Moni, 1962. *Factors affecting human fertility in nonindustrial societies: a cross-cultural study.* New Haven: Department of Anthropology, Yale University (YUPA 66).

Opler, Morris K., 1969. "Cross-cultural aspects of kissing." *Medical aspects of human sexuality* 3:11-21.

Ortner, Sherry, 1974. "Is female to male as nature is to culture?" In Michelle Rosaldo and Louise Lamphere, eds., *Woman, culture and society.* Stanford, California: Stanford University Press.

Parkes, Alan S., 1966. *Sex, science and society.* Newcastle upon Tyne: Oriel.

—— 1976. *Patterns of sexuality and reproduction.* London: Oxford University Press.

Patai, Raphael, 1960. *Family, love and the Bible.* London: MacGibbon & Kee.

Pomeroy, Wardell B., 1972. *Dr. Kinsey and the Institute for Sex Research*. New York: Harper and Row.

Reuben, David R., 1969. *Everything you always wanted to know about sex (but were afraid to ask)*. New York: David McKay.

Slater, Mariam K., 1959.

"Ecological factors in the origin of incest." *American anthropologist* 61:1042-1059.

Stephens, William N., 1969. *A cross-cultural study of modesty and obscenity*. Halifax: Dalhousie University Press.

Suggs, Robert C., 1966. *Marquesan sexual behavior*. New York:

Harcourt, Brace and World.

Symons, Donald, 1979. *The evolution of human sexuality*. New York & Oxford: Oxford University Press.

Ullerstam, Lars, 1966. *Erotic minorities*. New York: Grove.

Unwin, J. D., 1934. *Sex and culture*. London: Oxford University Press.

AUTHOR'S ACKNOWLEDGMENTS

I am happy to acknowledge at least some
of the many people and institutions that have helped
me in preparing this book.

Of institutions, the two most important are the Institute for Sex Research, now the Alfred C. Kinsey Institute, at the University of Indiana, in Bloomington (Paul Gebhard, the director, Joan Huntington, assistant to the director, and all the staff were extremely helpful, but particular thanks go to Joan Brewer); and the Human Relations Area Files housed in the library of the Graduate Center of the City University of New York (many thanks to Jane Moore, the chief librarian, for many favors). These institutions proved to be absolutely indispensable. Other important institutions: the New York Public Library, reference branch; Butler Library, Columbia University; Columbia-Presbyterian medical library; the New York Academy of Medicine; Bobst Library, New York University; Wilbour Library, Brooklyn Museum (with special thanks to Diane Guzman); the Fashion Institute of Technology; the General Theological Seminary, the Jewish Theological Seminary, and the Union Theological Seminary (all in New York); the Library of Congress; the British Museum; the Museum of Mankind (London); the Bibliothèque Nationale; the Musée de l'Homme (special thanks to Geneviève Domergue); the Louvre (especially Jean Louis de Cenival); Völkerkunde Museum, Berlin; Ägyptisches Museum, Berlin (special thanks to Karl Theodor Zauzich); Museo Missionario-etnologico, Vatican City (special thanks to Fr Jozef Penkowski).

Mariam K. Slater, Harvey Zuckerman, John Beatty, Frank Spencer, Alex Orenstein, Roger C. Owen, Ronald Waterbury, and Chad Hardin read sections of the manuscript and suggested revisions (some of which have been used) and often helped in other ways. Thomas M. Stutzbach cataloged a number of materials for me, which proved to be invaluable in the final production of the book.

The following people helped in various and sundry ways: Edmund White (who suggested the book in the first place), Robin Maugham, Raymond Firth, Geoffrey E. Gorer, George D. Spindler, Gilbert Herdt, Shirley Lindenbaum, Richard B. Lee, Marjorie Shostak, John M. Campbell, Moni Nag, Stanley M. Garn, Raphael Patai, John Money, Vern L. Bullough, Deborah Gewertz, Natasha Sadomskaya, Jonathan Katz, Arnie Kantrowitz, Philippe Derchain, Robert A. Day, Junichi Takahashi, Mervyn J. Meggitt, Robert M. Glasse, Bernadette Bucher, David D. Schieber, Alan R. Schulman, Pei-Yi Wu, Bernard S. Solomon, John M. O'Brien, Per Schelde Jacobsen, Lynn Ceci, Gloria Levitas, James Moore, Amal Rassam, D. Michael Steffy, Don Haarman, Robert Paynter, Jane Schneider, Edward C. Hansen, Paul E. Mahler, Randolph Trumbach, Paula Rubel, Abraham Rosman, Anne Chapman, Flora Kaplan, James deWoody, Walter Duncan, Carole Vance, William M. Davis, David and Barbara Ames, Gillian and David Gillison, Virginia Guilford, Kenneth E. Engel, Christine Mossaides, Evelyn Masana, Debbie J. Green, Arlene Zigmann, and Gus Rigas. My editors, Rachel Grenfell and James Hughes, were most diligent in cutting the manuscript down to manageable size while still accommodating many of my idiosyncracies. Rozelle Bentheim also proved to be most conscientious during the time she worked on the book.

I am indebted to Lila Rosenblum and members of "the group" for helping me through some very trying times associated with the book.

I am also indebted to the many and various kinds of aid provided at Queens College and particularly by the anthropology department and interlibrary loan service. Above all, I owe special gratitude to Dorothy Belfermann, who cheerfully and with incredible care produced a typed, proof-read manuscript from my handwritten version.

Illustration Acknowledgements
and Sources

CHAPTER ONE
7 top Natives fishing, Cape Van Diemen (Musée de l'Homme, Paris)
7 bottom Goddess Baubo, 5th c. BC Greek figurine (Bildarchiv Preussischer Kulturbesitz)
8 Serui native, Amazonia (Alan Hutchison)
10 Sex education, Central Africa (Musée de l'Homme, Paris)
11 top left Mesopotamian cylinder seal, 3rd millennium BC (Peter Webb Collection)
11 top right "Mars & Venus," detail, engraving, Enea Vico (after Parmigianino) Italy, 1543 (British Museum, London)
11 bottom Mochica pot, Peru, c. 500 (Rafael Larco Herrera Museum, Lima)
13 Indian miniature, Kangra style, 18th c. (Victoria & Albert Museum, London)
14 "Roman Charity," painting, Giaocchino Serangeli, Italy, 1824 (Charmettes Museum, Chambéry, France)

CHAPTER TWO
15 top "Adam & Eve," woodcut, European, 14th c.
15 bottom "Mother & Child," engraving, USA (Peter Webb Collection)
16 Mormon family, engraving, USA, 19th c. (Mary Evans Picture Library)
18 Jewish women bathing, engraving, Germany, 18th c. (Österreichische Nationalbibliothek, Vienna)
21 left "Lot & his daughters," painting, Lucas van der Leyden, Holland, 1530 (Peter Webb Collection)
21 right "Luxuria" (detail), wood engraving, Pieter Brueghel the Elder, Flemish, 16th c. (Fotomas Index)
22 top Burning of witches, woodcut, Germany, 16th c. (Historia-Photo, Bad Sachsa, West Germany)
22 left "Witches' sabbath," etching, Francisco de Goya, Spain, 18th c. (Mansell Collection)
22 right Kate Hamilton's Night House, London, 19th c. (Fotomas Index)
24 Greek red-figure vase, 5th c. BC (Ashmolean Museum, Oxford)
25 top "Burning of Sodomites," painting. Pedro Berruguete, Spain 15th c. (Prado Museum, Madrid)
25 Monk at fleshpots, woodcut, European, 15th c. (Mary Evans Picture Library)
26 Burning of monks, woodcut, Germany, 16th c. (Author's Collection)
28 Illustration from pamphlet, The Silent Friend, England, 19th c.
29 Ancient Egyptian figurine (British Museum, London)
30 Anti-masturbatory devices, England, 19th c. (Peter Webb Collection)

CHAPTER THREE
31 top Drawing of human sperm by Antonie van Leeuwenhoek, Holland, 1703 (Kinsey Institute for Sex Research, Bloomington, Indiana)
31 bottom Naked woman carrying phallus, vase painting, Greece, 5th c. BC (Peter Webb Collection)
32 Monsters, Nuremberg Chronicle, 1493 (Mansell Collection)
33 top Album painting, India, 18th c. (Werner Forman Archive)
33 bottom "Jupiter & Olympia," painting, Giulio Romano, Italy, 16th c. (Mansell Collection)
34 top "Aristotle & Phyllis," woodcut, Hans Baldung Grien, Germany, 16th c. (Mansell Collection)
34 bottom Drawing of sexual intercourse, Leonardo da Vinci, Italy, 16th c. (Copyright Reserved)

35 Magnus Hirschfeld, Germany, 20th c. (Bildarchiv Preussischer Kulturbesitz)
36 Alfred Kinsey with colleagues, USA (Popperfoto)
37 William Masters & Virginia Johnson, USA (Popperfoto)
38 Havelock Ellis, England (Mansell Collection)
39 Margaret Mead, USA (Wide World)

CHAPTER FOUR
41 top Human foetus, woodcut, Jacob Rueff, Europe, 16 c. (Author's Collection)
41 bottom African mouthbrooder (Jane Burton/ Bruce Coleman Ltd)
42 Paramoecium conjugation (I. Walker/ NHPA)
43 Amoeba fission (Peter Parks/Oxford Scientific Films)
46 Chastity Belt, wood engraving, Europe, Middle Ages (Mary Evans Picture Library)
47 Hymen, Anatomical drawing, France, 17th c. (Peter Webb Collection)
48 Deep-sea anglerfish (Seaphot/Planet Earth Pictures)
49 "Adam & Eve," painting, Matthias Grünewald, Germany, 16th c. (Mansell Collection)
50 Gorillas copulating, line drawing, John Field (after George Schaller, The Mountain Gorilla, Chicago, 1963)
51 top Female baboon in oestrus (M.P. Kahl/ Bruce Coleman Ltd.)
51 bottom Baboons mating (R. & M. Borland/ Bruce Coleman Ltd.)
53 Rhinos mating (Jacana)

CHAPTER FIVE
55 top Indian posture book, Orissa, India, 19th c. (Peter Webb Collection)
55 bottom Temple sculpture, Khajuraaho, India, 11th c. (Peter Webb Collection)
57 Sexual scene, woodblock, Japan, 17th c.
58 "Ledakant," drawing, Rembrandt, Holland, c. 1646 (Peter Webb Collection)
59 left "Departure of the husband," print, Thomas Rowlandson, England, c. 1815 (Peter Webb Collection)
59 right Mesopotamian cylinder seal, Sumeria, 5th millennium BC (Peter Webb Collection)
61 Sexual position, silk painting, China, 18th c. (C.T. Loo Collection)
62 left Seated intercourse, painting, China, 13th–14th c. (Dubosc Collection)
62 right "Meditations among the tombs," Thomas Rowlandson, England, c. 1815–20 (British Museum, London)
63 Couple in coitus, wood carving, Africa, 19th c. (Musée de l'Homme, Paris)
64 top The Swing, Silk painting, China, 18th c. (Roger Peyrefitte Collection, Paris)
64 middle Homosexual scene, Turkey, 19th c. (Peter Webb Collection)
64 bottom Temple sculpture, Khajuraaho, India, 11th c. (Peter Webb Collection)

CHAPTER SIX
65 top Indian female type, Orissa, India, 19th c. (Peter Webb Collection)
65 middle !Kung Bushman (Musée de l'Homme, Paris)
65 bottom Cerne Abbas giant, Dorset, England (Aerofilms)
66 "Long Dong Silver," USA (Peter Webb Collection)
67 "Hottentot apron," drawing (Peter Webb Collection)
68 Various breast shapes, Germany, 19th c. (Author's Collection)
71 Indian female types, Orissa, India, 19th c. (Peter Webb Collection)
73 Human sperm (Author's Collection)

75 top James Morris, author (John Topham Library)
75 bottom Jan Morris, author (Bruno de Hamel)
76 Shiva Ardhanaarisvara, bronze, India, 14th c. (Indian Museum, Calcutta)
77 Berdache, Crow Indian, USA (Museum of the American Indian, Heye Foundation)

CHAPTER SEVEN
81 top Willendorf "Venus," Europe, Aurignacian, c. 30,000 BC
81 Trobriand Island women (photo: Bronislaw Malinowski)
82 top Ghanaian beauty ideals (Author's Collection)
82 bottom Calabar girl, Africa (Kinsey Institute for Sex Research, Bloomington, Indiana)
85 Bath House, woodcut, Europe, Middle Ages (Author's Collection)
86 Amazonian Indians (Alan Hutchison)
87 Depilation of pubic hair, woodcut, Germany, 16th c. (Author's Collection)
88 "The Bath of Psyche," Lord Leighton, England, 1890 (Tate Gallery, London)
89 Lady with parasol, color plate, Europe, 20th c. (James Hughes Collection)
90 top left Female ideal, Vesalius, Italy, 16th c. (Fotomas Index)
90 top right Jane Russell, USA (Ronald Grant Archive)
90 bottom left Serpent goddess, Crete, 16th c. BC (Alan Hutchison)
90 bottom right Geisha girl, Japan (Popperfoto)
91 left Corseted woman, late 19th c. (Mary Evans Picture Library)
91 center Woman wearing bustle, late 19th c. (Mary Evans Picture Library)
91 right Hóttentot woman, South Africa (Peter Webb Collection)
92 Jayne Mansfield (James Hughes Collection)
93 top Male ideal, drawing, Vesalius, Italy, 16th c. (Fotomas Index)
93 bottom Alain Delon, French movie star, in 1967 (Popperfoto)
94 Kaama Suutra illustration, 19th c. (Peter Webb Collection)
95 top Ritual scarring, Germany, 19th c. (Ullstein Bilderdienst)
95 bottom Galla girl, Ethiopia (Alan Hutchison)
96 top left Eskimo Kwakiútl woman, Canada (Information Canada Photothèque)
96 top right Chinook woman and child, drawing, 19th c. (Peter Webb Collection)
96 bottom left Woman with ornamental lip plate (from Boris de Rachewiltz, Black Eros, 1964)
96 bottom right Padaung woman, Burma (Claus-Dieter Brauns)
97 Bound feet, China (Popperfoto)
98 top left Scarification, Sudan (O. Luz/ZEFA)
98 right Marquesan Islander, engraving, 19th c. (Mary Evans Picture Library)
98 bottom left Tatooed skin, Tokyo University Museum. (Camera Press)
99 top Steve Reeves, USA (Melvyn Bagshaw Collection)
99 bottom Fulani beauty contest, West Africa (Victor Englebert/Susan Griggs)
100 Circumcision, relief, Saqqara, Egypt (By courtesy of the Wellcome Trustees, London)
102 Circumcision ceremony, Arnhem Land, Australia (Axel Poignant)
103 top Circumcision, woodcarving, West Africa (Alan Hutchison)
103 bottom Circumcision instruments, Jewish, Europe, 1801 (By courtesy of the Wellcome Trustees, London)
104 Male statuette, Sudan (Musée de l'Homme, Paris)
105 left The Castrato Farinelli, Italy, 18th c.

(Peter Webb Collection)
105 right Altar, Rome, 3rd c. AD (C.M. Dixon)
106 Defeat of Philistines by Israelites (The Mansell Collection)
107 Clitoridectomy knife, Central Africa (from Boris de Rachewiltz, *Black Eros*, 1964)
109 Buli Girls, Ethiopia (from Boris de Rachewiltz, *Black Eros*, 1964)
110 Bwaka girl, Africa (from Boris de Rachewiltz, *Black Eros*, 1964)

CHAPTER EIGHT
111 top Masked woman, illustration from John Bulmer, *Anthropometamorphosis*, England, 1650 (Peter Webb Collection)
111 bottom "Streaker," Twickenham rugby ground, England, 1974 (Syndication International)
112 Dukhobors, Canada (Keystone)
114 Nudist family, England, 1950s (Popperfoto)
115 Dinka men, Sudan (Peter Fuchs)
116 Man & wife outside their hut, North Africa (Musée de l'Homme, Paris)
117 Naaga woman, India (photo: Prof. C. von Fürer Haimendorf)
118 Emperor Augustus of Rome, 1st c. AD (Mansell Collection)
119 Maasai tribesman, East Africa (Alan Hutchison)
120 Modeling women's underwear, Paris 1982 (Gamma/Frank Spooner)
121 Madonna, painting, Cristoforo Scacco, Italy, 15th c. (Peter Webb Collection)
122 Prostitute, Italy (Gamma/Frank Spooner)
123 Yahgan couple, South America (Musée de l'Homme, Paris)
124 Veiled women, Muscat & Oman (Bruno Barbey/Magnum)
125 Tuareg man, North Africa (Alan Hutchison)
126 Masked women, illustration from John Bulmer, *Anthropometamorphosis*, England, 1650 (Peter Webb Collection)
127 left Men with penis sheaths, Vanuatu (Alan Hutchison)
127 right Penis-tying on an Ancient Greek vase painting, *c.* 5th c. BC (Author's Collection)
128 top Henry VIII, engraving after Hans Holbein, England, 16th c. (Mansell Collection)
128 bottom Drunken peasant, painting, Pieter Brueghel the Elder, 16th c. (Mansell Collection)

CHAPTER NINE
129 Incest between Niece & Uncle, woodcut, Germany, 16th c. (Author's Collection)
130 Lee Marvin with his mistress Michele Trebiola (Popperfoto)
131 Mormon family, USA, 1978 (Camera Press)
132 Nigerian musician with wives (Mike Wells/Aspect)
134 Toda girl, India (Alan Hutchison)
135 Indian woman committing suttee, engraving, 18th c. (Mary Evans Picture Library)
136 Cleopatra, relief, Egypt, 1st c. AD (Mansell Collection)
139 !Kung Bushman woman (Gerald Cubitt/Bruce Coleman Ltd)
140 "Proof of virginity," woodcut, Chinese, 18th c. (Author's Collection)
145 top Amazonian Indian couple (Alan Hutchison)
145 Johann Sebastian Bach & Family (Mary Evans Picture Library)
147 "Christ & the Woman Taken in Adultery," painting, Rembrandt, Holland, 17th c. (National Gallery, London)
148 Zande adulterer, Africa (from E.E. Evans-Pritchard, *We the Zande*)

CHAPTER TEN
149 top Medieval brothel, woodcut, Germany, 15th c. (Author's Collection)
149 bottom Sacred prostitute, Babylonia, 1st millennium BC (Ancient Art & Architecture Collection)
152 left Moroccan dancing girl (Popperfoto)
152 right Egyptian dancer, engraving, 19th c. (Fotomas Index)
153 Temple sculpture, Khajuraaho, India, 11th c. (Alan Hutchison)
154 Courtesan & mirror, Orissa, India, 19th c. (Peter Webb Collection)
155 Chinese prostitutes, 20th c. (Peter Webb Collection)
156 Caged geisha girls, Tokyo, 20th c. (Mary Evans Picture Library)
157 Geisha girls, Japan, 20th c. (BBC Hulton Picture Library)
158 top Ancient Greek *hetaerae*, Attic vase painting, 6th c. BC. (Mansell Collection)
158 bottom Courtesan & customer, Attic vase painting, Greece, 5th c. BC (Peter Webb Collection)
159 top Brothel, frieze painting, Pompeii, Italy, 2nd c. AD (Peter Webb Collection)
159 bottom Medieval brothel, woodcut, Germany, *c.* 15th c. (Österreichische Nationalbibliothek, Vienna)
160 top "Lobby Loungers," engraving, George Cruikshank, England, 19th c. (British Museum, London)
160 middle Toulouse-Lautrec with model and painting, 1895 (Peter Webb Collection)
160 bottom Sale of prostitute, drawing, Félicien Rops, Belgium, *c.* 1880 (Peter Webb Collection)
162 Transvestite prostitutes, Singapore (Roger-Viollet)
163 Boulton & Park, transvestite prostitutes, contemporary engraving, London, 19th c. (Mary Evans Picture Library)
164 Goddess Ishtar, terracotta, Sumerian, 3rd millennium BC (Musée du Louvre, Paris)
165 top Sacred prostitute, bronze figurine, Mohenjo-Daro, Pakistan, *c.* 3000 BC (Bavaria-Verlag)
165 bottom Sacred prostitute, figurine, Ishtar temple, Assur, Mesopotamia, 1st millennium BC (Peter Webb Collection)
166 "Mary Magdalene," painting, Titian, Italy, 1554 (Peter Webb Collection)

CHAPTER ELEVEN
167 top Prostitutes' labor organization button, USA (Author's Collection)
167 bottom Christine Jorgensen, USA (Popperfoto)
168 top Test tube baby on 2nd birthday, England, 1981 (Associated Press)
168 bottom Women in *chadors*, Iran (Gamma/Frank Spooner)
170 Birth control poster, India (Gamma/Frank Spooner)
171 Condom collection, USA (Kinsey Institute for Sex Research, Bloomington, Indiana)
174 Ernest Röhm, Germany (Popperfoto)
175 top Nazi destruction of Hirschfeld Institute, Germany (*Anthropos I*)
175 bottom Scene from *Bent* by Martin Sherman, Royal Court Theatre, London 1979 (Chris Davies/Network)
176 Gay wedding, Holland (Popperfoto)
177 Gay Liberation buttons, USA (Author's Collection)
178 Manager of sperm bank, USA (Gamma/Frank Spooner)
179 Women's prison, Mexico (Gamma/Frank Spooner)
180 "Women against porn" demonstration, New York (Gamma/Frank Spooner)

182 Sex education rag doll, USA, 1981 (Gamma/Frank Spooner)

CHAPTER TWELVE
184 Fertility figures, Chad, Africa (Jorgen Basch)
185 top Petroglyphs, Fezzan, N. Africa, 8th millennium BC (John Field)
185 bottom Petroglyphs, Fezzan, N. Africa, 3rd millennium BC (John Field)
186 top & bottom Bushman Rock painting, Southern Africa (John Field)
187 left Faience figurine, ancient Egypt. (British Museum, London)
187 right Dancing girls, ancient Egypt, (British Museum, London)
188 top The Turin Papyrus, ancient Egypt (John Field)
188 center Erotic graffiti (Ostraka), ancient Egypt (John Field)
188 bottom Procreation of Horus, relief, ancient Egypt, 19th Dynasty (Private collection)
189 bottom Man, woman & harp, figurine, ancient Egypt (Brooklyn Museum)
190 Zande wives, E. Africa (E.E. Evans-Pritchard)
191 top Ithyphallic god Min, relief, Karnak, Egypt, 12th Dynasty (Private collection)
191 bottom Statuette, woodcarving, C. Africa (Musée de l'Homme, Paris)
192 Detail of Chokwe seat, W. Africa (Musée de l'Afrique Centrale, Tervuren, Belgium)
193 Yoruba royal stool, Nigeria (Michael Holford)
194 Royal chair, W. Africa (Musée de l'Homme, Paris)
195 Writer André Gide & companion on African trip
196 Transvestite shaaman, West Africa (Gert Chesi)
198 Anthropomorphic goblet, wood, Zaïre, Africa (Musée de l'Homme, Paris)
199 Erotic dance, C. Africa (Musée de l'Homme, Paris)
200 Bronze gold-weight, W. Africa, contemporary (Kinsey Institute for Sex Research, Bloomington, Indiana)

CHAPTER THIRTEEN
201 top Copulating couple, Natufian, Middle East, *c.* 8000 BC (John Field)
201 bottom Ritual copulation, Uruk, Mesopotamia, 5th millennium BC (John Field)
203 Sacred prostitute, Ishtar temple, Assur, Mesopotamia, 3rd millennium BC (John Field)
204 Priestess of Anahita, Sassanian vase, Persia, 6th c. AD (Hermitage Museum, Leningrad)
205 Arab men embracing (Keystone)
206 top Women's communal bathhouse, miniature, Turkey, 19th c. (Museum of Turkish & Islamic Art, Istanbul)
206 bottom Woman bathing, miniature, Ottoman, 18th c. (Topkapi Sarayi Library, Istanbul)
207 left Veiled Muslim woman, Egypt (Popperfoto)
207 right Woman with beaded veil, Chad, C. Africa (Documentation Francaise)
209 "Balrâm Gûr and the Princess of Rûm," miniature, Persia, Safavid period (17th c.) (Museum of Turkish & Islamic Art, Istanbul)
210 top "Dalliance," Afzal al-Husainî, miniature, Persia, 17th c. (Victoria & Albert Museum, London)
210 bottom Fragment of sex manual, Fayum, Egypt, 11th c. (Österreichische

Nationalbibliothek, Vienna)
211 "The Golden Chain," illustration to *Hafr Aurang* Ms by Jâmî, Persia, 16th c. (Smithsonian Institution, Freer Gallery of Art, Washington DC)
212 Two youths hand-in-hand, miniature, Qasvin, Persia, 16th c. (Musée Guimet, Paris)
213 Laquered playing card, Persian, Kajar period, 19th c. (Private Collection, Teheran)
214 Two lovers, miniature, Persia (Private Collection)

CHAPTER FOURTEEN
215 top Kaama Suutra position, Orissa, India, 19th c. (Peter Webb Collection)
215 bottom Yoni/Lingam miniature, India, 18th c. (Ajit Mookerjee Collection)
216 Sexually aroused ascetic, wood carving, India, 17th c. (Ajit Mookerjee Collection)
217 Lingga, Harappaa, Indus civilization, 3rd millennium BC (Private Collection)
218 Lingga, Madras, 1st c. BC (Department of Archaeology, Government of India)
219 top & bottom Temple sculptures, Konaarak, Orissa, India, 13th c.
220 top Temple sculpture, Khajuraaho, India, 11th c. AD (Max-Pol Fouchet)
220 left & bottom Temple relief, Khajuraaho, India, 11th c. AD (Max-Pol Fouchet)
221 Temple sculpture, Khajuraaho, India, 11th c. AD
222 Temple sculpture, Rati-Lila, carving, Katmandu, Nepal, 18th c.
223 Andaman Island males (Lidio Cipriani/Weidenfeld & Nicholson Archives)
225 Múria girl, Southwestern India (Stern)
226 left & right Lepcha men of the Himalayas (John Morris)
227 Toda woman, Tamil Nadu, South India (Alan Hutchison)
228 "Lovers on a Terrace," Mughal miniature, India, 18th c. (Victor Lownes Collection)
229 Temple sculpture, Khajuraaho, India, 11 c. AD (Max-Pol Fouchet)
230 Temple sculpture detail, Konaarak, Orissa, India, 13th c. AD
231 Transvestite prostitute, Bombay, India (Alan Hutchison)
232 Yoni mudra (Richard Lannoy)

CHAPTER FIFTEEN
233 top Chart of the body, engraving from Daoist Handbook of Internal Alchemy (Bibliothèque Nationale, Paris)
233 bottom Couple reading sex manual, painting on silk, Chinese, 17th c. (C.T. Loo Collection)
234 Yin and Yáng personified, engraving from "The Moon Lady," China, 1610 (University of Indiana Library, Bloomington, Indiana)
235 "Dosojin," Shinto phallic shrine, 1894
236 Shinto phallic procession, Japan, contemporary (Kinsey Institute for Sex Research, Bloomington, Indiana)
238 Yab-Yum, gilt bronze, Tibet, 16th c. AD (Property of Alistair McAlpine)
239 top Threesome on swing, erotic manual, China, Ming period, c. 16th c.
239 center Threesome, erotic manual, China, Ming Period, c. 16th c.
239 bottom Intercourse aloft, erotic manual, China, 18th c. (University of Indiana Library)
240 top "Golden Lotus," painting, China, 19th c. (University of Indiana Library, Bloomington, Indiana)
240 bottom Painting, China, late Yüan period (1280–1367) (Dubosc Collection, Paris)
241 "The Dream of the Fisherman's Wife," book illustration, Hokusai, Japan, 1824 (British Museum, London)
242 top & bottom Composite of illustrations

attributed to Hokusai (1746–1835) featuring sexual gymnastics (John Field)
244 top left Sado-masochism, print, Japanese, 19th c. (University of Indiana Library, Bloomington, Indiana)
244 top right Voyeurism, print, Japan, 19th c. (University of Indiana Library, Bloomington, Indiana)
244 bottom Sado-masochism, Japan, 20th c.
245 top "Two Actors," painting, China, 18th c. (University of Indiana Library, Bloomington, Indiana)
245 bottom Ainu girl, illustration by A.H. Savage Landor, England, 1893

CHAPTER SIXTEEN
247 top "The spirit of sex," rock carving, Central Australia
247 bottom Oceanic intercourse, illustration by Paul Gauguin, 19th c. (Cabinet des Dessins, Louvre Museum, Paris)
248 top Áranda girl and child (from Baldwin Spencer & F.J. Gillen, *The Arunta*, England 1927)
248 bottom Carved phalli, Australia, from *Man*, England, 1921 (John Field)
249 Coming of age ceremony, N. Australia. (Axel Poignant)
251 top Gable detail, "bai" clubhouse, Palau Islands, Micronesia
251 bottom Yapese girl, Caroline Islands, Melanesia (Eliot Elisofon)
252 left Girls in erotic dance, Solomon Islands, Melanesia (from Ove Brusendorf & Paul Herringsen, "*Love's Picture Book*", 1960)
252 right Chief's phallic necklace, Tubuatu, Central Polynesia (Peabody Museum, Salem, Massachusetts)
253 Yap women, Caroline Islands, Micronesia (David S. Boyer, National Geographic)
254 Doorpost carving, New Zealand
255 Huli woman suckling pig, New Guinea (Robert M. Glasse)
256 top Painting on rafter of "bai" clubhouse, Palau Is., Micronesia (John Field)
256 bottom Male image, Cook Islands, Central Polynesia (British Museum, London)
257 Staff god, Rarotonga, Cook Islands, Central Polynesia (Otago Museum, New Zealand)
258 Maori box lid with ancestors, New Zealand
259 left Female figure, wood, Tubuatu, (British Museum, London)
259 right Carving, Rapanui, Easter Island
260 Fertility symbol, Torres Straits, New Guinea (C.M. Dixon)

CHAPTER SEVENTEEN
261 top Tlazoltéotl, MS. Laud, misc. 679, folio 16, Nahua-Mixtec, 15th c. (Bodleian Library, Oxford)
261 bottom Caribou Eskimo family, Ennadai Lake, Canada (Fritz Goro/Time-Life)
262 left Paddle, Western Eskimo, mid-19th c. (British Museum, London)
262 right Totonác priest, Mexico, 12th c. AD
263 Conibo girl, Amazonia (Emil Schulthess)
264 top Mochica vessel, Peru (Rafael Larco Herrera Museum, Lima)
264 right Mochica shrimp pot, Peru (Kinsey Institute for Sex Research, Bloomington, Indiana)
264 bottom Mochica drinking vessel, Peru (Rafael Larco Herrera Museum, Lima)
265 Ithyphallic captive, Maya-Toltec, Mexico (Regional Museum, Campeche, Mexico)
266 Zuni war god, carving, New Mexico (Brooklyn Museum, New York)
267 Bowl showing Hopi fertility rite, Pueblo, New Mexico, 17th c. AD (Peter Webb Collection)

268 Rawhide cutouts from Sioux ceremonial lodge, USA, 19th c. (John Field)
270 Cherokee stone pipe, USA, 19th c. (Werner Forman Archive)
271 "Sioux dance to the berdache," by George Catlin from *Banners of the North American Indians*, London, 1876
272 Mimbres lottery bowl, Southwest USA, c. AD 800–1300 (Bill Faris Collection)
274 Portrait carving of Nootka women, NW USA (Museum für Völkerkunde, Berlin)

CHAPTER EIGHTEEN
275 top Erotic illustration, Giulio Romano, Italy, 1527 (reconstruction)
275 bottom Penitent, woodcut, A. Dürer, 16th c.
276 Balkan couple, Macedonia (H.B. Crook)
277 Balkan female partisan (BBC Hulton Picture Library)
278 Aran woman; still from film *Man of Aran*, dir. Robert J. Flaherty
279 top Feminist graffiti on "sexist" advertisement, London, 1980 (Jill Posener)
279 bottom Flagellation in London brothel, engraving, England, 18th c. (Gichner Foundation for Cultural Studies, Washington DC)
280 "Venus" figurine, Yugoslavia, Aurignacian period c. 30,000 BC (Werner Forman Archive)
281 top Carving from Laussel, Dordogne, France, Aurignacian c. 30,000 BC (Author's Collection)
281 Antler artifact, Gorge d'Enfer, Dordogne, France, c. 15,000 BC (Achille B. Weider)
282 top Anthropomorphic carving, wood, North Jutland, Denmark, c. 4th c. BC (Prof. Glob)
282 right "The Flagellation of Christ," painting, Luis Borassa (1396–1424), Spain (Musée Goya, Castres)
282 Shelah-na-gig figure, Kilpeck, England, 11th c.
283 Detail from "The Last Judgment," Michelangelo, Sistine Chapel, Rome, 1541 (Author's Collection)
284 The Adamites seized by guards, engraving, Amsterdam, 18th c. (Mansell Collection)
285 Ulla, prostitute activist, Lyons, France (Gamma/Frank Spooner)
286 Gay couple, Marseille, France, 1979 (Gamma/Frank Spooner)
288 Phallic rocket, painting, Alfred Beloch, Germany (International Museum of Erotic Art, San Francisco)

CHAPTER NINETEEN
289 Letters from alphabet, woodcut after Peter Flöther by Martin Weygel, Germany, 16th c. (Mansell Collection)
290 Coitus with animal, cave painting, Val Comonica, Italy, 7th c. BC (Kinsey Institute for Sex Research, Bloomington, Indiana)
292 Gays (M. Moishard/Explorer)
294 Woman with genital jewellery, Central Africa (Musée de l'Homme, Paris)
301 Phallic figurine, ancient Egypt (British Museum, London)
303 *Earl Lavender*, illustration by Aubrey Beardsley, England, 1895 (Peter Webb Collection)
306 Elephants mating, Africa (Kinsey Institute for Sex Research, Bloomington, Indiana)
Specially created maps appearing on pages 9, 56, 101 (two), 143, 144, 296 (two) and 301 were drawn up by Lovell Johns Ltd.
Line drawings on pages 50, 185 (2), 186, 188–9, 201 (2), 203, 242–3, 248, 256–7, 268 (2) were specially made by John Field.

INDEX

Page numbers in *italic* refer to the illustration captions.

A

Abkhasians (Caucasus), 68, 214
abortion, 17, 27, 168, 170, 291
abstinence, 289; *see also* celibacy; chastity
Achómawi (S. America), 270, 302
Adamites, 112, 284; *284*
adultery, 8–9; in Africa, 194–5, 197–8; in ancient Egypt, 188; in Middle East, 206; in Oceania, 255; punishment for, 146–8, 219; *147*; tabus, 192; *192*; western law, 23, 24, 26, 27
Afghans, 206
Africa, 40, 185–200; circumcision, 103; clitoridectomy, 106; coital positions, 60; eunuchs, 105; facial scars, 95; hemicastration, 104; homosexuality, 195–7, 198; infibulation, 107; marriage, 190; polyandry, 134; prostitution, 150–1; royalty, 193; sacred prostitution, 166; sex rituals, 193–5; tabus, 190–3, 242
Agrippina, 137
Ainu (E. Asia), 236–7, 242, 243, 244; *245*
Akhenaten 187
Akhvakh (Caucasus), 213
Alaskan Indians, 177
Albanians, 140, 270, 276, 277, 288
Aleút (N. America), 261, 262, 265, 266, 302
Alexander the Great, 83
Algeria, 151
Algonkians (N. America), 150
altitude, and sterility, 70
Amarakaire (S. America), 271
Amazon Indians, 128; *8, 145*
Amenhotep III, Pharaoh, 137
American Anthropological Association, 38, 40
American Law Institute, 27, 146, 147
"American Vice," the, 297
Amhara (Ethiopia), 87, 208
amoeba, 42–3; *43*
Anabaptists, 283
Anahita, goddess *204*
anal coitus (sodomy), 17, 24, 25, 26, 55, 56, 63–4; *25, 26*
Anangga rangga, 32, 70, 94, 228
anaphrodisiacs, 289
Andamanese, 222–3, 229, 231; *223*
Angola, *103*
Ankole (Africa), 193
Apache (N. America), 85, 272, 302, 305

aphrodisiacs, 29, 289–90
Apinayé (S. America), 61, 263, 269
Aquinas, St Thomas, 19, 34
Arabia, 126, 149, 208
Arabs, 66, 112, 165, 209, 302
Áranda (Australia), 8, 248, 249, 255; *248*
Arápaho (N. America), 268, 270
Araucanians (S. America), 150, 263, 265, 269, 271
Arawak Indians (N. America), 306
Aretino, Pietro, 13
ariori society, Tahiti 247, 304
Aristophanes, 222
Aristotle, 17, 31, 34, 38; *34*
Armenia, 151
Arnhem Land, 249; *249*
art, erotic, 221, 228, 239–40, 279, 282–3; *219–21, 240, 241, 282*; prehistoric, 281–2; *189, 201, 281, 290*
Artaxerxes, 137
Artha-shaastra, 152–3
artificial insemination, 167, 177–8; *178*
Aruba (Caribbean), 151
asceticism, 216; *216*
Ashanti (W. Africa), 148
Asia, 215–32, 233–46
Association Internationale de Droit Pénal, 27
Assyrians, 201
astringents, 290
Atatürk, Kemal, 125
Athapaskan Indians (N. America), 261–2
Athenaeus, 99
Attis *105*
attractiveness, physical, 81–100
Augustine, St, 20–1, 149
Augustus, Emperor, 24, 157
Aurelian, Emperor, 148
Australia, 8, 109, 288, 297
Australian aborigines, 8, 106, 108–9, 247–9, 256, 263, 281, 291, 297; *248*
Australopithecus, 47
autofellation, 48, 189
Avicenna, 34
Aymará (S. America), 136, 264, 265, 274, 306
Aztecs, 146, 147, 148, 150, 262, 265, 289; *261, 265*

B

Babylonians, 149, 163–4, 201; *164, 165*
Bach, Johann Sebastian, 145; *145*
Baer, Karl Ernst von, 34
Baganda (Africa), 116
Baiga, 146

Bakete (Africa), 133
Bakuba (Africa), 133
Bala (Zaire, Africa), 98, 197, 199
Balhika (Asia), 232
Balinese, 61, 82, 116, 136, 140, 229
Balkans, 275–7; *276, 277*
Baluchistan, 204
Bambara (Africa), 60, 191
Bantu, 66, 87, 103, 185, 190–5
Banyoro (Africa), 150–1
Basongye (Africa), 60
Baubo, goddess, 7
Beach, Frank A., 39, 269, 295, 298
beards, 83, 92–3
Beardsley, Aubrey, *303*
beauty, 81–4; *84*
beauty contests, 99–100; *99*
Beauvoir, Simone de, 80
Bediyas (Asia), 153
Beduins, 214
Bellacoola (N. America), 265, 267, 300
Bellagio Conference (1963), 27
Bemba, 192, 194, 200, 298
Benin, 193
Berbers (N. Africa), 190, 204
Berckmann, Noel, 60
berdache (transvestite) 270, 304; *271*
Berruguete, Pedro, *25*
bestiality, 16, 290; *290*; American Indians, 271, 273; in ancient Egypt, 189; in Asia, 232; in the Middle East, 211–12; *211*; in Oceania, 257–8; western law, 25, 26, 27
Bhutan, 218, 227
Bible, 16, 106, 126, 133, 137, 146, 149, 161, 204, 214, 302
Bick, Mario, 121–2, 127
bigamy, 27, 283
Bini (Africa), 191
Bira (Zaire, Africa), *96*
birth control *see* contraception
bisexuality, 291
Blackfoot Indians (N. America), 147, 268, 291
Bolivia, 70
bondage, 232, 243
Book of David, 25
Borassá, Luis *282*
Borneo, 102, 185, 294
Bororó (S. America), 11–12, 88, 150, 263, 272
Bororó Fulani (Africa), 99–100; *99*
boy-wives, 202–3, 249
Brazil, 8, 9, 11–12; *86*
breasts, 14; *14*; as buttock substitutes, 50–1; ideals of beauty, 91–2; nudity, 117, 120; position, 41; shapes, 66; *68*
bride capture, 250–1
brothels, 149, 154, 155, 157–60, 162–3; *22, 149, 156*

Brown, Louise, 177; *168*
Bruegel, Pieter (the Elder), *21*
Brues, Alice, 9?
Buddhism, 112, 153, 215–18, 234–5, 238, 289; *238*
Buganda (Africa), 193
Buka (Oceania), 8, 60, 61, 255, 257
Buli (Africa) *109*
Bulgaria, 275
Bundi (N. Guinea), 66
bundling, 291
Bunyoro (Africa), 193
Burmese, 7, 100–2, 218, 231
Burton, Sir Richard, 37, 39, 212, 230, 243, 290
Burundi (C. Asia), 193
Burusho, 213–14
Bush Negroes (S. America), 289, 292
Bushmen (Africa), 61, 65, 103, 139, 185, 186–7, 191, 199, 200; *65, 91, 139, 186*
buttocks, 50–1, 91; *51, 91*
Bwaka (Zaire, Africa), *110*
Byzantium, 105

C

Calabar (Nigeria), *82*
California Indians, 117
Caligula, Emperor, 137, 157
Cambodia, 218
Canaanites, 20
Canada, 112
cancer, and circumcision, 108
Canute, King, 147
Carib, 269
Caribbean, 131
Caribou Eskimo, *261*
Casanova, 120
castration, 24, 25, 105; *105*
Catholic Theological Society of America, 172
Cato, 158
Catullus, 148
Caucasus, 67, 213, 214, 237, 262, 291
Cayapa (S. America), 147, 269
celibacy, 20–1, 24–5, 44, 209, 215, 216, 218, 226, 289
Cencu or Chenchu (Asia), 61, 222
Central America, 267
Cewa (Africa), 199, 298
Chad, 125; *207*
Chaga (Africa), 58, 150, 193, 194, 199
Charlemagne, 158
Charles-Picard, G., 93
Chartham, Dr Robert, 65
chastity, 116, 215, 289
chastity belts, 46, 237, 262, 291; *46*
Cherkess (Caucasus), 214

Cherokee (N. America), *270*
Cheyenne (N. America), 147, 268, 272, 291, 305
Chicago Vice Commission, 123
child marriage, 291–2
childlessness, 24–5
China, 32, 233–5, 242, 246; birth control, 169; coital positions, 12, 62, 63; *61, 62*; erotic art, 239–40; *240*; eunuchs, 105, 295; footbinding, 97; *97*; homosexuality, 244–5; *245*; ideals of beauty, 81; marriage, 129, 238; masturbation, 244; prostitution, 153–4, 162; *155*; sex manuals, 239; *233, 239*; syphilis, 305–6; tabus, 242, 243
Chiricahua, 295
Chiriguano (S. America), 61, 269, 271
Chokwe (Africa), *102*
Christianity, and cleanliness, 85; marriage, 134, 283, 284; and nudity, 111–12; and prostitution, 158, 164–5; *see also* Judaeo-Christian world
chromosomes, 73–4, 77–8
Chukchi (N. America), 236, 237, 240, 242, 293
Church of England, 17–18, 177
cicatrization, 97; *98*
circumcision, 100–3, 107–10; *100–4*; in Africa, 191; American Indians, 262; Jews, 19–20, 102, 103, 108, 204; in Middle East, 205–6; in Oceania, 257
cisvestism, 292; *292*
class, and sexual behavior, 12–14
Claudius, Emperor, 137
cleanliness, 85–6; *85*
Clement II, Pope, 158
Clement VII, Pope, 33
Cleopatra, 136; *136*
climate, and sexual activity, 69–70
clitoridectomy, 106–7, 110, 263; *107, 109, 110*
clitoris, 47, 92
cloning, 167, 178
clothing, 119–28; *120–8*
codpieces, 128; *128*
coitus, definition, 55–6
coitus interruptus, 254, 290
Colombia, 10–11
Colorado, 269
Columban, St, 25
Columbus, Christopher, 32
Comanche Indians (N. America), 139, 147, 265, 300
Comfort, Dr Alex, 168, 232
Communism, 27
conception, 8–9
condom, 292; *171*
Confucianism, 154, 234, 235, 239
Conibo (S. America), 107, 263; *263*

Constantine, Emperor, 23, 24, 146, 164
contraception, 7, 17–18, 167–73, 290–2
Cook, Dr, 70
Cook Islands (Oceania), *256, 257*
Copper Eskimo, 146
Correns, Karl, 34
cousin marriages, 137, 138
Cree Indians (N. America), 299
Crow Indians (N. America), 58, 59, 60, 266, 267, 269, 271; *77*
Cruickshank, George, *160*
Cuba, 66
cults, sexual, 260
cunnilingus, 64, 182, 230, 246, 254, 258; *64*
Cyprus, 151
Czechoslovakia, 277–8

D

Dahomey, 92, 116, 129
Daka (Africa), 190
Dakota Indians (N. America), 291, 305
Dani (Oceania), 255
Daoism (Taoism), 233–5, 243; *233*
Dard (C. Asia), 207, 208, 213, 293
Darwin, Charles, 44, 48, 81, 82, 83, 91, 92–3, 124–5
Davenport, William 291
Dayaks, 102
de León, Cieza 264
de Vries, Hugo, 34
Dhegiha (N. America), 266
dildoes, 107, 292–3; *199*
Dinaric Serbs, 276–7, 286
Dinka (Africa), 115; *115*
Divale, William, 80
divorce, 16, 24, 26, 27, 132, 134, 172, 182
Dobuans (Oceania), 60, 89
Dogon (Africa), 60, 191, 298
Dravidians (India), 95
droit du seigneur, 293
Dukagini Albanians, 288
Dukhobors, 112, 113; *112*
Dürer, Albrecht, 275
Durkheim, Émile, 77
Durrell, Lawrence, 73
Dyuka Bush Negroes (S. America), 292

E

ear piercing, 95
Easter Islanders, (Rapa Nui, Oceania), 92, 251, 256, 295
Eastern Orthodox Church, 16, 20, 139, 140, 208, 280

Edda (Africa), 191
Edo (Africa), 191
Egypt, 151, 302; *152*
Egypt, ancient, 107, 187–9; *187–90*;
  circumcision, 100, 102; *100*;
  genital preservation, 295; incest,
  136, 137, 187, 204; masturbation,
  299; nekrophilia, 299–300;
  nudity, 118; pubic hair, 88;
  punishment for adultery, 148
Elizabeth I, Queen of England, 25
Ellis, Havelock, 31, 36, 39, 115,
  117, 120, 122–3, 141, 306; *38*
Engels, Friedrich, 149, 284
England, 9, 21–3, 25–6, 67, 159,
  162–3; *160, 163, 282*
Episcopal Church, 17–18
Eskimos, 66, 69–70, 124, 242,
  261–2, 265, 289, 298, 305; *261,
  262*
Essenes, 20, 205
Ethiopia, 106, 190, 205, 208, 295;
  106
Étoro (Oceania), 146, 256
Etruscans, 118, 151
Eulenspiegel Society, 176
eunuchs, 77, 105, 162, 231, 295
Europe, 275–88, 297
Ewe (Africa), 166

F

Falashas (Ethiopia), 106, 205
Fallopius, Gabriel, 34
Fang (Africa), 81–2, 191, 197, 199,
  200, 290, 298, 301
Farinelli, *105*
Fascism, 27
fatness, 83–4, 91; *82*
Faure, François Felix, 46–7
Fellahin, 206
fellation, 17, 19, 30, 48, 64, 182,
  189, 221, 230, 254, 264, 269–70,
  297; *230, 270*
fertilization, 45–6
festivals, erotic, 248–9, 251; *251,
  252*
fetishes, 120, 122, 179, 240, 279–80,
  293; *240*
Fijians, 63, 95
finger defloration, 263, 268
flagellation, 303; *279, 282*
folklore, western, 27–30
foot-binding, 97, 240, 293; *97*
foot fetishes, 240; *240*
"foration," 56, 63–4
Forberg, Friedrich Carl, 39
Ford, Clellan S., 39, 269, 295, 298
foreskin tying, 128, 263; *127*
Formosans, 244, 302
fornication, 24, 25, 26
France, 160, 165, 285–6, 287, 302;

285, 286
Frederik Barbarossa, Emperor, 147
French Revolution, 26
frequency of coitus, 209–10, 230,
  254, 269, 276
Freud, Sigmund, 23, 38, 39, 92,
  135–6, 141
Friedan, Betty, 167
frigidity, 293
Fuchs, Edward, 39
Fulani (Africa), 88–9

G

Gagnon, John L., 144
Galen, 34
Galla (Africa), 107
Ganda (Africa), 81, 92, 147, 191,
  192, 199–200, 293
Gandhi, Mahatma, 216
gang rape, 147, 272
"gantizing," 56–7; *57, 283*
Gauguin, Paul, 247
Gauls, 113
Gay Liberation movement, 77, 167,
  173–4, 175–7; *176, 177, 286*
Gebhard, Dr Paul, 31, 56, 264
geisha, 156, 157; *157*
genetics, 34, 43–5, 73–4, 77–8
genital modifications, 100–10,
  262–3; *100–10*
Germany, 35–6, 68, 95, 112, 113–14,
  163, 174–5; *95*
Gershom ben Judah, 19
Ghana, 166; *82*
ghost marriage, 214
gichigich, Oceanic sex technique,
  253; *253*
Gide, André, 196, 212; *195*
Gilgamesh, Epic of, 125
Gillen, F.J., 248
Gilyak, 236, 242, 243
Gipsies, 298–9
Goajiro (S. America), 60
Goldhammer, Florence, 151
gonorrhoea, 305
Gorer, Geoffrey, 92, 226, 230, 297
Great Basin Indians, 117
Greece, 277, 286
Greece, ancient, 12, 17, 19, 87; *7*;
  baths, 85; hermaphrodites, 74;
  homosexuality, 161–2, 297; ideals
  of beauty, 93, 94, 99, 100; incest,
  136; infibulation, 107; nudity,
  113, 118; *118*; pederasty, 24,
  31–2, 162; *24, 31*; penis tying,
  128; *127*; phallic cults, 302;
  prostitution, 157, 161–2, 165; *158*;
  study of sex, 34
Greek Orthodox Church, 280
Gregory I, Pope, 137
Gregory III, Pope, 137

grooming, 85–8
Gros Ventre Indians (N. America),
  268
Guatemala, 8–9, 131
Guayaki (S. America), 269
Guerra, Francisco, 150
Guinea, 200
gunabibi copulation ceremony
  (Australia) 248, 251
Guthrie, Dale, 83
gymnastics, sexual, 240; *188, 242*

H

Hadza, 146
hair, removal of, 86–8; *86, 87*
Haiti, 131
Hami (C. Asia), 32
Hammurabi Babylonian Code of,
  149; *149*
Haqqa (Kurdistan), 205
Harappaa, 217
Hare (N. America), 261–2, 267
Harni criminal caste (India), 153
Harris, Marvin, 80, 133
Hasidic Jews, 82
Hausa (Africa), 88–9, 94, 133, 151,
  193, 207, 298, 299
Havasupai Indians (N. America),
  99
Hawaii, 136, 251, 256
Hazara (Asia), 213
head-molding, 95; *96*
Hebrews, 125, 136, 146, 148, 149,
  164, 204, 208, 301, 302
Hedwig, Sophia (Herman Karl), 76
Heliopolis, 164
hemicastration, 104, 105
hermaphrodites, 74–5, 77
Herodotus, 32, 100, 134–5, 163–4,
  189
Hertwig, Oscar, 34
Hidatsa (N. America), 267–8
Hill Mariaa (Asia), 225
Himalayas, 134
Hinduism, 77, 108, 215–22; *76*;
  classification of sexual types,
  70–1; *71*; homosexuality, 231;
  incest, 218–19; kissing, 298;
  marriage, 134, 227, 228; *135*; and
  nudity, 112, 113; phallic cults,
  217, 302; *215, 217, 218*;
  prostitution, 152–3; sacred
  prostitution, 165–6; semen
  power, 216–17, 230; sexual laws,
  218–21; tabus, 230; veils, 125
Hippocrates, 34, 71
Hirschfeld, Magnus, 35–6, 174,
  292, 304; *35, 175*
Hittites, 211
Hokkien, 242–3
Hokusai, *241, 242*

Holland, 21, 112
Holy Roman Empire, 147
Homo erectus 47
homosexuality, 54, 74, 295–7;
   aborigines, 249; Africa, 195–7,
   198; American Indians, 270–1;
   anal foration, 63–4; in ancient
   Egypt, 189; in Asia, 223–4, 231–2;
   223; in China, 244–5; *245*;
   churches and, 171; clothing,
   122–3; Eskimo, 262; Gay Lib,
   173–4, 175–7; *177*; in Germany,
   174–5; homophilia, 279, 280, 297;
   in Japan, 245; in Middle East,
   212–13; *213*; in Oceania, 256–7;
   prostitution, 150, 161–3; *162*;
   punishment for, 146;
   sadomasochism, 56, 123, 176,
   303–4; Siwans, 202–3; in South
   America, 265; in Tibet, 238; in
   the West, 17, 18, 24, 25, 27, 35–6,
   76–7, 286–7, 297
Hong Kong, 66
Hopi Indians 59, 60, 132, 266, 267,
   269–70, 271, 272, 290, 300; *267*
Hóttentots, 66, 81, 91, 104, 185,
   186, 192, 196, 199, 293, 306; *67*
Huli (New Guinea), 255
Human Relations Area Files, 39–40
hunter-gatherers, 222–4, 236–7
Hunza (Asia), 213
hymen, 47, 302; *47*

I

Ibibio (Africa), 191
Igbo (Africa), 148, 166
Ijo (Africa), 290
Ila (Africa), 81, 87, 192, 193, 199,
   200, 289, 299
illegitimacy, 27, 131
impotence, 297–8
Incas, 136, 150, 262, 264–5, 271–2,
   290
incest, 10–11, 135–40; *129*; in
   Africa, 193; American Indians,
   268; in ancient Egypt, 136, 137,
   187, 204; in Asia, 223; Buddhism,
   218–19; milk incest, 139, 208, 280;
   myths, 47; in Oceania, 247, 251;
   punishment for, 147; in the
   West, 20, 23, 25, 27;
   Zoroastrians, 204
Index of prohibited books, 33
India, birth control, 169, 215–18,
   224, 229, 232; *170*; child
   marriage, 292; coital positions,
   12, 63; *13, 55, 215*; fellation, 230;
   230; homosexuality, 231;
   marriage, 227; prostitution,
   152–3; *153, 154*; sacred
   prostitution, 165–6; *165, 219*;

semen power, 216–17; sex and
   class, 13; sex manuals, 32, 70,
   215; *228*; sex shows, 304
Indians, North American, 81, 103,
   124, 150, 261–74, 305, 306; *77,
   271*
Indians, South American, 61, 106,
   124–5, 261–74, 306; *263*
Indonesia, 256
infanticide, 17, 79–80, 271, 291
infibulation, 46, 106, 107, 206, 263
Ingalik (N. America), 261
Innocent III, Pope, 137
Inquisition, *25*
Institut für Sexualwissenschaft, 35–6
Institute for Sex Research (USA),
   36–7
Iran, 125–6, 168, 211; *168*
Ireland, 21, 278, 286, 299; *278*
Iroquois (N. America), 79
Ishtar, goddess, 164, 201; *164, 203*
Isis 189; *188*
Islamic countries, 87, 168–9,
   201–14; abstinence, 289;
   adultery, 148; castration, 105;
   circumcision, 103, 108;
   homosexuality, 212–13; and
   incest, 139; infibulation, 107;
   marriage, 227; milk incest, 208;
   and prostitution, 149–50, 153; sex
   manuals, 32–3; temporary
   marriage, 208; veils, 125–6; *124,
   207*
Israel, 204
Iteso (Africa), 196

J

Jacobus, Dr, 65
Jainism, 112–13, 215, 216–17, 218,
   289
Jamaica, 9, 131, 306
Janjero (Ethiopia), 104, 105
Jansenism, 21
Japan, 235–6, 242, 245–6; *235, 236*;
   coital positions, 12, 58; dildoes,
   293; erotic art, 57, 240; *57, 241*;
   homosexuality, 245; marriage,
   238; phallic cults, 302;
   prostitution, 154–6, 162; *156, 157*;
   sadomasochism, *244*; sex
   manuals, 239; tatooing, 97, *98*
Java, 153
Jesus, 20
jewelry, genital, 294, *294*
Jews, 14, 79, 204–5, 209, 210–11;
   age of puberty, 66; and birth
   control, 170; circumcision, 19–20,
   102, 103, 108, 204; *103*
   clitoridectomy, 106; and
   homosexuality, 212; ideals of

beauty, 93; and incest, 20, 139;
   marriage, 19, 137, 145, 207; and
   masturbation, 147; and
   menstruation, 18–19, 28; *18*;
   nocturnal emissions, 19; and
   nudity, 111
Jibu (Africa), 190
Jívaro (S. America), 146, 267
Joan of Arc, 17
Johannesburg, 161
Jorgensen, Christine, 35, 76, 167;
   167
Joyce, James, 57
Judaeo-Christian world, 15–30,
   137, 141, 146
Junod, Henri, 39, 161
Juvenal, 148

K

Kaama suutra, 13, 32, 33–4, 55, 63,
   70, 94–5, 152, 215, 228, 230, 232,
   233, 304; *13, 55, 215*
Kabedile Pomo (N. America), 274
Kachin (Burma), 225
Kadar (Asia), 225, 291
Kágaba (S. America), 10–11, 58,
   139, 266, 268, 269, 272, 273, 290,
   293, 298, 299
Kainantu (Oceania), 257, 300
Kaindu (Asia), 32
Kaingáng (S. America), 265, 269,
   272, 295, 298
Kallinago (S. America), 269
Kamchadál (Asia), 236, 237
Kamul (Asia), 32
Kanuri (Africa), 58, 199, 207, 210
Karajá (S. America), 61
Karen (Burma), 225, 231
Karimoja (Africa), 196
Kariuki, Josiah, 113
Kaska, 146
Kautilya, 152–3
Kavirondo (Africa), 291
Kazakh (Asia), 213
Kenya, 113, 118, 119
Keraki (New Guinea), 299
Ket (Asia), 238
Kgatla-Tswana (Africa), 14, 60, 92,
   191, 197, 199, 200
Kiener, Franz, 115–16
Kikuyu (Africa), 113, 191, 193–4,
   197, 199, 200, 291, 295
Kinsey, Alfred, 12–13, 19, 36–7, 38,
   40, 65, 67, 68, 72, 115, 141–2,
   144, 145–6, 167, 181–2, 245–6,
   287, 290, 295; *39*
Kinsey Institute, 56, 57, 178, 287
kissing, 229, 244, 270, 298; *229*
Klamath (N. America), 265, 267,
   270
Klinefelter's syndrome, 73

Koka shastra, 32, 228, 232
Kolhatis, nomadic acrobats (India), 153
Kóniag Eskimo, 261, 262
Konso (Ethiopia), 103
Kopts (M. East) 103, 208, 302
Koran, 139, 148, 153, 206, 208, 212, 214, 235, 238, 242, 243, 246
Koryak (Asia), 236, 237, 243
Krafft-Ebing, Richard von, 31, 174, 303
Kroeber, Alfred L., 69, 85, 86, 95
Krzywicki, Ludwik, 145
Kubeo (S. America), 9, 135, 268–9, 270, 272, 289
Kuna (S. America), 264
!Kung (Africa), 139, 186; *139*
Kusaians (Oceania), 61, 92
Kushites, 109
Kuwait, 213
Kwakiútl (N. America), 81, 150
Kwoma (Africa), 60, 114–15, 251, 255, 295

L

labia minora, 66, 92, 102, 107, 258, 293; *259*
Lakher (Asia), 136
Lambeth Conference, 17–18, 169
Lamet (Asia), 136
Lango (Africa), 191, 196, 295
Lapps, 282
Latin America, *see* South America
Lau (Asia), 256, 300
leather fetishes, 122, 293
Leeuwenhoek, Antonie van, 34; *31*
legislation, 23–7, 219–21
legitimacy, 130–1
Leighton, Lord, *88*
Leonardo da Vinci, 34; *34*
Lepcha (Asia), 60, 61, 146, 218, 223, 224, 226–7, 230–1, 232, 290, 295, 298; *226*
lesbians, 16, 197, 198, 213, 271, 297
Lesu (Oceania), 61, 250, 255, 295
Lévi-Strauss, Claude, 80, 88, 133, 135
Leyburn, 131
Leyden, Lucas van der, *21*
lingga, 217, 302; *215, 217, 218*
Linnaeus, Carl, 33
lip plates, 95–7, 117; *96*
Louis IX, King, 158
Louis XIV, King, 29
love magic, 298–9
Lovejoy, Owen, 53–4
Lozi (Africa), 192
Luba (Africa), 193
Lunda (Africa), 193
Luo (Africa), 115–16, 300
Luther, Martin, 21

M

Maasai (Africa), 60, 81, 109–10, 118–19, 190, 191, 195; *119*
McLennan, J.F., 134
Mahaabhaarata, the, 153, 217–18
Malabar, 113
Malawi, 8
Malays, 227
Malaysia, 231
male prostitution, 161–3, 164; *162, 231*
Malekula, 257
Malinowski, Bronislaw, 40, 61, 81, 138, 248, 252, 256, 295; *81*
Malthus, Thomas, 169
Malwa (Asia), 232
Mam (S. America), 8–9, 263
Mandan (N. America), 263, 267–8, 305
Mang Garuda (India), 153
Mangaians (Oceania), 63, 64, 90, 92, 103, 252, 254, 295, 298, 300, 302, 306; *252*
Mansfield, Jayne, *92*
Maori (New Zealand), 97, 251, 254, 258; *254, 258*
Marind-anim (Oceania), 256–7
Marquesans (Oceania), 13–14, 59, 60, 62, 84, 91–2, 103, 249–50, 251, 253–4, 256, 257–8, 259, 290, 305; *98*
marriage, 129–34; in Africa, 190; American Indians, 265–6; in Asia, 227–8, 237, 238; child marriage, 291–2; Eskimos, 261–2; in Europe, 283–4; Judaeo-Christian tradition, 16; monogamy, 19, 52, 129, 132, 207, 283; in Oceania, 249–51; premarital virginity, 140–6; in Soviet Union, 27; temporary, 208; *see also* divorce; incest
Marshall, Donald S., 90, 254
Marshallese (Oceania), 47, 60, 136, 146, 250, 251, 260
Martinique, 131
Marvin, Lee, 129; *130*
Marx, Karl, 149, 284
Mary, Virgin, 121, 125, 145, 302–3; *121*
Mary I, Queen of England, 25
Mary Magdalene, 164–5; *166*
Masani, 113, 117
masks, 126
masochism, *see* sadomasochism
Masters and Johnson, 29, 37–8, 167, 293, 298; *37*
masturbation, 11, 107, 189, 299; in Asia, 232; attitudes to, 147; in China, 244; female, 16; myths, 28, 30; *28*; in the West, 17, 19

Mataco (N. America), 272
Matuntara (Australia), 248
maturation, 66–7
Maya, 81, 104, 150, 262–3, 265, 267, 300; *265*
Maya Kekchi (S. America), 263
Mbugwe (Africa), 190
Mbundu (Africa), 197
Mead, Margaret, 37, 40, 179, 300; *39*
Medina, Lina, 67
Mekhong, 117–18
Melanesia, 256, 257
men, beauty contests, 99–100; *99*; clothing, 120, 121, 126; physical attractiveness, 92–5; *93*; sex differences, 77–80
Mende (Africa), 208
Mendel, Abbé Gregor, 34
Menomini Indians (N. America), 111
menopause, 67
menstruation, Jewish rituals, 18–19, 28; *18*; myths and beliefs, 8, 28–9, 64, 223, 263; onset of, 66–7; tabus, 191, 209, 213–14, 230, 242, 247, 255, 280; in the West, 18–19
Mesopotamia, 12, 59, 125, 148, 298; *11, 59, 203*
Metropolitan Community Church, 77
Mexico, 8, 264
Miao (Asia), 244
Michelangelo, 57, 282–3; *283*
Micronesia, 8, 104
Middle East, 103, 201–14
milk incest, 139, 208, 280
Millington, Sir Thomas, 33
Min, god, 187, 188; *190*
Minangkabau (Sumatra), 227
missionaries, in the Pacific, 259, 260
missionary position, 11–12, 30, 58–9, 189, 229, 252, 253, 254, 269; *11, 58*
Moche (Peru), 103
Mochica, 262, 264–5, 298; *11, 264*
modesty, 114–17, 205
Mohave (N. America), 116
Mongo (Africa), 81, 295
Mongo-Nkundu (Africa), 190, 191, 192, 197, 199
Mongols, 238–9, 246
monogamy, 19, 52, 129, 132, 207, 283
Monomotapa (Africa), 133, 193
Montagu, Ashley, 67, 77–8, 80
Montenegro, 276, 286
Mormons, 16, 111, 129, 170, 283–4; *16, 131*
Morris, Desmond, 50, 51–2, 127
Morris, Jan, 75; *75*

Mosaic code, 24, 149
Mosś (Africa), 191, 212–13, 305
Muhammad, prophet, 138, 209
Mundurucú (S. America), 115, 146, 266
Murdock, G.P., 32, 137, 142–4, 145, 182
Múria (Asia), 224–6, 229, 230, 231, 232; *225*
Murngin (Australia), 59, 60, 248, 259, 281
Muscat, *124*
myths, 27–30, 31–2

N

Naaga (Asia), 117, 225; *117*
Naasik (India), 113
Naayar (Asia), 116, 130–1, 230
Nag, Moni, 145
Nager (Asia), 213
Nahane (N. America), 269, 270, 272
Nambikwara (S. America), 61, 266, 269
Námbutji (S. America), 249
Nambuutiri Braahmans (Asia), 130
Naples, 147
Napoleonic code, 23, 26–7
National Institute of Mental Health (USA), 37
Navaho (N. America), 14, 58, 146, 263, 267, 269, 270, 272, 291, 299, 300, 304, 305
Nazism, 27, 36, 174–5
necks, stretched, 98; *96*
Negritoes, 222
Negroes, 65
nekrophilia, 189, 257, 299–300
Nepal, 217, 221
Nero, Emperor, 75
Netsilik Eskimo, 261
New Guinea, 40, 63–4, 95, 120, 128, 191, 225, 242, 247, 256, 291, 297, 299
New Hebrides *see* Vanuatu
Ngonde (Africa), 8
Ngoni (Africa), 192, 195, 199, 200
Nigeria, 82–3, 88–9, 134; *82, 132*
night courting, 291
night-crawling, 258, 266, 300
Nilotes, 97, 103, 109
Ningyuen (Asia), 32
nipples, 41, 66; excision, 105
Nkundu (Africa), 192
nocturnal emissions, 12, 19, 25, 244
Nootka (N. America), 150, 274; *274*
Normanby islanders (Oceania), 251
North America, 261–3, 265–74, 297, 305
North Carolina, 28
Northwest Coast Indians, *96*
Norway, 288

nose plugs, 95, 117
nose-rubbing, 223–4, 229, 244, 298
Noyes, John Humphrey, 134
nudity, 111–19; *111–19*
Nuer (Africa), 117, 136, 295, 301
Nukuoro, 295
Nupe (Africa), 88–9, 190
Nurge, Ethel, 68
Nyakyusa (Africa), 194, 196–7, 200
Nyanga (Africa), 193
Nyika (Africa), 194, 199
Nyoro (Africa), 60

O

Oceania, 40, 247–60
"Oceanic position," 61–2, 229, 252, 254; *254, 260*
odors, 84–5
Ojibwa (N. America), 116, 266, 269, 271, 272
Okinawans, 238, 242, 243, 244
Omaha, 266, 305
Oman, 76, 162, 212
Ona (S. America), 61, 269
Oneida community (New York), 134, 284
Orakaiva (Oceania), 251
oral-genital acts, 64, 182; *see also* cunnilingus; fellation
orgasm, female, 9, 30, 38, 51, 253
orgies, 21, 203
Ortner, Sherry, 77, 80
Osiris 189; *188*
Ossetes (Asia), 214

P

Pacific Islands, 103, 247–60
Padaung (Burma), 98; *96*
paedophilia, American Indians, 272–3
Pahaarii, 134, 227
Pakistan, 231
Palau Islands (Oceania), 62; *250*
Pano (S. America), 106, 263
Papua New Guinea, 8, 260
paramoecium, 42; *42*
paraphilia, 244, 257, 300–1
Parkes, Alan S., 66–7, 68, 69
partialism, 293
paternity, 8
pathicism, 297
Paul, St, 20, 58, 125
Paul VI, Pope, 167, 171
Pawnee (N. America), 265, 274
peasants, clothing, 121; and nudity, 116
pederasty, 212, 297; *24*; in ancient Greece, 24, 31–2, 162; *24, 31*; in Asia, 231, 232; in China, 245; *245*;

in Egypt, 202–3; in Europe, 287; in Oceania, 256–7; in Roman Empire, 24, 162
penis, anatomy, 45, 47, 52; anti-erection appliances, *30*; circumcision, 100, 102–3; *100–4*; erections, 115; foreskin tying, 128, 263; *127*; genital locking, 46–7, 52; modifications, 100–6, 107–10; *100–5*; sheaths (phallocrypts), 126–8; *127, 128*; size, 29, 65–6, 93–5, 263; *29, 65–6, 94*; worship, 217, 218–2, 301–2; *215, 217, 218, 235, 236, 301*
penis holding, 301
penitentials, 33–4, 275; *275*
Pepys, Samuel, 126
The perfumed garden, 33, 34, 58, 210, 298
Persians, 136, 137, 203–4; *204*
Peru, 12, 64, 67, 84, 264–5, 298; *11*
phallic symbols, 120, 217, 281–2, 301–2; *215, 217, 218, 235, 236, 301*
phallocrypts, *see* penis sheaths
Philippines, 185, 256, 258, 294, 300
Phoenicians, 204
physical attractiveness, 81–100
physique, 70–2
Picts, 113
Pigmies, 103, 191, 197
Pima (S. America), 88, 266
Pincus, Gregory, 167
Plains Indians, 95, 147, 262, 272, 291, 305
Plato's Retreat (New York), 173
Playboy Magazine, 259
Pliny the Elder, 27, 28
Plutarch, 24, 137, 204
Poland, 280
Polo, Marco, 32, 68, 113, 140–1, 154
polyandry, 133–4, 227, 238, 265
polygamy, 10, 16, 19, 27, 132–4, 283–4; *16, 131, 132*
Polynesians, 55, 88, 97, 103, 150, 256, 297, 300, 302, 305
Pomo (N. America), 269
Ponapeans (Oceania), 59, 92, 104, 259
pornography, 180–1, 275, 278–9, 283
Portugal, 107
positions, coital, 11–12, 30, 50–1, 55, 57–63; *11, 50, 55–63*; American Indians, 269; in Asia, 229; in Europe, 285; in Oceania, 252–4
posture, and sexuality, 47, 49–51, 53, 54, 185
Potosí (Bolivia), 70
pregnancy, 8–9; male, 299; tabus, 191, 192, 267

prostitutes, 77, 149–66, 181–2; *149–66*, *167*; in ancient Egypt, 188; clothing, 122; *122*; male, 161–3, 164; *162*; in Middle East, 206; myths, 30; nineteenth-century England, 23; Roman law, 24, 157–8, 161–2; *159*; sacred, 19–20, 163–6, 188, 201; *164*, *165*, *203*
Protestants, 280
puberty, onset of, 66–7; rites of, 80, 110
pubic hair, 87–8, 240; *87*
public copulation, 302
Puerto Rico, 9
Pukapukans (Oceania), 59, 62, 63, 252, 255, 257, 289, 295, 300
Puna Indians (S. America), 274
punishment, for sexual misbehavior, 146–8, 219; *192*
purdah, 207
Puritans, 21, 26

QR

Quakers, 16
Rámkokamekra (S. America), 269
rape, 30; in animals, 54; in Oceania, 258; as punishment, 146, 147, 272; ritual, 193–4; in Roman law, 24
Raphael, 283
Rapport Simon, 285–6, 287
Raroia (Tuamotu, Oceania), 247
Rarotonga (Cook Islands, Oceania) 251; *257*
rear entry coitus, 60–1, 186; *61*, *186*
Reeves, Steve, *99*
Reformation, 21, 25
Rehoboam, King of Judah, 164
Reich, Wilhelm, 36
Rembrandt, *58*, *147*
Reuben, Dr David, 28, 100–2, 168
Rif (N. Africa), 210, 212, 213
ritual sex, aborigines, 248–9; in Africa, 193–5; American Indians, 263–4, 267–8; in Asia, 230–1; initiation rites, 55, 113
Riza, Shah of Iran, 125
Rockefeller Foundation, 37
Röhm, Ernst, 174; *174*
Roman Catholic Church, 17, 125; and birth control, 18, 167, 169, 170–1; castrati, 105; in Europe, 280; and incest, 140; Jansenism, 21; and marriage, 16, 20, 137; milk incest, 208; sexual behavior, 171–2
Roman Empire, 12, 99, 304; adultery, 148; aphrodisiacs, 289; baths, 85; birth control, 291; castration, 105; *105*;

hermaphrodites, 74; homosexuality, 286; incest, 136, 137; infibulation, 107; legislation, 23–5; marriage, 19, 129; and nudity, 118; onset of menstruation, 66; prostitution, 24, 157–8, 161–2; *159*
Romano, Giulio, 33, 283; *33*, *275*
romantic love, 302–3
Rops, Félicien, *160*
Rowlandson, Thomas, *59*, *62*
Royal Anthropological Institute, 129–30
Rueff, Jacob, *41*
Rumania, 275
Rundi (Africa), 192, 193, 199
Rusk, Dean, 37
Ruskin, John, 87
Russell, Jane, *90*
Rwanda (Africa), 193

S

sacred prostitution, 19–20, 163–6, 188, 201; *164*, *165*, *203*
sadomasochism, 300, 303–4; *303*; American Indians, 272; in Asia, 232; clothing, 122; in Europe, 279, 280; *279*; fetishes, 293; homosexuals, 56, 123, 176, 303–4; in Japan, *244*; in Oceania, 258
Salish (N. America), 266, 272
Samaritans, 204, 205, 208, 209, 210, 212
Samburu (Africa), 104
Samoans, 251, 256, 300; *98*
Samoyéd (Asia), 237
San Francisco, 176
Santal (Asia), 61, 225, 229, 230, 231, 232
Sarakatsani (Europe), 275–6, 286, 288
Sara (Africa), 97
satii (suttee), 134; *135*
Saudi Arabia, 206
Scandinavia, 280
scars, facial, 95; *95*
Schneider, Jane, 122
Scotland, 280, 293
sculpture, erotic, 221, 228, 279; *219–21*
Scythians, 134–5
seasonal sex, 52–3, 68–70
"seed raising," 214, 227, 262, 276
Semang (Asia), 140, 222–3, 225, 227
semen, myths and beliefs, 11, 23, 215–17, 233, 256; nocturnal emissions, 12, 19, 25, 244; rituals, 194
Serbians, 276, 306
Seri (N. America), 293

sex, study of, 31–40, 178–80
sex changes, 35, 178
sex hospitality, 190, 204, 213, 218, 236, 237, 251, 262, 266, 276
sex manuals, 32–3, 70, 210, 215, 228, 233, 239, 278–9; *210*, *228*, *233*, *239*
sexual differences, 48–9; *49*
sexual reproduction, 42–6
shaamans, 237, 242, 266–7
Shabbetaians, 205
Shakers, 16–17
Sheldon, William H., 71–2
Sherpa (Asia), 227
Shilluk (N. Africa), 193, 298
Shintoism, 154, 235–6, 302; *235*, *236*
Siberia, 236–7, 242, 282, 297, 305
Sichuan (China), 32
Sidamo (Africa), 104
Sikhs (India), 112
Simon, William, 144
Sioux (N. America), 305; *271*
Sirionó (S. America), 61, 84, 92, 94, 269, 272–3, 295, 298
Síssano (Oceania), 120
Siwans (Egypt), 132, 202–3
skin color, 88–9; *89*
skin decorations, 97–8; *98*
Skoptsý (Russia), 95, 105
Slater, Mariam, 38, 139
Smith, Sir Andrew, 91
Smith, Captain John, 150
sodomy, *see* anal coitus
soixante-neuf, 64
Solomon, King of Israel, 133, 149
Solomon Islands (Oceania), 8, 289; *252*
Solon of Athens, 157, 161
Somali (Africa), 107, 199, 298
Sons of Freedom, 112
South America, 55, 140, 242, 262–74, 297
Soviet Union, 27, 61, 159, 278, 280, 284–5, 287
Spain, 25, 280; *25*
sperm, *31*
Sri Lanka, 216, 217
Stalin, Joseph, 285
standing coitus, 63
steatopygia, 91; *91*
Stephens, William N., 116
"streaking", 111; *111*
subincision, 104, 108–9, 248; *248*
Sudan, *104*
Suetonius, 137, 187
Sumatra, 153
Sumerians, 201, 298
superincision, 103, 110, 256
surrogate mothers, 177–8
Sweden, 136–7
Symonds, Donald, 83
syphilis, 30, 159, 272, 305–6
Syrians, 81, 164

T

tabus, Africa, 190–3, 242; American
  Indians, 266–7; in Asia, 230;
  Eastern European, 280; in the Far
  East, 242–3; in Oceania, 255, 258–9
Tahiti, 150, 247, 256, 302, 304, 305
Tallensi (Africa), 61–2, 139, 191, 192
Tamil, 298
Tantrism, 222, 238–9; 222, 238
Tanzania, 118–19
Tarahumara (S. America), 266
Tarascan Indians (N. America), 7
Tasmanians, 61, 248
tatooing, 97, 295; 98
teeth, 97, 109
Telugu (India), 232
Tepoztecans (N. America), 116,
  263, 272
Tessman, 81–2
test-tube babies, 168, 177; 168
testicles, 71; removal, 104
Thai, 117–18, 217, 218–19, 229, 231–2
Thandan (Asia), 229
Thonga (Africa), 92, 193, 194, 199,
  298
Tiberius, Emperor, 24, 157, 187
Tibet, 32, 58, 140–1, 238–9, 244; 238
Tikopia (Oceania), 250–1, 254,
  258–9, 290, 293
Timbirá (S. America), 61, 263, 266,
  269, 295
Tiv (Africa), 81
Tiwi (Africa), 133, 250
Tlingit (N. America), 265, 267
Toda (India), 93, 227, 229, 231; 134,
  227
Tongans (Oceania), 89, 111, 255,
  256, 258, 259, 293, 295
Toraja (Oceania), 255, 257
Totonác (America), 103, 262, 263;
  262
Transkei, 139
transsexuality, 35, 74, 75–6, 77,
  178, 231, 304; 75
transvestism, 17, 74, 103, 122,
  304–5; 196; American Indians,
  270; 271; in Asia, 231, 232, 237;
  231; Eskimo, 262; in Muslim
  countries, 126, 212; in Oceania,
  256; prostitution, 162–3, 164; 162
Trinidad, 131
Trobriand islanders (Oceania), 8,
  12, 59, 60, 61, 81, 88, 146, 150,
  248, 251, 252, 254–7, 290, 295,
  298; 81
Trukese (Oceania), 10, 59, 61, 62,
  63, 92, 102, 250, 251–3, 255, 257,
  258, 289, 294, 295, 300
Trumai (S. America), 146, 273
Tuamotu, 305
Tuareg, 62, 126, 207, 210, 213; 125

Tuka movement (Oceania), 260
Tukano (S. America), 263, 268–9,
  270, 289, 302
Tupinambá (S. America), 10, 263,
  270
Turkana (Africa), 118
Turkey, 125, 212
Turnbull, Colin, 110
Turner's syndrome, 73
Turu (Africa), 60
Tuscany, 58
Tutsi (Watusi) (Africa), 135
Twi (Africa), 191, 192–3
twins, 9, 104, 136, 265
Tylor, Edward Burnett, 138, 140

U

Uganda, 306
Ulithi, 295, 298
Ulrichs, Karl Heinrich, 76–7, 174
United States of America, birth
  control, 18; cohabitation, 172;
  divorce, 172; homosexuality, 56,
  77, 122–3, 173–4, 175–7, 287, 297;
  ideals of beauty, 88, 92, 94, 95;
  nudity, 118; onset of puberty, 66,
  67; oral-genital acts, 64;
  polygamy, 16; 16; premarital
  sexuality, 143–4, 145;
  prostitution, 160, 163; sex and
  class, 12–13; sex in old age, 68;
  sexology, 36–8; transsexuals, 76
Unwin, J.D., 142, 143, 144
Ur, 12, 59, 201

V

vagina, Hindu classification, 70–1;
  71; infibulation, 46, 106, 107, 206,
  263; 106; introcision, 106, 248;
  myths, 29; structure, 47, 52;
  teeth, 35
Vanggaard, Thorkil, 161
Vanuatu, 127, 128, 260; 127
Vardhamaanaa Mahaaviira, 112–13
Vedda (India), 222, 223
Vedism, 217
veils, 125–6; 207; 124, 168, 207
Venda (Oceania), 92
venereal diseases, 64, 161, 260, 305–6
Vesalius, Andreas, 34
Victorian attitudes, 21–3, 31
Vietnamese, 60, 140, 147, 219, 229,
  235
virginity, 302; in Africa, 199;
  American Indians, 262; in the Far
  East, 243; in the Judaeo-Christian
  tradition, 16–17; in Middle East,
  206; in Oceania, 252; premarital,
  140–6; 140; in Siberia, 236–7

Volterra, Daniele da, 282
voyeurism, 243; 244

W

Walbiri (Australia), 249, 301
Wali, Ibn Muhammad, 117
Wallis, Captain Samuel, 150
Wandervogel movement, 113–14
warriors, nudity, 113; and tabus,
  255
Westermarck, Eduard, 39, 126, 138
Wickler, Wolfgang, 50, 127
widow-inheritance, 194
Wikan, Unni, 76, 162
Williams, George C., 43–4
Windsor, Duchess of, 84
witches, 21; 22
Wógeo (Oceania), 8, 59, 60, 88,
  104, 252, 253, 255, 257, 259, 295
Woleaians (Oceania), 254
Wolfenden report, 167, 175
Wolof (Africa), 298
women, beauty contests, 99;
  clothing, 120–1, 125–6, 124, 125;
  physical attractiveness, 89–92;
  88–90; sex differences, 77–80
Women's Liberation movement,
  79, 83, 99, 167, 170

XYZ

xaniith (M. East), 76
XYY-trisomy, 73
Yadaw, 116
Yahgan (S. America), 58, 124–5; 123
Yakut (Asia), 89, 237
Yānomamö (S. America), 8, 263,
  270–1, 272, 291
Yao (Africa), 47, 192, 193, 194, 200
Yapese (Oceania), 8, 62, 81, 139,
  251, 252–3, 254, 255, 258, 300,
  302; 251, 253
Yasodhara, 55
Yerkes, Robert, 36
yīn and yáng, 233–4; 234
Yoni 215, 232
Yoruba (Africa), 290; 193
Yugoslavia, 135
Yunnan, 32
Yurok (N. America), 69, 266, 269,
  270
Zande (Africa), 60, 92, 133, 140,
  148, 190, 192–9, 291, 293, 297;
  148, 190
Zardandan, 32
Zoöphilia, 306
Zoroastrianism, 203–4, 212, 214
Zulu, 12, 60, 87, 103, 111, 128, 148,
  191, 192, 195, 196, 305
Zuni (N. America), 266; 266